SBAC
SMARTER BALANCED
GRADE 8 MATH

Grinnell Public Library
2642 East Main Street
Wappingers Falls, NY 12590
www.Grinnell-Library.org

By Deborah Murphy Orr

BARRON'S

About the Author

Deborah Murphy Orr is a veteran Mathematics educator with thirty-seven years of experience inspiring middle school students in the Southern California area. From her undergraduate degrees in both Education and Theatre Arts Performance from State University of New York College at Fredonia to post-graduate work including a Masters in Education from California State University, Long Beach to a Mathematics Coaching Certification from Loyola Marymount University, Los Angeles, she has continued motivating two generations of students with the implementation of the best practices in Mathematics. Serving as Mentor Teacher, Mathematics Chair, and Mathematics Coach in ABC Unified School District, she has shared her expertise with parents, teachers, and the community. The Common Core Standards for Mathematics and the Standards for Mathematical Practice are the motivation for her student-centered learning with rigor, nurturing students to exceed their own expectations.

Acknowledgments

I would like to express my love, gratitude, and appreciation to my amazing husband, Stephen, and daughter, Winnie. Thanks to your love, encouragement, and unwavering faith, and the amazing grace of God, we're finally here! Thanks to Mom and Dad who always assured me that I could do anything. Love and appreciation to my siblings, extended family, friends, and colleagues for your continued support. And, thanks to my students—I continue to learn from you every day!

–Deborah Murphy Orr

The Smarter Balanced screenshots, on pages 4, 5, and 6, are reprinted with permission courtesy of The Regents of the University of California. The publishing of this information does not represent an endorsement of products offered or solicited by Barron's Educational Series, Inc.

© Copyright 2018 by Barron's Educational Series, Inc.

All rights reserved.
No part of this publication may be reproduced or distributed in any form or by any means without the written permission of the copyright owner.

All inquiries should be addressed to:
Barron's Educational Series, Inc.
250 Wireless Boulevard
Hauppauge, NY 11788
www.barronseduc.com

ISBN: 978-1-4380-1090-8
Library of Congress Control Number: 2017953369

Printed in the United States of America
9 8 7 6 5 4 3 2 1

Contents

Introduction — 1

- Overview for Students — 1
- Computer Adaptive Test Expectations — 1
- Performance Task Expectations — 2
- Overview for Parents and Teachers — 2
- Technology Expectations — 3
- Task Types — 3
- Scoring — 7
- How the SBAC Is Formatted — 8
- How to Use This Test Prep Guide — 8

Chapter 1
Functions and Proportional Relationships — 11

- Identifying Functions — 12
- Linear Functions and Slope — 22
- Function Analysis — 32
- Slope and Similarity — 44
- SBAC Challenge Questions — 46

Chapter 2
Linear Equations in One Variable — 49

- Solving Multi-Step Linear Equations — 49
- Determining the Number of Solutions to Linear Equations — 56
- SBAC Challenge Questions — 62

Chapter 3
Systems of Equations — 63

- Solving Systems of Equations by Substitution — 64
- Solving Systems of Equations by Elimination — 70
- Solving Systems of Equations by Graphing — 74
- Real-World and Mathematical Problems — 81
- SBAC Challenge Questions — 89

Chapter 4
Real Numbers and the Pythagorean Theorem — 91

- Rational and Irrational Numbers — 91
- Converting a Decimal to a Rational Number (Fraction Form) — 93
- Estimating Values of Expressions That Contain Irrational Numbers — 98
- Pythagorean Theorem and Its Converse — 101
- Distance Between Two Points in a Coordinate System — 106
- Pythagorean Theorem in Three Dimensions — 111
- SBAC Challenge Questions — 115

Chapter 5
Geometry—Transformations — 117

- Translations — 118
- Rotations — 125
- Reflections — 136
- Dilations — 146
- Congruence and Similarity — 157
- SBAC Challenge Questions — 171

Chapter 6
Patterns and Relationships in Data — 173

- Scatter Plots and Lines of Best Fit — 174
- Frequency and Relative Frequency Tables — 182
- SBAC Challenge Questions — 189

Chapter 7
Geometry—Two and Three Dimensions — 191

- Angles Formed by Intersecting Lines — 191
- Three or More Intersecting Lines — 194
- Volume of Rectangular Prisms, Cylinders, Cones, and Spheres — 203
- SBAC Challenge Questions — 210

Chapter 8
Integer Exponents and Scientific Notation — 211

- Properties of Integer Exponent Expressions — 211
- Scientific Notation — 228
- Operations with Scientific Notation — 232
- SBAC Challenge Questions — 237

Chapter 9
Performance Task Overview   **239**

Chapter 10
Practice Test   **245**
- Computer Adaptive Test   245
- Performance Task   251

Appendix A: Answers Explained for Chapters 1–8   **253**

Appendix B: Answers Explained for the Practice Test   **335**

Appendix C: Common Core Standards   **357**

Index   **363**

Introduction

Overview for Students

As your eighth-grade school year draws to a close, the vehicle for measuring your achievement in eighth-grade mathematics and comparing it to your previous years' learning is the SBAC Grade 8 Math exam (Summative Mathematics Exam) from the Smarter Balanced Assessment Consortium (SBAC). This SBAC Grade 8 Math exam will assess your understanding of the Grade 8 Common Core Standards for Mathematics along with your understanding of the Standards for Mathematical Practice. The SBAC exam will test your understanding of this year's mathematics curriculum by measuring:

- simple to more complex procedures and calculation skills
- conceptual understanding, including more than one way to solve a problem
- application of skills, concepts, and procedures to novel situations
- your ability to choose an appropriate method to solve a problem
- an explanation of your own mathematical reasoning or your ability to identify an error in someone else's reasoning

Some of the questions will feel easy and routine, while others will seem more rigorous. This is because the purpose of this assessment is not just to measure your skills, but also to assess your ability to apply the content you have mastered this year to new and unique real-world and mathematical problems.

The SBAC Grade 8 Math exam consists of two separate parts: the Computer Adaptive Test (CAT) and the Performance Task. Both parts of this exam are untimed. Though your school will have some type of testing schedule based on recommended test times, additional time will be provided to you if you need it.

Computer Adaptive Test Expectations

The first part of this exam is called a Computer Adaptive Test (CAT) because the computer will continue to "adapt" your test until it measures your success across all the required content. Based on your response to each question, it will either present a question with similar content in a different way (easier or more rigorous) or present a question to measure different content. The CAT portion of this exam will consist of approximately 30–35 questions.

Performance Task Expectations

The Performance Task portion of this exam will contain a series of 4–6 questions that revolve around one real-world situation. The series of questions about that theme will build to greater complexity and will require the application of multiple concepts from Grade 8 level content as well as concepts learned in previous grades. The first question, and sometimes the second question, is usually based on a calculation or an evaluation of information presented in the problem. Subsequent questions will require a mathematically supported decision based on the initial results and explanations or justifications based on further calculations or applications. In some cases, the response might require technology-enhanced elements, such as a "Draw or Connect Line" tool.

Overview for Parents and Teachers

The SBAC provides a summative assessment given in the spring of the school year, which measures students' understanding of grade-level mathematics content as well as their ability to apply the content to real-world and mathematical problems. Shifts required by the Grade 8 Common Core Standards for Mathematics and the Standards for Mathematical Practice are embedded in classroom instruction to prepare students for the SBAC assessments, which were created not only to measure student learning, but also to measure students' progress toward college and career readiness. Specifically, these required shifts are Deeper Focus, Coherence, and Rigor, as outlined in Table I-1 below.

Table I-1. Math Shifts

Deeper Focus	Coherence	Rigor
Students are building a deeper understanding of "why" and "how" the mathematical concepts and procedures work as well as an understanding of how to choose procedures and concepts for a specific situation.	Students are seeing the progression of math concepts across grade levels, to connect to previous learning, and are understanding how current learning will prepare them for future concepts.	Students are striving to achieve proficiency in fluency (procedures and skills), conceptual understanding, and the application of knowledge to novel, real-world, and mathematical problems.

Technology Expectations

All sections of this test will be taken on a computer or tablet. A lot of practice using a keyboard or a virtual keyboard (on a tablet) is important since you will want to be comfortable with the technology you will be using for this exam. Some of the technology tools will require you to click, drag-and-drop, or type responses using a regular keyboard or an equation keypad on the screen.

Ask your teacher what type of device you will be using for the actual SBAC assessment so that you will have plenty of time to practice using it.

Task Types

The SBAC assessment is designed to not only measure your ability to use specific mathematical procedures and facts to find the right answer, but also to assess how you can apply this same information in more complex situations that require critical thinking. For example, asking you to solve an equation demonstrates an important mathematical skill. However, giving you an equation, showing you all the procedures and steps to solve it, and then asking you to identify where one or more errors occurred within the procedure requires the demonstration of a far deeper understanding.

In a regular classroom setting, you should have experience with each of the types of tasks that might be on this assessment. This exam contains a variety of question types including **selected-response tasks**, **constructed-response tasks**, **technology-enhanced tasks**, and the **Performance Task**. Let's take a closer look at each of the four task types:

1. **Selected-Response Tasks**
   Selected-response tasks are typical multiple-choice questions that either require one correct response or multiple correct responses. If only one correct response is required, you will use the cursor to fill in a circle by clicking on it.

> Marco says that the interior angles of a triangle add up to 180°. He claims that the interior angles of a hexagon must add up to 360° because a hexagon has twice as many vertices as a triangle and can be divided into two triangles. Therefore, its interior angles must sum to twice the value of those of a triangle.
>
> Which statement, if any, explains Marco's error?
>
> Ⓐ A hexagon does not have 6 vertices.
>
> Ⓑ A hexagon can be divided into 4 triangles, not 2.
>
> Ⓒ The interior angles of a triangle do not add up to 180°.
>
> Ⓓ Marco's statement is correct and contains no error.

Figure I-1. Example of a selected-response task with one correct answer

If more than one correct response is required (i.e., a multi-select question that asks you to "choose all that apply"), you will use the cursor to click the open squares for all of the correct answers. The open circles and the open squares are the visual reminders of whether only one choice or more than one choice is required for a correct and complete response. Of course, the question itself will also contain these instructions.

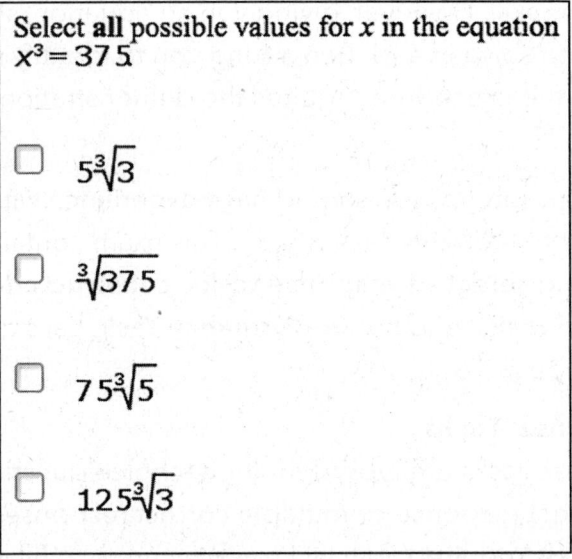

Figure I-2. Example of a selected-response task with more than one correct answer

 **HELPFUL HINT**

If you select one wrong response when answering a multiple-response (multi-select) question or if you do not select all the correct responses when answering a multiple-response (multi-select) question, you will receive zero points for that question.

2. Constructed-Response Tasks

Constructed-response tasks require a written response based on some analysis of the question. A complete and correct response may need to include some key vocabulary or other explanations.

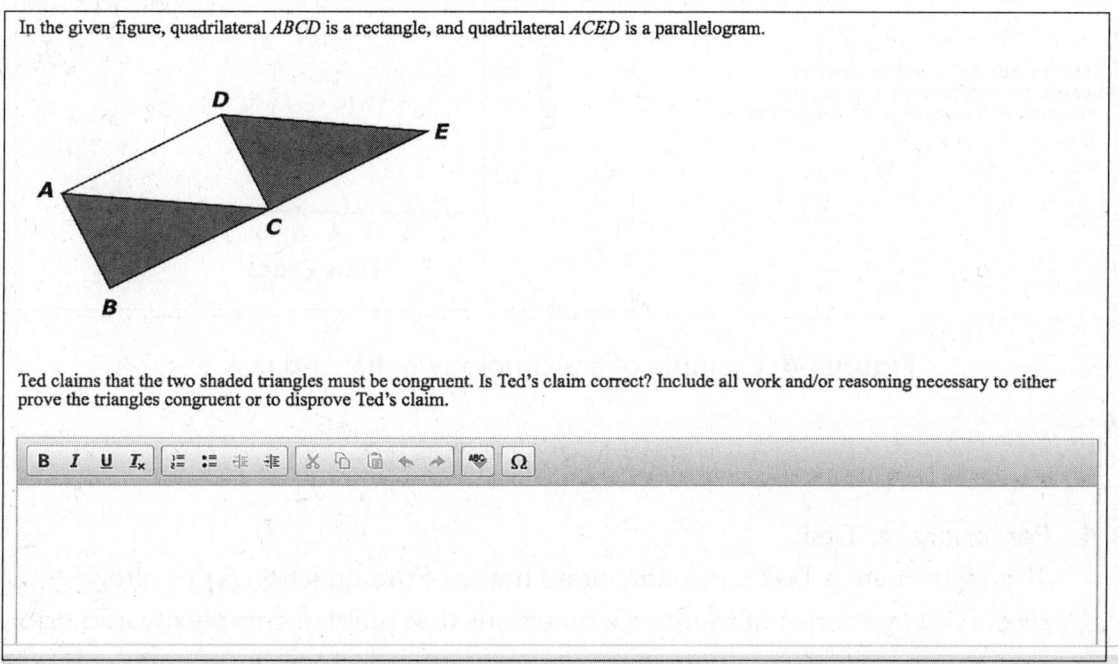

Figure I-3. Example of a constructed-response task

For **extended constructed-response tasks**, the question will contain a second part that will rely on or expand upon the response to the first part of the question.

3. Technology-Enhanced Tasks

Technology-enhanced tasks are nontraditional types of questions that require the use of technology to respond. For example, you may need to select and drag responses to place them into a chart or to order them. You might need to input an expression or an equation that requires the use of a drop-down list of choices. A "Draw or Connect Line" tool might be required to form a shape or to graph information. For Figure I-4, you would need to use the "Add Arrow" tool to graph the correct response.

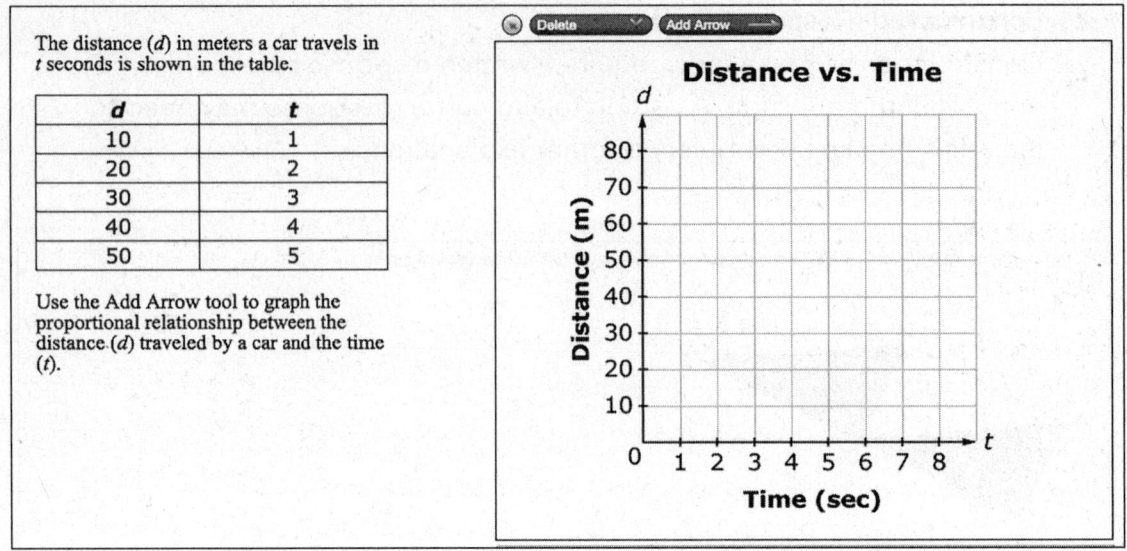

Figure I-4. Example of a technology-enhanced task

4. Performance Task

The Performance Task can incorporate many of the question types already discussed in a series of four to six questions that build in complexity and rigor, integrating multiple mathematics content standards. More information about the Performance Task can be found in Chapter 9.

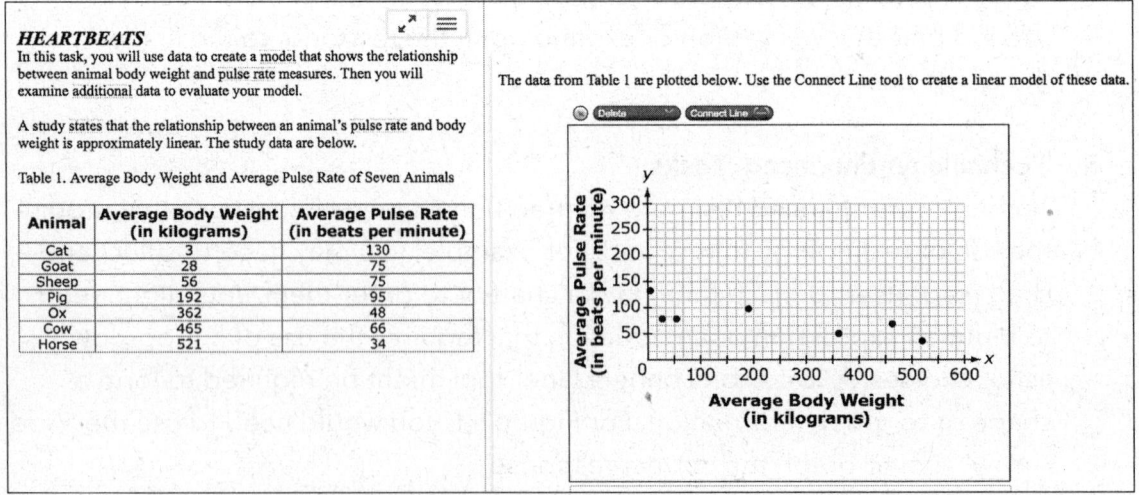

Figure I-5. Example of a Performance Task

Scoring

The scoring for this test is based on the types of questions on each test and the complexity required of the responses. Scoring for any of the CAT questions is, in most cases, based on a 0-point or 1-point score. For example, if a multi-select task requires that you select more than one correct response, but one of the two choices that you selected was an incorrect response OR if you did not select the correct number of responses, you would receive zero points for that question. Some of the constructed-response or extended constructed-response tasks are based on a 2-point, 1-point, or 0-point score. Two points would be awarded for a complete, clear, and correct answer with a precise explanation of the understanding of the concept or mathematical justification. One point would be awarded for a correct answer with a limited or partially demonstrated understanding, while zero points would be awarded for no demonstrated understanding. This is where the ability to use strong math vocabulary correctly will allow you to be successful.

Scoring for the Performance Task will have, depending on the question, a 3-point, 2-point, or 1-point value for each of the four to six questions. Though the Performance Task contains only four to six questions, it is considered its own untimed assessment, separate from the CAT portion. The Performance Task results count as a significant portion of the overall standardized scoring for the SBAC Grade 8 Math exam.

The SBAC assessment results will be delivered in an individual student report that will provide measures for the mathematics claims. The four claims are Concepts and Procedures, Problem Solving, Communicating Reasoning, and Modeling/Data Analysis. Student scoring results will be given as a range or a level based on a standardized score. These results will not be given in the form of a raw score of the number of questions answered correctly nor will they be given as a percentage of points earned.

Student reports will include an overall standardized score, and this score will be in a range for one of four performance levels. The performance levels are **Standard Exceeded**, **Standard Met**, **Standard Almost Met**, and **Standard Not Met**. These SBAC eighth-grade performance levels will be related to the Grade 8 Common Core Standards for Mathematics, which can be found in Appendix C of this book.

How the SBAC Is Formatted

The SBAC is formatted in a few different ways for the Computer Adaptive Test:

- The majority of the questions will be presented individually on a single screen that may need to be scrolled up and/or down to see the complete question and possible answer choices. At the top of the screen, there will be "zoom in" and "zoom out" buttons, which you can use to see more details.
- Some questions will be presented on a split screen. On the left, there will be text and data that explain the problem along with any relevant information. On the right, there will be the question or questions to answer. Each side of the split screen will have a separate scroll bar so that the information on the left is always readily available for reference.
- For some questions, a calculator symbol will be available for you to open and use an onscreen calculator.

The SBAC will be formatted in one split screen for the Performance Task:

- All of the data or information will be presented on the left.
- All of the questions will be presented on the right, and the right side of the screen will need to be scrolled down to see the rest of the questions.
- Each side of the split screen will have a separate scroll bar for ready access to the data and information.

How to Use This Test Prep Guide

This test prep guide is organized by content chapters. You have likely already received primary instruction for all the content in these chapters. The types of tasks and practice are designed to mirror the types of questions and the rigor of those questions on the actual SBAC exam.

Throughout the review chapters, you will find Helpful Hints with reminders to consider. Here is an example:

Read each question carefully. Determine what kind of response and how many responses are needed.

Chapters 1–8 will contain each of the following:

- A list of the **Grade 8 Common Core Standards for Mathematics** covered in that chapter
- **Key Concepts** to remember for each topic
- Worked out **Examples** with detailed explanations
- **Guided Practice** problems that are designed for you to work on after you review all of the examples in each section. The answer explanations are given immediately after each set of Guided Practice questions. These problems will guide you through how to answer each type of question on that particular topic.
- After reviewing the Guided Practice problems, try to answer the **Independent Practice** problems on your own. These questions are designed for you to work through without any help, and they should give you a better idea of what topics you know and what topics you need to review once more. These Independent Practice problems represent some of the common types of questions that you will encounter on the Computer Adaptive Test of the SBAC Grade 8 Math exam. You should attempt these questions on your own first before you review the correct answers. All of the answer explanations can be found in Appendix A.
- Once you have mastered the Independent Practice problems, you will then be ready to work on the **SBAC Challenge Questions**. The SBAC Challenge Questions are designed to mirror some of the more complex and rigorous questions that you will see on the actual exam. The SBAC Challenge Questions will synthesize multiple concepts, giving you the opportunity to demonstrate a deeper understanding of related ideas. These questions represent a variety of question types on the actual exam, including extended constructed-response questions and more traditional question types that may require an understanding of multiple concepts and procedures to answer. Attempt all of these questions on your own first, and then you may review the correct answers and explanations, which can be found in Appendix A.

Chapter 9 provides an overview of the Performance Task and sample practice questions. In Chapter 10, you will find a complete practice test with a CAT and a Performance Task. Worked out answer explanations for the practice test can be found in Appendix B. Finally, in Appendix C, you will find a complete list of the Grade 8 Common Core Standards for Mathematics.

Functions and Proportional Relationships

CHAPTER 1

Common Core Standard 8.EE.B.5

Graph proportional relationships, interpreting the unit rate as the slope of the graph. Compare two different proportional relationships represented in different ways. *For example, compare a distance-time graph to a distance-time equation to determine which of two moving objects has greater speed.*

Common Core Standard 8.EE.B.6

Use similar triangles to explain why the slope m is the same between any two distinct points on a non-vertical line in the coordinate plane; derive the equation $y = mx$ for a line through the origin and the equation $y = mx + b$ for a line intercepting the vertical axis at b.

Common Core Standard 8.F.A.1

Understand that a function is a rule that assigns to each input exactly one output. The graph of a function is the set of ordered pairs consisting of an input and the corresponding output. (Note that function notation is not required for Grade 8.)

Common Core Standard 8.F.A.2

Compare properties of two functions each represented in a different way (algebraically, graphically, numerically in tables, or by verbal descriptions). *For example, given a linear function represented by a table of values and a linear function represented by an algebraic expression, determine which function has the greater rate of change.*

Common Core Standard 8.F.A.3

Interpret the equation $y = mx + b$ as defining a linear function, whose graph is a straight line; give examples of functions that are not linear. *For example, the function $A = s^2$ giving the area of a square as a function of its side length is not linear because its graph contains the points (1, 1), (2, 4), and (3, 9), which are not on a straight line.*

Common Core Standard 8.F.B.4

Construct a function to model a linear relationship between two quantities. Determine the rate of change and initial value of the function from a description of a relationship or from two (x, y) values, including reading these from a table or from a graph. Interpret the rate of change and initial value of a linear function in terms of the situation it models, and in terms of its graph or a table of values.

Common Core Standard 8.F.B.5

Describe qualitatively the functional relationship between two quantities by analyzing a graph (e.g., where the function is increasing or decreasing, linear or nonlinear). Sketch a graph that exhibits the qualitative features of a function that has been described verbally.

Identifying Functions

Key Concepts

- Any set of ordered pairs is called a relation. Some relations are functions.
- A set of ordered pairs is called a function if for every input, there is exactly one output.
- Functions can be linear or nonlinear.
- Functions can be represented in a variety of ways including as tables, as graphs, algebraically, and by verbal description.

The simplest way to visualize the definition of a function is with a mapping diagram. If each input (x-coordinate) maps to exactly one output (y-coordinate), the set of ordered pairs represents a function.

For each of the following examples, determine whether the mapping diagram represents a function.

Example 1

2 ⟶ 6
3 ⟶ 8
4 ⟶ 3
5 ⟶ 7

Answer: **This represents a function.** Each input maps to exactly one output.

Example 2

2 ⟶ 6
3 ⟶ 8
4 ⟶ 3

Answer: **This does not represent a function.** The input 2 maps to two different outputs (6 and 8) as illustrated by the two arrows from one input.

Example 3

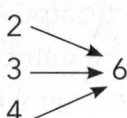

Answer: **This represents a function.** Each input maps to exactly one output. In this case, all the inputs map to the same output.

Example 4

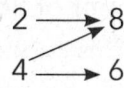

Answer: **This does not represent a function.** The input 4 maps to two different outputs (8 and 6) as illustrated by the two arrows from one input.

From a table, a function can be determined if each of the values for the independent variable (input) results in exactly one dependent variable (output).

Example 5

Determine whether each of the following tables represents a function.

Table A

Number of Tickets	Total Cost (in dollars)
2	9
5	22.50
11	49.50
2	9
4	18

Table B

Number of Questions Correct	Test Score
22	88
25	100
25	101
17	68
15	60

Answer: **The information in Table A represents a function.** The independent variable (input) is the number of tickets, and the dependent variable (output) is the total cost (in dollars). This is because the total cost *depends* on the number of tickets bought. Each input has exactly one output. The input 2 appears on the table twice, but it has the same output each time that it appears.

The information in Table B does not represent a function. The independent variable (input) is the number of questions correct, and the dependent variable (output) is the test score. This is because the test score *depends* on the number of questions correct. The input 25 has two different outputs, which is not reflective of a function.

From a set of ordered pairs, if each x-coordinate (input) has exactly one y-coordinate (output), the set of ordered pairs represents a function.

Example 6

Determine whether each set of ordered pairs represents a function.

(A) {(3, 5), (2, 7), (3, 5), (6, 3)}   (B) {(4, 3), (2, 6), (3, 6), (6, 3)}

Answer: **Set (A) represents a function.** Though the input 3 appears twice in the ordered pairs, it appears with the same output both times. **Set (B) also represents a function.** Each input has exactly one output.

Alternatively, a mapping diagram could be created from the sets of ordered pairs, or the ordered pairs could be graphed. *From a graph*, determining whether a function is represented can be accomplished by using a vertical line test. Create a vertical line by using a pencil held parallel to the y-axis and draw a vertical line to determine how many times it intersects the line or curve. If the vertical line intersects the given line or curve at only one point, that verifies that the line or curve represents a function. The one point represents that the *x*-coordinate (input) has exactly one *y*-coordinate (output). If the vertical line intersects the given line or curve at more than one point, that verifies that the line or curve does not represent a function because crossing multiple points means that there is more than one *y*-coordinate (output) for the *x*-coordinate (input). Also, from a graph, you can determine whether a function is linear or nonlinear. Linear functions must graph as a line.

Example 7

Determine whether each of the following graphs represents a function. Then, determine whether each graph is linear or nonlinear.

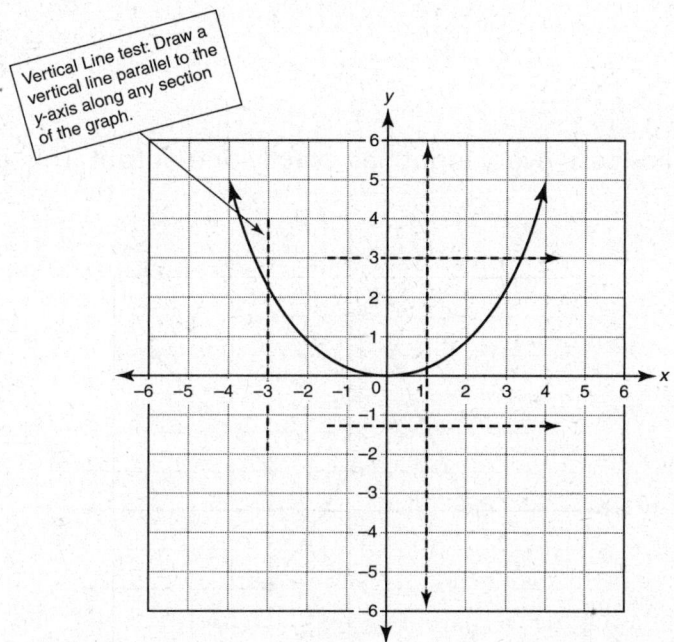

Answer:

Function, nonlinear

Using the vertical line test, every input has exactly one output. This graph is nonlinear. It is a curve.

Grinnell Public Library
2642 East Main Street
Wappingers Falls, NY 12590
www.Grinnell-Library.org

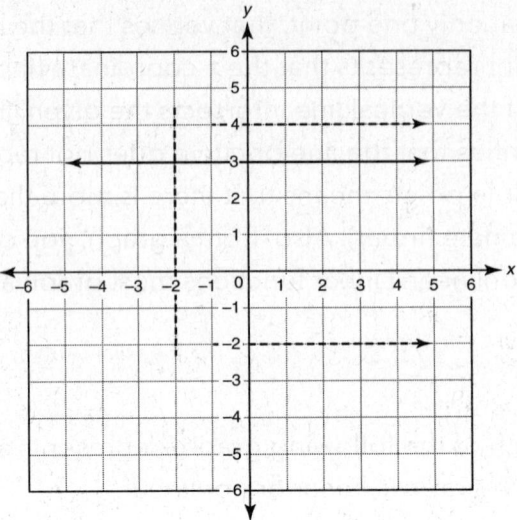

Answer:

Function, linear

Using the vertical line test, every input has exactly one output. This graph is linear. It is a line.

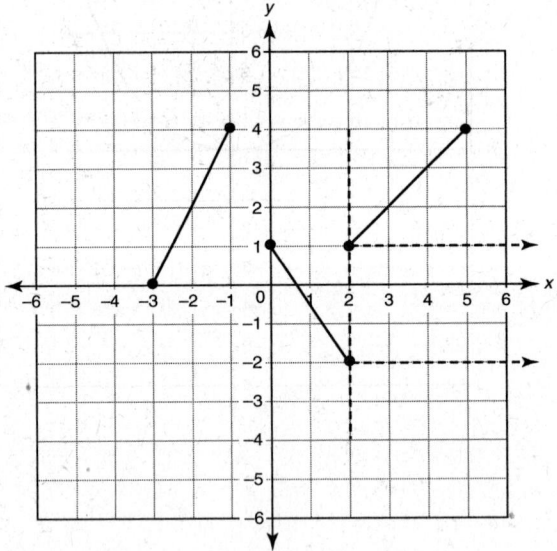

Answer:

Not a function, nonlinear

Using the vertical line test, the input 2 has two different outputs (1 and –2). This graph is not linear. It contains unconnected segments.

From an equation, a function can be determined if any value substituted for x results in a unique value for y.

Example 8

Do the following equations represent a function?

(A) $y = 4x + 7$ (B) $y = x^2 - 2$ (C) $y = |x| + 3$ (D) $x = 4$

Answers:

(A) **Represents a function** Each value substituted for x will result in a unique value for y.

$y = 4(-3) + 7$ $y = 4(3) + 7$ Viewed as a mapping diagram: $-3 \longrightarrow -5$

$y = -5$ $y = 19$ Each input extends an arrow to $3 \longrightarrow 19$
exactly one output.

(B) **Represents a function** Each value substituted for x will result in a unique value for y.

$y = (-3)^2 - 2$ $y = 3^2 - 2$ Viewed as a mapping diagram: -3

$y = 7$ $y = 7$ Each input extends an arrow to $3 \longrightarrow 7$
exactly one output.

(C) **Represents a function** Each value substituted for x will result in a unique value for y.

$y = |-3| + 3$ $y = |3| + 3$ Viewed as a mapping diagram: $-3 \longrightarrow 6$

$y = 6$ $y = 6$ Each input extends an arrow to 3
exactly one output.

(D) **Does not represent a function** This equation states that x is 4 for all values of y. This means that there are an infinite number of outputs {i.e., (4, 0), (4, −1), (4, 3), ...}.

Viewed as a mapping diagram: -1

This input extends arrows to multiple $4 \longrightarrow 0$
outputs. 3

From a verbal description, you can also determine whether a situation represents a function.

Example 9

A contest states that every winner will win $100 more than his or her age, verified by a driver's license or another form of identification. Winners must be 18 years of age or older. Robert says that the age of the winners cannot represent a function in terms of the prize because no one under 18 years of age can win. Janet says that the age of the winners cannot represent a function in terms of the prize because more than one winner could be the same age. Who is correct? Explain.

Answer: **Neither Robert nor Janet is correct.** Robert is incorrect because the contest limitation is on the input, limiting the inputs to be considered but not affecting the relationship between any winner and the prize. Since winners must be 18 years of age or older, and the output is $100 added to that number, any 18-year-old winner will get $118 (not any other amount), any 19-year-old winner will get $119, etc. This means that every input (age) has exactly one output (age + $100). Janet is also incorrect because there is no additional output if more than one winner is the same age (input). If four winners are all 25 years of age, they will each get the same amount ($125). This means that the input 25 will always generate an output of 125. This contest represents a function between the age of the winner and the amount of winnings.

Guided Practice

1. Determine whether each of the following represents a function. Explain why or why not.

A.

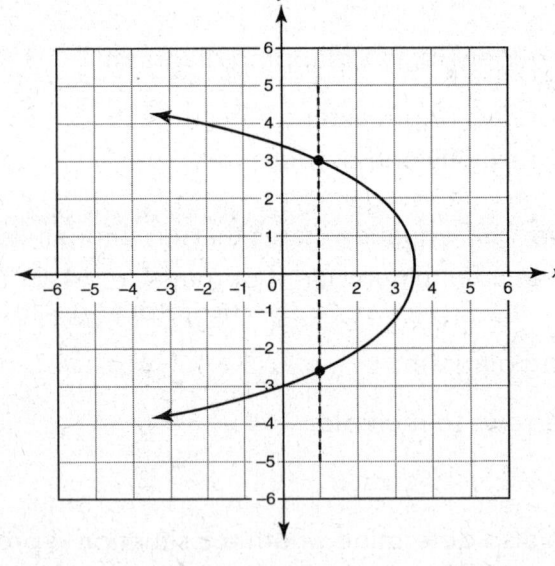

B.

x	3	5	7	1
y	2	2	2	2

C. {(−1, −5), (−2, −7), (−3, 6), (4, −3)}

D. {(8, 3), (2, 3), (3, 3), (6, 3)}

E. $y = 2x - 2$ F. $y = 1$ G. $x = 2$ H. $y = x^2$

2. Determine whether each of the following graphs represents a function. Then, determine whether the graph is linear or nonlinear.

A.
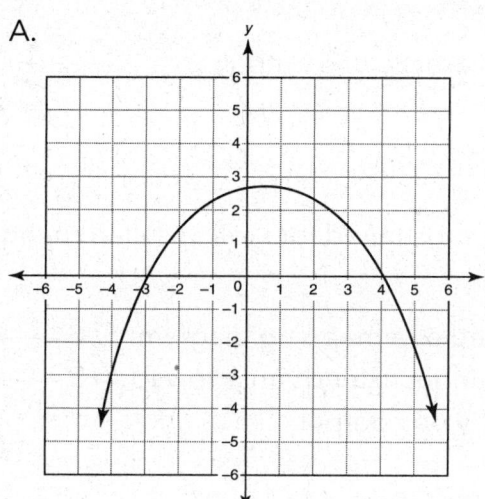

B.
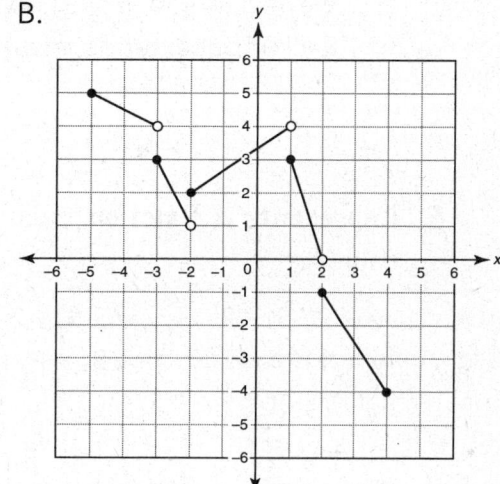

3. One point on the graph of a function is (4, 5). Which of the following points could not be on the graph of that function?

○ A. (−4, 7)   ○ B. (5, −2)   ○ C. (2, −1)   ○ D. (4, −6)   ○ E. (7, 5)

Guided Practice Answers Explained

1. **A. Does not represent a function** Using the vertical line test, a vertical line will intersect this graph at more than one point. For example, the ordered pairs (1, −2.75) and (1, 3) demonstrate that the x-coordinate (input) has more than one y-coordinate (output).

   B. Represents a function Each input (x) has exactly one output (y). Although the outputs are the same, there is no ordered pair where the input produces more than one output.

   C. Represents a function This set of ordered pairs has exactly one output for each input.

   Viewed as a mapping diagram:
   Each input extends an arrow to exactly one output.

   −1 ⟶ −5
   −2 ⟶ −7
   −3 ⟶ 6
   4 ⟶ −3

D. **Represents a function** This set of ordered pairs has exactly one output for each input.

> Viewed as a mapping diagram:
> Each input extends an arrow to exactly one output.

$$\begin{array}{l} 8 \\ 2 \rightarrow 3 \\ 3 \\ 6 \end{array}$$

E. **Represents a function** Each value substituted for x will result in a unique value for y.

$y = 2(-5) - 2 \quad y = 2(5) - 2$ Viewed as a mapping diagram: $-5 \longrightarrow -12$
$y = -12 \qquad\quad y = 8$ Each input extends an arrow to $5 \longrightarrow 8$
exactly one output.

F. **Represents a function** Each value substituted for x will result in a y value of 1, which is a unique output for that input.

$y = 1$ Viewed as a mapping diagram: $-5 \longrightarrow 1$
Each input extends an arrow to $5 \nearrow$
exactly one output, positive 1.

G. **Does not represent a function** This equation states that x is 2 for all values of y. This means that there are an infinite number of outputs {(2, 0), (2, −3), (2, 3), . . .}.

> Viewed as a mapping diagram:
> This input extends arrows to multiple outputs.

$$2 \begin{array}{l} \nearrow 0 \\ \rightarrow -3 \\ \searrow 3 \end{array}$$

H. **Represents a function** Each value substituted for x will result in a unique value for y.

$y = (-5)^2 \quad y = (5)^2$ Viewed as a mapping diagram: $-5 \searrow$
$y = 25 \qquad y = 25$ Each input extends an arrow to $5 \longrightarrow 25$
exactly one output.

Functions and Proportional Relationships • 21

2. **A. This graph represents a function. It is nonlinear.** Every input has exactly one output, using the vertical line test. It is nonlinear. It is a curve.

   B. This graph represents a function. It is nonlinear because the points are not consecutive. Notice where the points appear to overlap (i.e., the ordered pairs (2, 0) and (2, −1) have the same x-coordinate (input), but appear to have different y-coordinates (outputs)). However, since one is an open dot (meaning that it includes everything up to that point, but that it does not include that point) and the other is a closed dot (indicating that that endpoint is included), these segment endpoints indicate that there is only one output (−1) for the input (2).

3. **(D)** The ordered pair (4, 5) has the same input as (4, −6) but a different output. For a function to exist, each input must have exactly one output.

Independent Practice

1. Which of the following choices does not represent a function? Select all that apply.

   ☐ A.   ☐ B.

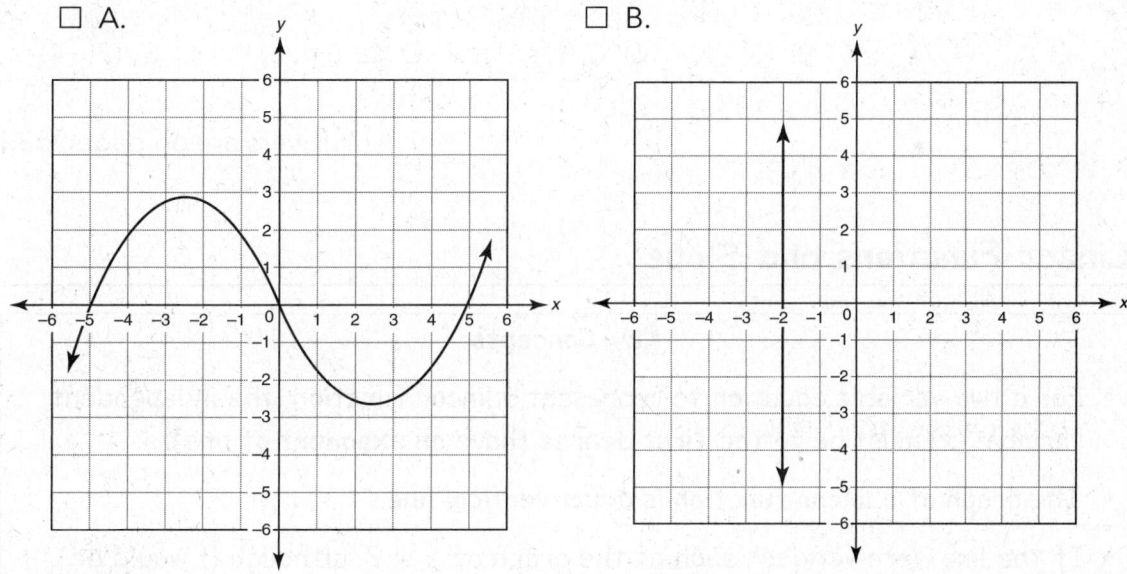

   ☐ C. {(−2, −5), (−3, −5), (−4, −5), (6, −5)}   ☐ D.

x	8	2	9	6	2
y	6	5	8	2	3

   ☐ E. $y = |x| - 3$

2. Which of the following choices represents a function? Select all that apply.

☐ A.

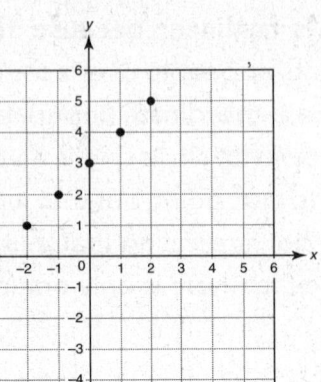

☐ B.

Number of pencils	4	7	9	2
Cost	$3.56	$6.23	$8.01	$1.87

☐ C. $y = x^2 + 1$ ☐ D. $x = y^2$ ☐ E. {(5, –2), (–7, 3), (5, 2), (10, 10)}

3. One point on the graph of a function is (–4, 7). Which of the following points could not be on the graph of that function?

○ A. (–4, 7)   ○ B. (5, 7)   ○ C. (2, –1)   ○ D. (–4, 5)   ○ E. (7, –4)

(Answers are on page 253.)

Linear Functions and Slope

Key Concepts

- For a two-variable equation to represent a linear function, the independent variable (x) must be to the first degree (have an exponent of one).
- The graph of a linear function is a non-vertical line.
- If the line were vertical, such as the graph of $x = 2$, although it would be linear, the graph would represent an infinite number of outputs for the input 2. Thus, this would not represent a function.

Functions and Proportional Relationships • 23

The **unit rate** or **rate of change** of a linear function is the same between any two points on the line and is represented by the ratio of the difference in the y-coordinate values to the difference in the respective x-coordinate values. The rate of change is also called the **slope** of the graph of the linear function. This rate of change, or slope, can be determined from different representations of the linear function by counting the units of change on a graph or by using the slope formula.

From a graph of a linear function, the rate of change (slope) can be determined by using two points on the line. Finding the difference in the y-coordinates, and the difference in the respective x-coordinates, can be done by counting or by calculation. Counting the units of change between the points up or down the y-axis, and the units of change to the left and right along the x-axis, is one way to determine this ratio.

Another method is calculating the rate of change (slope), using the following formula:

$$\text{slope} = \frac{y_2 - y_1}{x_2 - x_1}$$

This formula calculates the ratio between the change in the two y-coordinates and the change in the two respective x-coordinates, as indicated by the subscripts on the ordered pairs.

💡 **HELPFUL HINT**

The rate of change (slope) can be determined using the slope formula for a graph, for a table or other set of ordered pairs, for a context or verbal description, or for an equation.

Example 1

Determine the rate of change (slope) of this graph.

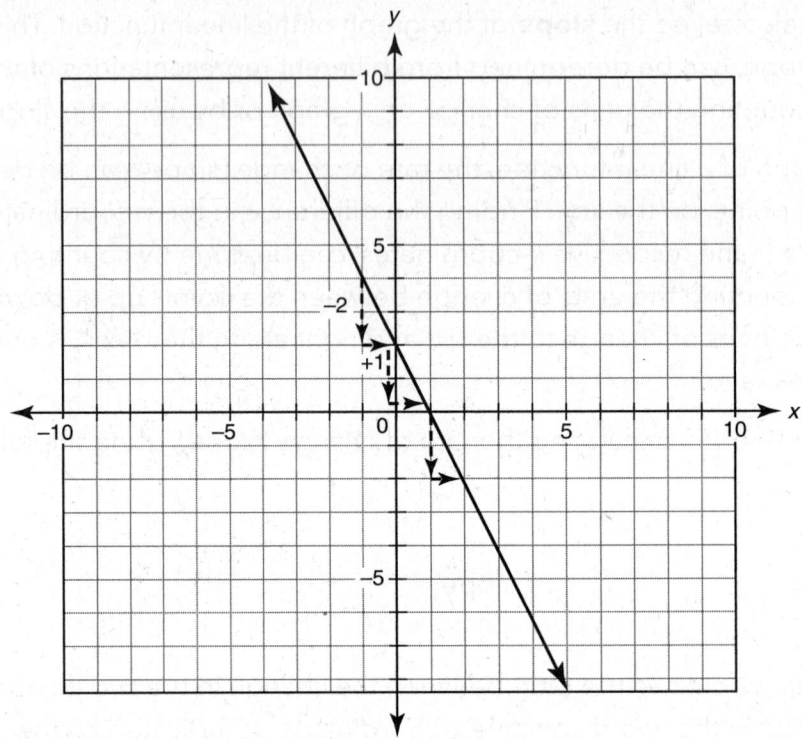

Answer: The rate of change (slope) of this graph can be counted as a decrease of two (down two units) along the y-axis and an increase of one (right one unit) along the x-axis. This represents a rate of change (slope) of $\frac{-2}{1}$. The rate of change (slope) can also be calculated by using two ordered pairs from the graph. By selecting two ordered pairs, for example, the x-intercept (1, 0) and the y-intercept (0, 2), it is possible to calculate the rate of change (slope). Use (1, 0) as (x_2, y_2) and (0, 2) as (x_1, y_1).

$$\text{slope} = \frac{y_2 - y_1}{x_2 - x_1}$$

$$\text{slope} = \frac{0 - 2}{1 - 0} \qquad \text{(Substitute.)}$$

$$\text{slope} = \frac{-2}{1} \qquad \text{(Simplify.)}$$

The rate of change (slope) is $\frac{-2}{1}$, which indicates a decrease of two units down the y-axis for every one unit increase (right one unit) along the x-axis.

Example 2

Determine the rate of change (slope) of this graph.

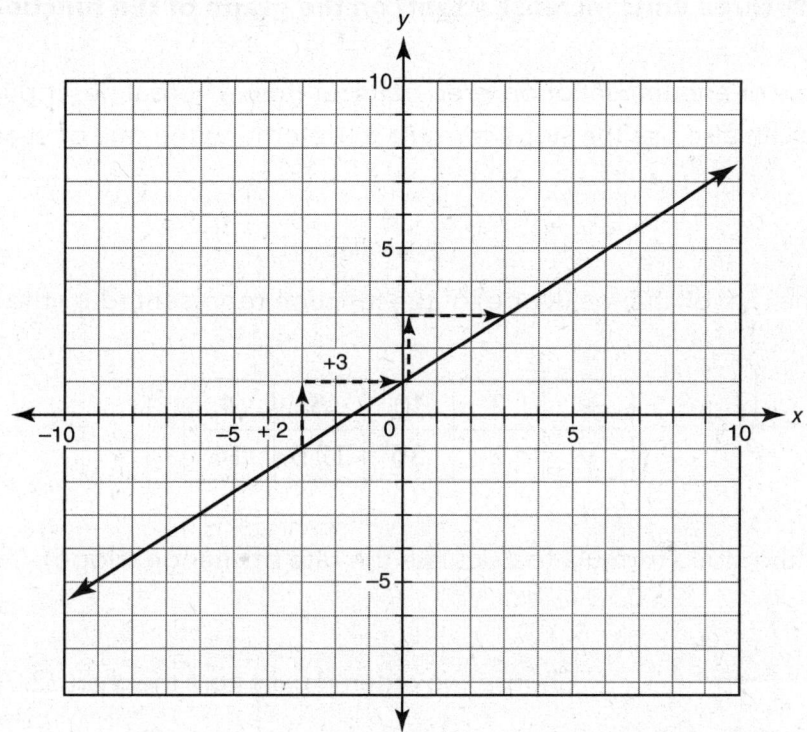

Answer: The rate of change (slope) of this graph can be counted as an increase of two (up two units) along the *y*-axis and an increase of three (right three units) along the *x*-axis. This represents a rate of change (slope) of $\frac{2}{3}$. The rate of change (slope) can also be calculated by using two ordered pairs from the graph. Choose two ordered pairs, such as (−3, −1) and (3, 3), and calculate the rate of change (slope) using the slope formula. Use (−3, −1) as (x_2, y_2) and (3, 3) as (x_1, y_1).

slope = $\frac{y_2 - y_1}{x_2 - x_1}$

slope = $\frac{-1 - 3}{-3 - 3}$ (Substitute.)

slope = $\frac{-4}{-6}$ (Simplify.)

slope = $\frac{2}{3}$

The rate of change (slope) is $\frac{2}{3}$, which indicates an increase of two units (up) for every three units increase (right) on the graph of the function.

From a table or another set of ordered pairs, or from a verbal description of a function, you can also use the slope formula to determine the rate of change (slope).

Example 3

Determine the rate of change (slope) of the function represented by the following table of values.

x	2	10	5	4
y	7	35	17.5	14

Answer: Use the slope formula to calculate the rate of change (slope).

$\text{slope} = \dfrac{y_2 - y_1}{x_2 - x_1}$ (Choose two ordered pairs from the chart: (2, 7) and (4, 14).)

$\text{slope} = \dfrac{14 - 7}{4 - 2}$ (Substitute.)

$\text{slope} = \dfrac{7}{2}$ (Simplify.)

The rate of change (slope) is $\frac{7}{2}$, which indicates an increase of seven units (up) for every two units increase (right) on a graph of the function.

Example 4

Determine the rate of change (slope) of the function represented by the following set of ordered pairs.

$$\{(5, 3.75), (-8, -6), (6, 4.5), (11, 8.25)\}$$

Answer: Use the slope formula to calculate the rate of change (slope).

$\text{slope} = \dfrac{y_2 - y_1}{x_2 - x_1}$ (Choose two ordered pairs from the set: (5, 3.75) and (−8, −6).)

$\text{slope} = \dfrac{-6 - 3.75}{-8 - 5}$ (Substitute.)

$\text{slope} = \dfrac{-9.75 \times 100}{-13 \times 100}$ (Multiply by a form of one to eliminate the decimal in the numerator.)

$\text{slope} = \dfrac{975}{1300}$ (Simplify.)

$\text{slope} = \dfrac{39}{52}$

$\text{slope} = \dfrac{3}{4}$

The rate of change (slope) is $\dfrac{3}{4}$, which indicates an increase of three units (up) for every four units increase (right) on a graph of the function.

Example 5

On Tuesday, Larry earned $105 for three hours of woodworking. On Wednesday, he earned $280 for eight hours of woodworking. On Thursday, he earned $385 for eleven hours of woodworking. If the amount he earned is a function of the time he worked, determine the unit rate.

Answer: Since the money Larry earned was dependent on the number of hours he worked, the money he earned is represented by the dependent variable *y* and the hours he worked is represented by the independent variable *x* for each ordered pair.

$$\text{slope} = \frac{y_2 - y_1}{x_2 - x_1}$$ (Create two ordered pairs from the context: (3, $105) and (8, $280).)

$$\text{slope} = \frac{280 - 105}{8 - 3}$$ (Substitute.)

$$\text{slope} = \frac{175}{5}$$ (Simplify.)

$$\text{slope} = \frac{35}{1}$$

The unit rate (slope) is $\frac{35}{1}$, which indicates an increase of $35 for every one hour he worked.

Key Concepts

- When a linear function is in the equation form **y = mx + b**, the slope can be determined from the equation by looking at the value of **m**.
- This form of an equation is called the slope-intercept form.
- The *y*-intercept for the function is represented by the value of **b** in the equation.

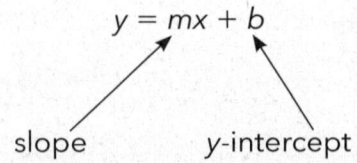

Example 6

Determine the slope for each linear function. Which is the greatest slope?

A. $y = 2x - 7$ B. $y = -\dfrac{4}{5}x + 1$ C. $y = 9x$

Answers:

A. The slope is 2. In slope-intercept form $y = mx + b$, the slope is the coefficient of x. For every increase of two units (up), the graph will increase one unit (right).

B. The slope is $-\dfrac{4}{5}$. In slope-intercept form $y = mx + b$, the slope is the coefficient of x. For every decrease of four units (down), the graph will increase five units (right).

C. The slope is 9. In slope-intercept form $y = mx + b$, the slope is the coefficient of x. For every increase of nine units (up), the graph will increase one unit (right).

Choice C has the greatest slope because it has the largest absolute value.

Guided Practice

1. Which of the following functions has the smallest rate of change (slope)? Which has the greatest rate of change (slope)?

    A.

    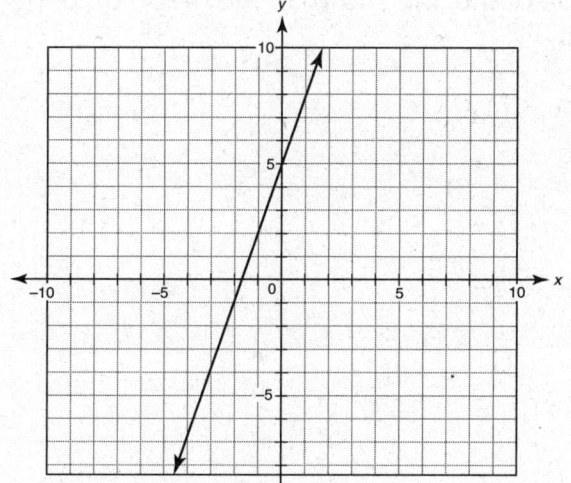

    B. {(2, 1), (3, 5), (4, 9), (1, −3)}

    C.

    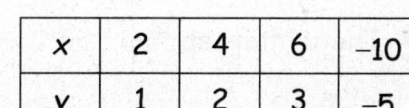

x	2	4	6	−10
y	1	2	3	−5

    D. $y = 5x - 8$

Guided Practice Answers Explained

1. **Choice C has the smallest rate of change (slope). Choice D has the greatest rate of change (slope).** For choices A, B, and C, choose two ordered pairs to use in the slope formula.

Choice A	Choice B	Choice C
(0, 5) and (1, 8)	(2, 1) and (3, 5)	(2, 1) and (4, 2)
slope = $\dfrac{y_2 - y_1}{x_2 - x_1}$	slope = $\dfrac{y_2 - y_1}{x_2 - x_1}$	slope = $\dfrac{y_2 - y_1}{x_2 - x_1}$
slope = $\dfrac{8 - 5}{1 - 0}$	slope = $\dfrac{5 - 1}{3 - 2}$	slope = $\dfrac{2 - 1}{4 - 2}$
slope = $\dfrac{3}{1}$	slope = $\dfrac{4}{1}$	slope = $\dfrac{1}{2}$

In choice D, given $y = mx + b$, with m = slope, the equation $y = 5x - 8$ has a slope of 5.

Independent Practice

1. Indicate whether the slope of each of the following linear functions is greater than, less than, or equal to the slope of the line shown in the graph on page 31. Fill in the correct circle for each function.

Functions and Proportional Relationships • 31

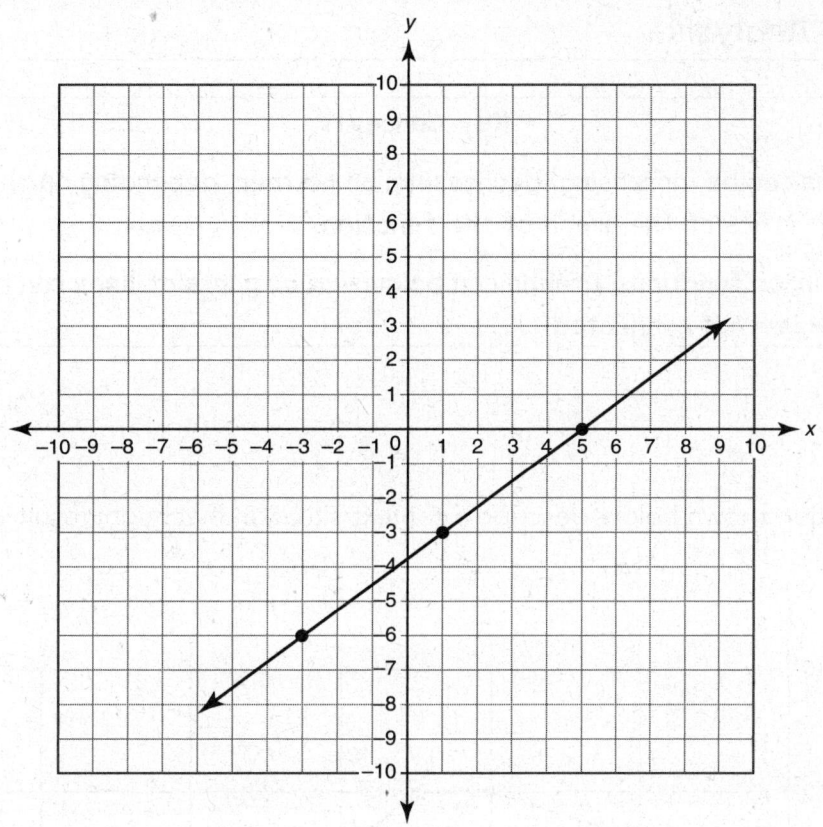

	Greater Than	Less Than	Equal To
A. $y = \dfrac{5}{8}x + 7$	O	O	O
B. $\{(3, 5), (0, -1), (4, 7)\}$	O	O	O

C. Lorraine's science experiment requires that she calculate the average height of her plants daily. On Day 4, the average height was 3 inches. On Day 12, the average height was 9 inches. On Day 15, the average height was 11.25 inches. The function represented by this experiment is the height in terms of time.

	Greater Than	Less Than	Equal To
	O	O	O

D.

x	−2	6	−8	4
y	0	4	−3	3

	Greater Than	Less Than	Equal To
	O	O	O

(Answers are on page 253.)

Function Analysis

> **Key Concepts**
> - Functions can be increasing, decreasing, or neither, depending on the characteristics of the graph of the function.
> - For nonlinear functions, graphs can be curved or parts of lines can be connected or not connected.

Example 1

For the function shown below, describe a context/situation that might result in this graph.

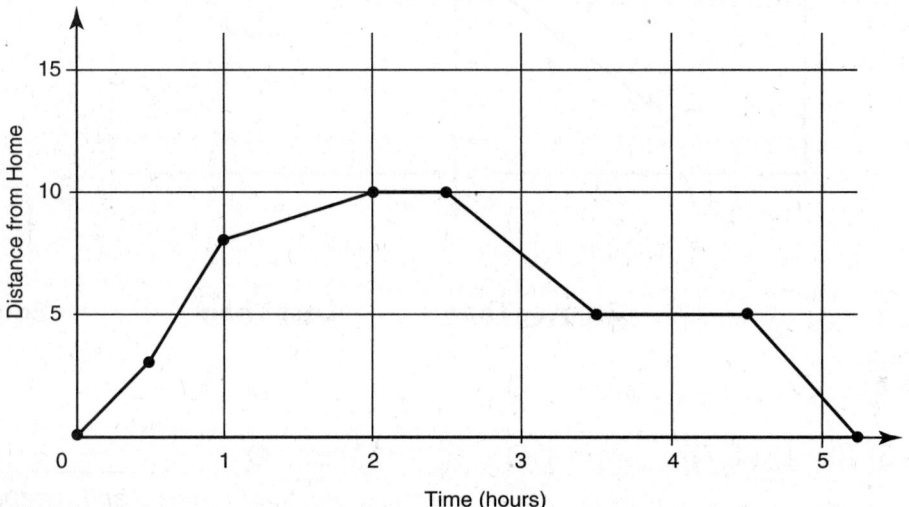

Answer: Leaving from home, Steve biked steadily for half an hour. Then, he increased to a steady higher speed for the next half hour. Next, he slowed significantly and rode steadily for an hour. Suddenly, he discovered he had a flat tire and stopped to change it. After half an hour, Steve started walking toward home. He walked steadily for an hour and then stopped to talk with a friend. After standing and talking for an hour, Steve rode leisurely the rest of the way toward home, arriving after about 40 minutes of biking.

Linear Functions

- If the slope is positive, the function is increasing (from left to right, the line goes up).
- If the slope is negative, the function is decreasing (from left to right, the line goes down).
- If there is a slope of zero (no increase or decrease along the y-axis with an increase (moving right) along the x-axis), the function is represented by a horizontal line.
- If there is an undefined slope (only an increase or decrease along the y-axis, but no change along the x-axis), the function is represented by a vertical line.

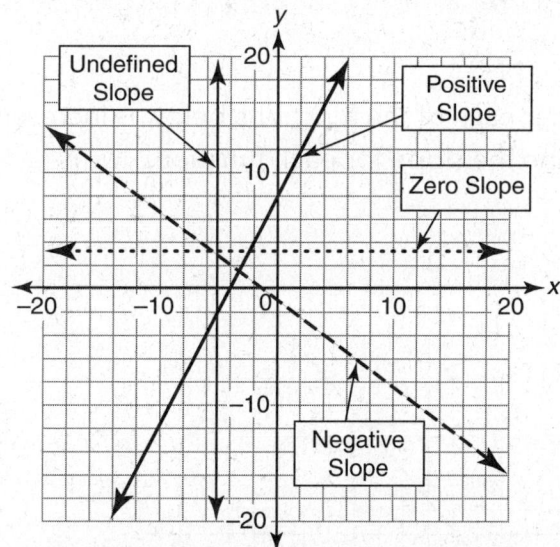

Note: *When comparing slopes to determine which slope is greater (steeper) or smaller (less steep), always determine the absolute value of the slope. When comparing steepness, the sign indicates direction, and the absolute value compares the steepness. For example, when comparing a slope of −3 with a slope of $\frac{1}{2}$, the comparison of the absolute values shows that a slope of −3 ($|-3| = 3$) is actually steeper (down three units, right one unit) than a slope of $\frac{1}{2}$ $\left(\left|\frac{1}{2}\right| = \frac{1}{2}\right)$ (up one unit, right two units). Although the line with a slope of −3 goes down (left to right), and the line with a slope of $\frac{1}{2}$ goes up (left to right), in this case, the line with the negative slope will be steeper because its absolute value is greater.*

Linear functions can either be parallel, or they can intersect. This characteristic can be determined by looking at the slopes of the functions.

> **Key Concepts**
> - Linear functions with the same slope but a different y-intercept are parallel. The y-intercept is where the function intersects the y-axis (the point where the x-coordinate is 0).
> - Linear functions that have different slopes will intersect at one point.
> - Linear functions that have slopes that are opposite reciprocals will intersect and will be perpendicular.

Example 2

First, determine whether each of the functions below is increasing, decreasing, or neither. Then, determine the slope for each function.

(i)

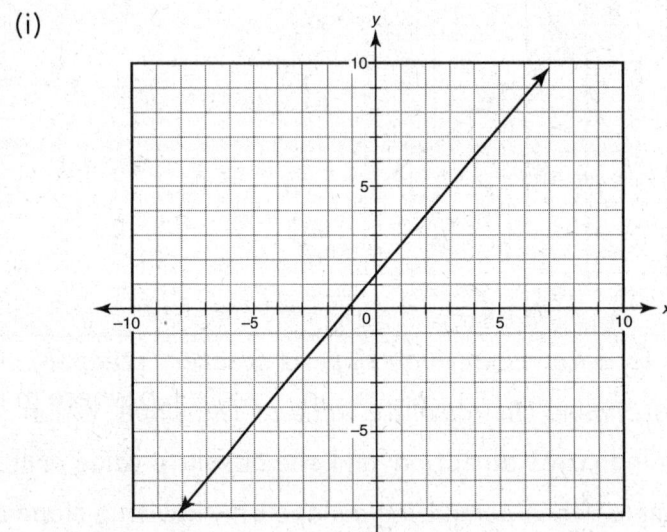

(ii) $y = -\dfrac{5}{6}x + 2$

(iii) $\{(1, -3), (6, 3), (-4, -9)\}$

(iv) $y = 2x - 3$

Answers: **Linear functions (i), (iii), and (iv) are increasing because the slopes are positive. Also, for linear function (i), the graph can be seen, from left to right, increasing. Linear function (ii) is decreasing because the slope is negative.**

(i) Choose two ordered pairs on the line, (−2, −1) and (3, 5), and then use the slope formula to determine the slope:

$$\text{slope} = \frac{y_2 - y_1}{x_2 - x_1}$$

$$\text{slope} = \frac{-1 - 5}{-2 - 3}$$

$$\text{slope} = \frac{-6}{-5} = \mathbf{\frac{6}{5}}$$

(ii) Using the slope-intercept form of a linear equation, $y = mx + b$ where m is the slope, in the equation $y = -\frac{5}{6}x + 2$, the slope is $\mathbf{-\frac{5}{6}}$.

(iii) Choose two ordered pairs from the set, (6, 3) and (−4, −9), and then use the slope formula to determine the slope:

$$\text{slope} = \frac{y_2 - y_1}{x_2 - x_1}$$

$$\text{slope} = \frac{-9 - 3}{-4 - 6}$$

$$\text{slope} = \frac{-12}{-10} = \mathbf{\frac{6}{5}}$$

(iv) Using the slope-intercept form of a linear equation, $y = mx + b$ where m is the slope, in the equation $y = 2x - 3$, the slope is **2**.

Example 3

Determine the relationship (parallel, intersecting and not perpendicular, or intersecting and perpendicular) between each pair of linear functions from Example 2.

- A. (i) and (ii)
- B. (i) and (iii)
- C. (ii) and (iii)
- D. (i) and (iv)
- E. (ii) and (iv)
- F. (iii) and (iv)

Answers:

A. **The slopes of (i) and (ii) are slopes of intersecting and perpendicular functions.** They are opposite reciprocals.
B. **The slopes of (i) and (iii) are slopes of parallel functions.** The slopes are the same. Since none of the ordered pairs from (iii) would appear on the graph of (i), if plotted, (i) and (iii) are not collinear, which means they will not have the same *y*-intercept.
C. **The slopes of (ii) and (iii) are slopes of intersecting and perpendicular functions.** They are opposite reciprocals.
D. **The slopes of (i) and (iv) are different, so the functions will intersect but are not perpendicular because the slopes are not opposite reciprocals.**
E. **The slopes of (ii) and (iv) are different, so the functions will intersect but are not perpendicular because the slopes are not opposite reciprocals.**
F. **The slopes of (iii) and (iv) are different, so the functions will intersect but are not perpendicular because the slopes are not opposite reciprocals.**

Example 4

Sherril and her parents have $40,000 in savings for college. She plans to take $10,000 per year for tuition. Write a linear function that gives the balance *y* in the savings account after *x* years of withdrawals. Identify whether it is an increasing or decreasing function.

Answer: **This linear equation will represent a decreasing function. The linear function will be *y* = $40,000 − $10,000*x*** or written in slope-intercept form:

$$y = -\$10{,}000x + \$40{,}000$$

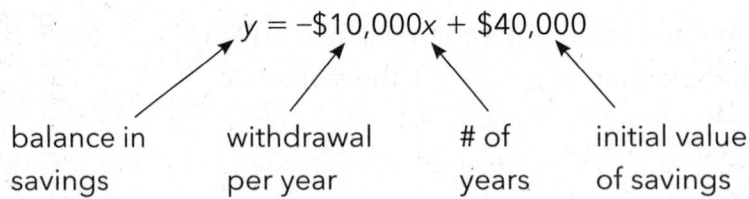

balance in savings | withdrawal per year | # of years | initial value of savings

The slope is −$10,000, and the *y*-intercept is $40,000. This *y*-intercept is referred to as the initial value because it is the starting amount for the problem when *x* (number of years of withdrawals) is 0.

Example 5

Geordie's savings are recorded in the following table. Given this information, write a linear function that will represent his total savings s after w weeks.

Number of Weeks w	4	6	9	10
Total Savings s	$100	$150	$225	$250

Answer: **The linear function would be y = $25x.** Choose two ordered pairs from the table, (4, $100) and (6, $150), and use the slope formula:

$$\text{slope} = \frac{y_2 - y_1}{x_2 - x_1}$$

$$\text{slope} = \frac{\$150 - \$100}{6 - 4}$$

$$\text{slope} = \frac{\$50}{2} = \frac{\$25}{1}$$

From the ordered pairs, a positive slope indicates an increase of $25 per week. With no initial savings given in the problem, the y-intercept, or initial value at x = 0 weeks, is $0.

Example 6

Determine which of the following statements are supported by the graph below. Fill in the correct circle next to each statement.

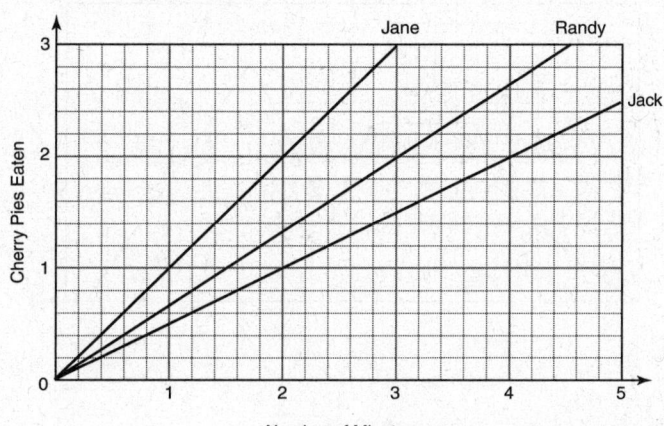

	Supported	Not Supported
A. Jack finished 2 pies in 1 minute.	○	○
B. Randy finished 2 pies in 3 minutes.	○	○
C. Jane finished one pie each minute.	○	○
D. Jane finished 3 pies first.	○	○
E. The slope for each line is represented by $\frac{\text{\# of minutes}}{\text{\# of cherry pies eaten}}$.	○	○

Answers:

A. Not Supported
B. Supported
C. Supported
D. Supported
E. Not Supported

The slope for Jane's line is 1, the slope for Randy's line is $\frac{2}{3}$, and the slope for Jack's line is $\frac{1}{2}$. Since the slope is the change in the *y*-coordinates (the number of cherry pies eaten) over the change in the *x*-coordinates (the number of minutes), that means that Jane ate 1 pie per minute, Randy ate 2 pies in 3 minutes (or 1 pie every 1.5 minutes), and Jack ate 1 pie every 2 minutes.

Guided Practice

1. Describe a situation that might be represented by the following graph.

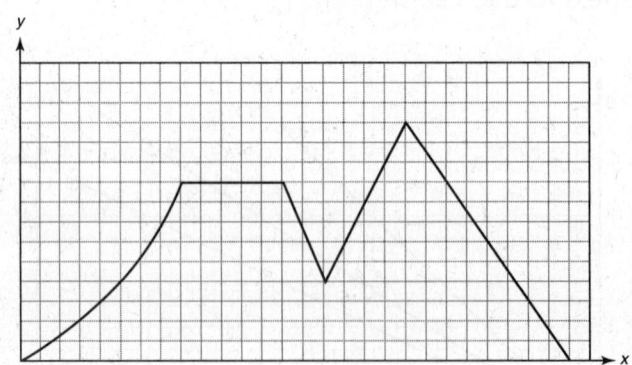

2. Determine whether each of the following linear functions is increasing, decreasing, or neither.

   A. $y = \frac{2}{3}x + 7$

   B.
   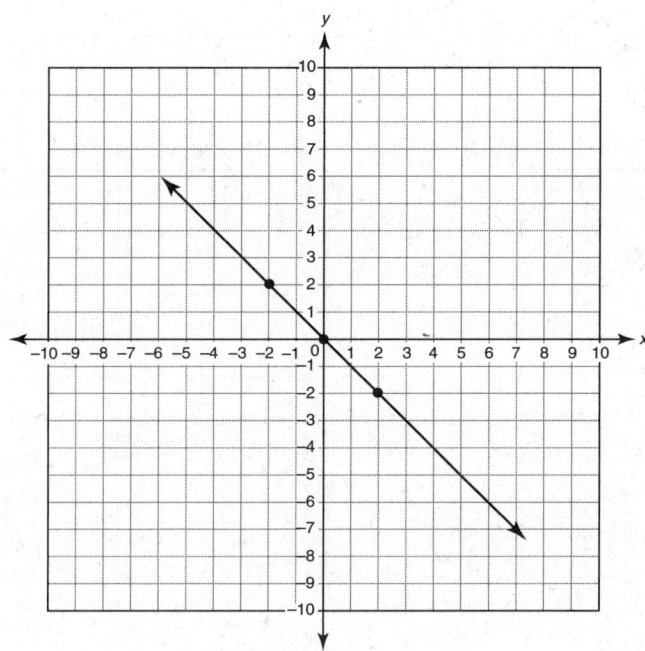

   C.

x	1	2	3	−4
y	7	7	7	7

3. Ken says that two linear equations ($3x + 4y = 12$ and $4x − 3y = 12$) represent parallel lines. Kevin says that these two linear equations represent perpendicular lines. Who is correct and why?

4. Hannah's parents started a savings account for her with an initial deposit of $1,000. If she adds $200 per month, create an equation to represent this linear function where t is the total amount in her account after m months.

5. For each of the following representations of linear functions, indicate whether the function is parallel, intersecting but not perpendicular, or intersecting and perpendicular to the linear function $y = 3x + 4$ by writing the letter that corresponds to each function in the appropriate section of the following table.

Parallel	Intersecting, but Not Perpendicular	Intersecting and Perpendicular

A.

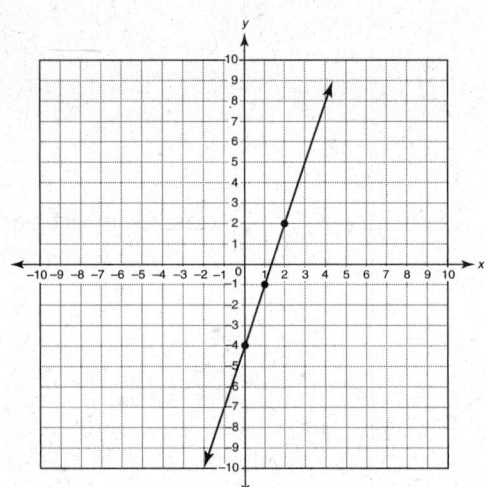

B.

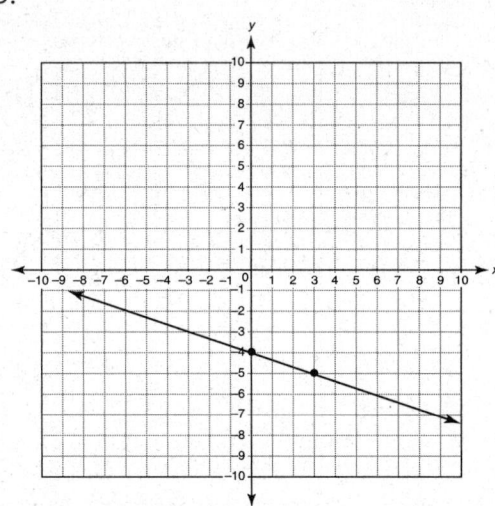

C. {(0, −5), (1, −1), (3, 7), (−2, −13)} D. $y = \frac{2}{3}x + 4$ E. $-9x + 3y = 15$

Guided Practice Answers Explained

1. **Answers will vary.** Sample Situation: Use x for time, and use y for water pressure. Donna gradually increases the water flow through her hose. She then maintains the desired water pressure for cleaning the driveway. Next, she steadily decreases the water pressure to water the plants along the driveway. Then, she steadily increases the water pressure to clean the sidewalk. Finally, she steadily decreases the water pressure as she waters the grass until the water flow stops completely.

2. **A. increasing**   **B. decreasing**   **C. neither**

   A. The slope is $\frac{2}{3}$ according to the slope-intercept form of the equation $y = mx + b$, in which the coefficient of x is the slope. Since the slope is positive, this linear function is increasing.

   B. The slope is negative, as indicated by the graph. Since, from left to right, the line is moving down, this linear function is decreasing.

c. From the table, choose two ordered pairs, (1, 7) and (2, 7), and calculate the slope:

$$\text{slope} = \frac{y_2 - y_1}{x_2 - x_1}$$

$$\text{slope} = \frac{7 - 7}{2 - 1}$$

$$\text{slope} = \frac{0}{1} = 0$$

This linear function is neither increasing nor decreasing. A graph of this function will be a horizontal line. Note that, in the table, the y-coordinates are all the same. This indicates no change along the y-axis.

3. **Kevin is correct.** These equations represent perpendicular lines. Convert each of the equations to $y = mx + b$ form.

$$3x + 4y = 12 \qquad\qquad 4x - 3y = 12$$
$$\underline{-3x \qquad = -3x} \qquad\qquad \underline{-4x \qquad = -4x}$$
$$\frac{4y}{4} = \frac{-3x + 12}{4} \qquad\qquad \frac{-3y}{-3} = \frac{-4x + 12}{-3}$$
$$y = -\frac{3}{4}x + 3 \qquad\qquad y = \frac{4}{3}x - 4$$

The slope of the first equation is $-\frac{3}{4}$, and the slope of the second equation is $\frac{4}{3}$. Since the slopes are opposite reciprocals, these equations represent perpendicular lines.

4. **t = $200m + $1,000** The slope is an increase of $200 every month, and the y-intercept is the initial value of $1,000. The y-intercept is where the number of months is equal to 0.

5.

Parallel	Intersecting, but Not Perpendicular	Intersecting and Perpendicular
A, E	C, D	B

The slope of the given equation is 3. In slope-intercept form of the equation, $y = mx + b$, 3 is the value of m, which represents the slope. The y-intercept is 4, the value of b.

A. The slope of the graphed linear function is 3. Choose two points on the line, (0, −4) and (2, 2), and calculate the slope.

$$\text{slope} = \frac{y_2 - y_1}{x_2 - x_1}$$

$$\text{slope} = \frac{2 - (-4)}{2 - 0}$$

$$\text{slope} = \frac{6}{2} = \frac{3}{1}$$

The y-intercept shown on the graph is −4. Since the slopes are the same and the y-intercepts are different, the graphs of the linear functions will be parallel.

B. The slope of the graphed linear function is $-\frac{1}{3}$. Choose two points on the line, (0, −4) and (3, −5), and calculate the slope.

$$\text{slope} = \frac{y_2 - y_1}{x_2 - x_1}$$

$$\text{slope} = \frac{-5 - (-4)}{3 - 0}$$

$$\text{slope} = -\frac{1}{3}$$

Since the slopes of the graphs are opposite reciprocals, the lines will be intersecting and perpendicular.

C. The slope for the linear function represented by this set of ordered pairs is 4. Using two points from the set, (0, −5) and (3, 7), the slope can be calculated as follows:

$$\text{slope} = \frac{y_2 - y_1}{x_2 - x_1}$$

$$\text{slope} = \frac{7 - (-5)}{3 - 0}$$

$$\text{slope} = \frac{12}{3} = 4$$

Since the slopes are different (3 and 4, respectively), the graphs of the linear functions will intersect, but will not be perpendicular since the slopes are not opposite reciprocals.

D. The slope of the given equation is $\frac{2}{3}$. In slope-intercept form of this equation, $y = mx + b$, $\frac{2}{3}$ is the value of m, which represents the slope. Since the slopes are different $\left(3 \text{ and } \frac{2}{3}, \text{ respectively}\right)$, the graphs of the linear functions will intersect, but will not be perpendicular since the slopes are not opposite reciprocals.

E. The slope of this equation is 3. Transform the equation to slope-intercept form, $y = mx + b$, and 3 is the value of m, which represents the slope. The y-intercept is 5, which is the value of b. Since these equations have the same slope, but different y-intercepts, these equations represent linear functions that are parallel.

$$-9x + 3y = 15$$
$$\underline{+9x = +9x}$$
$$\frac{3y = 9x + 15}{3}$$
$$y = 3x + 5$$

Independent Practice

1. Sketch a graph that represents the following situation with speed as a function over time:

   Kalon is riding his motorcycle at a consistent speed. He sees a pedestrian in a crosswalk ahead and slows gradually as he approaches the crosswalk. Stopped, he waits for the pedestrian to cross. Then gradually he brings the bike back to the same consistent speed that he was riding at initially, riding for approximately the same amount of time that he did before until he gets to his destination. As he turns into his destination, he slows down gradually and comes to a complete stop when he parks the motorcycle.

2. Give a linear equation *or* a graphical representation for each of the following situations:

   A. Increasing linear function
   B. Decreasing linear function
   C. Increasing nonlinear function
   D. Decreasing nonlinear function
   E. Linear function that neither increases nor decreases
   F. Increasing and decreasing nonlinear function

3. Write a linear equation that represents a linear function for each of the following situations related to $y = -\frac{4}{5}x + 1$:

   A. Parallel
   B. Perpendicular
   C. Intersecting, but not perpendicular
   D. Having a steeper slope
   E. Having a less steep slope
   F. Having a slope of zero

(Answers are on page 255.)

Slope and Similarity

Key Concepts

- The idea that the slope between any two points on a line is constant can be verified by using similar triangles.

Example 1

Given Triangle *AEF* ~ Triangle *ABC*, demonstrate that the slope between *AE* and *AB* is the same.

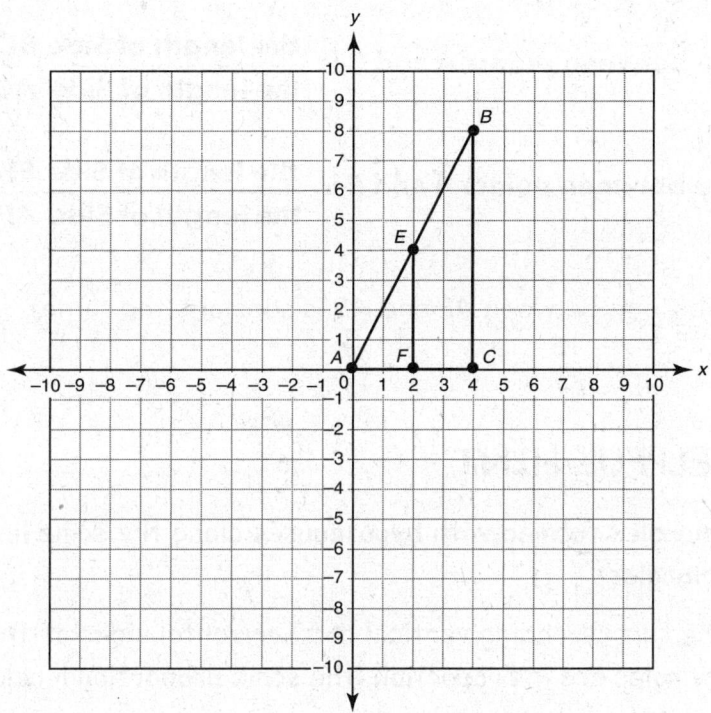

Answer: Triangle *AEF* is similar to Triangle *ABC*, so the corresponding vertical and horizontal sides are in proportion:

$$\frac{\text{Side } BC}{\text{Side } EF} = \frac{\text{Side } AC}{\text{Side } AF}$$

$$\frac{8}{4} = \frac{4}{2}$$

$$\frac{2}{1} = \frac{2}{1}$$

Since the corresponding side lengths of the larger triangle are in proportion to those of the smaller triangle, it is also true that the relationship between the sides of the larger triangle is the same as the relationship between the sides of the smaller triangle.

The vertical distance of each right triangle will relate to the horizontal distance of each triangle. The slope represents the relationship between the vertical and horizontal distances of all right triangles (slope triangles) on a line.

The slope between points A and B is $\dfrac{\text{the length of Side } BC}{\text{the length of Side } AC} = \dfrac{8}{4} = \dfrac{2}{1}$

The slope between points A and E is $\dfrac{\text{the length of Side } EF}{\text{the length of Side } AF} = \dfrac{4}{2} = \dfrac{2}{1}$

Therefore, the slope between AE and AB is constant (the same).

💡 HELPFUL HINT

Right triangles formed with hypotenuses along the same line are called **slope triangles**.

Since the corresponding vertical and horizontal sides of these similar right triangles are in proportion, the same proportional relationship exists with the hypotenuses.

The slope (the ratio between the vertical and horizontal sides) will be the same along any two points along the line.

SBAC Challenge Questions

1. Customers at a movie theater will pay $8 for admission for children under 12, $12 for regular admission, or $10 for senior citizens over the age of 60. Dale states that the cost of admission is a function of the age of the customer. Patti states that the age of the customer is a function of the cost of admission. Who is right? Explain.

2. Elaine has the following set of ordered pairs {(2, 6), (−4, 9), (12, −5), (1, 1)}. She states that they make a function. She also claims that she can add any ordered pair to the set, and it will still be a function. She gives the examples of (−1, 3) and (5, −1). Given this evidence, Matt initially agrees with Elaine but then starts

to question her statement. Which of the following ordered pairs can Matt use to prove that Elaine's claim is false? Select all that apply.

☐ A. (2, 9)   ☐ B. (1, −1)   ☐ C. (10, −4)   ☐ D. (4, 9)   ☐ E. (12, −4)

3. Write a linear equation in slope-intercept form that is parallel to $y = 0.5x + 4$ and for which the ordered pair (4, 1) is a solution.

4. Write a linear equation in slope-intercept form that is perpendicular to $y = -\frac{2}{3}x + 5$ and for which the ordered pair (6, −1) is a solution.

5. Write a linear equation in standard form that intersects, but is not perpendicular to, the linear equation $y = 3x - 9$ and for which the ordered pair (3, −2) is a solution. (Remember: Standard form of an equation is $Ax + By = C$, where A, B, and C must all be integers.)

(Answers are on page 262.)

Linear Equations in One Variable

CHAPTER 2

Common Core Standard 8.EE.C.7

Solve linear equations in one variable.

Common Core Standard 8.EE.C.7.A

Give examples of linear equations in one variable with one solution, infinitely many solutions, or no solutions. Show which of these possibilities is the case by successively transforming the given equation into simpler forms, until an equivalent equation of the form $x = a$, $a = a$, or $a = b$ results (where a and b are different numbers).

Common Core Standard 8.EE.C.7.B

Solve linear equations with rational number coefficients, including equations whose solutions require expanding expressions using the distributive property and collecting like terms.

Solving Multi-Step Linear Equations

Key Concepts

- Before solving linear equations, both sides of the equation must be simplified using the order of operations.
- Then, all variables must be collected to one side of the equation and the constants must be collected to the other side of the equation.
- Solving an equation uses inverse operations and related properties of equality.
- Solving equations for real-life or mathematical problems is based on a variable which must be defined before writing the equation.

Example 1

Solve: $3x - 2 = 5x + 2$

Answer: **The solution to this equation is –2.**

$$3x - 2 = 5x + 2$$
$$\underline{-5x = -5x}$$

(Collect all variables on one side. Use the Subtraction Property of Equality to subtract $5x$ from both sides.)

$$-2x - 2 = 2$$
$$\underline{+ 2 = +2}$$

(Simplify. Use the Addition Property of Equality to add 2 to both sides.)

$$-2x = 4$$

(Simplify.)

$$\frac{-2x}{-2} = \frac{4}{-2}$$

(Use the Division Property of Equality to divide both sides by –2.)

$$x = -2$$

Example 2

Solve: $4\left(x + \dfrac{1}{2}\right) - 3 = 2(x + 5) - 1$

Answer: **The solution to this equation is 5.**

$$4\left(x + \frac{1}{2}\right) - 3 = 2(x + 5) - 1$$

(Simplify each side of the equation.)

$$4x + 2 - 3 = 2x + 10 - 1$$

$$4x - 1 = 2x + 9$$
$$\underline{-2x = -2x}$$

(Collect all variables on one side. Use the Subtraction Property of Equality to subtract $2x$ from both sides.)

$$2x - 1 = 9$$
$$\underline{+ 1 = +1}$$

(Simplify. Use the Addition Property of Equality to add 1 to both sides.)

$$2x = 10$$

(Simplify.)

$$\frac{2x}{2} = \frac{10}{2}$$

(Use the Division Property of Equality to divide both sides by 2.)

$$x = 5$$

Example 3

Solve: $\dfrac{2}{3}(x + 6) = \dfrac{1}{3}(3x + 9)$

<u>Answer:</u> **The solution to this equation is 3.**

$\dfrac{2}{3}(x + 6) = \dfrac{1}{3}(3x + 9)$ (Simplify each side of the equation.)

$3\left(\dfrac{2}{3}x + 4 = x + 3\right)$ (Use the Multiplication Property of Equality to eliminate the denominator of the remaining fraction by multiplying each term of the equation by 3.)

$2x + 12 = 3x + 9$ (Collect all variables on one side. Use the Subtraction Property of Equality to subtract $3x$ from both sides.)
$\underline{-3x \qquad\quad = -3x}$

$-1x + 12 = 9$ (Simplify. Use the Subtraction Property of Equality to subtract 12 from both sides.)
$\underline{\qquad -12 = -12}$

$-1x = -3$ (Simplify.)

$\dfrac{-1x}{-1} = \dfrac{-3}{-1}$ (Use the Division Property of Equality to divide both sides by -1.)

$x = 3$

Example 4

The length of a rectangle is 8 centimeters longer than the width. Determine the length and width of this rectangle if the perimeter is 28 centimeters.

<u>Answer:</u> **The width of the rectangle is 3 centimeters and the length of the rectangle is 11 centimeters.**

First, define the variables:

$$x = \text{width in centimeters}$$

$$x + 8 = \text{length in centimeters}$$

$$\text{Perimeter} = 2(\text{length}) + 2(\text{width})$$

Perimeter = 2(length) + 2(width)   (Use the perimeter formula as the basis of the equation.)

$28 = 2(x + 8) + 2x$ (Substitute the variables into the perimeter equation.)

$28 = 2x + 16 + 2x$ (Simplify.)

$28 = 4x + 16$ (Use the Subtraction Property of Equality to subtract 16 from both sides.)
$\underline{-16 = -16}$

$12 = 4x$ (Simplify.)

$\dfrac{12}{4} = \dfrac{4x}{4}$ (Use the Division Property of Equality to divide both sides by 4.)

$3 = x$ (Simplify.)

If $x = 3$, then the width is 3 centimeters and the length is $x + 8 = 11$ centimeters.

Guided Practice

For Questions 1–3, solve each equation.

1. $2(2a - 2) + 15 + a = 8 + 2a$

2. $\dfrac{2}{5}v = 45 - \dfrac{1}{2}v$

3. $\dfrac{9z + 6 - 4z}{2} = 8$

4. Roberta weighs $\dfrac{3}{5}$ as many pounds as Jonathan. If their weight totals 240 pounds, how much does Jonathan weigh?

5. The width of a patio is one-fourth of the patio's length. If the perimeter of the patio is 150 feet, find the dimensions of the patio.

Guided Practice Answers Explained

1. **−1**

   $2(2a − 2) + 15 + a = 8 + 2a$ (Simplify each side of the equation.)

   $4a − 4 + 15 + a = 8 + 2a$

   $5a + 11 = 8 + 2a$ (Collect all variables on one side. Use the Subtraction Property of Equality to subtract $2a$ from both sides.)

   $\underline{ −2a = −2a}$

   $3a + 11 = 8$ (Simplify. Use the Subtraction Property of Equality to subtract 11 from both sides.)

   $\underline{ −11 = −11}$

   $3a = −3$ (Simplify.)

   $\dfrac{3a}{3} = \dfrac{−3}{3}$ (Use the Division Property of Equality to divide both sides of the equation by 3.)

   $a = −1$

2. **50**

   $10\left(\dfrac{2}{5}v = 45 − \dfrac{1}{2}v\right)$ (To eliminate the fractional coefficients in the equation, use the Multiplication Property of Equality to multiply each term of the equation by the common denominator (10) of the two fractions.)

   $4v = 450 − 5v$ (Use the Addition Property of Equality to add $5v$ to both sides.)

   $\underline{+ 5v = + 5v}$

   $9v = 450$ (Simplify.)

   $\dfrac{9v}{9} = \dfrac{450}{9}$ (Use the Division Property of Equality to divide both sides of the equation by 9.)

   $v = 50$

3. **2**

$$\frac{9z + 6 - 4z}{2} = 8 \qquad \text{(Simplify.)}$$

$$2\left(\frac{5z + 6}{2} = 8\right) \qquad \text{(Use the Multiplication Property of Equality to multiply each term of the equation by 2 to eliminate the fraction.)}$$

$$5z + 6 = 16 \qquad \text{(Use the Subtraction Property of Equality to subtract 6 from both sides.)}$$
$$\underline{-6 = -6}$$

$$5z = 10 \qquad \text{(Simplify.)}$$

$$\frac{5z}{5} = \frac{10}{5} \qquad \text{(Use the Division Property of Equality to divide both sides of the equation by 5.)}$$

$$z = 2$$

4. **Jonathan weighs 150 pounds.**

Define the variables:

$$j = \text{Jonathan's weight}$$

$$\frac{3}{5}j = \text{Roberta's weight}$$

The equation $j + \frac{3}{5}j = 240$ represents their total weight.

Solve the equation for j.

$$5\left(j + \frac{3}{5}j = 240\right) \qquad \text{(To eliminate the fractional coefficient in the equation, use the Multiplication Property of Equality to multiply each term of the equation by 5.)}$$

$$5j + 3j = 1{,}200 \qquad \text{(Simplify.)}$$

$$\frac{8j}{8} = \frac{1{,}200}{8} \qquad \text{(Use the Division Property of Equality to divide both sides of the equation by 8.)}$$

$$j = 150$$

Since $j =$ Jonathan's weight, Jonathan weighs 150 pounds.

5. **The dimensions of the patio are a length of 60 feet and a width of 15 feet.**

Define the variables:

$$x = \text{the length of the patio}$$

$$\frac{1}{4}x = \text{the width of the patio}$$

The formula for perimeter is $P = 2(\text{length}) + 2(\text{width})$.

Therefore, the equation to represent the perimeter of this patio is $150 = 2x + 2\left(\frac{1}{4}x\right)$. Solve the equation for x.

$$150 = 2\left(\frac{1}{4}x + x\right) \quad \text{(Simplify.)}$$

$$150 = \frac{1}{2}x + 2x \quad \text{(Combine like terms.)}$$

$$2\left[150 = \frac{5}{2}x\right] \quad \text{(Use the Multiplication Property of Equality to eliminate the denominator of the fraction by multiplying each term in the equation by 2.)}$$

$$\frac{300}{5} = \frac{5x}{5} \quad \text{(Use the Division Property of Equality to divide both sides by 5.)}$$

$$60 = x$$

Since $x = 60$, the length of the patio is 60 feet. The width is represented by $\frac{1}{4}x = \frac{1}{4}(60) = 15$, so the width of the patio is 15 feet.

Independent Practice

1. Solve: $3x + 9x + 3 = \frac{1}{2}(6x - 18) + 5x$

2. Which of the following equations has the same solution as $-4x + 5 = 2x + 17$? Fill in the circle next to Yes or No for each equation.

	Yes	No
A. $6(x - 3) + 4 = \frac{1}{2}(6x - 8) + 8x$	○	○
B. $3x - 5 = 12x + 11$	○	○
C. $5x + 5 + 9x + 2 = 13x + 5$	○	○
D. $\frac{2}{3}x + \frac{3}{4}x = 17$	○	○

3. An online game club charges a $33 membership fee and $2.50 to rent each game. Nonmembers pay $4 for each game rental. For how many games will the charge be the same?

4. Solve: $3x - 2(x + 7) = 3(x - 5) - (x - 9)$

(Answers are on page 266.)

Determining the Number of Solutions to Linear Equations

When solved, some linear equations will have one solution, some will have no possible real number solution(s), and others will have infinite solutions. The process for solving these equations remains the same.

> **Key Concepts**
>
> - When a linear equation is solved, and the variable is equal to a constant, the equation has one solution.
>
> - When a linear equation is solved, and the variable cancels from both the left and right sides of the equation, the remaining constants determine the number of solutions.
>
> - If the remaining constants do not make a true statement, the equation has no real number solutions. This means that no matter what value is substituted for the variable, the two sides of the equation will not be equivalent.
>
> - If the remaining constants make a true statement, the equation has infinite solutions. This means that no matter what value is substituted for the variable, the two sides of the equation will be equivalent.

This information is condensed in Table 2-1.

Linear Equations in One Variable • 57

Table 2-1. Determining the Number of Solutions to Linear Equations

Number of Solutions	Variable	Constant
One solution	Solves to a coefficient of one	One constant on the side opposite the variable
No real number solutions	Cancels to a zero coefficient	Constants on both sides of the equal sign do not make a true statement
Infinite solutions	Cancels to a zero coefficient	Constants on both sides of the equal sign make a true statement

Example 1

Determine the number of solutions: $10 - (x - 2) = 4 - 2x + 5 + x$

<u>Answer:</u> **No solutions**

> 💡 **HELPFUL HINT**
>
> When subtracting an expression, you must **add the inverse of each term** in the expression OR consider it as distributing a negative one over each term in the parentheses.

$10 - (x - 2) = 4 - 2x + 5 + x$	(Simplify both sides of the equation before solving.)
$10 + (-x) + 2 = -x + 9$ 	(Use the Addition Property of Equality to add x to both sides.)
$12 \neq 9$	(Simplify. The remaining constants do not make a true statement.)

The variables canceled. The constants on either side of the equal sign do not make a true statement. Therefore, this equation has no solutions.

Example 2

Determine the number of solutions: $4x - 3 + 2x = 3(2x - 1)$

<u>Answer:</u> **Infinite solutions**

$4x - 3 + 2x = 3(2x - 1)$	(Simplify both sides of the equation before solving.)
$6x - 3 = 6x - 3$ $\underline{-6x = -6x}$	(Use the Subtraction Property of Equality to subtract $6x$ from both sides.)
$-3 = -3$	(Simplify. The remaining constants make a true statement.)

The variables canceled. The constants on either side of the equal sign make a true statement. Therefore, this equation has infinite solutions.

Guided Practice

For Questions 1–3, determine the number of solutions for each equation.

1. $2f - 15 + f = -8 + 3f - 7$

2. $\frac{3}{4}x - \frac{5}{6} = \frac{2}{3}x$

3. $3(2m + 4) = 2(3m - 6)$

4. Determine which of the following equations have no solutions. Select all that apply.

☐ A. $3(6x - 2) - x = 15x - 5 + 2x$
☐ B. $3x - 12 = 3(x - 4)$
☐ C. $\frac{3}{5}m - \frac{1}{10}m = \frac{2}{5}m + 2$
☐ D. $\frac{3}{8}x = \frac{1}{4}x + \frac{3}{8}$
☐ E. $8 + 9x - 2 = 3(3x + 1)$

Guided Practice Answers Explained

1. **Infinite solutions**

   $2f - 15 + f = -8 + 3f - 7$ (Simplify both sides of the equation before solving.)

   $3f - 15 = 3f - 15$ (Use the Subtraction Property of Equality to subtract $3f$ from both sides.)
   $\underline{-3f = -3f}$
   $-15 = -15$ (Simplify. The remaining constants make a true statement.)

   The variables canceled. The constants on either side of the equal sign make a true statement. Therefore, this equation has infinite solutions.

2. **One solution**

   $12\left(\dfrac{3}{4}x - \dfrac{5}{6} = \dfrac{2}{3}x\right)$ (Eliminate the fractional coefficients by using the common denominator and the Multiplication Property of Equality to multiply each term in the equation by 12.)

   $9x - 10 = 8x$ (Simplify. Use the Subtraction Property of Equality to subtract $8x$ from both sides.)
   $\underline{-8x = -8x}$
   $x - 10 = 0$ (Simplify. Use the Addition Property of Equality to add 10 to both sides.)
   $\underline{+ 10 = +10}$
   $x = 10$ (Simplify. There is only one constant on the side opposite the variable.)

   The variable is equal to 10. This equation has one solution.

3. **No solutions**

   $3(2m + 4) = 2(3m - 6)$ (Simplify both sides of the equation before solving.)

   $6m + 12 = 6m - 12$ (Use the Subtraction Property of Equality to subtract $6m$ from both sides.)
   $\underline{-6m = -6m}$

   $12 \neq -12$ (Simplify. The remaining constants do not make a true statement.)

The variables canceled. The constants on either side of the equal sign do not make a true statement. Therefore, this equation has no solutions.

4. **(A) and (E)**

A. $3(6x - 2) - x = 15x - 5 + 2x$ (Simplify both sides of the equation before solving.)

$18x - 6 - x = 17x - 5$

$17x - 6 = 17x - 5$ (Use the Subtraction Property of Equality to subtract $17x$ from both sides.)

$\underline{-17x = -17x}$

$-6 \neq -5$ (Simplify. The remaining constants do not make a true statement.)

The variables canceled. The constants on either side of the equal sign do not make a true statement. Therefore, this equation has no solutions.

B. $3x - 12 = 3(x - 4)$ (Simplify both sides of the equation before solving.)

$3x - 12 = 3x - 12$ (Use the Subtraction Property of Equality to subtract $3x$ from both sides.)

$\underline{-3x = -3x}$

$-12 = -12$ (Simplify. The remaining constants make a true statement.)

The variables canceled. The constants on either side of the equal sign make a true statement. Therefore, this equation has infinite solutions.

C. $10\left(\dfrac{3}{5}m - \dfrac{1}{10}m = \dfrac{2}{5}m + 2\right)$ (Eliminate the fractional coefficients by using the common denominator and the Multiplication Property of Equality to multiply each term in the equation by 10.)

$6m - m = 4m + 20$ (Combine like terms.)

$5m = 4m + 20$ (Simplify. Use the Subtraction Property of Equality to subtract $4m$ from both sides.)

$\underline{-4m = -4m}$

$m = 20$ (Simplify. There is only one constant on the side opposite the variable.)

The variable is equal to 20. This equation has one solution.

Linear Equations in One Variable • 61

D. $8\left(\dfrac{3}{8}x = \dfrac{1}{4}x + \dfrac{3}{8}\right)$ (Eliminate the fractional coefficients by using the common denominator and the Multiplication Property of Equality to multiply each term in the equation by 8.)

$3x = 2x + 3$ (Simplify. Use the Subtraction Property of Equality to subtract $2x$ from both sides.)
$\underline{-2x = -2x}$
$x = 3$ (Simplify. There is only one constant on the side opposite the variable.)

The variable is equal to 3. This equation has one solution.

E. $8 + 9x - 2 = 3(3x + 1)$ (Simplify both sides of the equation before solving.)

$9x + 6 = 9x + 3$ (Use the Subtraction Property of Equality to subtract $9x$ from both sides.)
$\underline{-9x \quad\quad = -9x}$
$6 \ne 3$ (Simplify. The remaining constants do not make a true statement.)

The variables canceled. The constants on either side of the equal sign do not make a true statement. Therefore, this equation has no solutions.

Independent Practice

1. Ellie states that the solution $x = 0$ means that the equation has no solutions. Do you agree or disagree with Ellie? Explain your reasoning.

2. Determine the number of solutions for each equation. Choose your answer by filling in the correct circle next to each equation.

	One	None	Infinite
A. $12 - 2x + 5 = -2x + 7$	○	○	○
B. $-x + 7 = -(-7 + x)$	○	○	○
C. $x - 2x = -5x + 4 + 2x$	○	○	○
D. $6x + 3x - 5 = 6(3x - 2) + 1$	○	○	○

(Answers are on page 269.)

SBAC Challenge Questions

1. Each of the two congruent sides of an isosceles triangle is 5 feet less than three times the length of the base of the triangle. If the perimeter is 60 feet, how long is each of the congruent sides?

2. The length of a painting is six less than four times the width. A second painting has a length that is three times the width of the first painting. The width of the second painting is 30 inches more than the width of the first. Both paintings have the same perimeter. Determine the dimensions of each painting.

3. Determine which of the following steps contains the first error that leads to an incorrect solution.

   Step One: $2.6 - 3x = -2(x - 1.3)$
   Step Two: $2.6 - 3x = -2x + 2.6$
   Step Three: $\underline{\quad -2x = +2x \quad}$
   Step Four: $2.6 - 5x = 2.6$
   Step Five: $\underline{-2.6 \quad\quad = -2.6}$
   Step Six: $\dfrac{-5x}{-5} = \dfrac{0}{-5}$
   $x = 0$

   - A. Step One
   - B. Step Two
   - C. Step Three
   - D. Step Four

(Answers are on page 270.)

Chapter 3: Systems of Equations

Common Core Standard 8.EE.C.8.A

Understand that solutions to a system of two linear equations in two variables correspond to points of intersection of their graphs, because points of intersection satisfy both equations simultaneously.

Common Core Standard 8.EE.C.8.B

Solve systems of two linear equations in two variables algebraically, and estimate solutions by graphing the equations. Solve simple cases by inspection. For example, $3x + 2y = 5$ and $3x + 2y = 6$ have no solution because $3x + 2y$ cannot simultaneously be 5 and 6.

Common Core Standard 8.EE.C.8.C

Solve real-world and mathematical problems leading to two linear equations in two variables. *For example, given coordinates for two pairs of points, determine whether the line through the first pair of points intersects the line through the second pair.*

Key Concepts

- Two or more equations that are related in some way are called a **system of equations**.
- Each equation in the system has an infinite number of ordered pairs that are solutions to that unique equation.
- When one ordered pair is a solution to *both* of the equations in the system, it is called the **solution** to the system.

There are three main ways to solve a system of equations. These methods are **substitution**, **elimination**, and **graphing**.

 **HELPFUL HINT**

Always use an original equation when substituting in any process.

Always alternate between the two equations in the system. *Always* switch equations for consecutive steps.

Solving Systems of Equations by Substitution

Steps for Solving Systems of Equations by Substitution

- **Isolate** one variable in one of the equations to a coefficient of one.
- **Substitute** the expression equal to this isolated variable into the second equation and solve it for a numerical result.
- **Substitute** this numerical value into the original first equation and solve it for a numerical result.
- The **solution** to the system is the ordered pair made from the pair of numerical results.
- **Check** the ordered pair by substituting it into the original second equation.
- This is the best method choice when one of the variables has a coefficient of one.

Example 1

Solve the following system of equations by substitution:

$$x = y - 2$$
$$3x - 2y = -9$$

<u>Answer:</u> The solution to this system is **(−5, −3)**.

<u>Step One:</u> **Isolate**

$x = y - 2$ (One of the equations already has x isolated in terms of y.)

Step Two: Substitute

$3x - 2y = -9$ (Substitute the expression $y - 2$ for x into the original second equation.)

$3(y - 2) - 2y = -9$

$3y - 6 - 2y = -9$ (Simplify.)

$y - 6 = -9$

$\underline{+ 6 = +6}$ (Use the Addition Property of Equality to add 6 to both sides.)

$y = -3$ (The result is a numerical value of -3 for y.)

Step Three: Substitute

$x = y - 2$ (Substitute the numerical value -3 for y into the original first equation.)

$x = -3 - 2$

$x = -5$ (The result is a numerical value of -5 for x.)

Step Four: Solution

$(-5, -3)$ (Use -5 for the x-coordinate and -3 for the y-coordinate of the ordered pair.)

Step Five: Check

$3x - 2y = -9$ (Substitute the ordered pair $(-5, -3)$ into the original second equation to determine if the ordered pair makes the equation true.)

$3(-5) - 2(-3) = -9$

$-15 + 6 = -9$

$-9 = -9$ (The statement is true. The ordered pair $(-5, -3)$ checks.)

Guided Practice

1. Solve the following system of equations by substitution:

$$2x + y = 19$$
$$2x - y = 1$$

2. Determine the x-coordinate for the solution for the following system of equations:

$$3x + 2y = 1$$
$$5y - 4x = 14$$

Guided Practice Answers Explained

1. **(5, 9)**

 HELPFUL HINT

When subtracting an expression, you must **add the inverse of each term** in the expression OR consider it as distributing a negative one over each term in the parentheses.

Step One: **Isolate**

$2x + y = 19$	(In this equation, the y has a coefficient of one, so isolate the y by using the Subtraction Property of Equality to subtract 2x from both sides.)
$\underline{-2x \quad = -2x}$	
$y = -2x + 19$	

Step Two: **Substitute**

$2x - y = 1$	(Substitute the expression $-2x + 19$ for y into the original second equation.)
$2x - (-2x + 19) = 1$	
$2x + 2x + (-19) = 1$	(See the Helpful Hint above for this answer explanation.)
$4x + (-19) = 1$	
$\underline{+19 = +19}$	(Use the Addition Property of Equality to add 19 to both sides.)
$\dfrac{4x}{4} = \dfrac{20}{4}$	(Simplify. Use the Division Property of Equality to divide both sides by 4.)
$x = 5$	(The result is a numerical value of 5 for x.)

Step Three: **Substitute**

$2x + y = 19$ (Substitute the numerical value 5 for x into the original first equation.)

$2(5) + y = 19$

$10 + y = 19$ (Simplify. Use the Subtraction Property of Equality to subtract 10 from both sides.)

$\underline{-10 = -10}$

$y = 9$ (The result is a numerical value of 9 for y.)

Step Four: **Solution**

$(5, 9)$ (Use 5 for the x-coordinate and 9 for the y-coordinate of the ordered pair.)

Step Five: **Check**

$2x - y = 1$ (Substitute the ordered pair (5, 9) into the original second equation to determine if the ordered pair makes the equation true.)

$2(5) - 9 = 1$

$10 - 9 = 1$

$1 = 1$ (The statement is true. The ordered pair (5, 9) checks.)

The solution to this system is (5, 9).

2. The x-coordinate is −1.

Step One: **Isolate**

$3x + 2y = 1$ (Isolate the variable x in terms of y.)

$\underline{-2y = -2y}$ (Use the Subtraction Property of Equality to subtract $2y$ from both sides.)

$\dfrac{3x}{3} = \dfrac{-2y + 1}{3}$ (Use the Division Property of Equality to divide both sides by 3.)

$x = -\dfrac{2}{3}y + \dfrac{1}{3}$ (Simplify.)

Step Two: **Substitute**

$5y - 4x = 14$ (Substitute the expression $-\frac{2}{3}y + \frac{1}{3}$ for x into the original second equation.)

$5y - 4\left(-\frac{2}{3}y + \frac{1}{3}\right) = 14$ (When distributing multiplication of a negative, be certain to multiply each term by the negative.)

$5y + \frac{8}{3}y - \frac{4}{3} = 14$ (Simplify.)

$3\left(5y + \frac{8}{3}y - \frac{4}{3} = 14\right)$ (To eliminate the denominators, use the common denominator 3 and the Multiplication Property of Equality to multiply each term by 3.)

$15y + 8y - 4 = 42$ (Simplify.)

$23y - 4 = 42$ (Use the Addition Property of Equality to add 4 to both sides.)
$\underline{+4 = +4}$

$\frac{23y}{23} = \frac{46}{23}$ (Simplify. Use the Division Property of Equality to divide both sides by 23.)

$y = 2$ (The result is a numerical value of 2 for y.)

Step Three: **Substitute**

$3x + 2y = 1$ (Substitute the numerical value 2 for y into the original first equation.)

$3x + 2(2) = 1$

$3x + 4 = 1$ (Simplify. Use the Subtraction Property of Equality to subtract 4 from both sides.)
$\underline{-4 = -4}$

$\frac{3x}{3} = \frac{-3}{3}$ (Simplify. Use the Division Property of Equality to divide both sides by 3.)

$x = -1$ (The result is a numerical value of -1 for x.)

Step Four: **Solution**

(−1, 2) (Use −1 for the x-coordinate and 2 for the y-coordinate of the ordered pair.)

Step Five: **Check**

$5y - 4x = 14$ (Substitute the ordered pair (−1, 2) into the original second equation to determine if the ordered pair makes the equation true.)

$5(2) - 4(-1) = 14$

$10 + 4 = 14$

$14 = 14$ (The statement is true. The ordered pair (−1, 2) checks.)

The solution to this system is (−1, 2). That means that the x-coordinate is −1. It is good practice to complete the entire solution to check that both coordinates are correct before writing your answer.

Independent Practice

1. Solve the following system of equations by substitution: $3.5x - 4y = 56$ and $2x + y = 9$

2. Solve the following system of equations by substitution: $y - x = -2$ and $4x + 3y = -6$

3. Which of the following systems of equations have a solution with either an x-coordinate of −2 or a y-coordinate of −2? Select all that apply.

☐ A. $3x - 6y = 30$
      $6x + y = 34$

☐ B. $2y - 4x = 0$
      $6x = y + 8$

☐ C. $-4x + y = 12.5$
      $2y = 0.5x + 10$

(Answers are on page 272.)

Solving Systems of Equations by Elimination

> **Steps for Solving Systems of Equations by Elimination**
>
> - Create opposite coefficients for one variable in the system by **multiplying** one or both equations by factors. Then combine the two equations to eliminate that variable.
> - **Solve** the resulting equation for a numerical result for the other variable.
> - **Substitute** this numerical result into the original first equation, and solve for a numerical result.
> - The **solution** to the system is the ordered pair made from the pair of numerical results.
> - **Check** the ordered pair algebraically in the original second equation by substitution.
> - This is the best method choice when the coefficients of like variables in the equations will cancel easily or can be multiplied to cancel.

Example 1

Solve the following system of equations by elimination:

$$5x + 3y = 11$$
$$2x + 7y = -13$$

<u>Answer:</u> The solution to this system is **(4, −3)**.

<u>Step One:</u> **Multiply**

$-2(5x + 3y = 11) = -10x - 6y = -22$ (Multiply the first equation by −2 and the second equation by 5 to create opposite coefficients for x.)

$5(2x + 7y = -13) = 10x + 35y = -65$

<u>Step Two:</u> **Solve**

$-10x - 6y = -22$ (Combine the equations to eliminate the x-terms.)

$\underline{+10x + 35y = -65}$

$\dfrac{29y}{29} = \dfrac{-87}{29}$ (Use the Division Property of Equality to divide both sides by 29.)

$y = -3$ (The result is a numerical value of −3 for y.)

Systems of Equations · 71

Step Three: **Substitute**

$5x + 3y = 11$ (Substitute −3 for y into the original first equation.)

$5x + 3(-3) = 11$

$5x - 9 = 11$ (Use the Addition Property of Equality to add 9 to both sides.)

$\underline{+9 = +9}$

$\dfrac{5x}{5} = \dfrac{20}{5}$ (Use the Division Property of Equality to divide both sides by 5.)

$x = 4$ (The result is a numerical value of 4 for x.)

Step Four: **Solution**

$(4, -3)$ (Use 4 for the x-coordinate and −3 for the y-coordinate of the ordered pair.)

Step Five: **Check**

$2x + 7y = -13$ (Substitute the ordered pair (4, −3) into the original second equation to determine if the ordered pair makes the equation true.)

$2(4) + 7(-3) = -13$

$8 + (-21) = -13$

$-13 = -13$ (The statement is true. The ordered pair (4, −3) checks.)

Guided Practice

1. Solve the following system of equations by elimination:

$$3x + 2y = 14$$
$$x - y = -17$$

2. Solve the following system of equations by elimination:

$$5x - 6y = -59$$
$$2x - 2y = -22$$

Guided Practice Answers Explained

1. **(−4, 13)**

<u>Step One:</u> **Multiply**

$(3x + 2y = 14) = 3x + 2y = 14$ (Multiplying the second equation by 2 and leaving the first equation alone results in opposite coefficients for the variable y, which will cancel when simplified.)

$2(x − y = −17) = 2x − 2y = −34$

<u>Step Two:</u> **Solve**

$3x + 2y = 14$ (Combine the equations to eliminate the y-terms.)

$+2x − 2y = −34$

$\dfrac{5x}{5} = \dfrac{−20}{5}$ (Use the Division Property of Equality to divide both sides by 5.)

$x = −4$ (The result is a numerical value of −4 for x.)

<u>Step Three:</u> **Substitute**

$3x + 2y = 14$ (Substitute −4 for x in the original first equation.)

$3(−4) + 2y = 14$

$−12 + 2y = 14$ (Use the Addition Property of Equality to add 12 to both sides.)

$+12 = +12$

$\dfrac{2y}{2} = \dfrac{26}{2}$ (Use the Division Property of Equality to divide both sides by 2.)

$y = 13$ (The result is a numerical value of 13 for y.)

<u>Step Four:</u> **Solution**

$(−4, 13)$ (Use −4 for the x-coordinate and 13 for the y-coordinate of the ordered pair.)

Step Five: Check

$x - y = -17$ (Substitute the ordered pair (−4, 13) into the original second equation to determine if the ordered pair makes the equation true.)

$-4 - 13 = -17$

$-17 = -17$ (The statement is true. The ordered pair (−4, 13) checks.)

2. **(−7, 4)**

Step One: Multiply

$-1(5x - 6y = -59) = -5x + 6y = 59$ (Multiply the first equation by −1 and the second equation by 3 to create opposite coefficients for y.)

$3(2x - 2y = -22) = 6x - 6y = -66$

Step Two: Solve

$-5x + 6y = 59$ (Combine the equations to eliminate the y-terms.)

$+6x - 6y = -66$

$x = -7$ (The result is a numerical value of −7 for x.)

Step Three: Substitute

$5x - 6y = -59$ (Substitute −7 for x into the original first equation.)

$5(-7) - 6y = -59$

$-35 - 6y = -59$ (Use the Addition Property of Equality to add 35 to both sides.)

$+35 \quad\quad = +35$

$\dfrac{-6y}{-6} = \dfrac{-24}{-6}$ (Use the Division Property of Equality to divide both sides by −6.)

$y = 4$ (The result is a numerical value of 4 for y.)

Step Four: Solution

(−7, 4)   (Use −7 for the x-coordinate and 4 for the y-coordinate of the ordered pair.)

Step Five: **Check**

$2x - 2y = -22$ (Substitute the ordered pair (–7, 4) into the original second equation to determine if the ordered pair makes the equation true.)

$2(-7) - 2(4) = -22$

$-14 - 8 = -22$

$-22 = -22$ (The statement is true. The ordered pair (–7, 4) checks.)

Independent Practice

1. Solve the following system of equations by elimination: $3x + 5y = 32$ and $-7x - 8y = -49$

2. Solve the following system of equations by elimination: $2x + 5y = -22$ and $10x + 3y = 22$

3. Which of the following systems of equations has a solution with an *x*-coordinate or a *y*-coordinate that has a value of 1? Select all that apply.

   ☐ A. $-2x = -15y - 32$
   $-7x + 5y = -17$

   ☐ B. $2x + 5y = 17$
   $2y - 3x = -16$

   ☐ C. $9x + 4y = 29$
   $-8x + 2y = 2$

   (Answers are on page 277.)

Solving Systems of Equations by Graphing

Steps for Solving Systems of Equations by Graphing

- **Graph** and label each equation independently.
- The **solution** to the system is the ordered pair at the point of intersection of the two lines.
- **Check** the ordered pair algebraically in both equations.
- This is the best method choice when both equations are in slope-intercept form or can easily be transformed to slope-intercept form.

Systems of Equations • 75

 **HELPFUL HINT**

Graphing only gives a close estimation of the solution. It is always best to test the point of intersection algebraically in both equations.

Example 1

Solve the following system of equations by graphing:

$$x + 2y = 6$$
$$2x + y = 6$$

Answer: The ordered pair **(2, 2)** is the solution to this system.

Step One: **Graph**

Determine the slope and y-intercept for each equation. This is done by transforming each equation into slope-intercept form ($y = mx + b$).

$$x + 2y = 6 \qquad\qquad 2x + y = 6$$
$$\underline{-x \quad\quad = -x} \qquad\qquad \underline{-2x \quad\quad = -2x}$$
$$\frac{2y}{2} = \frac{-x + 6}{2} \qquad\qquad y = -2x + 6$$
$$y = \frac{-1}{2}x + 3$$

The slope = $\frac{-1}{2}$; the y-intercept = (0, 3)   The slope = $\frac{-2}{1}$; the y-intercept = (0, 6)

Use the y-intercept and slope to graph each equation on the same Cartesian plane. Label each line with the original equation.

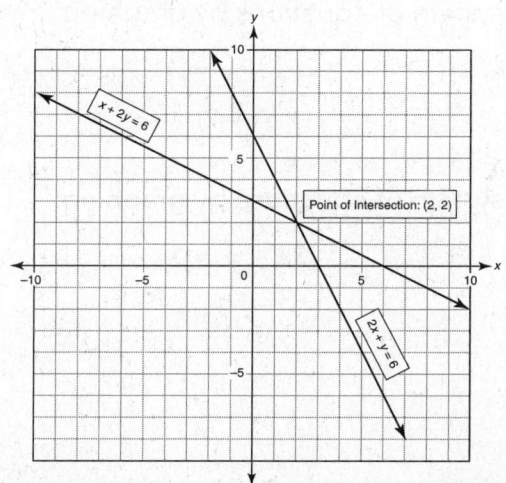

Step Two: **Solution**

Determine the point of intersection. Each line represents an infinite number of ordered pairs, each of which is a solution to that unique equation. The point of intersection is the one ordered pair that is a solution to both equations in the system. The solution to this system of equations is (2, 2).

Step Three: **Check**

Check the ordered pair (2, 2) algebraically in each equation.

$$x + 2y = 6 \qquad\qquad 2x + y = 6$$
$$2 + 2(2) = 6 \qquad\qquad 2(2) + 2 = 6$$
$$2 + 4 = 6 \qquad\qquad 4 + 2 = 6$$
$$6 = 6 \qquad\qquad 6 = 6$$

Remember

- If both equations have the same slope but different y-intercepts, the equations will be parallel and will have no point of intersection → There will be **no solutions** to the system.

- If both equations have the same slope and the same y-intercept, the equations will be the same line, having all the same points → There will be **infinite solutions** to the system.

- If the equations have different slopes, the equations will have one point of intersection → That point of intersection will be the **one solution** to the system.

Guided Practice

1. Solve the following system of equations by graphing:

$$-x + y = 1$$
$$y = 2x - 1$$

2. Solve the following system of equations by graphing:

$$3x + y = 1$$
$$-3x + y = 7$$

Guided Practice Answers Explained

1. **(2, 3)**

Step One: **Graph**

Determine the slope and *y*-intercept for each equation. This is done by transforming each equation into slope-intercept form ($y = mx + b$).

$$-x + y = 1 \qquad\qquad y = 2x - 1$$

$$\underline{+x \qquad\quad = +x}$$

$$y = x + 1$$

The slope = $\frac{1}{1}$; the *y*-intercept = (0, 1)   The slope = $\frac{2}{1}$; the *y*-intercept = (0, –1)

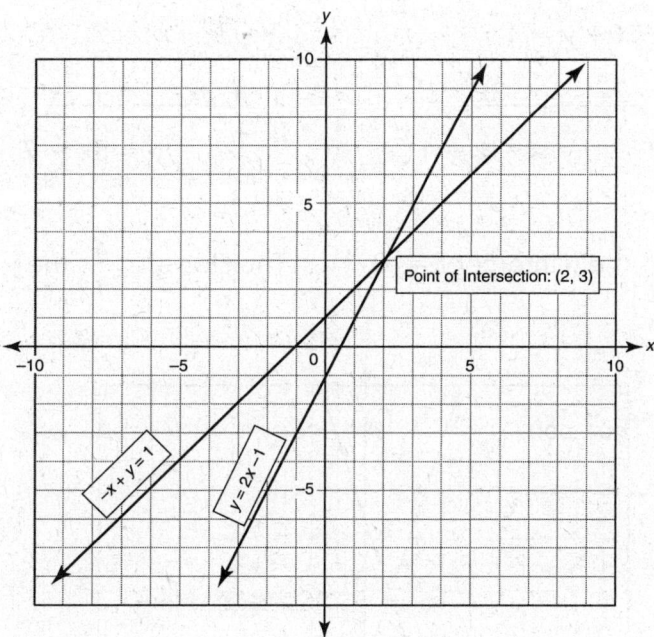

Step Two: **Solution**

Determine the point of intersection. Each line represents an infinite number of ordered pairs, each of which is a solution to that unique equation. The point of intersection is the one ordered pair that is a solution to both equations in the system. The solution to this system of equations is (2, 3).

78 • SBAC Grade 8 Math

Step Three: **Check**

Check the ordered pair (2, 3) algebraically in each equation.

$$-x + y = 1 \qquad\qquad y = 2x - 1$$
$$-(2) + 3 = 1 \qquad\qquad 3 = 2(2) - 1$$
$$-2 + 3 = 1 \qquad\qquad 3 = 4 - 1$$
$$1 = 1 \qquad\qquad 3 = 3$$

2. (−1, 4)

Step One: **Graph**

Determine the slope and y-intercept for each equation. This is done by transforming each equation into slope-intercept form ($y = mx + b$).

$$3x + y = 1 \qquad\qquad -3x + y = 7$$
$$\underline{-3x \quad\;\; = -3x} \qquad\qquad \underline{+\,3x \quad\;\; = +\,3x}$$
$$y = -3x + 1 \qquad\qquad y = 3x + 7$$

The slope = $\dfrac{-3}{1}$; the y-intercept = (0, 1)   The slope = $\dfrac{3}{1}$; the y-intercept = (0, 7)

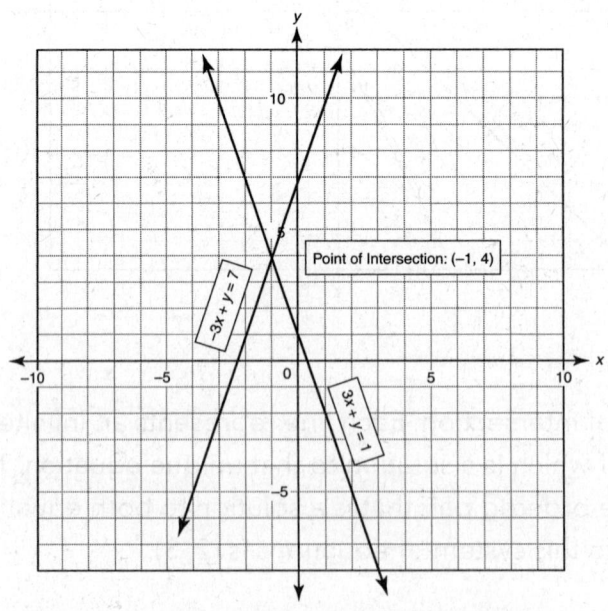

Step Two: **Solution**

Determine the point of intersection. Each line represents an infinite number of ordered pairs, each of which is a solution to that unique equation. The point of intersection is the one ordered pair that is a solution to both equations in the system. The solution to this system of equations is (−1, 4).

Step Three: **Check**

Check the ordered pair (−1, 4) algebraically in each equation.

$$3x + y = 1 \qquad\qquad -3x + y = 7$$
$$3(-1) + 4 = 1 \qquad\qquad -3(-1) + 4 = 7$$
$$-3 + 4 = 1 \qquad\qquad 3 + 4 = 7$$
$$1 = 1 \qquad\qquad 7 = 7$$

Independent Practice

1. Solve the following system of equations by graphing: $-x + 3y = -15$ and $4x + y = 8$

2. Solve the following system of equations by graphing:
$y = -\dfrac{1}{3}x + 1$ and $-x + 3y = -9$

3. By inspection (without graphing), determine the number of solutions for each system of equations.

   A. $y = 3x + 4$
   $-12x + 4y = 16$

   B. $2x + y = 7$
   $y = -2x + 3$

   C. $3x + 4y = 12$
   $2x + 4y = 8$

(Answers are on page 282.)

Let's sum up what we have learned so far:

Table 3-1. Solving Systems of Equations

Substitution	Elimination	Graphing
Best method choice when one of the variables has a coefficient of one.	*Best method choice* when the coefficients of like variables in the equations will cancel easily or can be multiplied to cancel.	*Best method choice* when both equations are in slope-intercept form or can easily be transformed into slope-intercept form.
Isolate one variable in one of the equations.	**Multiply** one or both equations by a factor, if necessary, to result in the elimination of one variable (by creating opposite coefficients) when the equations are combined.	**Graph** and label each equation independently.
Substitute the expression equal to the isolated variable into the second equation. Solve the new equation for a numerical result.	**Solve** the resulting equation for a numerical result for the other variable.	The **solution** to the system is the ordered pair at the point of intersection of the two graphs.
Substitute this numerical result into the original first equation. Solve for a numerical result.	**Substitute** this numerical result into the original first equation, and solve for a numerical result.	**Check** the ordered pair algebraically in both equations.
The **solution** to the system is the ordered pair made from the pair of numerical results.		
Check the ordered pair by substituting it into the original second equation.	**Check** the ordered pair algebraically in the original second equation by substitution.	

It is also possible to analyze a system of equations (by inspection on a Cartesian plane or by transforming the equations into slope-intercept form) for specific characteristics that will determine the number of solutions that the system of equations will have.

Table 3-2. Number of Solutions to a System of Equations

	No Solutions	Infinite Solutions	One Solution
Characteristics	Same slope	Same slope	Different slopes
	Different y-intercepts	Same y-intercept	Same or different y-intercepts
	Graph: parallel lines	Graph: same line	Graph: intersecting lines

Real-World and Mathematical Problems

Systems of equations can be used to solve real-world and mathematical problems that have multiple parts to the solution. The answer is usually presented as an ordered pair, with each variable defining one part of the solution.

Example 1

The Coffee family purchased five sandwiches and three bags of chips for $27.75. The Hamad family purchased three sandwiches and four bags of chips for $20.50. What is the cost for one sandwich, and what is the cost for one bag of chips?

Answer: **A sandwich costs $4.50, and a bag of chips costs $1.75.**

Define the variables:

s = the cost of one sandwich and c = the cost of one bag of chips

The Coffee family's purchase can be represented by the equation $5s + 3c$ = $27.75, because their total cost, $27.75, is five times the cost of one sandwich added to three times the cost of one bag of chips.

The Hamad family's purchase can be represented by the equation $3s + 4c$ = $20.50, because their total cost, $20.50, is three times the cost of one sandwich added to four times the cost of one bag of chips.

 **HELPFUL HINT**

The *best method choice* is elimination for this situation.

Neither of the equations has a variable with a coefficient of one, so solving by substitution would not be an appropriate method choice.

Graphing with decimals may not be accurate enough for this situation.

Step One: **Multiply**

$3(5s + 3c = \$27.75) = 15s + 9c = \$83.25$ (Multiply the first equation by 3 and the second equation by −5 to create opposite coefficients for s.)

$-5(3s + 4c = \$20.50) = -15s - 20c = -\$102.50$

Step Two: **Solve**

$15s + 9c = \$83.25$ (Combine the equations to eliminate the s-term.)

$+\ -15s - 20c = -\$102.50$

$\dfrac{-11c}{-11} = \dfrac{-19.25}{-11}$ (Use the Division Property of Equality to divide both sides by −11.)

$c = \$1.75$ (The result is a numerical value of $\$1.75$ for c.)

Step Three: **Substitute**

$5s + 3c = \$27.75$ (Substitute $\$1.75$ for c into the original first equation.)

$5s + 3(\$1.75) = \$27.75$

$5s + \$5.25 = \$27.75$ (Use the Subtraction Property of Equality to subtract $\$5.25$ from both sides.)

$\underline{\quad -\$5.25 = -\$5.25}$

$\dfrac{5s}{5} = \dfrac{\$22.50}{5}$ (Use the Division Property of Equality to divide both sides by 5.)

$s = \$4.50$ (The result is a numerical value of $\$4.50$ for s.)

Step Four: **Solution**

($4.50, $1.75)   (Use $4.50 for the *x*-coordinate representing the cost of a sandwich and $1.75 for the *y*-coordinate representing the cost of a bag of chips for the ordered pair.)

Step Five: **Check**

$3s + 4c = \$20.50$ (Substitute the ordered pair ($4.50, $1.75) into the original second equation to determine if the ordered pair makes the equation true.)

$3(\$4.50) + 4(\$1.75) = \$20.50$

$\$13.50 + \$7.00 = \$20.50$

$\$20.50 = \$20.50$ (The statement is true. The ordered pair ($4.50, $1.75) checks.)

Guided Practice

1. Zachary has 31 coins in his piggy bank that total $5.80. If they are all dimes and quarters, how many dimes does he have and how many quarters does he have? Use *x* to represent the number of dimes he has and *y* to represent the number of quarters he has.

2. Chelsea has 250 pounds of flour for her bakery. She needs 80 more pounds of flour for baking cakes than she needs for baking pies. How much flour does she need for baking cakes?

3. Caleb records that a fruit tree measures 3 feet tall and grows at 0.75 feet per year. He records that another fruit tree is 5 feet tall and grows at 0.25 feet per year. When will the trees be the same height? What will the height be when they are the same height? Use graphing to estimate your solution.

Guided Practice Answers Explained

1. **Zachary has 13 dimes and 18 quarters.**

Using the given variables, the equation $x + y = 31$ represents the total number of coins and the equation $0.10x + 0.25y = \$5.80$ represents their worth.

HELPFUL HINT

The *best method choice* is substitution. Since both *x* and *y* have coefficients of one, the first equation will be simple to solve for one variable in terms of the other.

Step One: **Isolate**

$x + y = 31$ (Isolate one variable. Use the Subtraction Property of Equality to subtract *x* from both sides.)

$\underline{-x = -x}$

$y = -x + 31$

Step Two: **Substitute**

$0.10x + 0.25y = \$5.80$ (Substitute the expression $-x + 31$ for *y* into the original second equation.)

$0.10x + 0.25(-x + 31) = \$5.80$

$0.10x + (-0.25x) + 7.75 = \$5.80$ (Simplify.)

$-0.15x + 7.75 = \$5.80$ (Use the Subtraction Property of Equality to subtract 7.75 from both sides.)

$\underline{ - 7.75 = -7.75}$

$\dfrac{-0.15x}{-0.15} = \dfrac{-\$1.95}{-0.15}$ (Use the Division Property of Equality to divide both sides by −0.15.)

$x = 13$ (The result is a numerical value of 13 for *x*.)

Step Three: **Substitute**

$x + y = 31$ (Substitute the numerical value 13 for *x* into the original first equation.)

$13 + y = 31$ (Use the Subtraction Property of Equality to subtract 13 from both sides.)

$\underline{-13 = -13}$

$y = 18$ (The result is a numerical value of 18 for *y*.)

Step Four: **Solution**

(13, 18)   (Use 13 for the x-coordinate and 18 for the y-coordinate of the ordered pair.)

Step Five: **Check**

$0.10x + 0.25y = \$5.80$ (Substitute the ordered pair (13, 18) into the original second equation to determine if the ordered pair makes the equation true.)

$0.10(13) + 0.25(18) = \$5.80$

$\$1.30 + \$4.50 = \$5.80$

$\$5.80 = \$5.80$ (The statement is true. The ordered pair (13, 18) checks.)

The solution to this system of equations is (13, 18). This ordered pair represents (x, y) or (number of dimes, number of quarters) that Zachary has. Therefore, he has 13 dimes and 18 quarters.

2. **Chelsea needs 165 pounds of flour for baking cakes.**

Define the variables:

x = the number of pounds of flour she will use for baking pies
y = the number of pounds of flour she will use for baking cakes

Chelsea can relate the two amounts she needs by the equation $y = x + 80$. To represent the total quantity of flour that she needs, she can use the equation $x + y = 250$.

 **HELPFUL HINT**

The *best method choice* is substitution since one of the variables is already isolated in one of the equations.

Step One: **Isolate**

$y = x + 80$ (The variable y is already isolated in the first equation.)

Step Two: **Substitute**

$x + y = 250$ (Substitute the expression $x + 80$ for y into the original second equation.)

$x + x + 80 = 250$

$2x + 80 = 250$ (Use the Subtraction Property of Equality to subtract 80 from both sides.)

$\underline{-80 = -80}$

$\dfrac{2x}{2} = \dfrac{170}{2}$ (Use the Division Property of Equality to divide both sides by 2.)

$x = 85$ (The result is a numerical value of 85 for x.)

Step Three: **Substitute**

$y = x + 80$ (Substitute the numerical value 85 for x into the original first equation.)

$y = 85 + 80$

$y = 165$ (The result is a numerical value of 165 for y.)

Step Four: **Solution**

$(85, 165)$ (Use 85 for the x-coordinate and 165 for the y-coordinate of the ordered pair.)

Step Five: **Check**

$x + y = 250$ (Substitute the ordered pair (85, 165) into the original second equation to determine if the ordered pair makes the equation true.)

$85 + 165 = 250$

$250 = 250$ (The statement is true. The ordered pair (85, 165) checks.)

The solution to this system is (85, 165). This ordered pair represents (x, y) or (pounds of flour for pies, pounds of flour for cakes). Therefore, Chelsea needs 165 pounds of flour for baking cakes.

3. **The trees will both be 6 feet tall in 4 years.**

Define the variables: t = the time measured in number of years that the trees will grow after the initial measure; h = the total height of the trees. The equation $h = 0.75t + 3$ represents the height of the first tree because we multiply the growth rate of 0.75 feet per year by the number of years and add the starting height. The equation $h = 0.25t + 5$ represents the height of the second tree because we multiply the growth rate of 0.25 feet per year by the number of years and add the starting height.

HELPFUL HINT

The *best method choice* is graphing.

Since the numbers are so small, adjusting the scale on the graph so that each box represents 0.25 allows the slope to be easily counted and spreads out the graph, making the solution easier to read.

Also, recognizing that the initial height will be the y-intercept, and that time will only be measured from zero (starting time) through positive numbers, limits the graph to the first quadrant.

Step One: **Graph**

Determine the slope and *y*-intercept for each equation. This is done by recognizing that each equation is in slope-intercept form ($y = mx + b$).

$$h = 0.75t + 3 \qquad\qquad h = 0.25t + 5$$

The slope = $\dfrac{0.75}{1}$; the *y*-intercept = (0, 3)   The slope = $\dfrac{0.25}{1}$; the *y*-intercept = (0, 5)

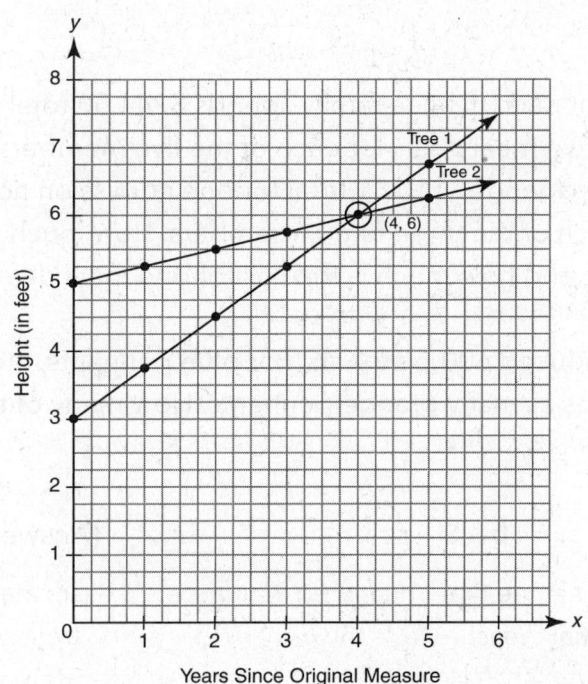

Years Since Original Measure

Step Two: **Solution**

Determine the point of intersection. The solution to this system of equations is (4, 6). This is equivalent to 4 years and 6 feet, as seen on the graph.

Step Three: **Check**

Check the ordered pair (4, 6) algebraically in each equation.

$$h = 0.75t + 3 \qquad\qquad h = 0.25t + 5$$
$$6 = 0.75(4) + 3 \qquad\qquad 6 = 0.25(4) + 5$$
$$6 = 3 + 3 \qquad\qquad 6 = 1 + 5$$
$$6 = 6 \qquad\qquad 6 = 6$$

The ordered pair (4, 6) is the solution to this system of equations. This represents (time in years, height in feet), which means that in 4 years the trees will be the same height of 6 feet tall.

Independent Practice

1. Sarah has $90 in her savings account. She plans to save $25 each month from her allowance. Camber has $120 in her savings account and plans to save $15 each month from her allowance. When will they have the same amount of money in their savings accounts? Graph a system of equations to estimate the solution.

2. At an amusement park, the Lee family spends $244.50 total for one admission ticket each and two meal deals for each of the five members of the family. The Nogal family spends $110.85 total for one admission ticket each and one meal deal for each of the three family members. How much is the cost of one admission ticket, and how much is the cost of one meal deal?

3. Taylor's Toys produced 600 pennants. For blue pennants, they produced 60 more than 3 times as many orange pennants. How many of the pennants were blue?

(Answers are on page 285.)

SBAC Challenge Questions

1. Colin and Daniel are working for the same digital media company. When Colin was hired in January, he was given a $4,000 signing bonus, and he earns $500 for every project that he designs. Daniel was also hired in January, but he only received a $1,500 signing bonus, and he earns $1,000 for every project that he designs. If they design one project per month (after January), after how many monthly projects will Daniel have the same total earnings as Colin?

2. A football player's career statistics show that he had 790 career passes for touchdowns and interceptions. Of these, the number of touchdown passes was twice the number of interception passes increased by 37. How many of the career passes were for touchdowns?

3. Jamie collects dolls. She has eight more dolls than her sister Deirdre. Together they display the dolls on three shelves of six dolls each. How many of the dolls on display are Jamie's?

(Answers are on page 289.)

Real Numbers and the Pythagorean Theorem

CHAPTER 4

Common Core Standard 8.NS.A.1

Know that numbers that are not rational are called irrational. Understand informally that every number has a decimal expansion; for rational numbers show that the decimal expansion repeats eventually, and convert a decimal expansion which repeats eventually into a rational number.

Common Core Standard 8.NS.A.2

Use rational approximations of irrational numbers to compare the size of irrational numbers, locate them approximately on a number line diagram, and estimate the value of expressions (e.g., π^2).

Common Core Standard 8.G.B.6

Explain a proof of the Pythagorean Theorem and its converse.

Common Core Standard 8.G.B.7

Apply the Pythagorean Theorem to determine unknown side lengths in right triangles in real-world and mathematical problems in two and three dimensions.

Common Core Standard 8.G.B.8

Apply the Pythagorean Theorem to find the distance between two points in a coordinate system.

Rational and Irrational Numbers

The set of real numbers can be divided into two types of numbers: rational numbers and irrational numbers. Every real number has a decimal expansion. The decimal expansion can be a terminating or a nonterminating decimal. Nonterminating decimals can be repeating or nonrepeating.

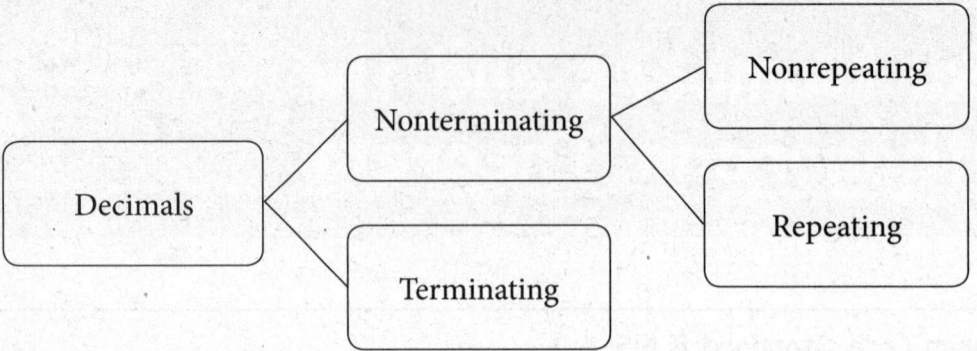

Rational numbers are all numbers that can be represented in the form of a fraction with an integer as the numerator and an integer as the denominator (where the denominator is not 0). Rational numbers include decimals (both repeating and terminating) and square roots of perfect squares or cube roots of perfect cubes.

Irrational numbers are all numbers that cannot be represented in the form of a fraction. They include nonterminating, nonrepeating decimals (like π), as well as square roots of numbers that are not perfect squares or cube roots of numbers that are not perfect cubes. Although the radical form is the more exact answer, irrational numbers may be estimated to use in ordering or for many mathematical solutions.

Example 1

Determine whether each of the following numbers is rational or irrational:

A. $\sqrt{16}$ B. $\sqrt{22}$ C. $\sqrt[3]{8}$

D. $\dfrac{5}{4}$ E. $0.9745\overline{3}$ F. 0.97453

Answers:

A. **Rational** This radical can be simplified because it contains the perfect square 16. The square root 4 can be written in the form of a fraction.
B. **Irrational** This radical cannot be simplified because 22 is not a perfect square. There is no real number that, when multiplied by itself, is 22.
C. **Rational** This radical contains the perfect cube 8. The cube root 2 can be written in the form of a fraction.
D. **Rational** $\dfrac{5}{4}$ is written in the form of a fraction, with integers as the numerator and as the denominator, and the denominator does not equal 0.
E. **Rational** All repeating decimals can be written in fraction form.
F. **Rational** All terminating decimals can be written in fraction form.

Guided Practice

Determine whether each of the following numbers is rational or irrational. Fill in the correct circle for each number.

	Rational	Irrational
1. $\frac{2}{3}$	○	○
2. $0.\overline{4}$	○	○
3. $\sqrt[3]{27}$	○	○
4. $\sqrt{149}$	○	○
5. π	○	○

Guided Practice Answers Explained

1. **Rational** The answer is already in fraction form.
2. **Rational** Repeating decimals can be converted into fraction form.
3. **Rational** The cube root is 3 because 3^3 is 27. Three can be written in fraction form.
4. **Irrational** This is not a perfect square. There is no real number that, when squared, gives a product of 149.
5. **Irrational** π (pi) is a nonterminating, nonrepeating decimal.

Converting a Decimal to a Rational Number (Fraction Form)

To convert a terminating decimal to a rational number (fraction form) the digits after the decimal become the numerator, and the denominator is the place value of the last digit.

The number 46 is the numerator.

$$0.\underline{46} \longrightarrow \frac{46}{100} = \frac{23}{50}$$

The place value (hundredths) is the denominator.

This process cannot be used with a repeating decimal. When converting a repeating decimal into a rational number (fraction form), the goal is to eliminate or "cancel out" the repeating part of the decimal.

> **Steps for Converting a Repeating Decimal to Fraction Form**
>
> 1. Set the repeating decimal equal to x. Write the repeating digits followed by an ellipsis, rather than a repetend (repeat bar), to see the repeating digits.
> 2. Multiply the equation by a power of 10 equal to the number of digits that repeat.
> 3. Subtract the original equation from the transformed equation, thus eliminating the repeat.
> 4. Solve the new equation for x. Simplify the fraction.

Example 1

Convert $0.\overline{7}$ to fraction form.

Answer: $\dfrac{7}{9}$

$x = 0.777\ldots$	(Set the repeating decimal equal to x. Write any repeated digits, followed by an ellipsis.)
$10(x = 0.777\ldots)$	(Multiply by 10^1 because only one digit repeats.)
$10x = 7.777\ldots$	(Subtract the original equation from the transformed equation, eliminating the repeating part of the decimal.)
$-(x = 0.777\ldots)$	
$9x = 7$	
$\dfrac{9x}{9} = \dfrac{7}{9}$	(Solve the new equation for x.)
$x = \dfrac{7}{9}$	

Example 2

Convert $0.\overline{45}$ to a fraction in simplest form.

Answer: $\dfrac{5}{11}$

$x = 0.454545\ldots$ (Set the repeating decimal equal to x. Write any repeated digits, followed by an ellipsis.)

$100(x = 0.454545\ldots)$ (Multiply by 10^2 because two digits repeat.)

$100x = 45.4545\ldots$
$-(x = 0.4545\ldots)$
$\overline{99x = 45}$ (Subtract the original equation from the transformed equation, eliminating the repeating part of the decimal.)

$\dfrac{99x}{99} = \dfrac{45}{99}$ (Solve the new equation for x.)

$x = \dfrac{45 \div 9}{99 \div 9}$ (Simplify.)

$x = \dfrac{5}{11}$

Example 3

Convert $0.8\overline{3}$ to a fraction in simplest form.

Answer: $\dfrac{5}{6}$

Note: This repeating decimal has a digit that does **not** repeat. In this case, multiply by the power of 10 that corresponds to the **first repeating digit**.

$x = 0.8333\ldots$ (Set the repeating decimal equal to x. Write any repeated digits, followed by an ellipsis.)

$100(x = 0.8333\ldots)$ (Multiply by 10^2 because the first repeating digit is the second digit after the decimal point.)

$100x = 83.333\ldots$
$-(x = 0.833\ldots)$
$\overline{99x = 82.5}$ (Subtract the original equation from the transformed equation, eliminating the repeating part of the decimal. Note: Although the repeating part of the decimal is eliminated, the difference has a terminating decimal.)

$$\frac{99x}{99} = \frac{82.5}{99}$$ (Solve the new equation for x.)

$$x = \frac{82.5 \cdot 10}{99 \cdot 10}$$ (Eliminate the decimal in the numerator by multiplying the equation by 10 over 10, which is equal to 1.)

$$x = \frac{825 \div 5}{990 \div 5}$$ (Simplify.)

$$x = \frac{165 \div 3}{198 \div 3}$$ (Simplify.)

$$x = \frac{55 \div 11}{66 \div 11}$$ (Simplify.)

$$x = \frac{5}{6}$$

Guided Practice

1. Convert each of the following repeating decimals into fraction form.

   A. $0.1\overline{6}$ B. $1.\overline{2}$

Guided Practice Answers Explained

1.
   A. $\dfrac{1}{6}$

   $x = 0.1666\ldots$ (Set the repeating decimal equal to x. Write any repeated digits, followed by an ellipsis.)

   $100(x = 0.1666\ldots)$ (Multiply by 10^2 because the first repeating digit is the second digit after the decimal point.)

   $100x = 16.666\ldots$
   $-(x = 0.166\ldots)$
   $\overline{99x = 16.5}$

   (Subtract the original equation from the transformed equation, eliminating the repeating part of the decimal. Note: Although the repeating part of the decimal is eliminated, the difference has a terminating decimal.)

$$\frac{99x}{99} = \frac{16.5}{99}$$ (Solve the new equation for x.)

$$x = \frac{16.5 \cdot 10}{99 \cdot 10}$$ (Eliminate the decimal in the numerator by multiplying the equation by 10 over 10, which is equal to 1.)

$$x = \frac{165 \div 5}{990 \div 5}$$ (Simplify.)

$$x = \frac{33 \div 3}{198 \div 3}$$ (Simplify.)

$$x = \frac{11 \div 11}{66 \div 11}$$ (Simplify.)

$$x = \frac{1}{6}$$

B. $1\frac{2}{9}$

$x = 1.222\ldots$ (Set the repeating decimal equal to x. Write any repeated digits, followed by an ellipsis.)

$10(x = 1.222\ldots)$ (Multiply by 10^1 because only one digit repeats.)

$10x = 12.222\ldots$ (Subtract the original equation from the transformed equation, eliminating the repeating part of the decimal.)
$-(x = 1.222\ldots)$

$9x = 11$

$$\frac{9x}{9} = \frac{11}{9}$$ (Solve the new equation for x.)

$x = 1\frac{2}{9}$

Estimating Values of Expressions That Contain Irrational Numbers

Expressions that contain irrational numbers cannot be fully simplified. These expressions can be approximated using a calculator or a chart of approximations. Use the chart below to complete the examples and practice problems.

$\sqrt{2} \approx 1.4142135\ldots$	$\sqrt{7} \approx 2.6457513\ldots$	$\sqrt{12} \approx 3.4641016\ldots$	$\sqrt{17} \approx 4.1231056\ldots$
$\sqrt{3} \approx 1.7320508\ldots$	$\sqrt{8} \approx 2.8284271\ldots$	$\sqrt{13} \approx 3.6055512\ldots$	$\sqrt{18} \approx 4.2426406\ldots$
$\sqrt{5} \approx 2.2360679\ldots$	$\sqrt{10} \approx 3.1622776\ldots$	$\sqrt{14} \approx 3.7416573\ldots$	$\sqrt{19} \approx 4.3588989\ldots$
$\sqrt{6} \approx 2.4494897\ldots$	$\sqrt{11} \approx 3.3166247\ldots$	$\sqrt{15} \approx 3.8729833\ldots$	$\sqrt{20} \approx 4.4721359\ldots$

Example 1

Determine which of the following expressions has the greatest value:

   ○ A. $\dfrac{\sqrt{5}}{2}$ ○ B. $\dfrac{\sqrt{6}}{3}$ ○ C. $\dfrac{\sqrt{8}}{3}$ ○ D. $\dfrac{\sqrt{16}}{\sqrt[3]{8}}$

<u>Answer:</u> **(D)**

A. $\dfrac{\sqrt{5} \approx 2.2360679\ldots}{2} \approx 1.1180$, which has an estimated value of slightly greater than 1.

B. $\dfrac{\sqrt{6} \approx 2.4494897\ldots}{3} \approx 0.8165$, which has an estimated value less than 1.

C. $\dfrac{\sqrt{8} \approx 2.8284271\ldots}{3} \approx 0.9428$, which has an estimated value less than 1.

D. $\dfrac{\sqrt{16}}{\sqrt[3]{8}} = \dfrac{4}{2} = 2$. This expression has the greatest value.

Example 2

Write the following expressions where they belong on the number line below. Identify whether each expression represents a rational or irrational number.

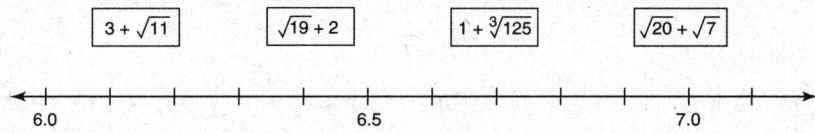

Answer:

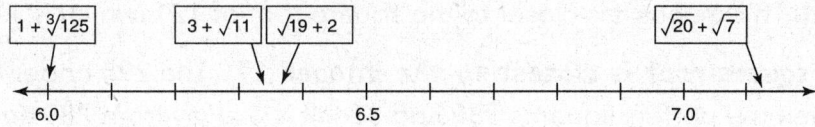

- $3 + \sqrt{11} \approx 3 + (\approx 3.3166247\ldots) \approx 6.32$ (irrational number, approximated, since $\sqrt{11}$ is irrational)
- $\sqrt{19} + 2 \approx 4.3588989 + 2 \approx 6.36$ (irrational number, approximated, since $\sqrt{19}$ is irrational)
- $1 + \sqrt[3]{125} = 1 + 5 = 6$ (rational number, approximated, since all expressions are rational numbers)
- $\sqrt{20} + \sqrt{7} \approx 4.4721359 + 2.6457513 \approx 7.12$ (irrational number, approximated, since both radicals are irrational numbers)

Guided Practice

1. Which of the following choices lists these expressions from least to greatest?

$$3 + \sqrt{15} \qquad \sqrt{6} + 5 \qquad 8 - \sqrt{3} \qquad 11 - \sqrt{11}$$

- A. $3 + \sqrt{15}, \sqrt{6} + 5, 8 - \sqrt{3}, 11 - \sqrt{11}$
- B. $8 - \sqrt{3}, 11 - \sqrt{11}, 3 + \sqrt{15}, \sqrt{6} + 5$
- C. $8 - \sqrt{3}, 3 + \sqrt{15}, \sqrt{6} + 5, 11 - \sqrt{11}$
- D. $3 + \sqrt{15}, 8 - \sqrt{3}, 11 - \sqrt{11}, \sqrt{6} + 5$

2. To which integer is each of the following irrational roots closest?

  A. $\sqrt{112}$ B. $\sqrt{295}$ C. $\sqrt{350}$ D. $\sqrt{1{,}000}$

Guided Practice Answers Explained

1. **(C)** The approximations are as follows:

   $3 + \sqrt{15} \approx 6.87$ $\sqrt{6} + 5 \approx 7.45$ $8 - \sqrt{3} \approx 6.27$ $11 - \sqrt{11} \approx 7.68$

2.
   A. The square root is closest to the integer 11. The 112 under the radical is between the perfect squares 100 and 121. It is 12 away from 100 and 9 away from 121. This means it is closer to the square root of 121, which is 11.

   B. The square root is closest to the integer 17. The 295 under the radical is between the perfect squares 289 and 324. It is 6 away from 289 and 29 away from 324. This means it is closer to the square root of 289, which is 17.

   C. The square root is closest to the integer 19. The 350 under the radical is between the perfect squares 324 and 361. It is 26 away from 324 and 11 away from 361. This means it is closer to the square root of 361, which is 19.

   D. The square root is closest to the integer 32. The 1,000 under the radical is between 900 and 1,600, which are the perfect squares with square roots 30 and 40. Closer to 900, you could test the next integers, 31 and 32, calculating the squares of these numbers. $31^2 = 961$ and $32^2 = 1{,}024$. The 1,000 is 39 away from 961 and 24 away from 1,024. This means it is closer to the square root of 1,024, which is 32.

Independent Practice

1. Convert each of the following repeating decimals into fraction form.

   A. $0.\overline{148}$ B. $2.\overline{6}$

2. List the following expressions in order from least to greatest.

   $\left(\sqrt{17}\right)^2 + 1$ $2(\pi)^2$ $5\left(\sqrt{13}\right)$ $\sqrt[3]{216} + \sqrt{20} + 2\left(\sqrt{18}\right)$

   (Answers are on page 293.)

Pythagorean Theorem and Its Converse

The Pythagorean theorem is used to determine unknown side lengths in right triangles. The Pythagorean theorem states that "the sum of the squares of the lengths of the two legs of a right triangle is equal to the square of the length of the hypotenuse." The hypotenuse is opposite the right angle, and it is the longest side length of the triangle.

The converse of the Pythagorean theorem is used to prove that a triangle is a right triangle. The converse of the Pythagorean theorem states that "if the sum of the squares of the lengths of two sides of a triangle is equal to the square of the length of the longest side, then the triangle is a right triangle."

Using a and b to represent the lengths of the legs of the right triangle, and using c to represent the length of the hypotenuse, the Pythagorean theorem is stated as follows:

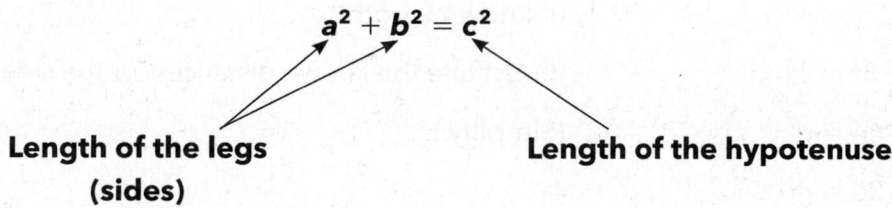

$$a^2 + b^2 = c^2$$

Length of the legs (sides)   **Length of the hypotenuse**

The converse of the Pythagorean theorem uses the same equation for a different purpose. When trying to determine the measure of a missing side length, only two values will be available, and the third will be a variable. When using the converse, however, all three side lengths will be available, and the statement will be proven true or false when determining whether or not the lengths form a right triangle.

 **HELPFUL HINT**

If the lengths of all three sides of a right triangle can be represented by integers, the side lengths are called **Pythagorean triples**.

Example 1

Jim travels eight miles due north of his campsite. He then turns and hikes six miles due west. Assuming a direct route, how far is Jim from his campsite?

<u>Answer:</u> **Assuming a direct route, Jim is 10 miles from his campsite.**

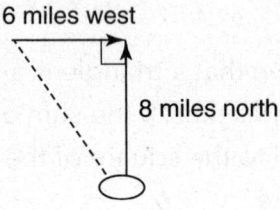

(Knowing that due north and due west directions form a right angle, it can be determined that the distance directly to the campsite will be the hypotenuse of the right triangle.)

$a^2 + b^2 = c^2$ (Use the Pythagorean theorem to find the unknown length.)

$6^2 + 8^2 = c^2$ (Substitute the known distances for the side lengths.)

$36 + 64 = c^2$ (Simplify.)

$100 = c^2$

$\sqrt{100} = \sqrt{c^2}$ (Take the square root of each side.)

$10 = c$ (The length of the hypotenuse is 10.)

Note: Because all three side lengths are integers (6, 8, and 10 miles), they represent a Pythagorean triple.

Example 2

Determine the width of a rectangular park to the nearest whole block if its length is 15 blocks and its diagonal is 20 blocks.

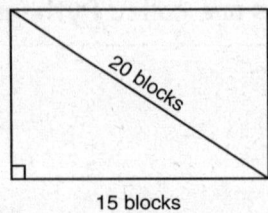

Answer: **To the nearest whole block, the width is 13 blocks.**

By definition, a rectangle has four right angles, so the triangle formed by the length and width of the rectangle and its diagonal is a right triangle. Use the Pythagorean theorem to find the length of the unknown side.

$a^2 + b^2 = c^2$	(Use the Pythagorean theorem to find the unknown length.)
$15^2 + b^2 = 20^2$	(Substitute the known distance for the length of the park (as either *a* or *b*) and the diagonal of the park, which is the hypotenuse, *c*.)
$225 + b^2 = 400$	(Simplify.)
$\underline{-225\quad = -225}$	(Use the Subtraction Property of Equality to subtract 225 from both sides.)
$b^2 = 175$	(Simplify.)
$\sqrt{b^2} = \sqrt{175}$	(Take the square root of each side.)
$b \approx 13$	($\sqrt{175}$ is an irrational number. 175 is between the two perfect squares 169 (13^2) and 196 (14^2). It is 6 away from 169 and 21 away from 196, so it is closer to 13. To the nearest whole block, the width is 13 blocks.)

Example 3

Dana wants to be certain that her blueprint of a project has the correct lengths indicating right angles at the corners of every room. One of the rooms, already built, is a living room that has side walls of 10 feet and 24 feet, and a decorative diagonal ceiling brace 26 feet long. Another room is shown to scale on the blueprint with side walls of 4 centimeters and 6 centimeters, with a diagonal measure on the blueprint of 10 centimeters. Will both rooms have right angles? Justify your answer.

Answer: **The room already built has right angles. The room on the blueprint will not have right angles with the given measurements.**

To use the converse of the Pythagorean theorem to prove a right angle, set up each set of measures in the equation $a^2 + b^2 = c^2$, using the longest measure as the hypotenuse (*c*).

Room Already Built	**Blueprint Room**
$a^2 + b^2 = c^2$	$a^2 + b^2 = c^2$
$10^2 + 24^2 = 26^2$	$4^2 + 6^2 = 10^2$
$100 + 576 = 676$	$16 + 36 = 100$
$676 = 676$	$52 \neq 100$
The room already built creates a true statement. It proves there are right triangles within the rectangular room divided in half by the decorative diagonal ceiling brace.	The blueprint room does not create a true statement. It does not prove there are right triangles within the rectangle of the room if it were divided in half by a diagonal.

Guided Practice

1. A flat screen television is 22 inches high and 30 inches wide. Use a calculator to determine how long the diagonal of the television screen is (to the nearest whole inch).

2. A photo is placed in a rectangular wooden frame with a length of 12 inches and a diagonal of 15 inches. What is the width of the photo frame?

3. Which of the following statements is true based on the converse of the Pythagorean theorem? Select all that apply.

    ☐ A. If the sum of the squares of the two sides that form the right angle is equal to the square of the length of the third side, then the triangle is a right triangle.
    ☐ B. The square of the side opposite the right angle is greater than the sum of the squares of the other two sides.
    ☐ C. The sum of the lengths of any two sides of a triangle must be greater than the length of the third side.
    ☐ D. The longest side length of a right triangle must be opposite the right angle.

Guided Practice Answers Explained

1. **To the nearest whole inch, the diagonal of the television screen is 37 inches.**

    $a^2 + b^2 = c^2$ (Use the Pythagorean theorem to find the unknown length.)

    $22^2 + 30^2 = c^2$ (Substitute the known lengths for the height and width.)

    $484 + 900 = c^2$ (Simplify.)

    $1{,}384 = c^2$

    $\sqrt{1{,}384} = \sqrt{c^2}$ (Take the square root of each side.)

    $37 \approx c$ ($\sqrt{1{,}384}$ is an irrational number. 1,384 is between the two perfect squares 1,369 (37^2) and 1,444 (38^2). It is closer to 1,369, so, to the nearest whole inch, the diagonal is 37 inches.)

2. **The width of the photo frame is 9 inches.**

    $a^2 + b^2 = c^2$ (Use the Pythagorean theorem to find the unknown length.)

    $12^2 + b^2 = 15^2$ (Substitute the known values for the length of the frame and the diagonal of the frame, which is the hypotenuse.)

    $144 + b^2 = 225$ (Simplify.)

    $-144 = -144$ (Use the Subtraction Property of Equality to subtract 144 from both sides.)

    $b^2 = 81$ (Simplify.)

    $\sqrt{b^2} = \sqrt{81}$ (Take the square root of each side.)

    $b = 9$ (The width is 9.)

3. **(A)** and **(D)**

   (A) True. This statement proves that a triangle is a right triangle. The longest side of the right triangle is the hypotenuse.

   (B) False. The square of the longest side (across from the right angle) is equal to, not greater than, the sum of the squares of the other two sides.

   (C) False. This statement does not prove the converse of the Pythagorean theorem.

   (D) True. When substituting the side lengths into the converse of the Pythagorean theorem, the side opposite the right angle is the hypotenuse. It is used to substitute for c in the Pythagorean formula.

Distance Between Two Points in a Coordinate System

On a Cartesian plane, the vertical distance between two points is the absolute value of the difference between the y-coordinates. The horizontal distance between two points is the absolute value of the difference between the x-coordinates. The x-axis and the y-axis form a right angle at the origin.

The Pythagorean theorem can be used to find the distance between any two points on the plane. The horizontal and vertical distances between the two points can be visualized as line segments parallel to the x-axis and the y-axis, respectively, forming a right angle. This means that the line segment between the two points forms the hypotenuse of a right triangle, opposite the right angle.

Example 1

Determine the distance between (3, 4) and (−2, −1). Round your answer to the nearest tenth, if necessary.

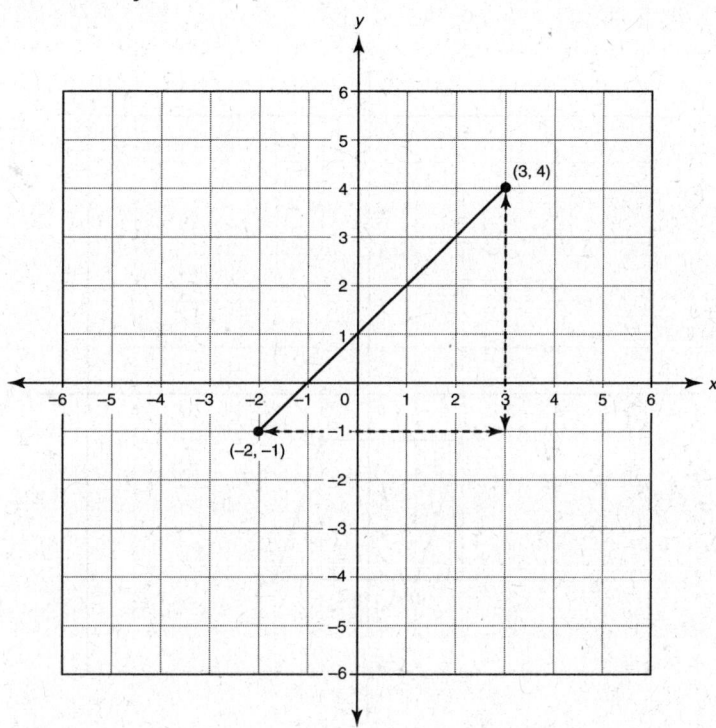

Answer: **Approximately 7.1 units**

The horizontal distance is 5 (3 − (−2) = 5), and the vertical distance is 5 (4 − (−1) = 5). Use the Pythagorean theorem to find the length of the hypotenuse.

$a^2 + b^2 = c^2$

$5^2 + 5^2 = c^2$ (Substitute the lengths of the two legs that form the right angle.)

$25 + 25 = c^2$ (Simplify.)

$50 = c^2$

$\sqrt{50} = \sqrt{c^2}$ (Take the square root of each side.)

$7.1 \approx c$ ($\sqrt{50}$ is irrational. $(7.0)^2 = 49$ and $(7.1)^2 = 50.41$. To the nearest tenth, $\sqrt{50}$ is closer to 7.1.)

Example 2

Given Parallelogram *ABCD*, determine the length of Diagonal *AC*. Round your answer the nearest tenth, if necessary.

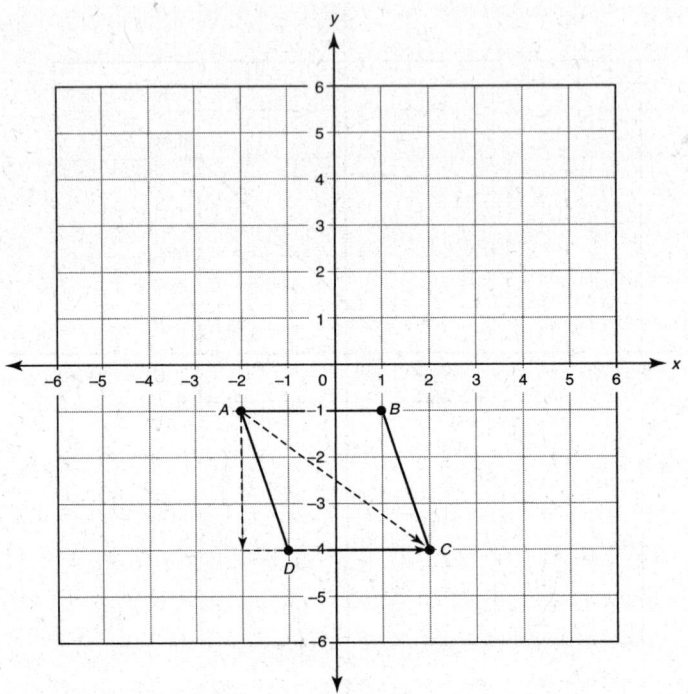

Answer: **5 units**

A right triangle is created on the grid using the height of the parallelogram as one leg and the diagonal of the parallelogram as the hypotenuse. Note: The second leg of the triangle is *not* the base of the parallelogram, but includes it. The horizontal distance from the vertex of the right angle to *C* is 4 (2 − (−2) = 4). The vertical distance from *A* to the vertex of the right angle is 3 (−1 − (−4) = 3). Use the Pythagorean theorem to find the length of the hypotenuse.

$a^2 + b^2 = c^2$

$4^2 + 3^2 = c^2$ (Substitute the lengths of the two legs that form the right angle.)

$16 + 9 = c^2$ (Simplify.)

$25 = c^2$

$\sqrt{25} = \sqrt{c^2}$ (Take the square root of each side.)

$5 = c$ (The diagonal is 5.)

Real Numbers and the Pythagorean Theorem • 109

Guided Practice

1. Determine the length of Segment PQ with the Endpoints P (−4, 4) and Q (3, 2). Round your answer to the nearest tenth, if necessary.

2. Given Right Triangle MNP with Vertices M (−4, 1), N (4, 1), and P (4, −3), determine the length of the hypotenuse. Round your answer to the nearest tenth, if necessary.

Guided Practice Answers Explained

1. **7.3 units**

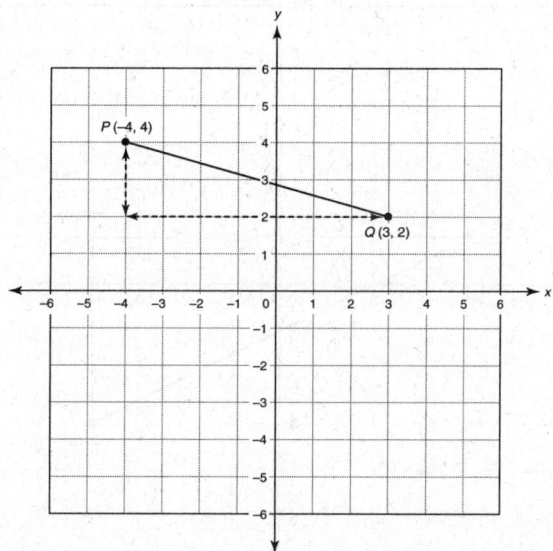

The horizontal distance is 7 (3 − (−4) = 7), and the vertical distance is 2 (2 − 4 = −2, |−2| = 2).

Use the Pythagorean theorem to find the length of the hypotenuse. (Note: Distance will always be the absolute value.)

$a^2 + b^2 = c^2$

$7^2 + 2^2 = c^2$ (Substitute the lengths of the two legs that form the right angle.)

$49 + 4 = c^2$ (Simplify.)

$53 = c^2$

$\sqrt{53} = \sqrt{c^2}$ (Take the square root of each side.)

$7.3 \approx c$ ($\sqrt{53}$ is irrational. $(7.2)^2 = 51.84$, and $(7.3)^2 = 53.29$. To the nearest tenth, $\sqrt{53}$ is closer to 7.3.)

2. **8.9 units**

Without graphing, it can be determined that Side *MN* is parallel to the *x*-axis because the *y*-coordinates are the same and because the slope between these two points is 0. Side *NP* is parallel to the *y*-axis because the *x*-coordinates are the same and because the slope between these two points is undefined. This means that Side *MN* and Side *NP* form the right angle of the right triangle and that Side *MP* is the hypotenuse.

Graphing verifies this:

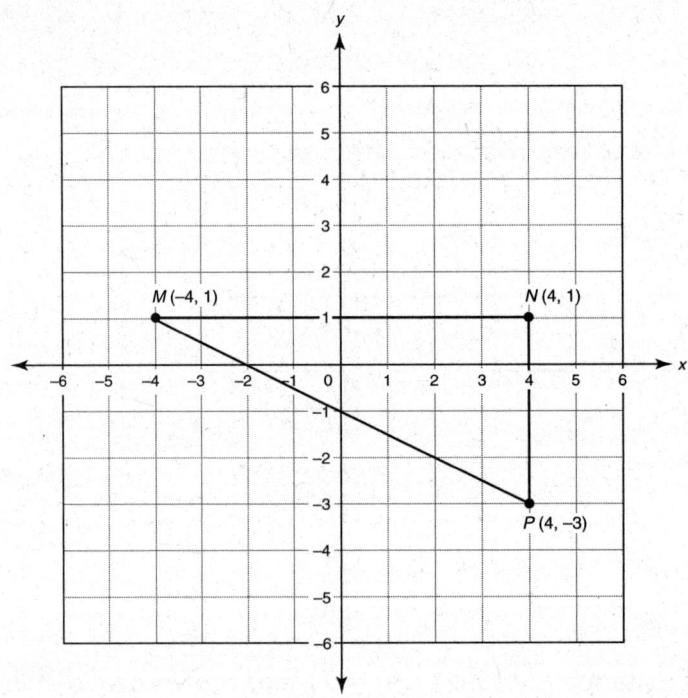

The horizontal distance between points *M* and *P* is 8 ($-4 - 4 = -8$, $|-8| = 8$), and the vertical distance is 4 ($1 - (-3) = 4$). Use the Pythagorean theorem to find the length of the hypotenuse.

$a^2 + b^2 = c^2$

$8^2 + 4^2 = c^2$ (Substitute the lengths of the two legs that form the right angle.)

$64 + 16 = c^2$ (Simplify.)

$80 = c^2$

$\sqrt{80} = \sqrt{c^2}$ (Take the square root of each side.)

$8.9 \approx c$

($\sqrt{80}$ is irrational. $(8.9)^2 = 79.21$, and $(9.0)^2 = 81$. To the nearest tenth, $\sqrt{80}$ is closer to 8.9.)

Real Numbers and the Pythagorean Theorem • 111

Pythagorean Theorem in Three Dimensions

The Pythagorean theorem is used to determine the length of any side of a right triangle. In previous examples, these right triangles were formed by diagonals of squares or rectangles. In three-dimensional solids, such as a right rectangular prism or cube, each face of the solid is a rectangle or square. It would be easy to find the length of a diagonal on any of those rectangular faces using the Pythagorean theorem.

Since right rectangular prisms have six faces that meet at right angles, it is also possible to use the Pythagorean theorem to find a three-dimensional diagonal within a right prism that connects vertices that do not share a face. A three-dimensional diagonal does not share a plane with any side on which the figure is drawn.

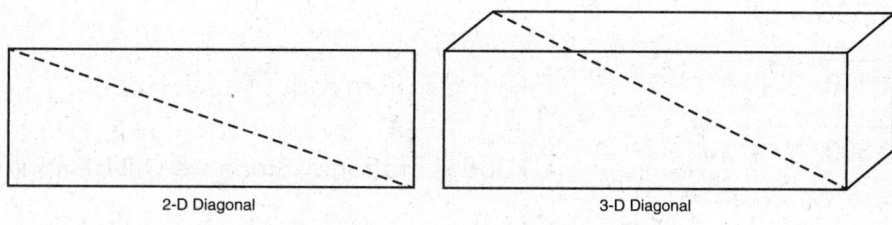

2-D Diagonal   3-D Diagonal

Example 1

A string of pennants is going to be strung from the southwest floor corner of the barn to the northeast ceiling corner. If the barn is 30 feet long, 20 feet wide, and 10 feet high, how long must the string of pennants be? Round your answer to the nearest foot, if necessary.

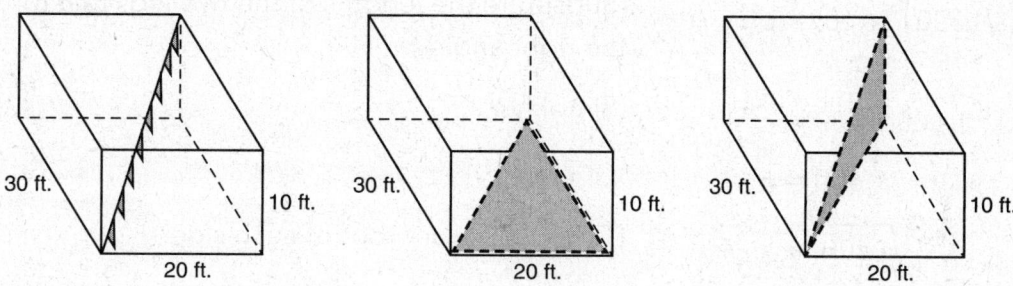

Answer: **37 feet long**

The barn is a rectangular prism, with all faces at right angles. The string of pennants is the hypotenuse of the right triangle formed with the height of the barn and the diagonal of the rectangle formed by the floor. It can be viewed as a three-dimensional diagonal of the rectangular prism.

First, use the Pythagorean theorem to calculate the diagonal of the floor, using the length and width of the barn as the legs that form the right angle.

$a^2 + b^2 = c^2$

$30^2 + 20^2 = c^2$ (Substitute the lengths of the two legs that form the right angle.)

$900 + 400 = c^2$ (Simplify.)

$1{,}300 = c^2$

$\sqrt{1{,}300} = \sqrt{c^2}$ (Take the square root of each side.)

$\sqrt{1{,}300} = c$ ($\sqrt{1{,}300}$ is irrational. Since we will be squaring this value in the next step, it can be left in radical form.)

Now, use the Pythagorean theorem to calculate the three-dimensional diagonal of the barn. Use the length of the pennant as the hypotenuse of the right triangle formed. Use the floor diagonal as one leg and the height of the barn as the other leg.

$a^2 + b^2 = c^2$

$\left(\sqrt{1{,}300}\right)^2 + 10^2 = c^2$ (Substitute the lengths of the two legs that form the right angle.)

$1{,}300 + 100 = c^2$ (Simplify.)

$1{,}400 = c^2$

$\sqrt{1{,}400} = \sqrt{c^2}$ (Take the square root of each side.)

$\sqrt{1{,}400} = c$ ($\sqrt{1{,}400}$ is irrational. $(37)^2 = 1{,}369$, and $(38)^2 = 1{,}444$. To the nearest whole number, $\sqrt{1{,}400}$ is closer to 37.)

$37 \approx c$

Guided Practice

1. An aerial photo drone can fly directly from its launch on the ground to the top of a 20 foot high building located diagonally across a rectangular park 30 feet wide and 40 feet long. How far will the direct drone path be to reach the building? Round your answer to the nearest foot, if necessary.

Guided Practice Answers Explained

1. **54 feet** The drone's path can be viewed as a three-dimensional diagonal of a rectangular prism. The park represents the base of a rectangular prism, and the building is a perpendicular face. The path of the drone is the hypotenuse of the right triangle formed, and the height of the building and the diagonal of the park are the legs.

    Use the Pythagorean theorem to calculate the diagonal of the park, using the length and width of the park as the legs that form the right angle.

    $a^2 + b^2 = c^2$

    $30^2 + 40^2 = c^2$ (Substitute the lengths of the two legs that form the right angle.)

    $900 + 1{,}600 = c^2$ (Simplify.)

    $2{,}500 = c^2$

    $\sqrt{2{,}500} = \sqrt{c^2}$ (Take the square root of each side.)

    $50 = c$ (The diagonal of the park is 50 feet.)

    Use the Pythagorean theorem to calculate the drone's path as the hypotenuse of the right triangle formed, and the diagonal of the park as one leg and the height of the building as the other leg.

    $a^2 + b^2 = c^2$

    $50^2 + 20^2 = c^2$ (Substitute the lengths of the two legs that form the right angle.)

    $2{,}500 + 400 = c^2$ (Simplify.)

    $2{,}900 = c^2$

    $\sqrt{2{,}900} = \sqrt{c^2}$ (Take the square root of each side.)

    $54 \approx c$ ($\sqrt{2{,}900}$ is irrational. $(53)^2 = 2{,}809$, and $(54)^2 = 2{,}916$. To the nearest whole number, $\sqrt{2{,}900}$ is closer to 54.)

Independent Practice

1. A roofer uses a 17 foot ladder to reach the top of a building. If the base of the ladder is placed 4 feet from the base of the building, how high is the building? Round your answer to the nearest tenth of a foot, if necessary.

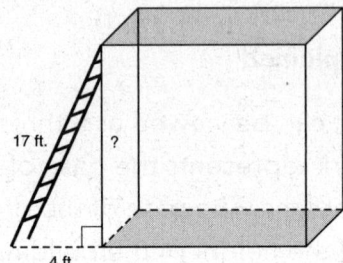

2. Rope connects the top of a badminton net to the ground stakes. If the top of the net is about 5 feet high off of the ground, and the stakes are placed 3 feet from the base of the net, how much rope is needed for the two stake ropes? Round your answer to the nearest foot, if necessary.

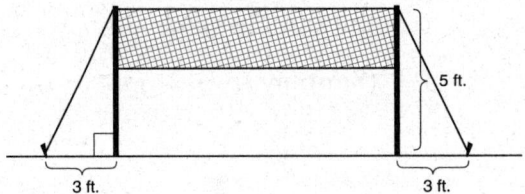

3. A snail crawls diagonally across a square patio stone with an area of 144 square inches. To the nearest tenth of an inch, how far does the snail crawl?

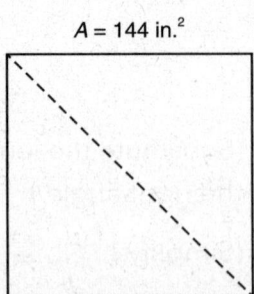

4. A bouquet of flowers must fit in a delivery box that is 15 inches long, 6 inches wide, and 6 inches high. If the longest stem is 17 inches long, how much of the longest stem will need to be trimmed so that the bouquet can fit in diagonally across the three dimensions?

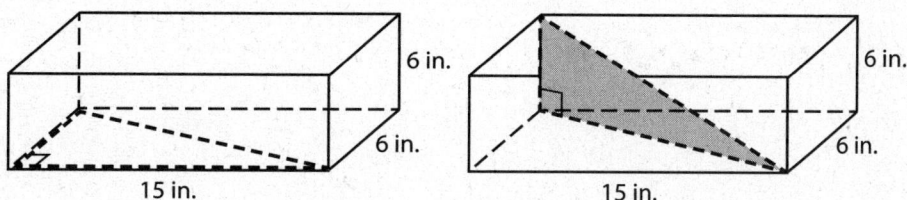

(Answers are on page 294.)

SBAC Challenge Questions

1. Triangle STU is formed with S (−4, 10), T (3, 1), and U (−6, 4).

    A. Determine the perimeter of the triangle.
    B. Order the lengths of the sides in order from least to greatest.
    C. Determine if this triangle is a right triangle.

2. Which of the following sets of ordered pairs results in a distance between 9 and 10 units? Select all that apply.

    ☐ A. (−4, 5) and (4, 10)
    ☐ B. (−1, 10) and (−3, 4)
    ☐ C. (−6, 7) and (1, 1)
    ☐ D. (3, 2) and (−4, −5)

(Answers are on page 297.)

Chapter 5: Geometry—Transformations

Common Core Standard 8.G.A.1

Verify experimentally the properties of rotations, reflections, and translations.

Common Core Standard 8.G.A.1.A

Lines are taken to lines, and line segments to line segments of the same length.

Common Core Standard 8.G.A.1.B

Angles are taken to angles of the same measure.

Common Core Standard 8.G.A.1.C

Parallel lines are taken to parallel lines.

Common Core Standard 8.G.A.2

Understand that a two-dimensional figure is congruent to another if the second can be obtained from the first by a sequence of rotations, reflections, and translations; given two congruent figures, describe a sequence that exhibits the congruence between them.

Common Core Standard 8.G.A.3

Describe the effect of dilations, translations, rotations, and reflections on two-dimensional figures using coordinates.

Common Core Standard 8.G.A.4

Understand that a two-dimensional figure is similar to another if the second can be obtained from the first by a sequence of rotations, reflections, translations, and dilations; given two similar two-dimensional figures, describe a sequence that exhibits the similarity between them.

Key Concepts

- Transformations are methods by which points, lines, and shapes are managed or manipulated.
- The original point, line, or shape is called the **pre-image**.
- The resulting point, line, or shape is called the **image**.
- Four types of transformations are **translations**, **rotations**, **reflections**, and **dilations**.

Translations

Key Concepts

- Translations are horizontal or vertical slides of a pre-image, point by point, to an image.
- With horizontal translations, the x-coordinate of the pre-image ordered pair will change.
- With vertical translations, the y-coordinate of the pre-image ordered pair will change.
- The image vertices are notated with a single tick mark, indicating "prime." For example, pre-image Vertex A would become image Vertex A' ("Vertex A prime").
- Translations move the position of the image, but preserve its size and shape.
- The pre-image and image affected by a translation are congruent because both the size and the shape are preserved.

Example 1

Line Segment AB, with Endpoints A (4, 3) and B (−1, −2), is translated four units left to create Line Segment A'B'. What are the coordinates of the endpoints of Line Segment A'B'?

Answer: **A' (0, 3) and B' (−5, −2)**

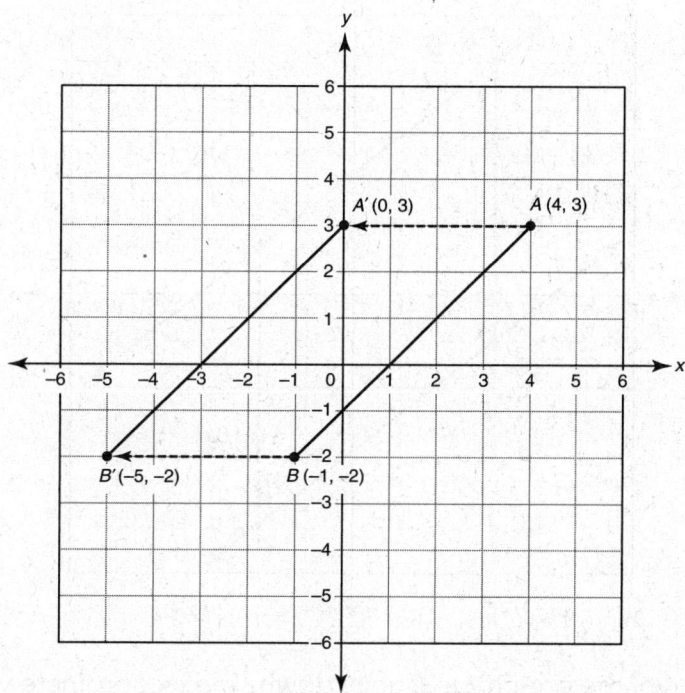

Slide each endpoint of the pre-image four units to the left. A translation left or right is a change along the x-axis only. Moving left along the x-axis gives an x-coordinate value that is less than the pre-image value. The x-coordinate values of the image are 4 less than the x-coordinate values of the pre-image, and the y-coordinates stay the same. Another notation for the ordered pairs of the image is (x − 4, y).

Example 2

Line EF, containing Points E (2, 1) and F (−3, 5), is translated 6 units down to create Line E'F'. What are the coordinates of Line E'F'?

<u>Answer:</u> **E' (2, −5) and F' (−3, −1)**

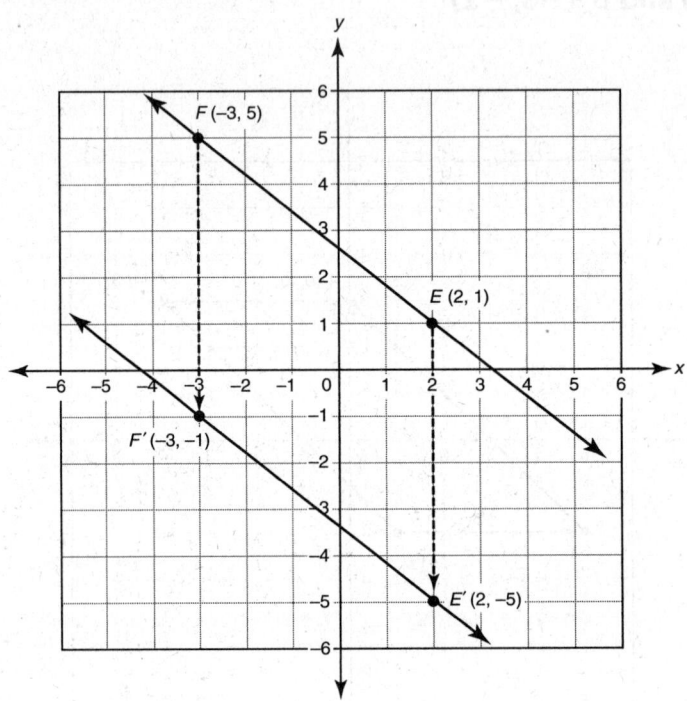

Slide each point of the pre-image 6 units down. The y-coordinate values of the image are 6 less than the y-coordinate values of the pre-image, and the x-coordinates stay the same. Another notation for the ordered pairs of the image is (x, y − 6).

 **HELPFUL HINT**

A translation up or down is a change along the y-axis only.

Moving down along the y-axis gives a y-coordinate value that is less.

Moving up along the y-axis results in a y-coordinate value that is greater.

A translation left or right is a change along the x-axis only.

Moving left along the x-axis results in an x-coordinate value that is less.

Moving right along the x-axis results in an x-coordinate value that is greater.

Example 3

Angle QRS, with Vertex R (−4, −2), Ray RQ, containing Point Q (−2, −3), and Ray RS, containing Point S (−1, 1), is translated three units up and one unit right to create Angle Q'R'S'. What are the coordinates of Vertex R' and the corresponding points on Ray R'Q' and Ray R'S'?

<u>Answer</u>: **Vertex R' (−3, 1), Point Q' (−1, 0), and Point S' (0, 4)**

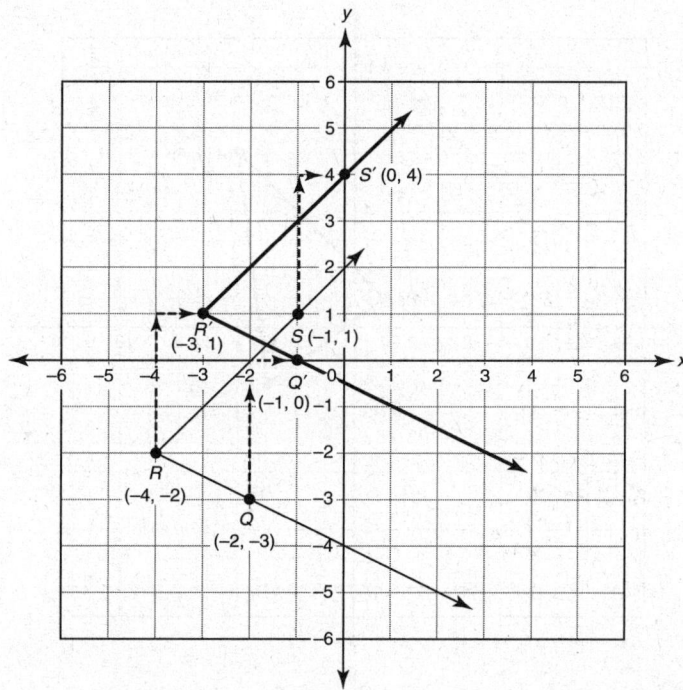

Slide each point of the pre-image 3 units up and 1 unit right. The y-coordinate values of the image are 3 greater than the y-coordinate values of the pre-image, and the x-coordinate values of the image are 1 greater than the x-coordinate values of the pre-image. Another notation for the ordered pairs of the image is $(x + 1, y + 3)$.

Guided Practice

1. Graph Triangle A'B'C', which was translated 5 units left and 3 units up from the pre-image Triangle ABC at A (4, 6), B (−1, 1), and C (3, −2). Determine the coordinates of the vertices of Triangle A'B'C'.

2. Parallelogram EFGH is translated 3 units right and 5 units down, creating Parallelogram E'F'G'H' with E' (−2, 5), F' (4, 5), G' (1, 2), and H' (−5, 2). Determine the coordinates of the vertices of Parallelogram EFGH by graphing.

3. Triangle Q'R'S' with Q' (7, −2), R' (3, −3), and S' (4, −5) was translated from Triangle QRS with Q (9, −3), R (5, −4), and S (6, −6). Give the translation of the image as an ordered pair without graphing. Explain.

Guided Practice Answers Explained

1. **The coordinates are A' (−1, 9), B' (−6, 4), and C' (−2, 1).**

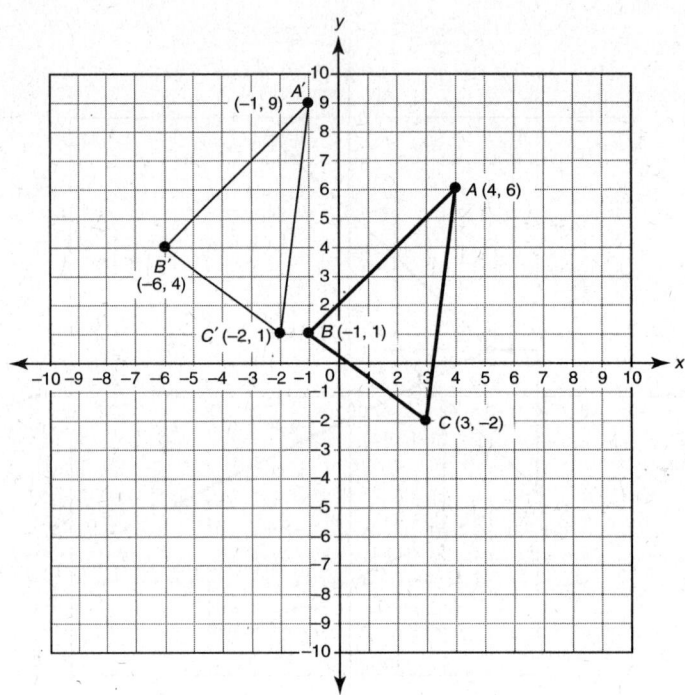

Each vertex was translated to the left 5 and up 3. The alternate notation for this is $(x − 5, y + 3)$.

2. **The coordinates of the pre-image (Parallelogram *EFGH*) are *E* (−5, 10), *F* (1, 10), *G* (−2, 7), and *H* (−8, 7).**

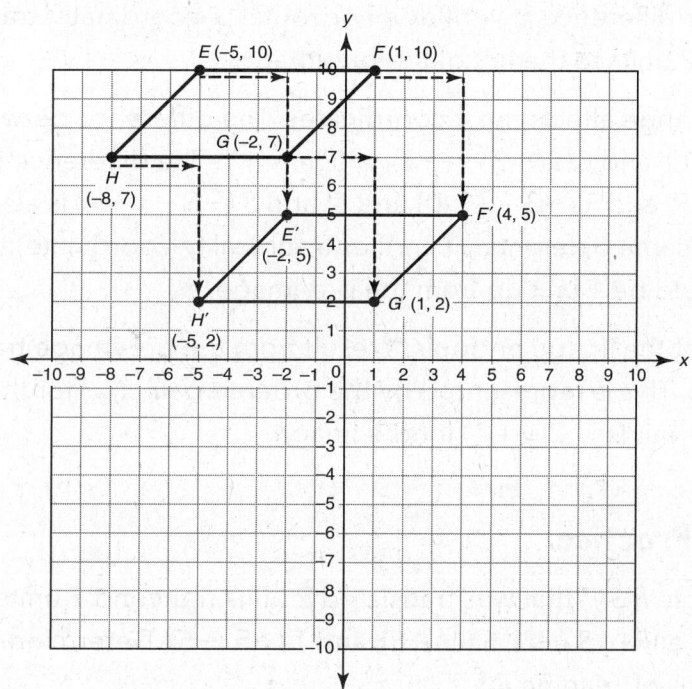

To determine the pre-image coordinates, use the translation 3 units right and 5 units down. The alternate notation would be $(x + 3, y - 5)$, resulting in the image coordinates *E'* (−2, 5), *F'* (4, 5), *G'* (1, 2), and *H'* (−5, 2). In this case, because the *image* coordinates were given, you need to work backward, moving up and left from the image to get to the pre-image.

3. **The ordered pair notation is $(x - 2, y + 1)$.**

Pre-Image	Image	
Q (9, −3)	Q' (7, −2)	To determine the translation, calculate the differences in the coordinates for each vertex by subtracting the pre-image coordinates from the image coordinates.
R (5, −4)	R' (3, −3)	
S (6, −6)	S' (4, −5)	

The horizontal change affects the x-coordinates. The difference between the x-coordinates of Q' and Q is 7 − 9, which is −2. The difference between the x-coordinates of R' and R (3 − 5) and between S' and S (4 − 6) is also −2. Since they all have the same difference, it verifies a horizontal (x-coordinate) translation of −2, which would be 2 units to the left of the pre-image.

The vertical change affects the y-coordinates. The difference between the y-coordinates of Q' and Q is −2 − (−3), which is +1. The difference between the y-coordinates of R' and R (−3 − (−4)) and S' and S (−5 − (−6)) is also +1. Since they all have the same difference, it verifies a vertical (y-coordinate) translation of +1, which would be 1 unit up from the pre-image.

This means that the image endpoints result from the pre-image translated 2 units left and 1 unit up. This is represented by the ordered pair (x, y) for the pre-image and the ordered pair $(x − 2, y + 1)$ for the image.

Independent Practice

1. Graph Triangle R'S'T' that was translated 2 units right and 7 units up from Triangle RST at R (−3, −2), S (1, −5), and T (−5, −5). Determine the coordinates of the vertices of Triangle R'S'T'.

2. Line Segment YX, with Y (3, 5) and X (6, 0), is translated 8 units left and 1 unit down, creating Line Segment Y'X'. Determine the coordinates of the endpoints of Line Segment Y'X' by graphing.

3. Triangle K'L'M', with K' (−2, −1), L' (2, 1), and M' (−1, −3), was translated from Triangle KLM, with K (−5, 3), L (−1, 5), and M (−4, 1). Give the translation of the image as an ordered pair without graphing. Explain.

(Answers are on page 301.)

Rotations

> **Key Concepts**
>
> - Rotations are clockwise or counterclockwise transformations that move a specific number of degrees along the edge of an invisible circle formed by the distance of the pre-image from the center (called the **point of rotation**).
>
> - Every point, line, or segment of a shape moves the same number of degrees and the same direction around the point of rotation.
>
> - The point, or center, of rotation can be located on the shape, within the shape, or outside the shape.
>
> - A rotation moves the position of the image, but preserves its size and shape.
>
> - The pre-image and the image created by a rotation are congruent because a rotation preserves both shape and size.

Some rotation images are made from the ordered pairs or segments from pre-images relative to the *x*-axis or *y*-axis. Some rotations require the use of a protractor to make them accurate. Other rotations, specifically those *around the origin,* have a specific relationship. This relationship can be noted using the *x*-coordinates and *y*-coordinates of the vertices from the pre-image and those of the image without the use of any tools.

Example 1

Rotate Triangle CAM (with C (2, 5), A (5, 1), and M (2, 1)) 90° counterclockwise around Point M.

Answer:

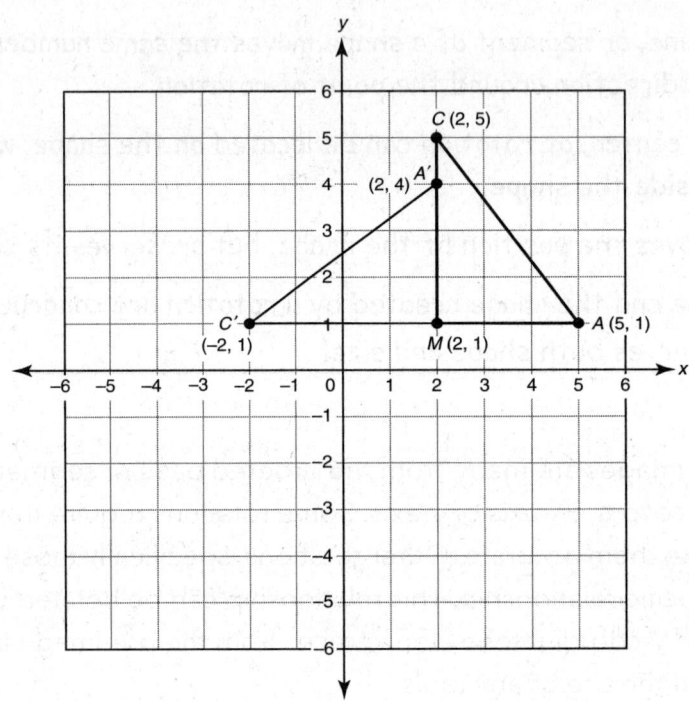

On the image, Vertex M is the same ordered pair, Vertex C' is (−2, 1), and Vertex A' is (2, 4). This example is a rotation around a point *on* the shape. Vertex M is the point of rotation. Moving Side MC 90° counterclockwise means leaving Vertex M stationary. Since Side MC is parallel to the y-axis, a 90° counterclockwise rotation means that it will now be parallel to the x-axis. On the image, Vertex C' is (−2, 1). Side MA is parallel to the x-axis, and a 90° counterclockwise rotation will move it parallel to the y-axis. On the image, Vertex A' is (2, 4).

One of the most common rotations on, within, or outside of a shape uses the origin as the point of rotation. There is specific notation that can be used for a rotation around the origin so that a protractor is not required.

Geometry—Transformations • 127

Table 5-1. Notation Shortcuts for a Rotation Around the Origin

Degrees	Direction	Image Coordinate Notation
90	Clockwise	(y, −x)
90	Counterclockwise	(−y, x)
180	Clockwise or Counterclockwise	(−x, −y)

Example 2

Triangle *CAM* is rotated clockwise 90° around the origin.

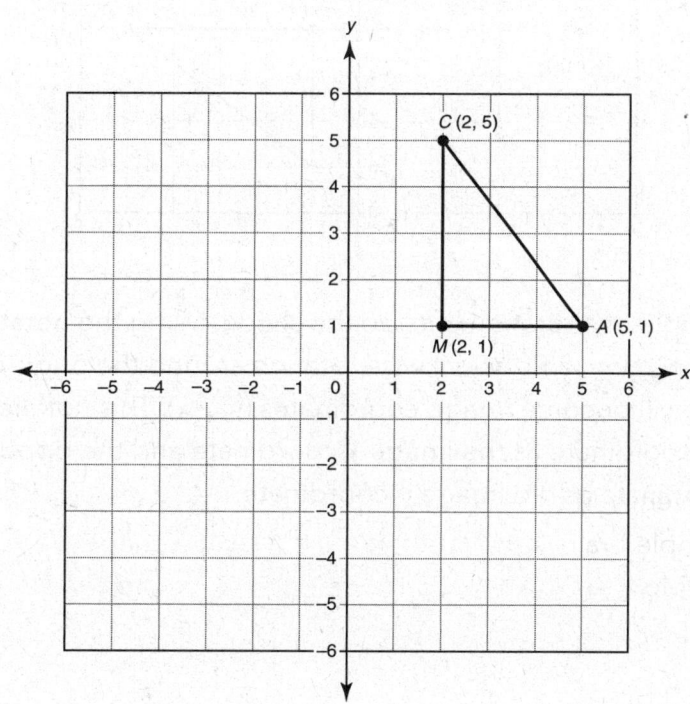

Give the coordinates of Triangle *C'A'M'*.

Answer: **The coordinates of Triangle C'A'M' are C' (5, −2), A' (1, −5), and M' (1, −2).**

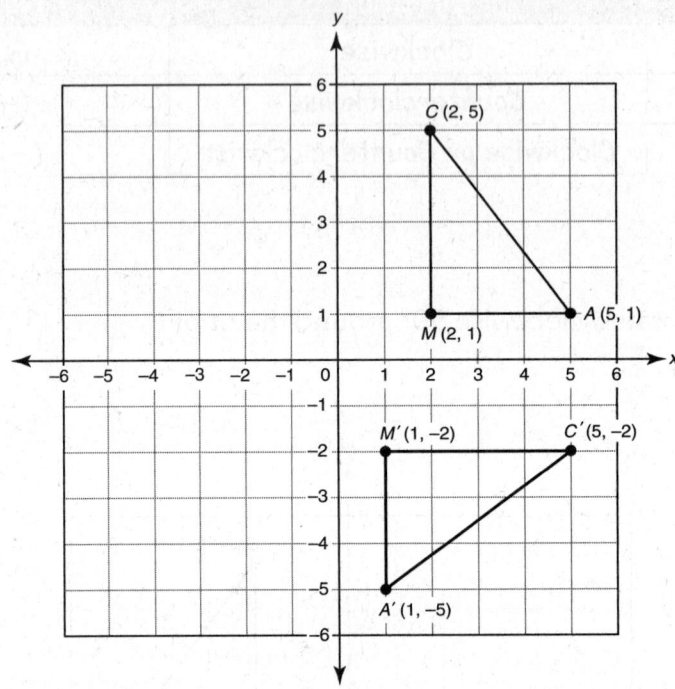

This is an example of a rotation *outside* the shape. Using the notation guidelines for images resulting from a 90° clockwise rotation around the origin, the pre-image coordinates (x, y) will become image coordinates $(y, -x)$. This notation uses the pre-image *y*-coordinate as the image *x*-coordinate and the opposite of the pre-image *x*-coordinate as the image *y*-coordinate.

Example 3

Rotate Triangle *WIN* 180° counterclockwise around the origin.

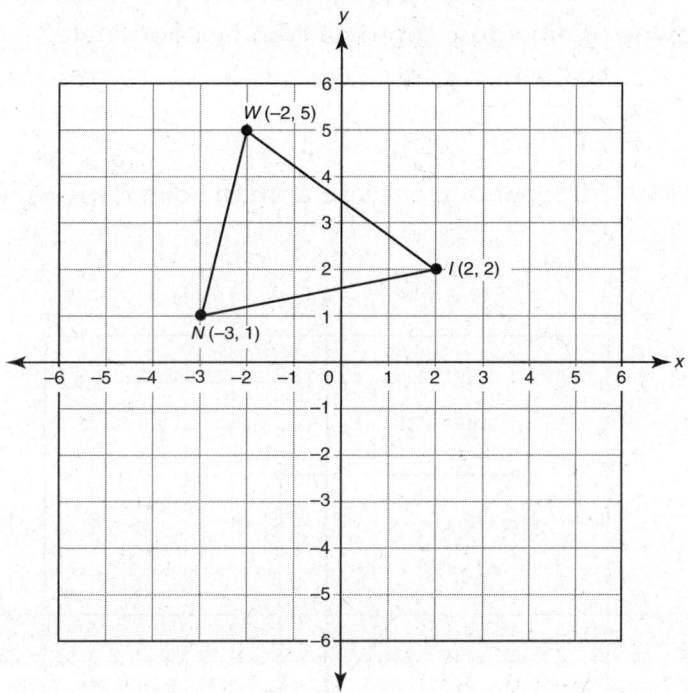

Give the coordinates of Triangle *W'I'N'*.

<u>Answer:</u> **The coordinates of Triangle *W'I'N'* are *W'* (2, −5), *I'* (−2, −2), and *N'* (3, −1).**

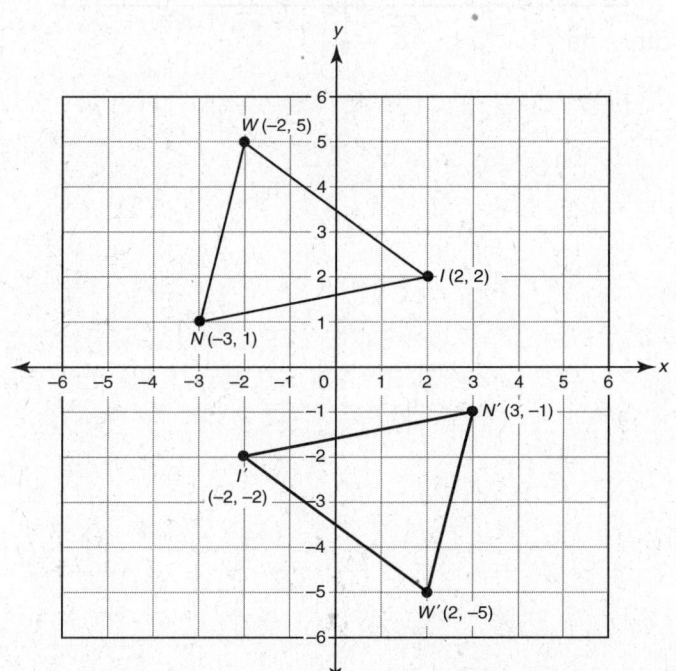

This is another example of a rotation *outside* the shape. Using the notation guidelines for images resulting from a 180° counterclockwise rotation around the origin, the pre-image coordinates (x, y) will become image coordinates (−x, −y) or the opposites of the pre-image x-coordinate and y-coordinate.

Example 4

Rotate Triangle MNT 90° counterclockwise around Point R at (−1, 0).

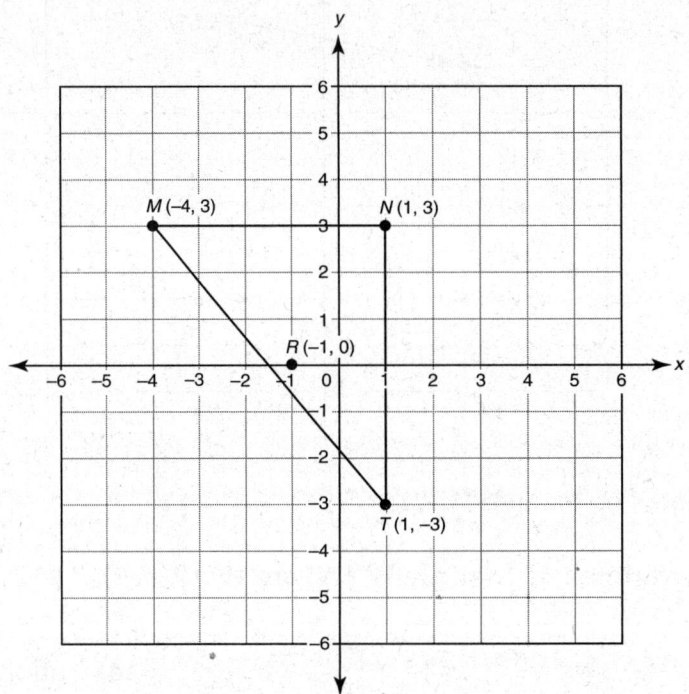

Answer: **The coordinates of Triangle M'N'T' are M' (−4,−3), N' (−4, 2), and T' (2, 2).**

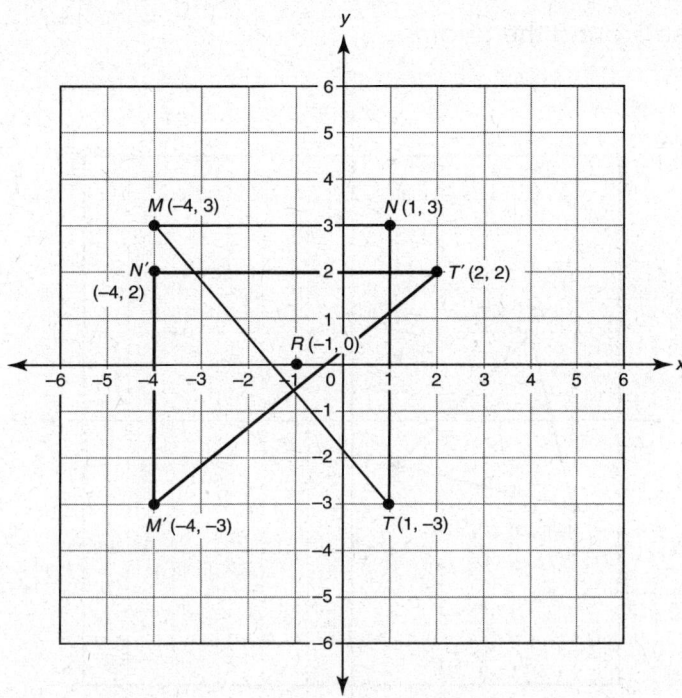

This is an example of a point of rotation *within* the shape. Side MN is parallel to the x-axis, so a 90° counterclockwise rotation moves it parallel to the y-axis. Side MN is located 3 units away from Point R and maintains that distance with the rotation. This results in M' (−4, −3) and N' (−4, 2).

Side NT is parallel to the y-axis, so a 90° counterclockwise rotation moves it parallel to the x-axis. Side NT is located 2 units away from Point R and maintains that distance with the rotation. This results in N' (−4, 2) and T' (2, 2).

Guided Practice

1. Determine the coordinates of Triangle T'A'Y' after a rotation of Triangle TAY 180° clockwise around the origin.

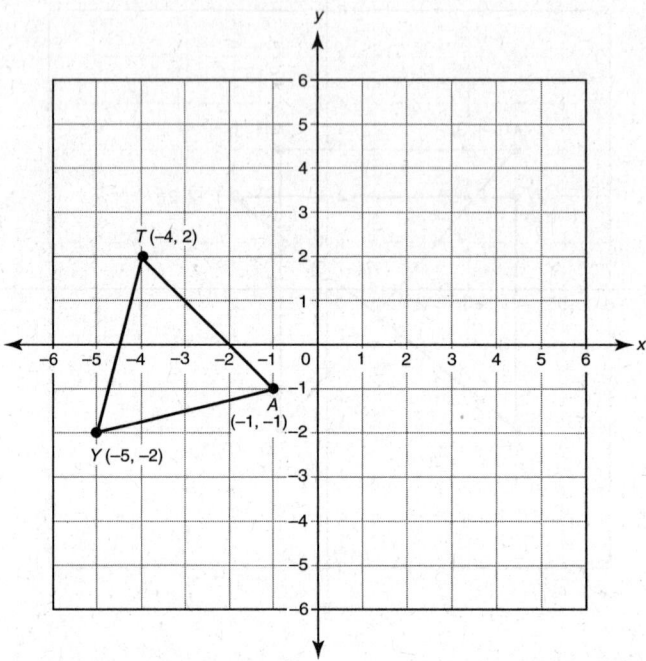

2. Rotate Rectangle EFGH 90° counterclockwise around Point R at (2, 2). Give the coordinates of the image.

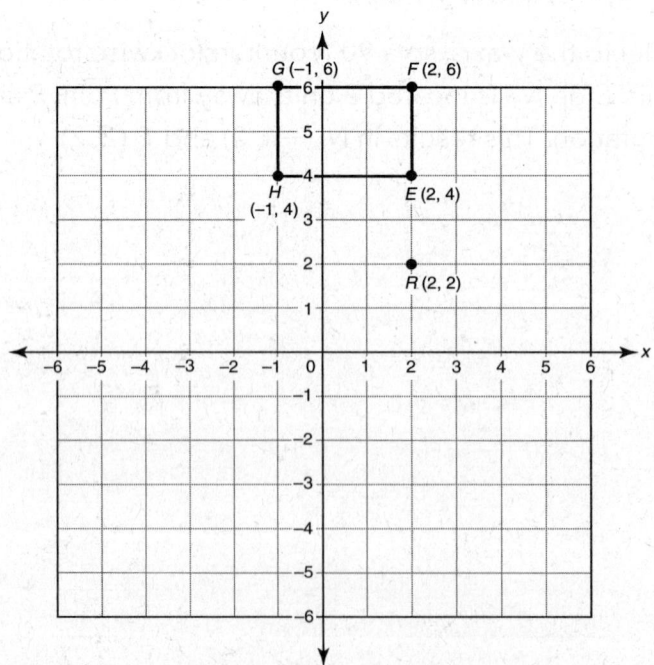

3. Describe the rotation of Triangle ABC resulting in Triangle A'B'C'. Include the degrees, direction, and point of rotation.

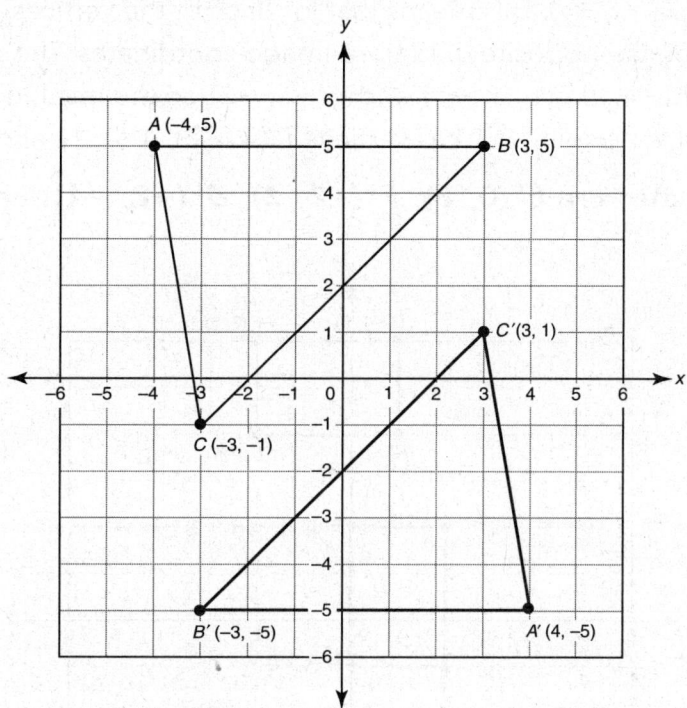

Guided Practice Answers Explained

1. **The coordinates are T' (4, −2), A' (1, 1), and Y' (5, 2).**

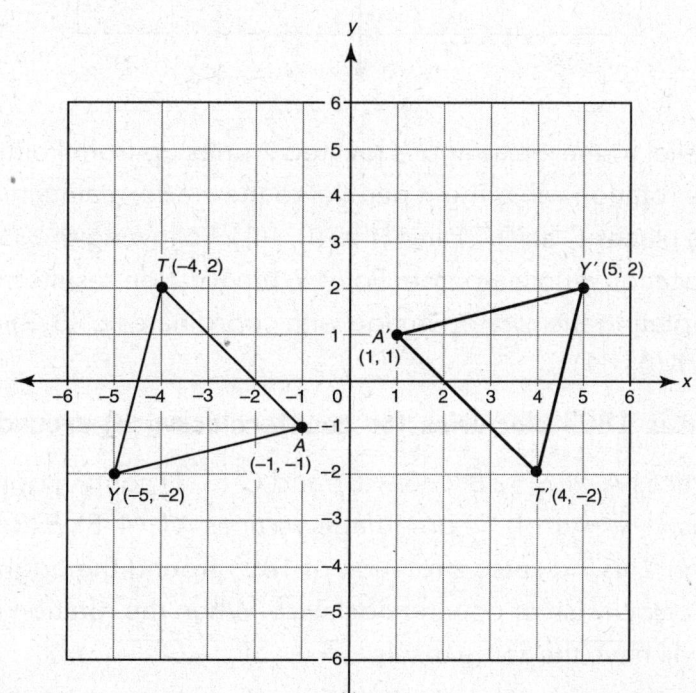

Using the coordinate notation from Table 5-1, a 180° clockwise rotation around the origin causes a change in the coordinates of each pre-image vertex (x, y) to each image vertex $(-x, -y)$. This means that for each of the vertices, the image coordinates will be the opposite of the pre-image coordinates. The pre-image coordinates are $T(-4, 2)$, $A(-1, -1)$, and $Y(-5, -2)$, so the resulting image rotated clockwise around the origin 180° has vertices $T'(4, -2)$, $A'(1, 1)$, and $Y'(5, 2)$.

2. **The coordinates are $E'(0, 2)$, $F'(-2, 2)$, $G'(-2, -1)$, and $H'(0, -1)$.**

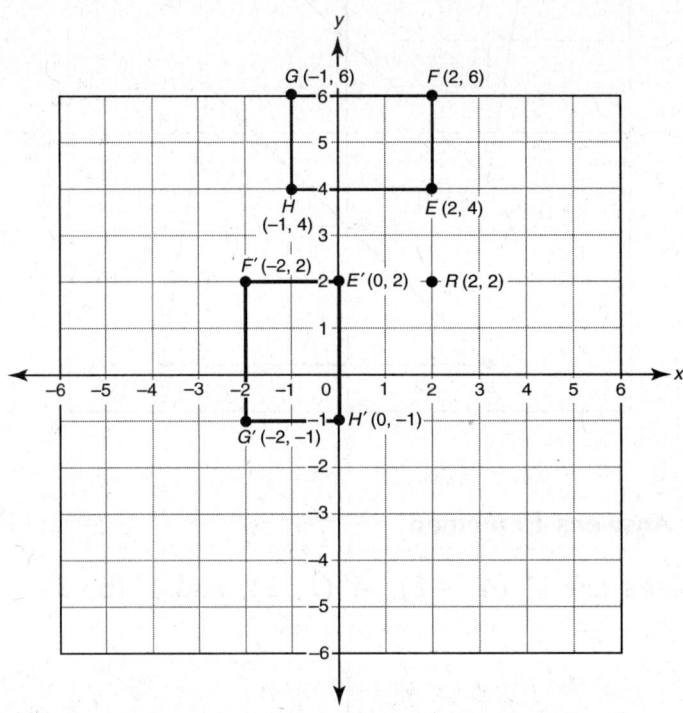

Side EH is parallel to the x-axis and is located 2 units up from Point R. A 90° counterclockwise rotation will bring it parallel to the y-axis, maintaining the distance from Point R. This places E' at $(0, 2)$ and H' at $(0, -1)$. Following the same rotation for Side FG, with a location 4 units up from Point R, the rotation results in $F'(-2, 2)$ and $G'(-2, -1)$, completing the rotated image with coordinates $E'(0, 2)$, $F'(-2, 2)$, $G'(-2, -1)$, and $H'(0, -1)$.

3. **The rotation is 180° clockwise (or counterclockwise) around the origin.**

The image vertices $A'(4, -5)$, $B'(-3, -5)$, and $C'(3, 1)$ contain opposite coordinate values, $(-x, -y)$, of the pre-image vertices $A(-4, 5)$, $B(3, 5)$, and $C(-3, -1)$ as (x, y). This indicates a rotation of 180° around the origin, and the direction is either clockwise or counterclockwise. When the rotation is 180°, either direction will have the same result.

Independent Practice

1. Determine the endpoints of Line Segment R'S' after a rotation of Line Segment RS 90° clockwise around the origin.

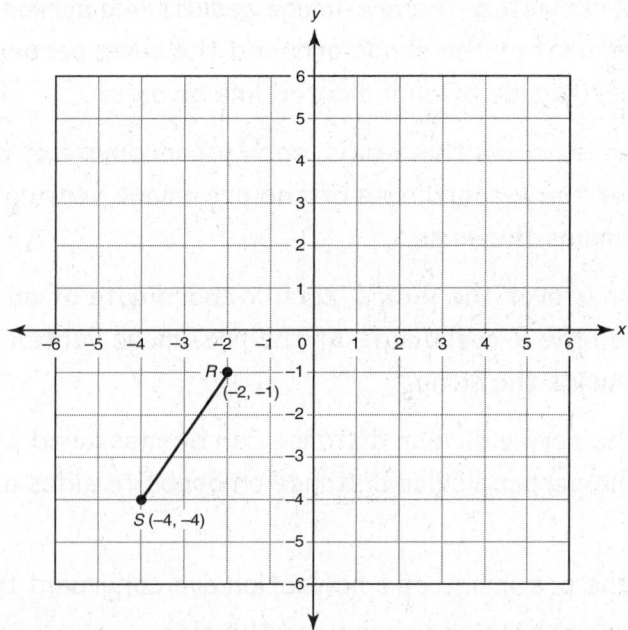

2. Describe the rotation of Angle JKL resulting in Angle J'K'L'. Include the degrees, direction, and point of rotation.

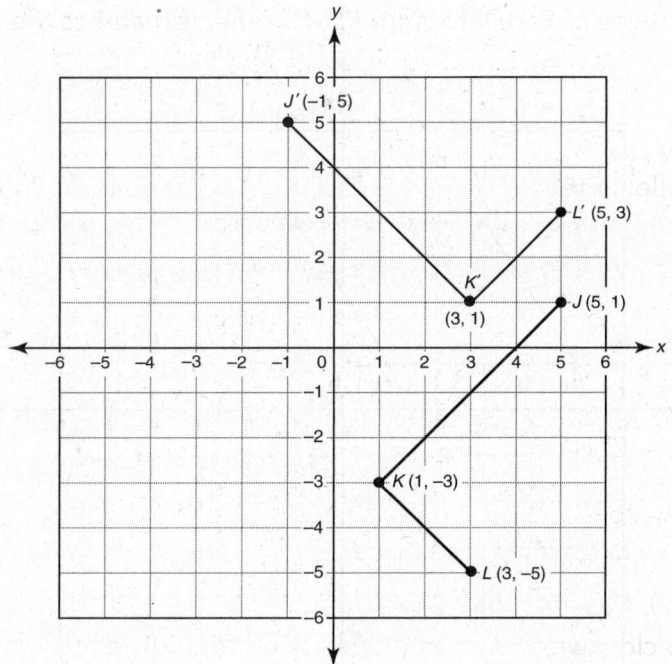

(Answers are on page 302.)

Reflections

> **Key Concepts**
>
> - When a shape is reflected, the pre-image results in a mirror image of every point, line, or segment of the shape graphed the same perpendicular distance away on the opposite side of an indicated line or axis.
>
> - If the reflection is across the x-axis, each y-coordinate of an image vertex is the opposite of the y-coordinate of the pre-image vertex, and the x-coordinate remains the same.
>
> - If the reflection is over the y-axis, each x-coordinate of an image vertex is the opposite of the x-coordinate of the pre-image vertex, and the y-coordinate remains the same.
>
> - Alternatively, the perpendicular distance can be measured by counting or by calculating the perpendicular distance on opposite sides of the line of reflection.
>
> - The image and the pre-image of a reflection are congruent because a reflection preserves both the shape and the size.

Example 1

Determine the vertices of Parallelogram *KLMN* reflected across the x-axis.

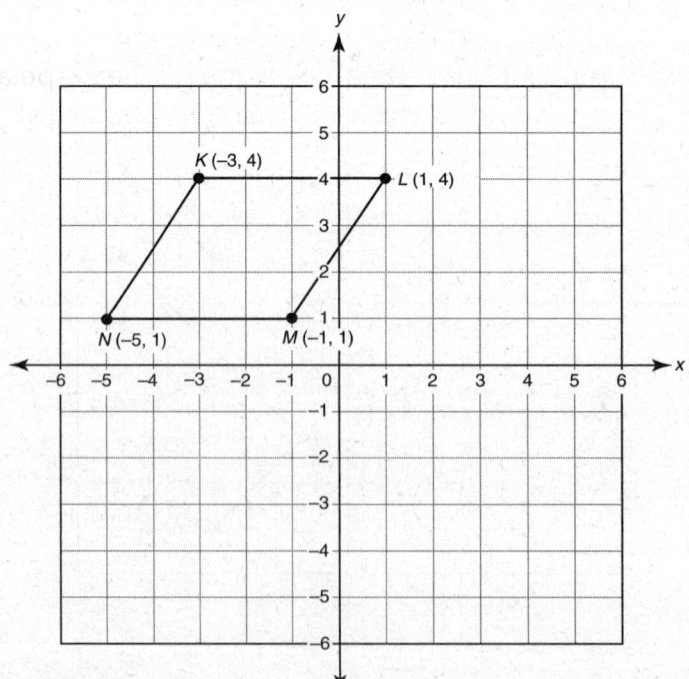

Answer: **The vertices are K' (−3, −4), L' (1, −4), M' (−1, −1), and N' (−5, −1).**

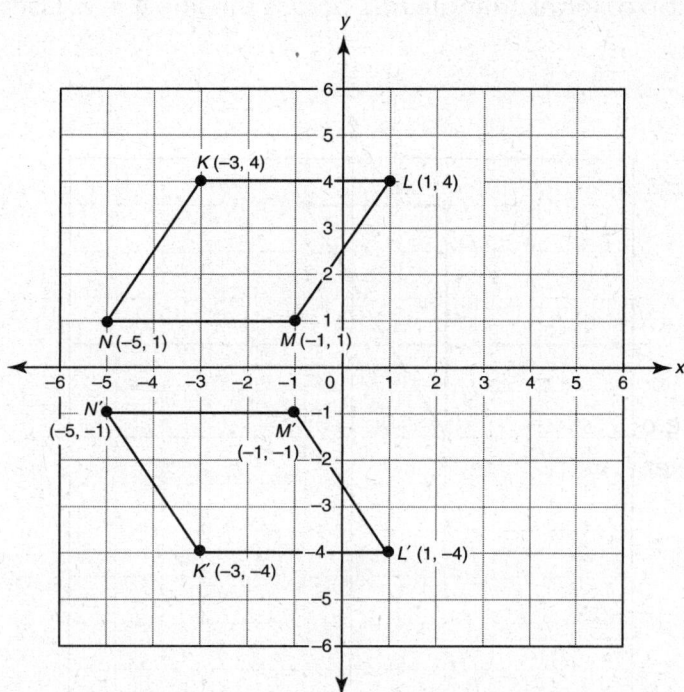

In a reflection across the x-axis, the x-coordinate values of the image are the same as the x-coordinate values of the pre-image, and the y-coordinate values of the image are the opposite of the y-coordinate values of the pre-image. The perpendicular distance from each vertex to the x-axis is preserved by using the opposite y-coordinate value for each vertex of the image. The pre-image and the image are congruent because both the size and the shape are preserved in the reflection.

Example 2

Graph the reflection of Right Triangle *RST* across the line $y = 2$. List the vertices of the image.

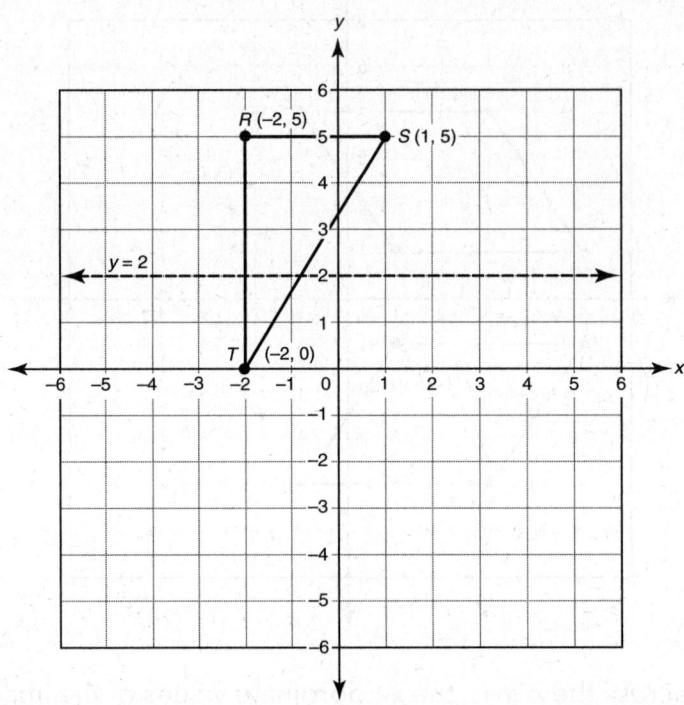

Answer: **The vertices are *R'* (−2, −1), *S'* (1, −1), and *T'* (−2, 4).**

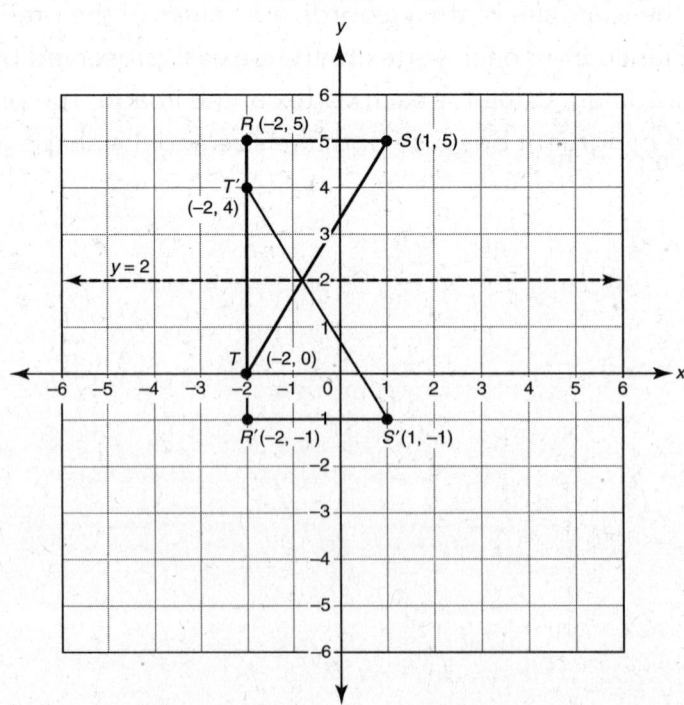

In a reflection across the graph of a line that is not an axis, count or calculate the perpendicular distance from the line of reflection to a vertex of the pre-image, and then count or calculate the same perpendicular distance on the opposite side of the line of reflection to the image.

In this example, Vertex R is located 3 units above the line of reflection, $y = 2$, so Vertex R' should be located 3 units below that line at the same x-coordinate as R. Vertex S is also located 3 units above the line of reflection, $y = 2$, so S' should be located 3 units below that line at the same x-coordinate as S. Vertex T is located 2 units below the line of reflection, $y = 2$, so it should be reflected to 2 units above that line at the same x-coordinate as T.

This gives the reflection R'S'T', which is congruent to RST. The pre-image and the image are congruent because both the size and the shape are preserved in the reflection.

Example 3

Line Segment UV is reflected across the x-axis and then across the y-axis, resulting in Line Segment U"V". Give the endpoints for Line Segment U"V".

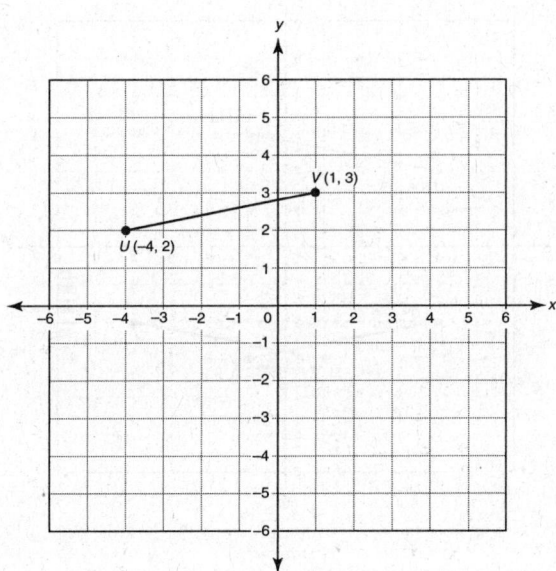

Answer: **The endpoints are U" (4, −2) and V" (−1, −3).**

The first reflection across the x-axis kept the x-coordinates of the pre-image vertices the same and used the opposite of the pre-image y-coordinates for the image U' (−4, −2) and V' (1, −3).

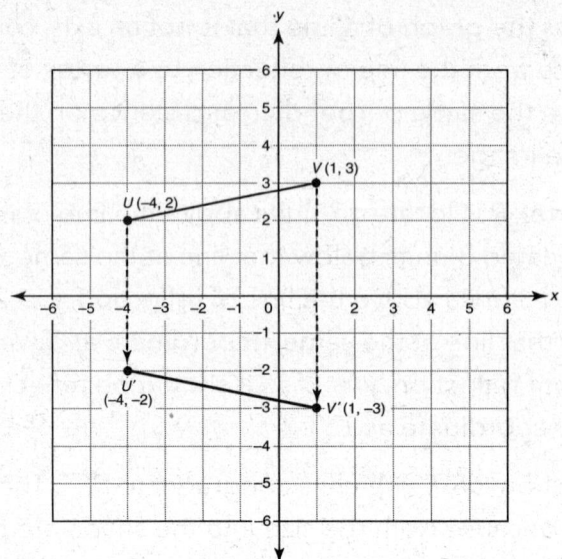

The second reflection across the y-axis preserved the new y-coordinates from U' and V' and used the opposite of their x-coordinates for the final image U" (4, −2) and V" (−1, −3).

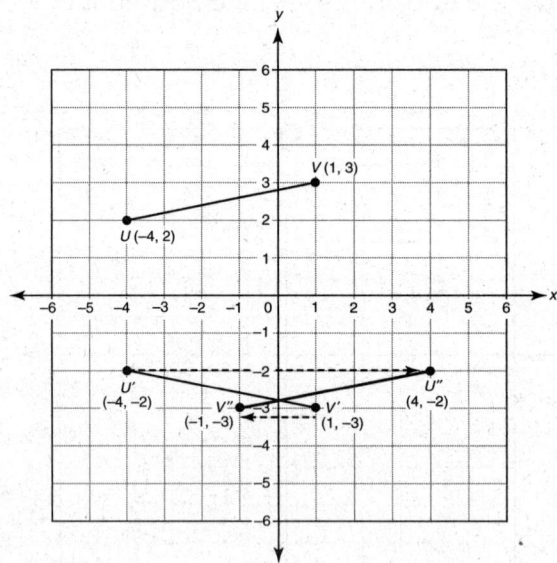

This reflection preserves the size, so the pre-image, U'V', and U"V" are all congruent.

Geometry—Transformations • 141

Guided Practice

1. Determine the vertices of the image of Quadrilateral WXYZ reflected across the line $x = -3$.

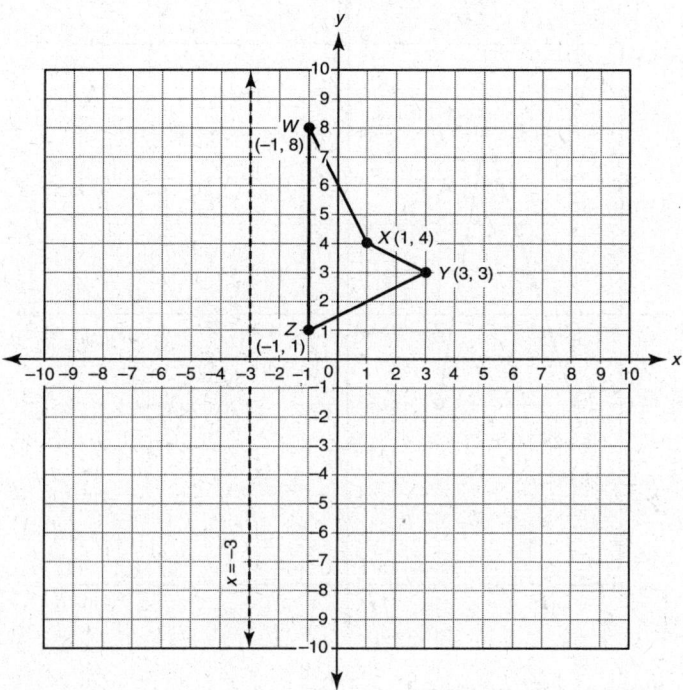

2. Graph the reflection of Triangle DEF across the line $y = -1$. Determine the vertices of the image.

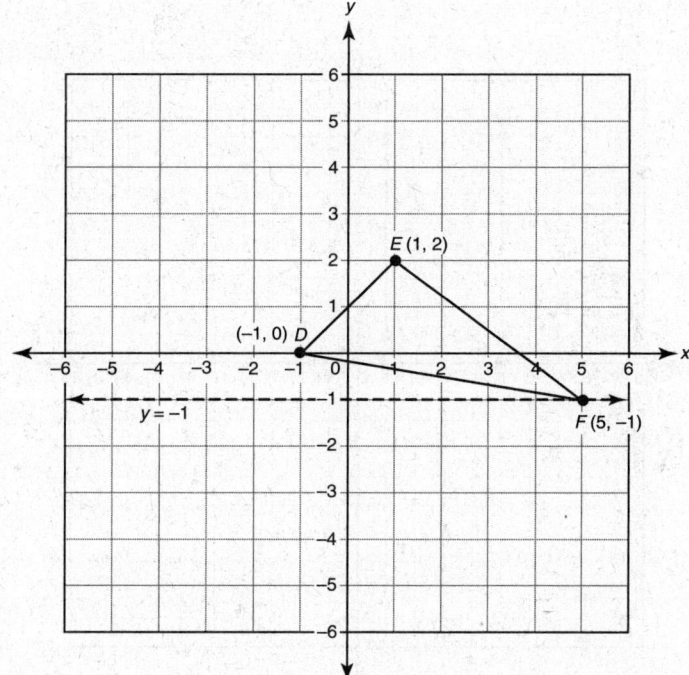

3. Angle RST is reflected across the y-axis. Determine the vertices of the image, Angle R'S'T'.

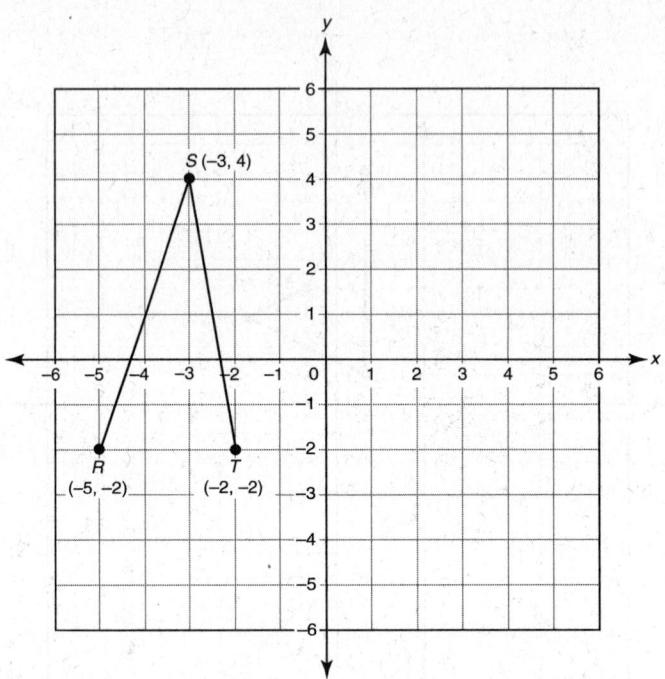

Guided Practice Answers Explained

1. **The vertices of the image are W' (−5, 8), X' (−7, 4), Y' (−9, 3), and Z' (−5, 1).**

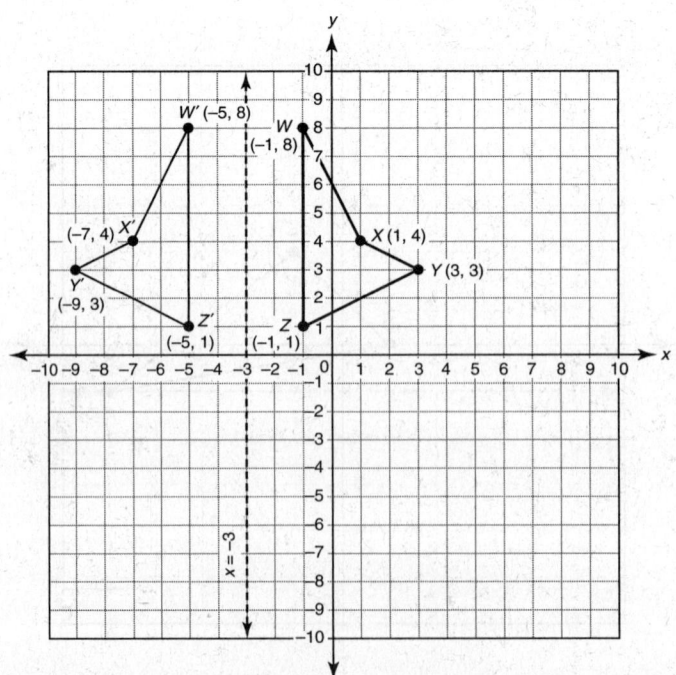

Geometry—Transformations • 143

In a reflection across a line that is not an axis, count or calculate the perpendicular distance from the line of reflection to a vertex of the pre-image, and then count or calculate the same perpendicular distance on the opposite side of the line of reflection to the image.

In this example, Vertex W is located 2 units to the right of the line $x = -3$, so Vertex W' should be 2 units to the left of that line, but the y-coordinate remains the same.

Vertex X is located 4 units to the right of the line $x = -3$, so Vertex X' should be 4 units to the left of that line, but the y-coordinate remains the same.

Vertex Y is located 6 units to the right of the line $x = -3$, so Vertex Y' should be located 6 units to the left of that line, but the y-coordinate remains the same.

Finally, Vertex Z is located 2 units to the right of the line $x = -3$, so Vertex Z' should be located 2 units to the left of that line, but the y-coordinate remains the same.

The pre-image and the image are congruent because both the size and the shape are preserved in the reflection.

2. **The vertices are D' (−1, −2), E' (1, −4), and F (5, −1). Vertex F is on the line of reflection and thus is the same point in both the pre-image and the image.**

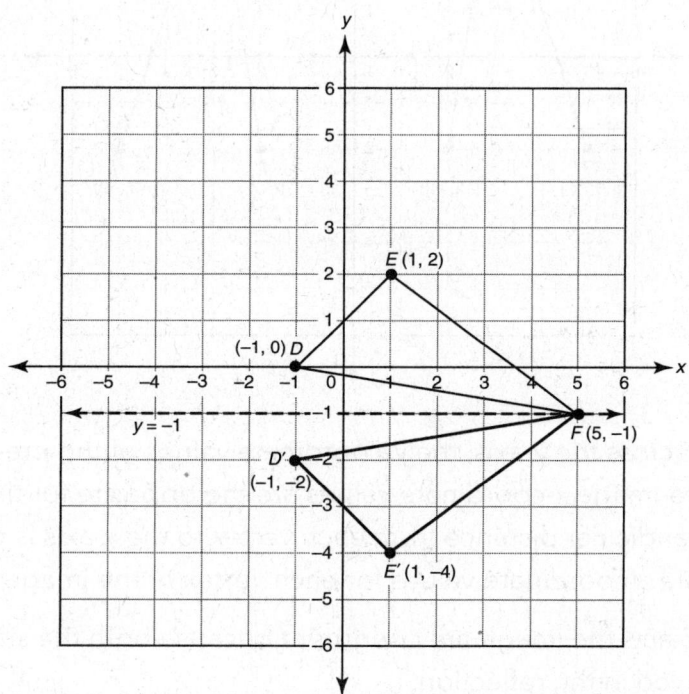

In a reflection across a line that is not an axis, count or calculate the perpendicular distance from the line of reflection to a vertex of the pre-image, and then count or calculate the same perpendicular distance on the opposite side of the line of reflection to the image.

In this example, Vertex D is located 1 unit above the line $y = -1$, so Vertex D' should be 1 unit below that line, but the x-coordinate remains the same.

Vertex E is located 3 units above the line $y = -1$, so Vertex E' is 3 units below that line, but the x-coordinate remains the same.

Uniquely, Vertex F is on the line of reflection, so it does not move.

The pre-image and the image are congruent because both the size and the shape are preserved in the reflection.

3. **The vertices are R' (5, −2), S' (3, 4), and T' (2, −2).**

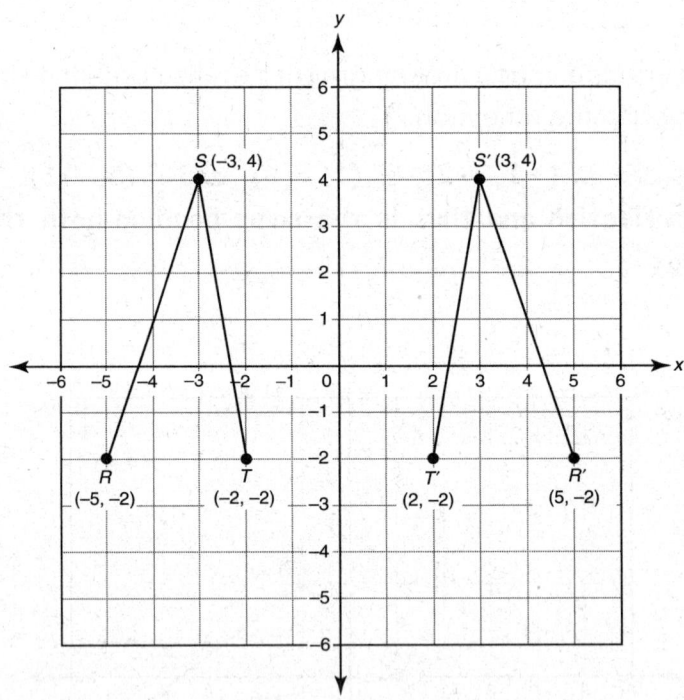

In a reflection across the y-axis, the y-coordinate values of the pre-image stay the same, and the pre-image x-coordinate values are the opposite for the vertices of the image. The perpendicular distance from each vertex to the y-axis is preserved by using the opposite x-coordinate values for each vertex of the image.

The pre-image and the image are congruent because both the size and the shape are preserved in the reflection.

Independent Practice

1. Determine the vertices of the image of Triangle UVW reflected across the line $y = -1$.

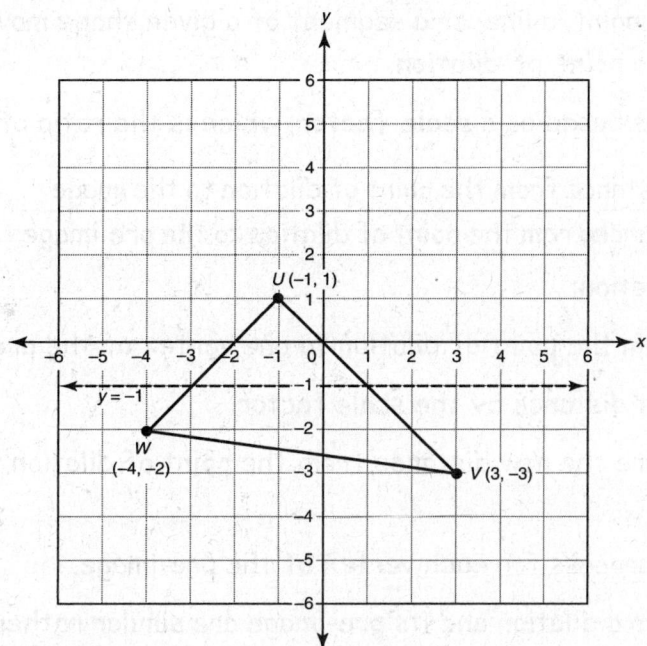

2. Angle A″B″C″ is the image after two reflections of Angle ABC. Determine the two reflections.

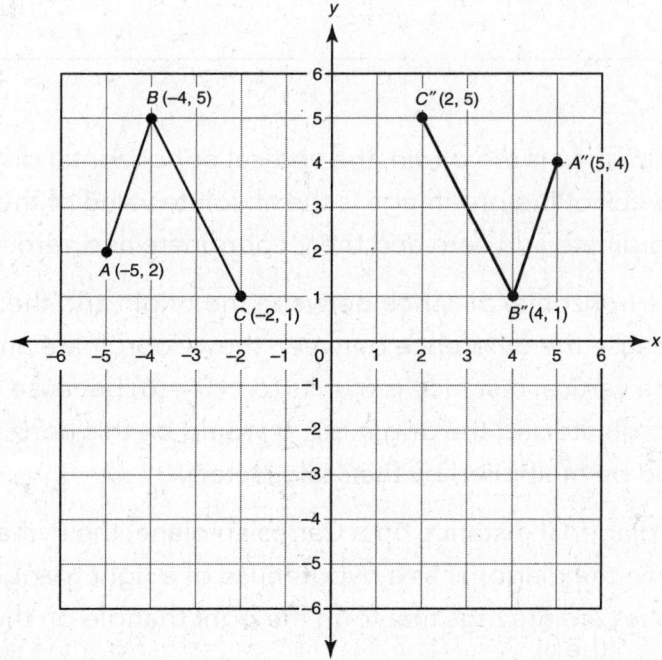

(Answers are on page 303.)

Dilations

> **Key Concepts**
>
> - In a dilation, a point, a line, or a segment of a given shape moves the same distance from a **point of dilation**.
> - This distance is based on a **scale factor**, which is the ratio of:
>
> $$\frac{\text{the distance from the point of dilation to the image}}{\text{the distance from the point of dilation to the pre-image}}$$
>
> - To create a dilation:
>   - Measure from the point of dilation to one vertex of the pre-image.
>   - Multiply that distance by the scale factor.
>   - Then, measure the new distance from the point of dilation to the vertex of the image.
>   - Repeat the process for each vertex of the pre-image.
> - The image from a dilation and its pre-image are similar rather than congruent.
> - In a dilation, the angles are congruent, but the side lengths of the image and the pre-image are in proportion, resulting from the multiplication by the scale factor.

When the point of dilation is the origin, the vertical or horizontal distance between the origin and a vertex of the pre-image is the absolute value of the difference between the *x*-coordinate and zero and the *y*-coordinate and zero.

For example, the horizontal distance between the origin and the ordered pair (4, 6) is 4 units because the difference between the *x*-coordinate and the origin (4 − 0 = 4) is 4. The vertical distance is 6 units (6 − 0 = 6) because the difference between the *y*-coordinate and the origin is 6. It would be this horizontal or vertical distance that would be multiplied by the scale factor.

To determine a diagonal distance on a Cartesian plane, the Pythagorean theorem is used to determine the diagonal as a hypotenuse of a right triangle. The horizontal and vertical distances are the legs that form the right triangle on the plane.

If the scale factor, or dilation factor, is less than 1, the image will be smaller than the pre-image and is called a **reduction**. An example of a reduction is when a photograph is resized to fit a wallet. The size of the original photograph is reduced.

If the scale factor is greater than 1, the image will be larger than the pre-image and is called an **enlargement**. An example of an enlargement is when a poster size image is created from a favorite photo. The size of the original photo is enlarged.

Example 1

Dilate Triangle *HJK* using a scale factor of 5. Give the vertices of Triangle *H'J'K'* if the point of dilation is the origin.

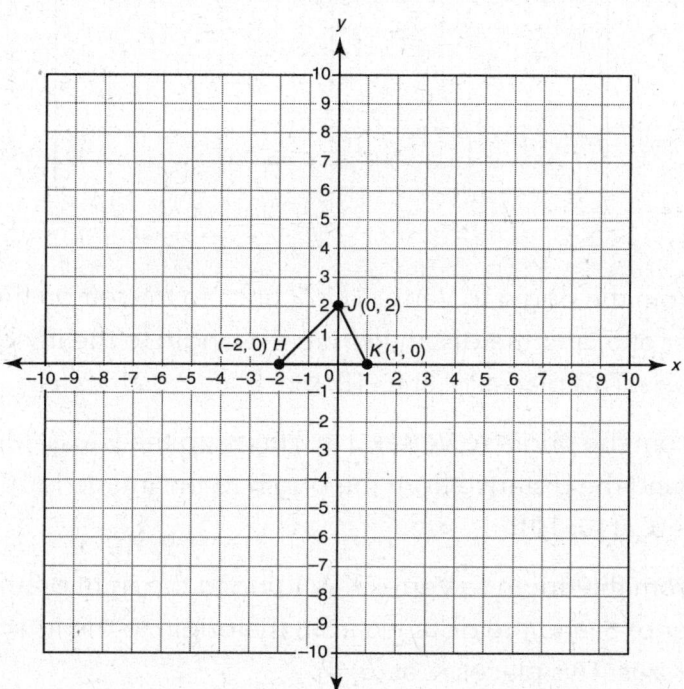

Answer: **The vertices are H' (−10, 0), J' (0, 10), and K' (5, 0).**

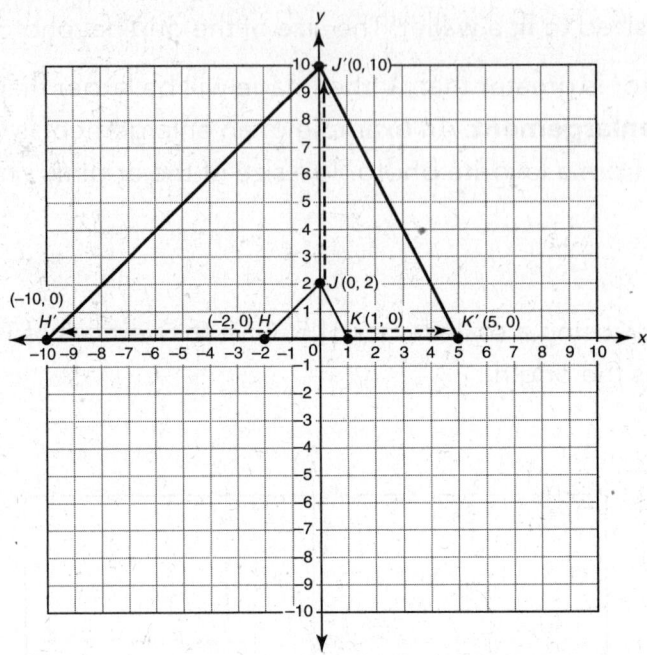

The distance from the origin to Vertex H is 2 units to the left on the x-axis. Multiply by the scale factor of 5, and the distance from the origin to the image is 10 units to the left on the x-axis. This places H' at (−10, 0).

The distance from the origin to Vertex J is 2 units up the y-axis. Multiply by the scale factor of 5, and the distance from the origin to the image is 10 units up the y-axis. This places J' at (0, 10).

The distance from the origin to Vertex K is 1 unit to the right on the x-axis. Multiply by the scale factor of 5, and the distance from the origin to the image is 5 units to the right on the x-axis. This places K' at (5, 0).

The angles of the triangle are congruent, but the side lengths are in proportion, using the scale factor of 5. Thus, the pre-image and the image are similar. This dilation results in an enlargement.

Example 2

Rectangle *RSTU* is dilated using a scale factor of $\frac{1}{3}$. If the point of dilation is Vertex *R*, determine the vertices of the image.

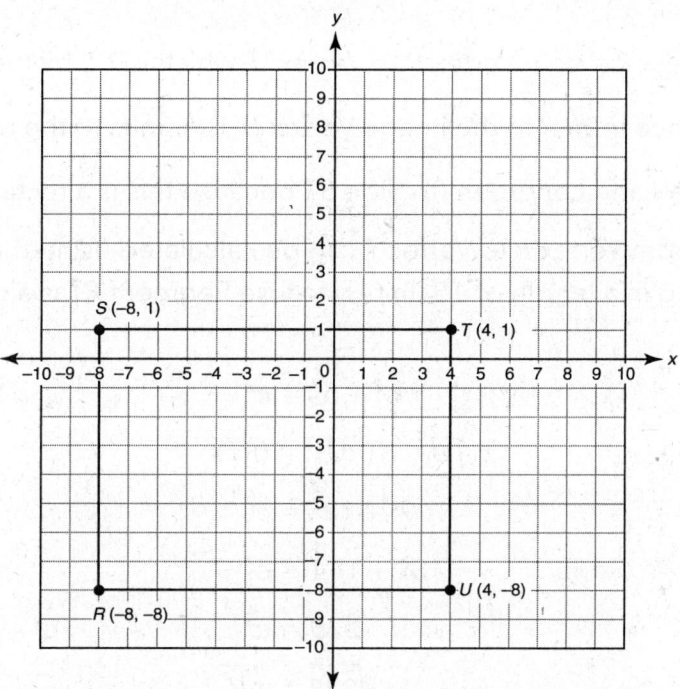

Answer: **The vertices of the image are R (−8, −8), S' (−8, −5), T' (−4, −5), and U' (−4, −8).** Notice that since Vertex *R* is the point of dilation, it remains fixed.

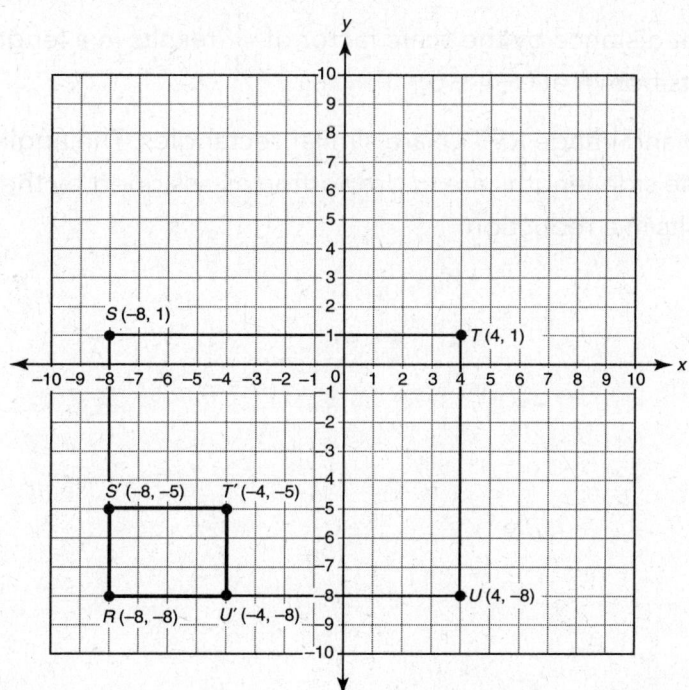

The distance from Vertex R to Vertex S is 9 units. Multiply by the scale factor of $\frac{1}{3}$, and the distance from R to the image Vertex S' is 3 units up at (−8, −5). This side is parallel and congruent to Side TU because this is a rectangle.

Multiply the distance from Vertex R to Vertex U, which is 12, by the scale factor of $\frac{1}{3}$, and the distance from R to the image Vertex U' is 4 units to the right at (−4, −8). This side is parallel and congruent to Side ST because this is a rectangle.

The distance from Vertex R to Vertex T can be calculated using the Pythagorean theorem, resulting in a length of 15 units because Segment RT is a diagonal of the rectangle.

$$a^2 + b^2 = c^2$$
$$(\overline{TU})^2 + (\overline{RU})^2 = (\overline{RT})^2$$
$$9^2 + 12^2 = c^2$$
$$81 + 144 = c^2$$
$$225 = c^2$$
$$\sqrt{225} = \sqrt{c^2}$$
$$15 = c$$

Multiplying that distance by the scale factor of $\frac{1}{3}$ results in a length for the image Vertex T' of 5 units from R at (−4, −5).

The pre-image and image RS'T'U' are similar rectangles. The angles are congruent and the side lengths are in proportion as assigned by the scale factor $\frac{1}{3}$. This dilation results in a reduction.

Guided Practice

1. Determine the image of Triangle VWX if dilated using a scale factor of $\frac{1}{2}$, with Vertex X as the point of dilation.

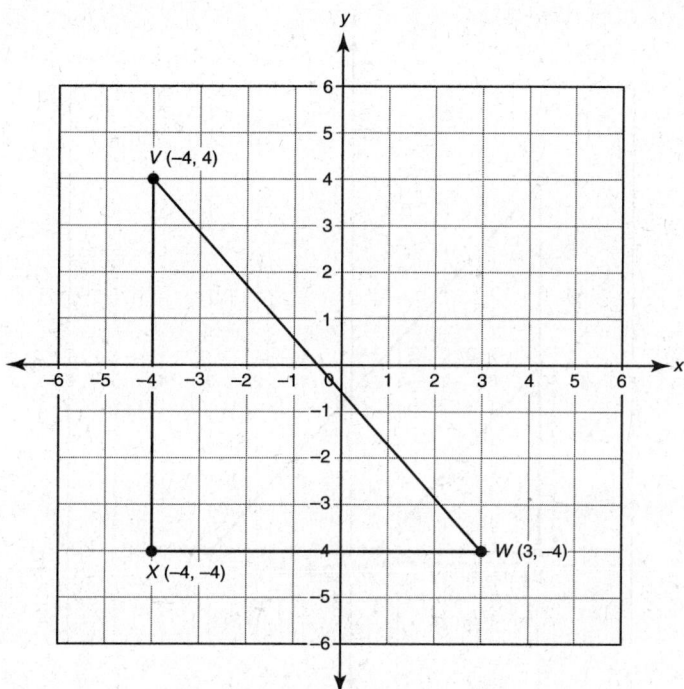

2. Determine the vertices of Triangle A'B'C' using a scale factor of 3 and the origin as the point of dilation for Triangle ABC.

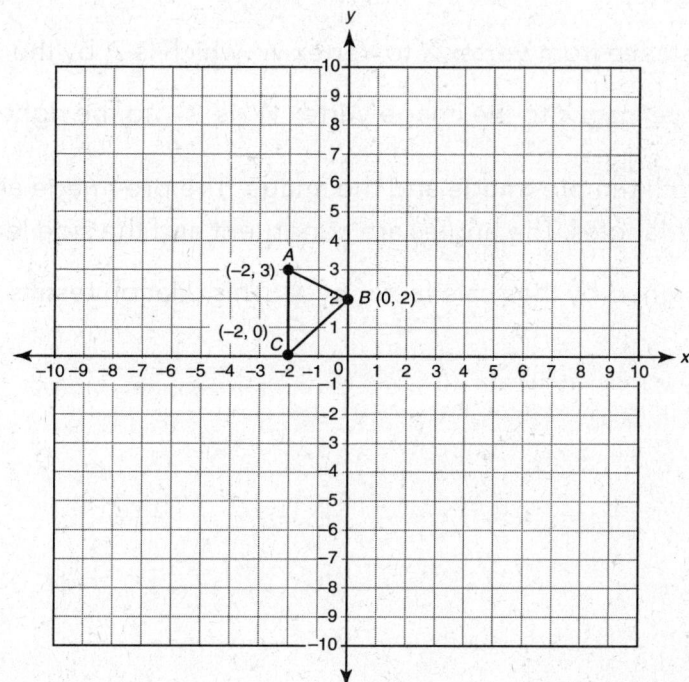

Guided Practice Answers Explained

1. **The vertices are V' (−4, 0), W' (−0.5, −4), and X (−4, −4).** Notice that since Vertex X is the point of dilation, it remains fixed.

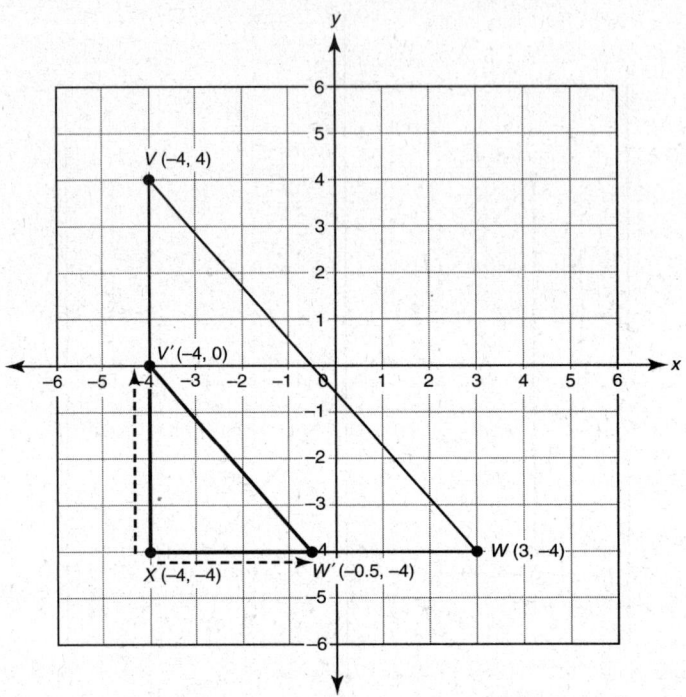

The distance from Vertex X to Vertex V is 8 units. Multiply by the scale factor of $\frac{1}{2}$, and the distance from X to the image Vertex V' is 4 units up at (−4, 0).

Multiply the distance from Vertex X to Vertex W, which is 7, by the scale factor of $\frac{1}{2}$, and the distance from X to the image Vertex W' is $3\frac{1}{2}$ to the right at (−0.5, −4).

Vertex X is in both the pre-image and the image. The pre-image and the image V'W'X are similar triangles. The angles are congruent and the side lengths are in proportion as assigned by the scale factor of $\frac{1}{2}$. This dilation results in a reduction.

2. **The vertices are A' (−6, 9), B' (0, 6), and C' (−6, 0).**

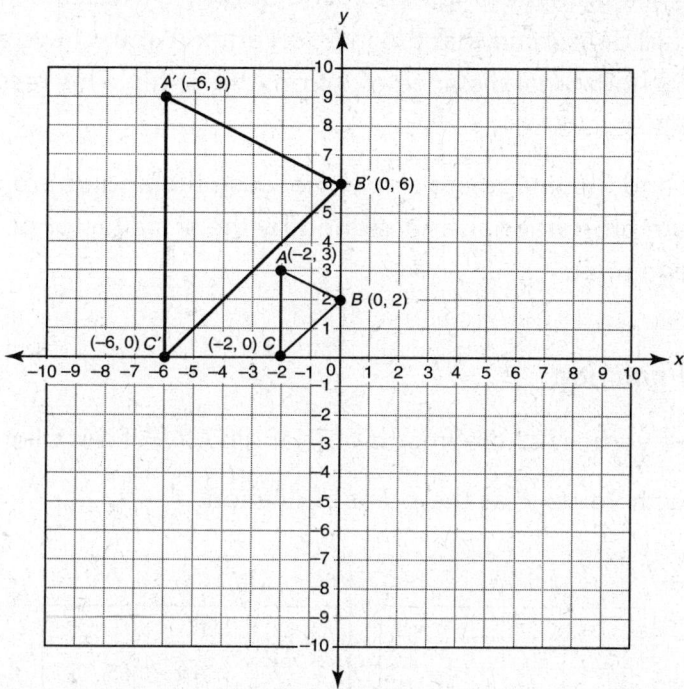

The perpendicular distance from the origin to Vertex B is 2 units up the y-axis. Multiplying by the scale factor of 3, the distance from the origin to the image Vertex B' is 6 at (0, 6).

The perpendicular distance from the origin to Vertex C is 2 units to the left on the x-axis. Multiplying by the scale factor of 3, the distance from the origin to the image Vertex C' is 6 at (−6, 0).

The perpendicular distance from the origin to Vertex A, calculated using the Pythagorean theorem, is an irrational number.

$$a^2 + b^2 = c^2$$

$$(|0 - 2|)^2 + (|0 - 3|)^2 = c^2$$

$$2^2 + 3^2 = c^2$$

$$4 + 9 = c^2$$

$$13 = c^2$$

$$\sqrt{13} = \sqrt{c^2}$$

$$\sqrt{13} = c$$

Alternatively, determining Vertex A's vertical distance from the origin as 3 and its horizontal distance from the origin as 2, and applying the scale factor to these distances, you could determine that the image Vertex A' must have a vertical distance of 9 and a horizontal distance of 6 from the origin. This results in the image Vertex A' at (−6, 9).

The pre-image and the image are similar because the angles are congruent, and the side lengths are proportional, as assigned by the scale factor of 3. The dilation results in an enlargement.

Independent Practice

1. Determine the vertices of the image of Triangle *MNP* if it is dilated using a scale factor of $\frac{1}{3}$, with Vertex *P* as the point of dilation.

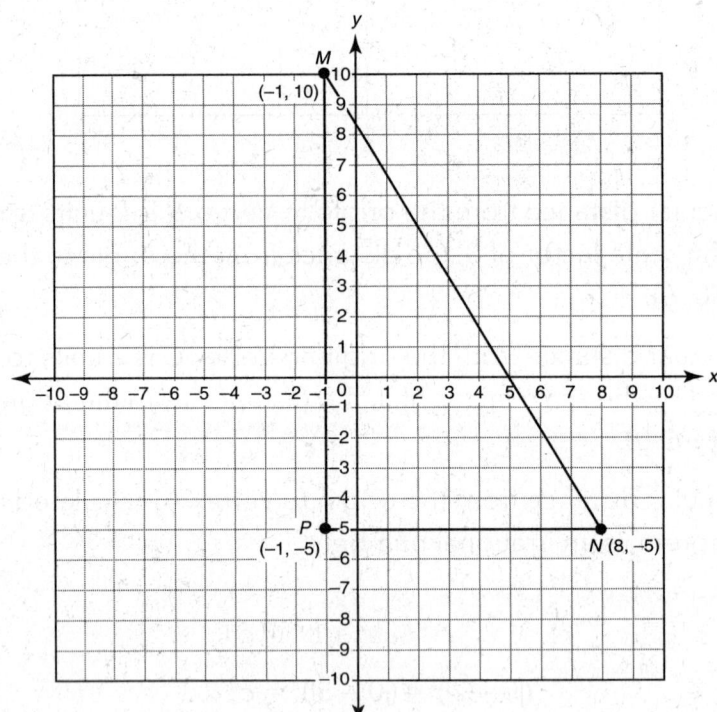

2. Determine the vertices of Parallelogram *A'B'C'D'* using a scale factor of 2 and the origin as the point of dilation for Parallelogram *ABCD*.

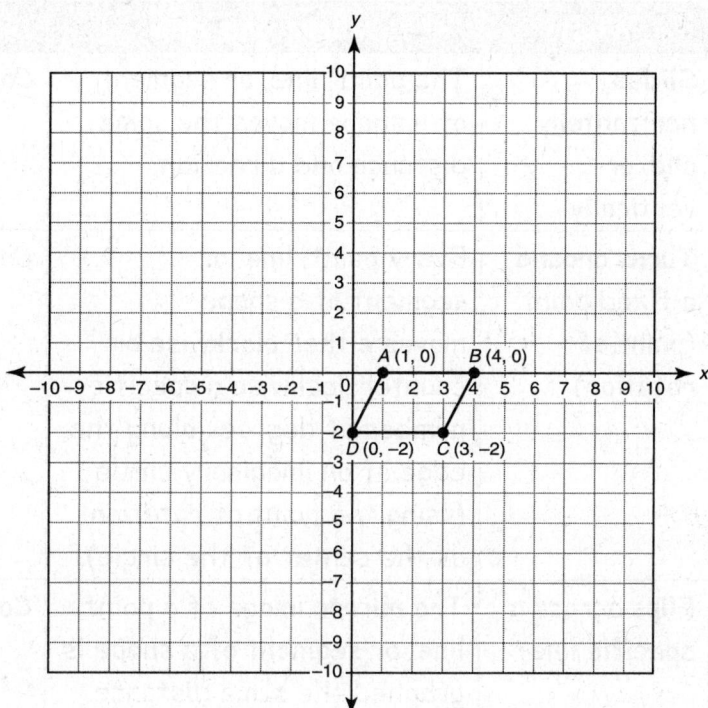

(Answers are on page 304.)

Types of Transformations Overview

Table 5-2. Types of Transformations

	What	Where and How	Size and Shape
Translation	**Slides** horizontally and/or vertically	The point, line, or segment of a shape moves the same distance and direction.	Congruent
Rotation	**Turns around** a fixed point (point of rotation)	Every point, line, or segment of a shape moves either clockwise or counterclockwise a specific number of degrees along the edge of an imaginary circle (using the point of rotation as the center of the circle).	Congruent
Reflection	**Flips** across a specific line	The mirror image of a point, line, or segment of a shape is graphed the same distance away on the other side of an indicated axis or line.	Congruent
Dilation	**Shrinks** or **stretches** from a fixed point (point of dilation).	Every point, line, or segment of the shape is moved, according to a ratio (scale factor), from the point of dilation.	Similar

Geometry—Transformations

Congruence and Similarity

> **Key Concepts**
>
> - For shapes to be **congruent**, the corresponding angles must be congruent in measure, and the corresponding sides must be congruent in length.
>
> - For shapes to be **similar**, the corresponding angles must be congruent in measure, and the corresponding sides must have length measures that are in proportion.
>
> - Translations, rotations, and reflections are all moves of location, but they preserve size. Therefore, one or even a series of these transformations will result in an image that is *congruent* to the pre-image. (Note: The symbol ≅ means congruent.)
>
> - A dilation, involved in any transformation or any series of transformations, will change the size of the image and will result in an image that is *similar* to the pre-image. The angles will be congruent, but the sides will be proportional based on the scale factor. (Note: The symbol ~ means similar.)

Example 1

Determine whether Right Triangle $M'''N'''P''$ can be demonstrated as congruent based on transformations from Right Triangle MNP. If so, describe the sequence of transformations that will exhibit the congruence between both. If not, explain why not.

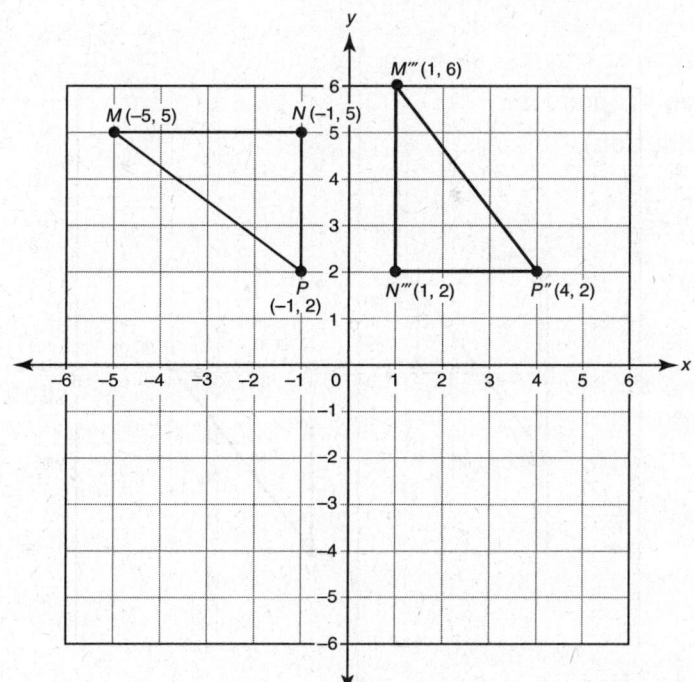

Answer: **Right Triangle *MNP* ≅ Right Triangle *M'''N'''P''***

The sequence of transformations is:

A. Triangle *MNP* is rotated 90° counterclockwise around *P*.

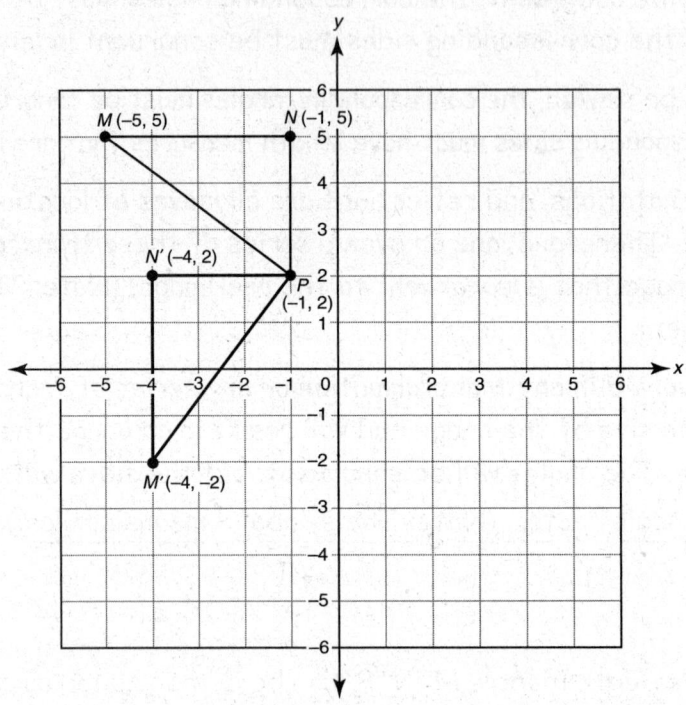

B. This image is then translated 2 units down and 5 units right.

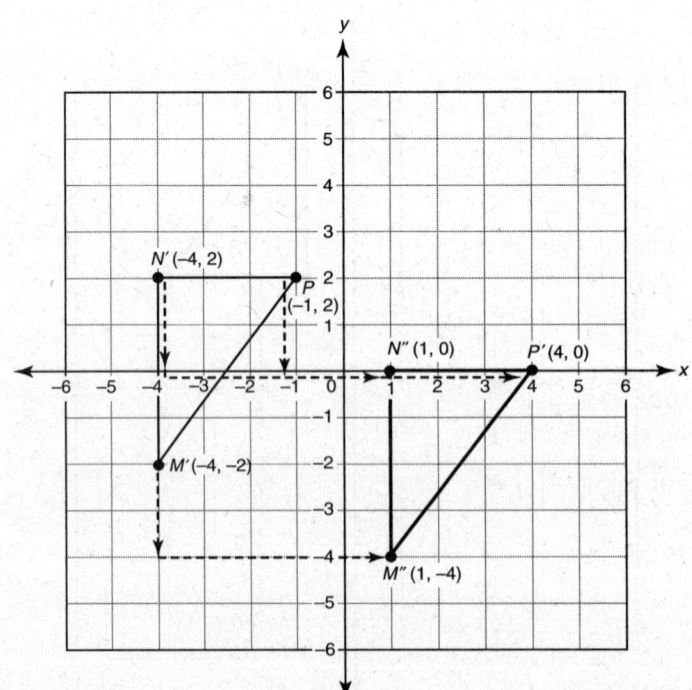

C. This image is then reflected over $y = 1$.

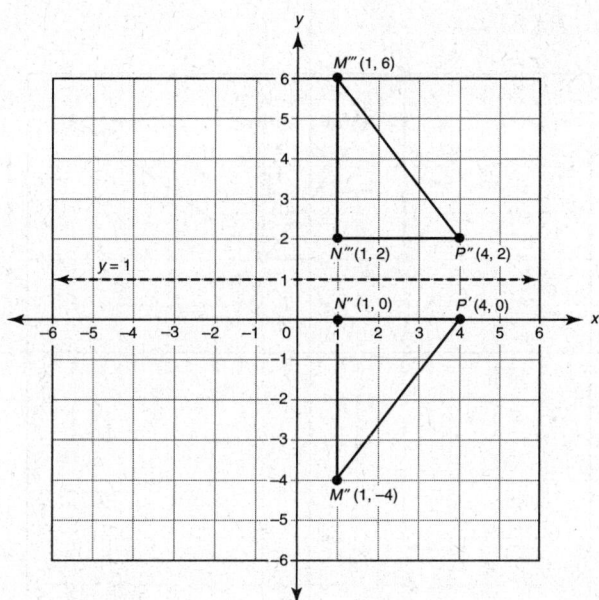

Since each of these transformations individually preserves congruence, the pre-image and the resulting images are congruent. Since each individually preserves congruence, this set of transformations will produce the same congruent image, regardless of the order of the transformations.

An alternate sequence of transformations that will result in the same congruency statement is:

A. Triangle *MNP* is reflected across the *y*-axis.

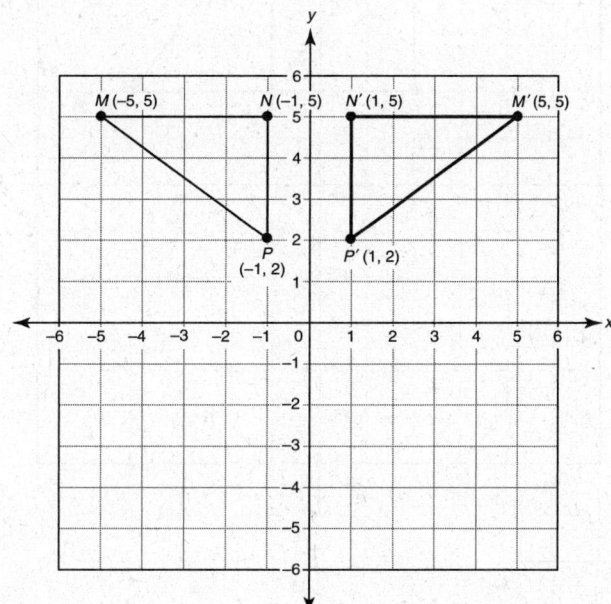

B. This image is then rotated 90° counterclockwise around P.

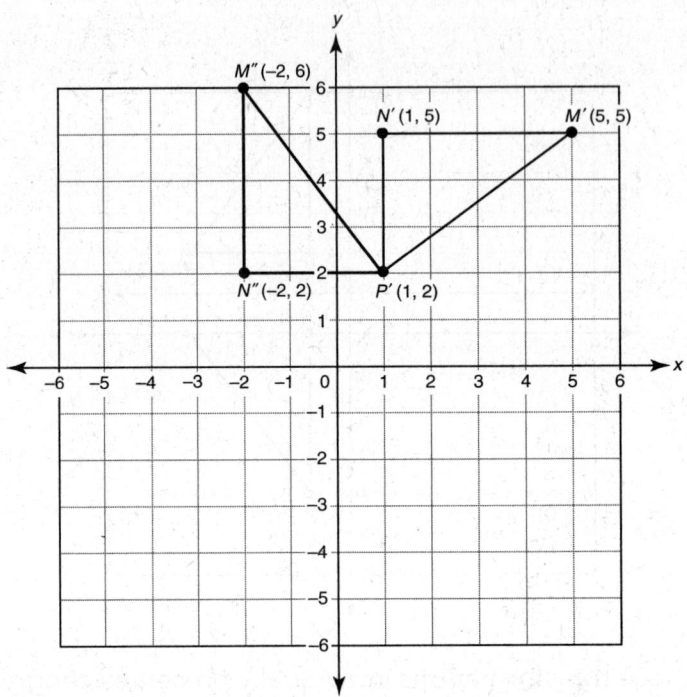

C. This image is then translated 3 units to the right.

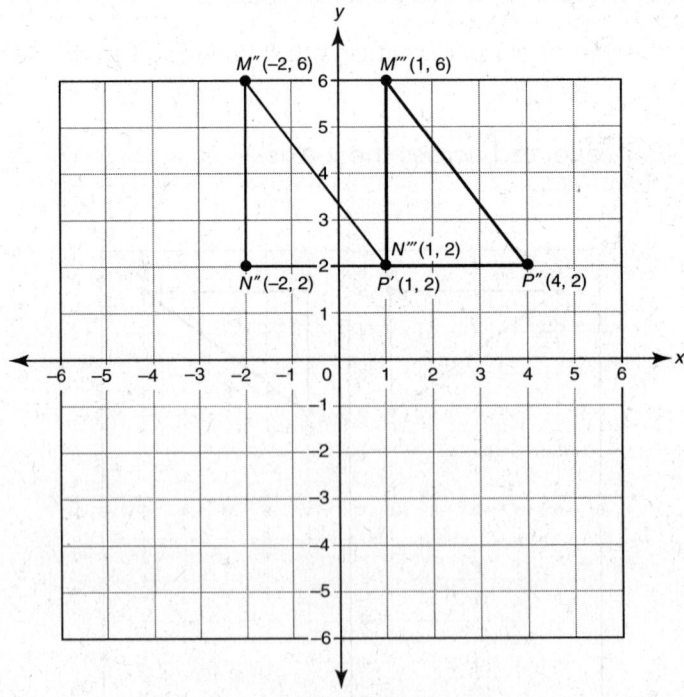

Since each of these transformations individually preserves congruence, the pre-image and the resulting images are congruent. Since each individually preserves congruence, this set of transformations will also produce the same congruent image, regardless of the order of the transformations.

Note that there are other alternate sequences of transformations that will result in this same congruency statement, but these are two sample sequences.

Example 2

Determine if Rectangle *ABCD* is congruent or similar to Rectangle *A'''B''C'''D'''* by describing the sequence of transformations that exhibits the congruence or similarity between them. Explain your reasoning.

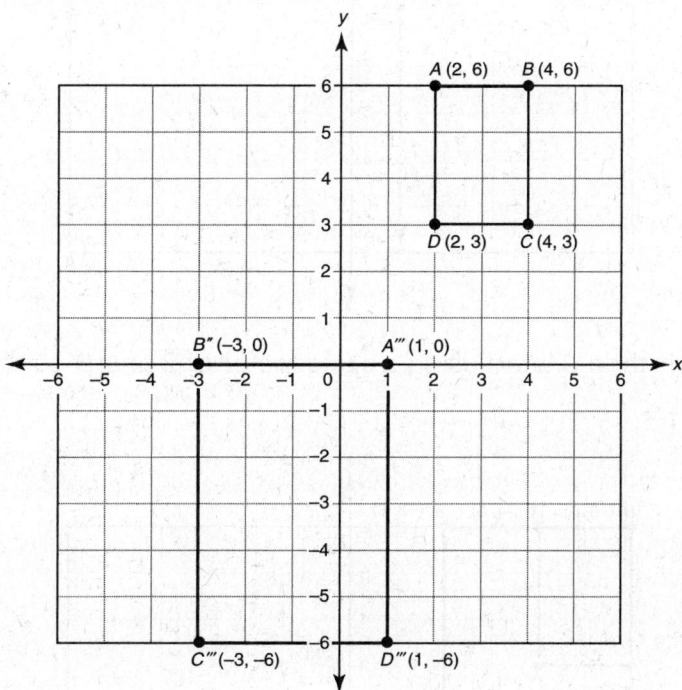

Answer: **Rectangle *ABCD* ~ Rectangle *A'''B''C'''D'''***

The sequence of transformations can occur in any order and will still result in Rectangle A'''B''C'''D'''. One sequence of transformations is:

A. Rectangle ABCD is reflected over $x = -1$.

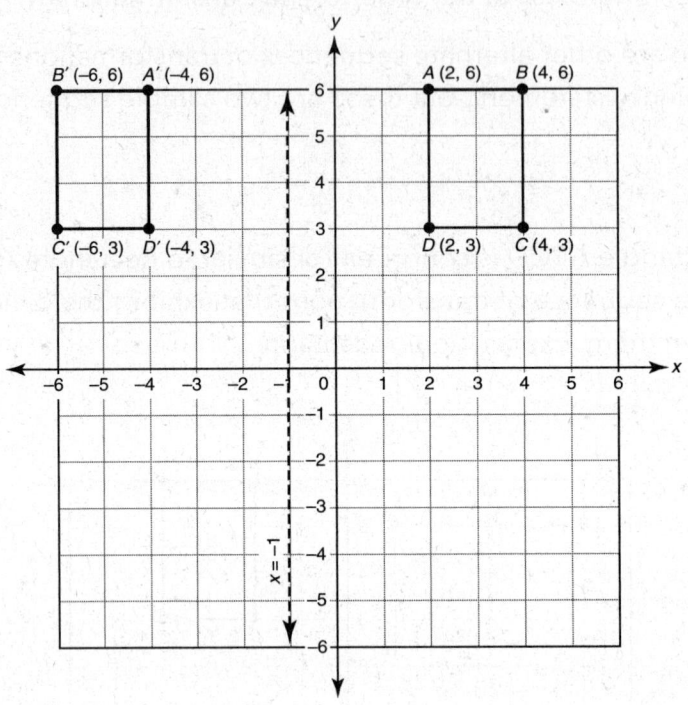

B. This image is then dilated using a scale factor of 2 and B' as the point of dilation.

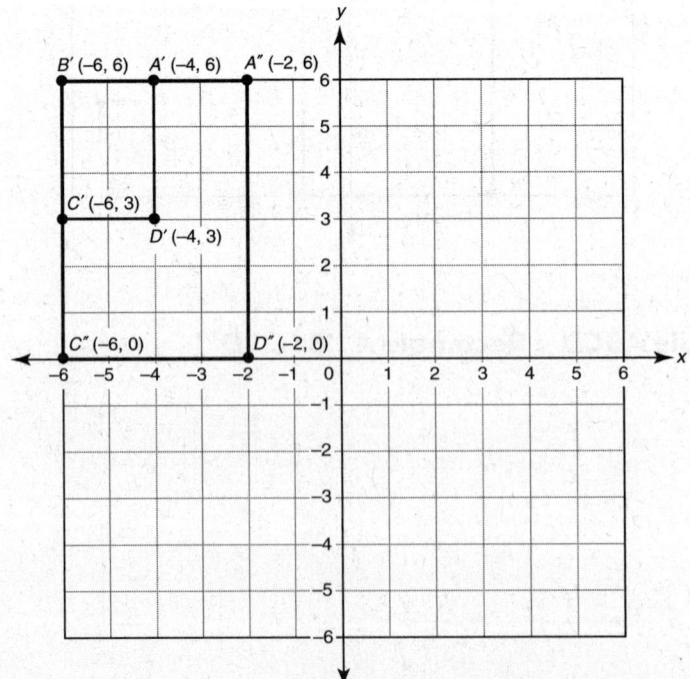

C. This image is then translated 6 units down and 3 units right.

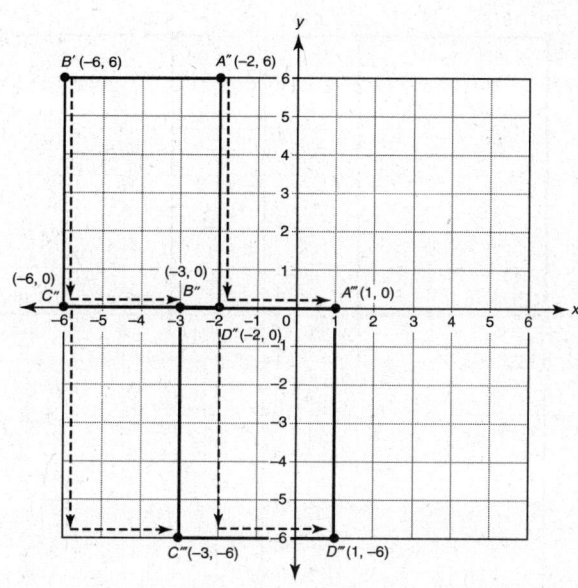

Reasoning: Multiple transformations are performed, but the dilation using a scale factor of 2 results in congruent angles and sides that are proportional, but not equal. By definition, this means that the rectangles are similar, but not congruent.

An alternate sequence of transformations is:

A. Rectangle *ABCD* is dilated using a scale factor of 2 and *A* as the point of dilation.

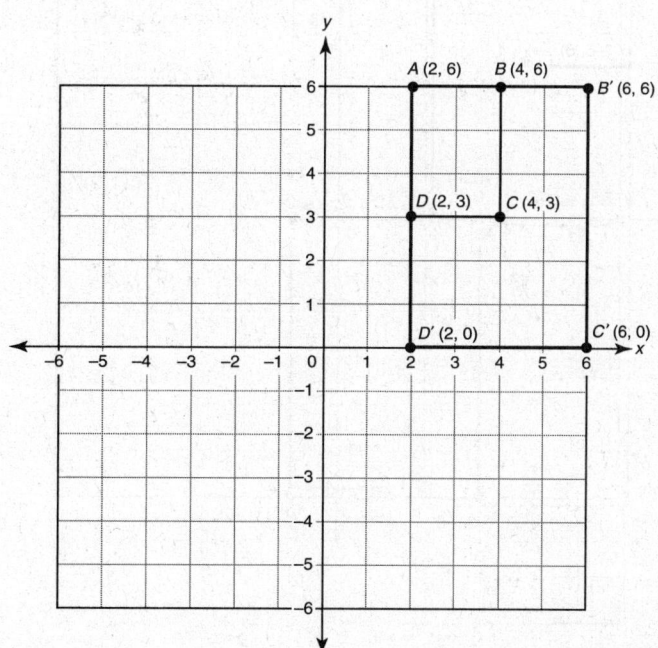

B. This image is then reflected over the y-axis.

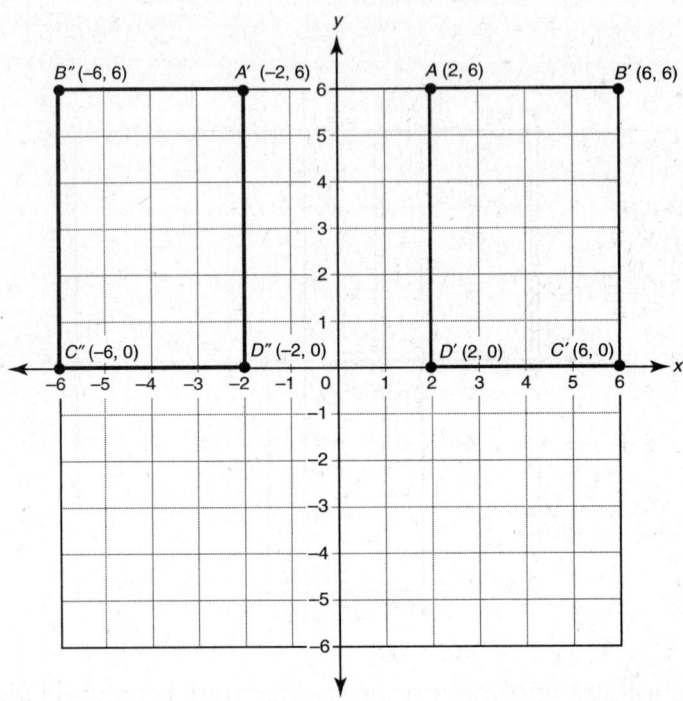

C. This image is then translated 6 units down and 3 units right.

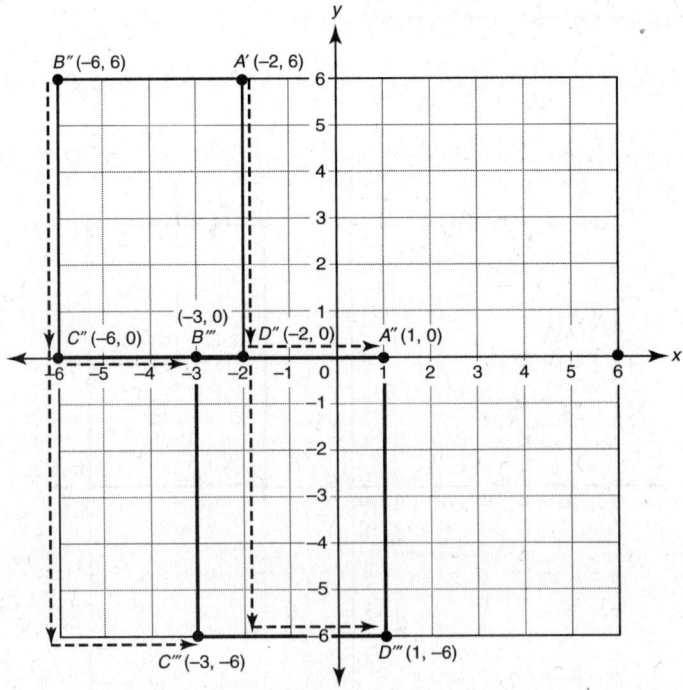

Guided Practice

1. Describe the sequence of transformations that will result in Triangle G"H"J. Determine whether Triangle G"H"J is similar to or congruent to Triangle GHJ. Explain your reasoning.

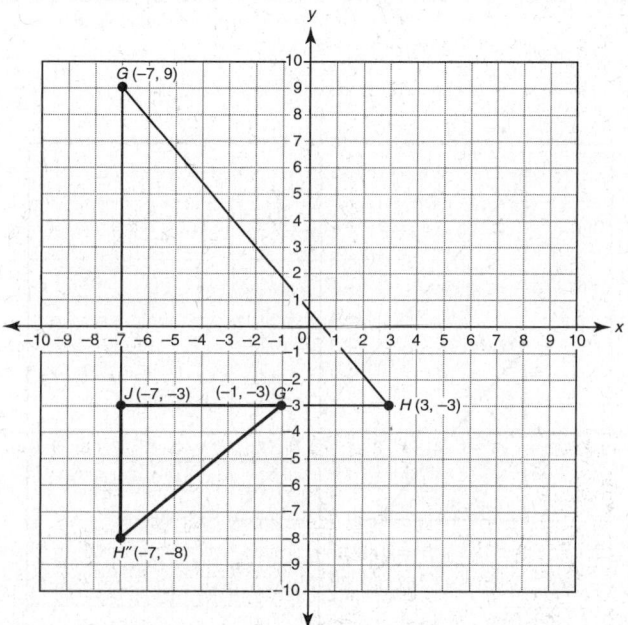

2. Determine whether Triangle B"C"D" can be an image of a sequence of transformations to Triangle BCD. Are they congruent or similar? Explain your reasoning.

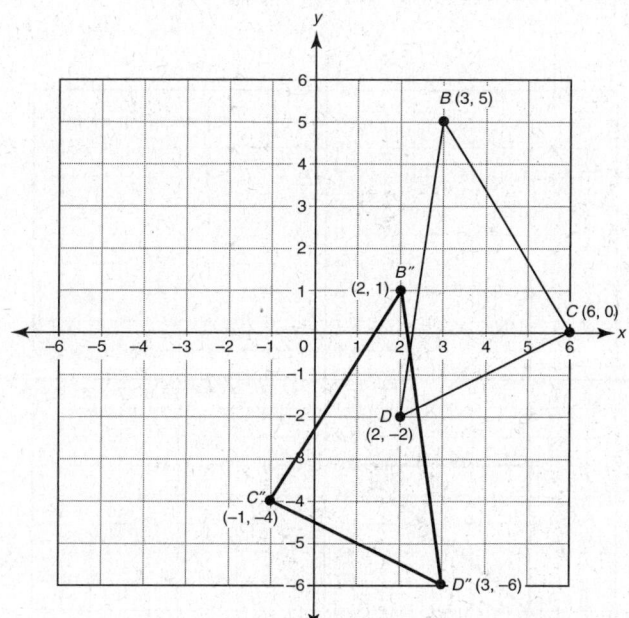

Guided Practice Answers Explained

1. **Triangle G"H"J is similar to Triangle GHJ.** The sequence of transformations was:

   A. Triangle GHJ is dilated from Point J with a scale factor of 0.5, resulting in a reduction.

   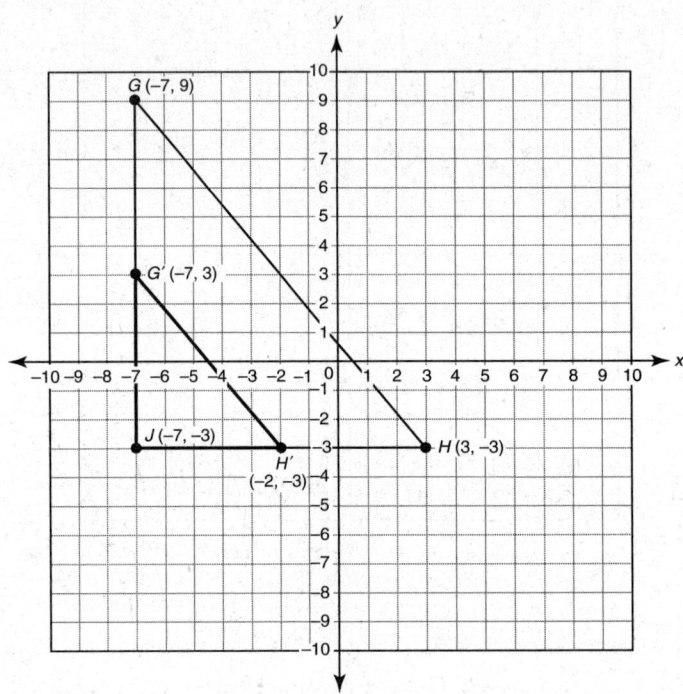

   B. This image is then rotated 90° clockwise around J.

   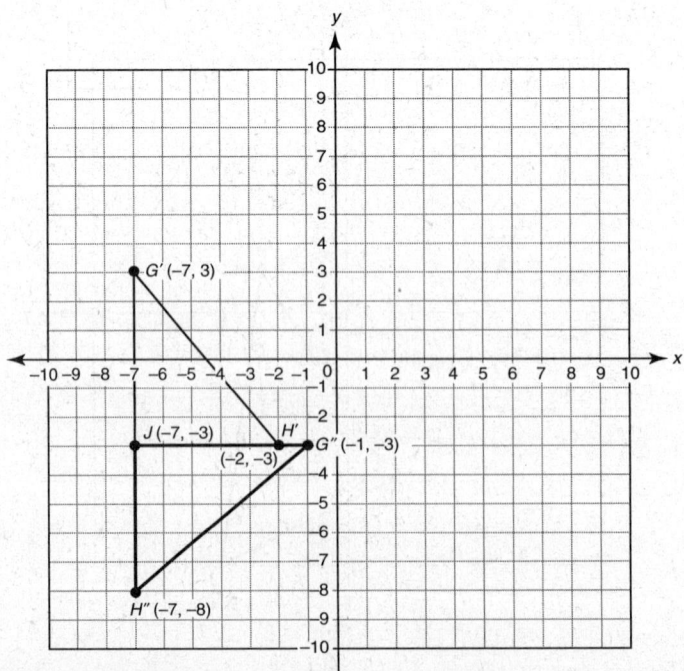

Triangle G″H″J is similar to Triangle GHJ. Both transformations (the dilation and the rotation) result in corresponding congruent angles, but the dilation using a scale factor of 0.5 means that the sides are not congruent (although they are proportional). By definition, the image is similar to the pre-image.

2. **Yes, Triangle B″C″D″ is a result of a sequence of transformations from Triangle BCD. They are congruent.**

The sequence of transformations was:

   A. Triangle BCD is translated 4 units down and 5 units left.

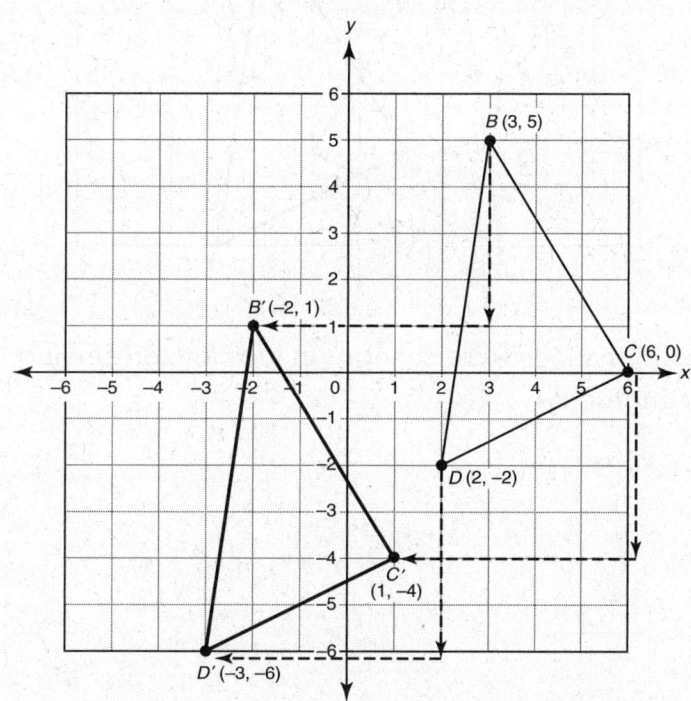

B. This image is then reflected over the y-axis.

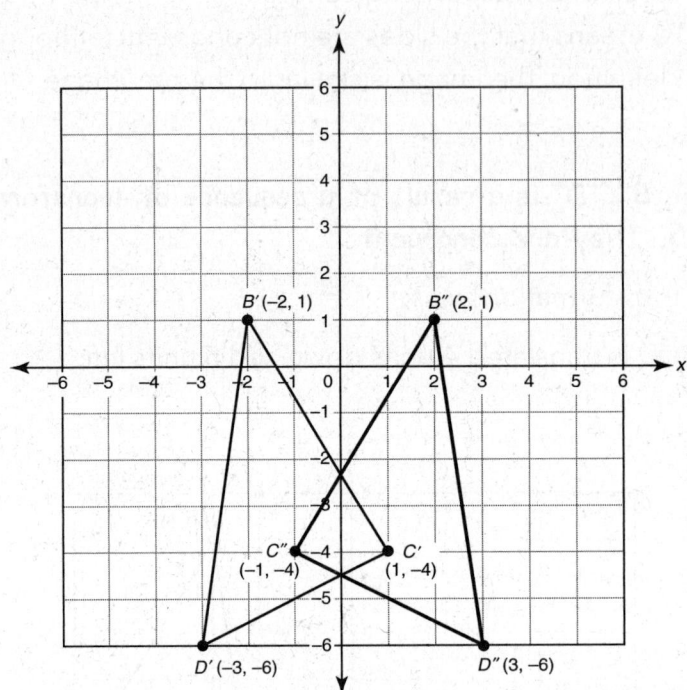

Both of the transformations were changes in location, preserving congruence, so the triangles are congruent.

Independent Practice

1. Describe the sequence of transformations that will result in Quadrilateral $F'''G'''H'''J'''$. Determine whether Quadrilateral $F'''G'''H'''J'''$ is similar to or congruent to Quadrilateral $FGHJ$. Explain your reasoning.

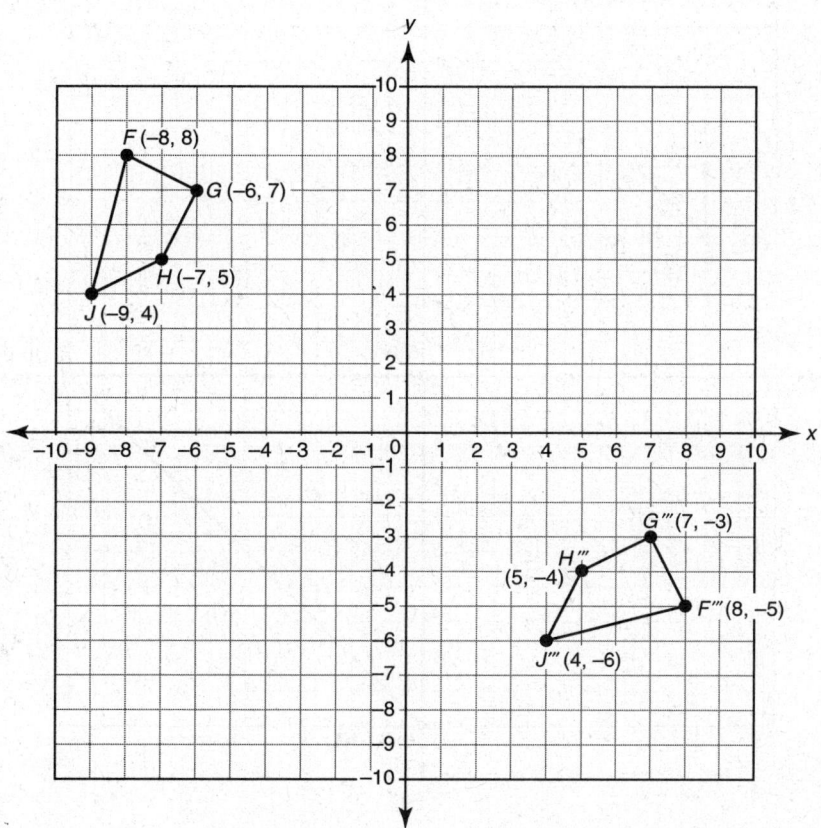

2. Determine whether Triangle E'F"G" can be an image of a sequence of transformations to Triangle EFG. Are the two triangles congruent or similar? Explain your reasoning.

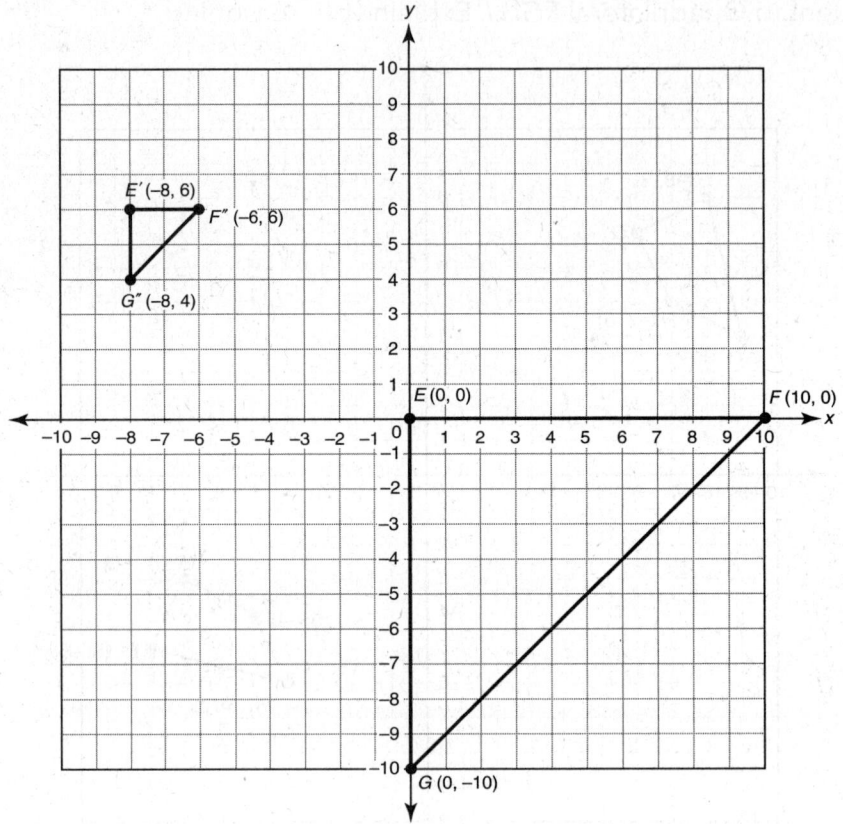

(Answers are on page 305.)

SBAC Challenge Questions

1. Line Segment *WV* has Endpoints *W* (5, 6) and *V* (−1, −1). Without graphing, determine the translation that will result in the image *W'V'* with Endpoints *W'* (7, 2) and *V'* (1, −5). Explain.

2. Which of the following sequences of transformations will result in an image that is similar to the pre-image, but with a larger area? Select all that apply.

   ☐ A. Translation 3 units to the left and 4 units up followed by a dilation from the origin with a scale factor of $\frac{1}{5}$, followed by a reflection across the x-axis

   ☐ B. Rotation of 180° counterclockwise around the origin, followed by a dilation from the origin using a scale factor of $\frac{3}{2}$, followed by a translation 4 units to the right

   ☐ C. Dilation from the origin using a scale factor of $\frac{2}{3}$, followed by a counterclockwise rotation of 90°, followed by a reflection across the line $y = 4$

   ☐ D. Translation 6 units to the right and 2 units down, followed by a reflection across the line $x = 3$, followed by a dilation from the origin with a scale factor of $\frac{7}{5}$

   ☐ E. Rotation 90° clockwise, followed by a dilation from the origin with a scale factor of 3, followed by a translation 3 units up

3. Wendy says that the rotation of a shape 180° clockwise around the origin will result in the same image as a reflection of the shape first over the x-axis and then over the y-axis. Scott disagrees with Wendy's statement. Who is correct? Explain your reasoning.

(Answers are on page 307.)

Patterns and Relationships in Data

CHAPTER 6

Common Core Standard 8.SP.A.1

Construct and interpret scatter plots for bivariate measurement data to investigate patterns of association between two quantities. Describe patterns such as clustering, outliers, positive or negative association, linear association, and nonlinear association.

Common Core Standard 8.SP.A.2

Know that straight lines are widely used to model relationships between two quantitative variables. For scatter plots that suggest a linear association, informally fit a straight line, and informally assess the model fit by judging the closeness of the data points to the line.

Common Core Standard 8.SP.A.3

Use the equation of a linear model to solve problems in the context of bivariate measurement data, interpreting the slope and intercept.

Common Core Standard 8.SP.A.4

Understand that patterns of association can also be seen in bivariate categorical data by displaying frequencies and relative frequencies in a two-way table. Construct and interpret a two-way table summarizing data on two categorical variables collected from the same subjects. Use relative frequencies calculated for rows or columns to describe possible association between the two variables.

 HELPFUL HINT

A calculator should be used for all the examples and practice questions in this chapter.

Scatter Plots and Lines of Best Fit

Key Concepts

- **Bivariate data** is data that has two variables. Two types of bivariate data are numerical data and categorical data.

- **Numerical data** (or **quantitative data**) contains dependent and independent variables. These ordered pairs of data can be graphed on a Cartesian plane for the purposes of analysis or comparison. An example of numerical data might be determining one or more plants' height over a number of weeks. This information can be graphed.

- **Categorical data** (or **qualitative data**) is data that is not numerical, so it is best organized by categories. It can best be represented in a frequency or relative frequency table for the purposes of analysis or comparison. An example of categorical data might be determining the number of students in a class who have a smartphone and those who have a curfew. Some students will have one or the other, some will have both, and some will have neither. This information is best analyzed in a chart or in a table.

Visual Display of Quantitative (Numerical) Data

Key Concepts

- A **scatter plot** is a graphical representation of a set of quantitative data where each ordered pair is represented by a dot. It is used to demonstrate a visual relationship, if any exists, between the x-coordinates and the y-coordinates of the quantitative data.

- An **outlier** is a piece of data that, when graphed, appears far away from the cluster of data.

- Data is said to have a **positive association** when as the x-coordinates increase, the y-coordinates also increase. Generally, from left to right, the data appears to be moving up, as in Figure 6-1.

- Data is said to have a **negative association** when as the x-coordinates increase, the y-coordinates decrease. Generally, from left to right, the data appears to be moving down, as in Figure 6-2.

- When there is no apparent upward or downward clustering of the data, it is said that the data has **no correlation**, as in Figure 6-3.

Patterns and Relationships in Data • 175

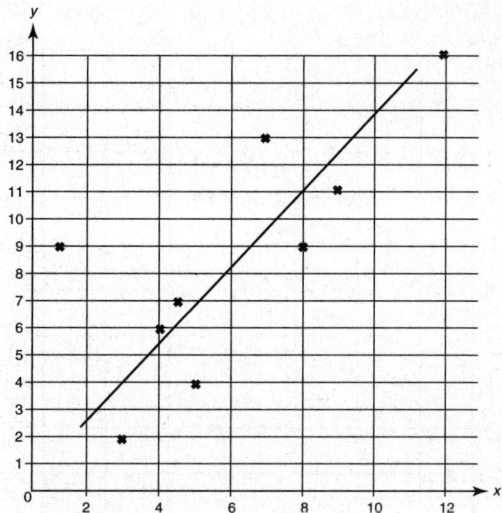

Figure 6-1. This scatter plot shows a positive association. As the x-values increase, the y-values also increase. There is an outlier at (1, 9).

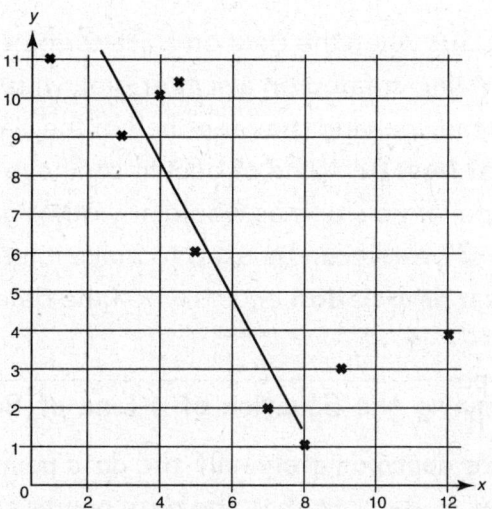

Figure 6-2. This scatter plot shows a negative association. As the x-values increase, the y-values decrease.

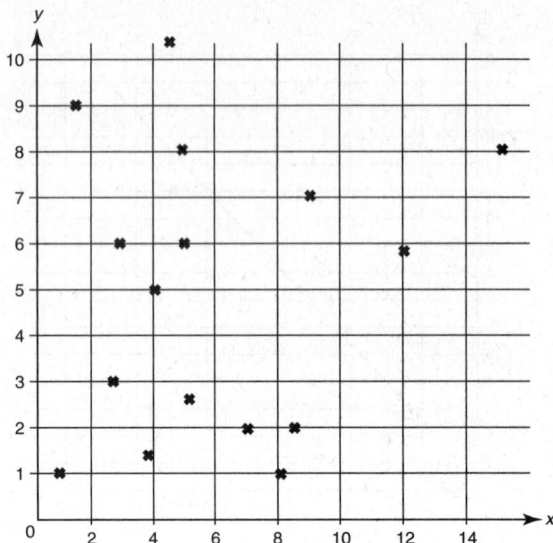

Figure 6-3. This scatter plot shows no association. There is no pattern of increase or decrease.

Linear association occurs when the data on a scatter plot generally clusters in a way to appear as a line. A line created on a scatter plot, with approximately half the data points on or above the line, and the other half of the data points on or below the line, is called a **line of best fit**. A line of best fit can have a positive slope, a negative slope, zero slope, or no slope as would any other graphed line. The slope and y-intercept of a line of best fit can be used to make inferences and predictions about the data. **Nonlinear association** occurs when the data clusters in a curve.

Determining the Equation of a Line of Best Fit

- Sketch a line that has approximately half the data points above it and half the data points below it. Be sure that the data points are clustered as close as possible to the line.

- Choose two points on the line sketched. These points may be part of the data or not, but must be on the sketched line. Use these two points to determine the slope of the line.

- Extend the line to determine the y-intercept.

- Write the equation of the line in slope-intercept form.

Example 1

Determine the equation of the line of best fit for the scatter plot below, which represents the number of practice problems a student answered correctly and the student's score on a quiz. Interpret the slope and the y-intercept in this context.

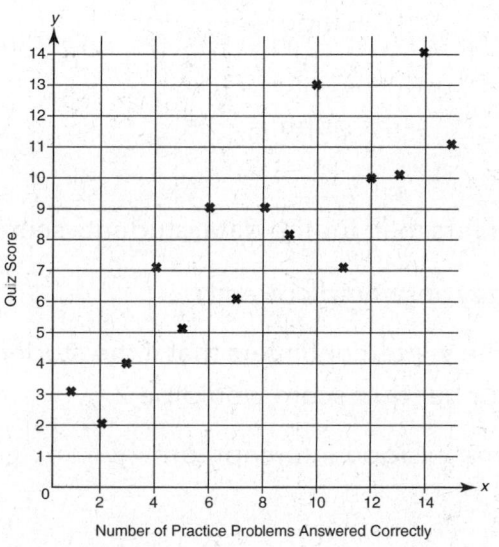

Answer: **The equation is $y = \frac{2}{3}x + 2$. The slope is $\frac{2}{3}$, and the y-intercept is 2.**

Sketch a line that divides the data points so that approximately half are above and half are below the line, and so that the data points are clustered near the line.

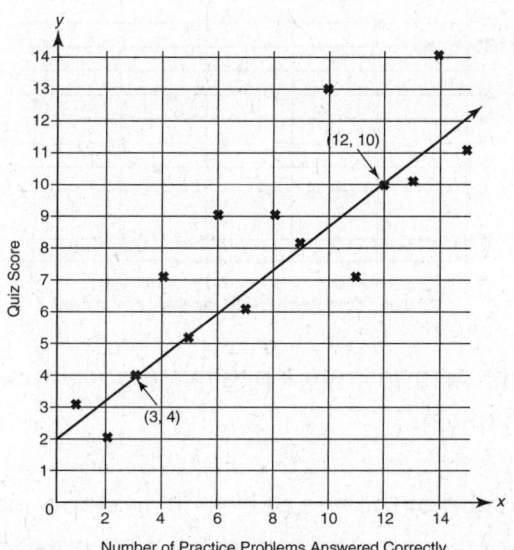

Choose two ordered pairs *on* the sketched line. The points (3, 4) and (12, 10) are on the line of best fit. Find the slope of the line.

$$\text{slope} = \frac{y_2 - y_1}{x_2 - x_1}$$

$$\text{slope} = \frac{10 - 4}{12 - 3}$$

$$\text{slope} = \frac{6}{9} = \frac{2}{3}$$

The slope is $\frac{2}{3}$. This infers that, for the data, students scored two points higher for every three questions they answered correctly.

The *y*-intercept is 2. The *y*-intercept infers that if the student answered zero questions correctly, his or her quiz score would be 2.

The equation of the line in slope-intercept form ($y = mx + b$) is $y = \frac{2}{3}x + 2$.

Guided Practice

Use the following scatter plot to answer Questions 1–3.

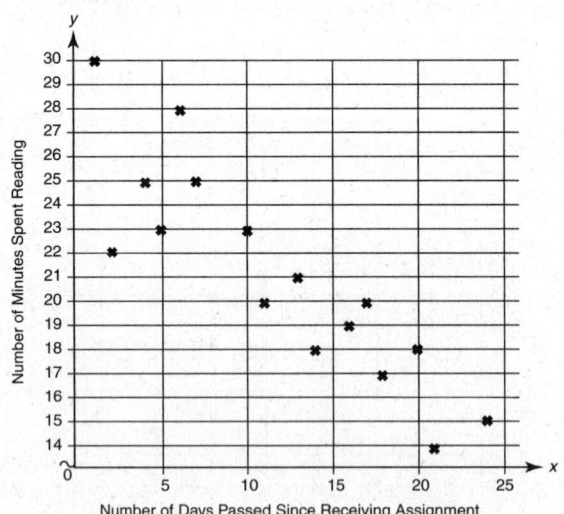

1. Does this scatter plot demonstrate a positive association, a negative association, or no correlation? Explain.

2. Determine the equation of the line of best fit, in slope-intercept form, for this scatter plot. The data represents the number of minutes spent reading an

assigned novel compared to the number of days passed since receiving the assignment.

3. Interpret the meaning of the slope and *y*-intercept for this situation.

4. A sandwich shop is trying to keep its prices low enough to attract new customers, but to still maintain its profit. After graphing a scatter plot of ordered pairs of its data (cost of ingredients, sandwich prices), the store determines that the equation $y = 1.4x + 3$ is the line of best fit for the data. Use this equation to determine how much the shop will charge for a sandwich containing $2.25 worth of ingredients. Interpret what the slope and the *y*-intercept mean in this situation.

Guided Practice Answers Explained

1. **This scatter plot shows a negative association.** Generally, from left to right, as the *x*-values increase, the *y*-values decrease. An outlier appears to be at (1, 30) and at (2, 22), which are both further away from the data clustered generally in a line with a negative slope.

2. **The equation of the line of best fit is $y = -\frac{1}{2}x + 27$.**

   Equations may vary somewhat. However, if approximately half the data points are above the line and half are below the line, and all of the data points are clustered near the line, it will be a valid line of best fit.

   Sketch a line so that approximately half of the data points are above the line and half the data points are below the line, and so that the data points are clustered near the line.

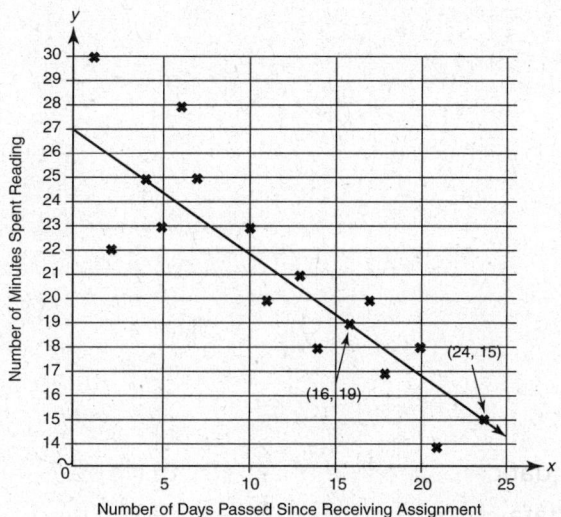

Choose two points *on* the line to find the slope: (16, 19) and (24, 15).

$$\text{slope} = \frac{y_2 - y_1}{x_2 - x_1}$$

$$\text{slope} = \frac{15 - 19}{24 - 16} = \frac{-4}{8} = \frac{-1}{2}$$

Extend the line to determine the *y*-intercept of 27. Then, write the equation of the line in slope-intercept form:

$$y = -\frac{1}{2}x + 27$$

3. **The slope represents that about 1 minute less of reading occurs for every two days that passed. The *y*-intercept represents that at 0 days (or the day the novel was assigned), 27 minutes were spent reading.**

4. **The store should charge $6.15 for this sandwich. The slope represents that for each $1 of ingredients, the cost of the sandwich will increase by $1.40. The *y*-intercept represents the maintained profit of at least $3 per sandwich.**

   $y = 1.4x + 3$ (Use the equation of the line of best fit.)

   $y = 1.4(2.25) + 3$ (Substitute $2.25 for *x*, the cost of ingredients.)

   $y = 3.15 + 3$ (Simplify.)

   $y = 6.15$ (The sandwich shop should charge $6.15 for a sandwich that uses $2.25 worth of ingredients.)

Independent Practice

1. Determine which of the following choices places the line of best fit correctly. Explain why each of the other selections is placed incorrectly.

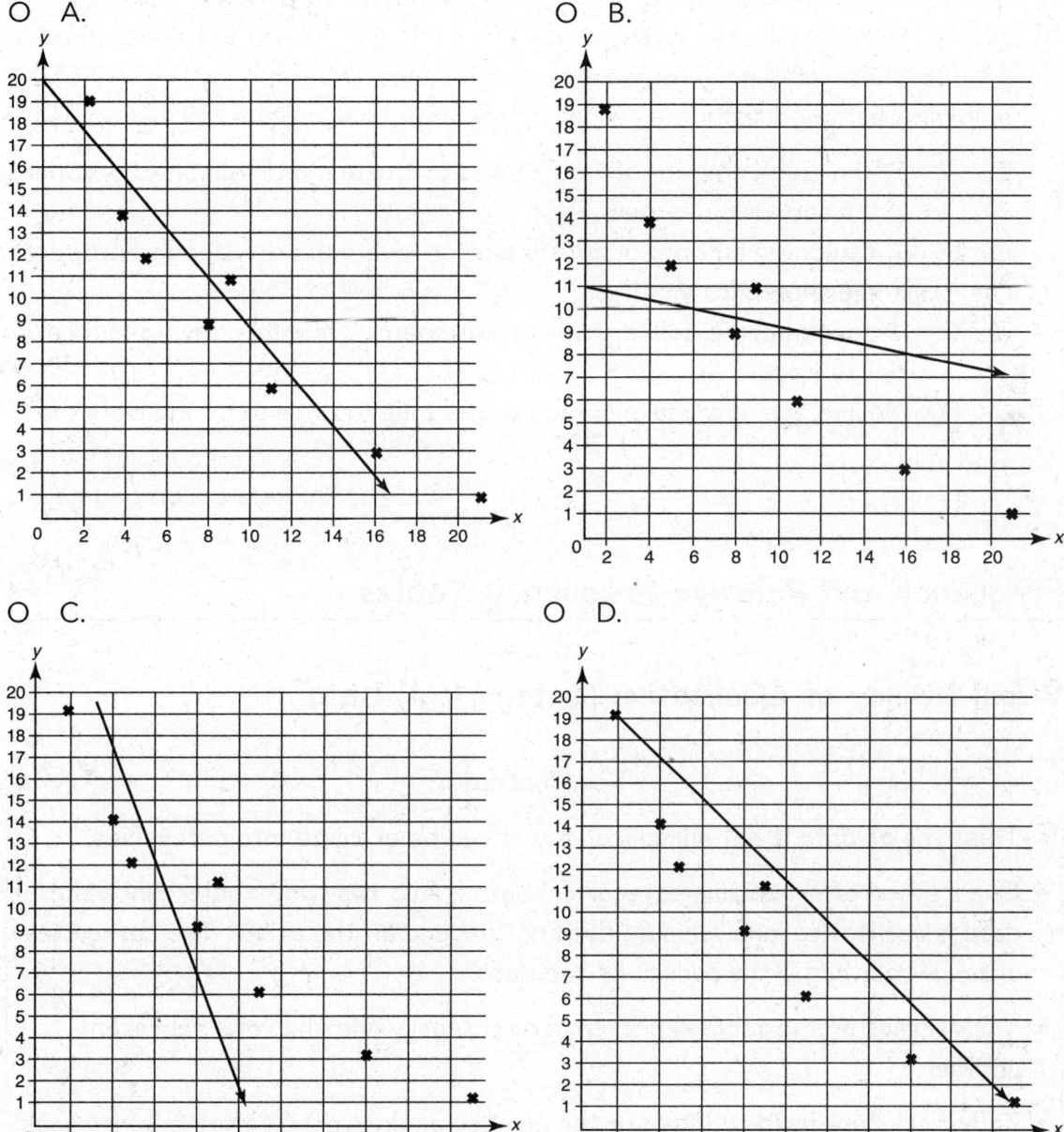

2. Write the line of best fit for the correct answer to Question 1.

3. A dry-cleaning service is considering expanding its delivery service to a larger area. The average time between locating the dry-cleaned product in the shop and the time it takes to deliver it is represented by the equation $y = 5x + 20$, where x is the distance in miles the driver will travel to deliver the dry-cleaned product and y is the entire delivery time in minutes. Determine which of the following statements are true according to this equation. Select all that apply.

- ☐ A. The average amount of time it takes to locate the dry-cleaned product in the shop is 5 minutes.
- ☐ B. The average amount of time it takes to locate the dry-cleaned product in the shop is 20 minutes.
- ☐ C. On average, the delivery person will spend 5 minutes driving to the delivery site.
- ☐ D. On average, it will take 5 minutes per mile to drive to the delivery site.

(Answers are on page 309.)

Frequency and Relative Frequency Tables

Visual Display of Qualitative (Categorical) Data

Key Concepts

- This type of data is not numerical, but it can be grouped into categories.
- One method of organizing categorical data is in a **two-way table**. Since the data is qualitative, one variable does not depend on the other. The categories are only related by the source of the data.
- The columns of the table represent one category and the rows represent another.
- Tally marks are used to indicate the number of data points that fall into each of the boxes formed where the columns and rows overlap.

Example 1

People were asked what type of movie genre they preferred and their age category. The two categories for this data are Movie Genre Preferred and Age of Respondent. Each tally mark on the two-way table indicates one responder's age and his or her movie genre preference.

The **two-way table** lists one category horizontally and the other vertically.

Two-Way Table

Movie Genre Preferred	Age of Respondent		
	21 and Under	22–40	Over 40
Romance	///	////	//
Horror	////	////	////
Comedy	//	///	//// ///
Action	//// ////	/	///

From this initial two-way table, a **frequency table** can be generated with numbers replacing the tally marks. Although these are numerical responses, it is not numerical data because the data is generated within a category, not by quantities.

Frequency Table

Movie Genre Preferred	Age of Respondent			Total Respondents
	21 and Under	22–40	Over 40	
Romance	3	5	2	10
Horror	4	5	5	14
Comedy	2	3	8	13
Action	9	1	3	13
Total	18	14	18	50

Relative frequency is calculated by the ratio or percent of how often something occurs divided by the total possible things that could occur. Each number from the frequency table is set up in a ratio to the total number of responses in that category. The total of the relative frequency ratios should be 1.

Example 2

Determine the relative frequency for the age of the responders from Example 1. Give the results in fraction and percent form.

Answer:

Relative Frequency Table by Age of Respondent

Movie Genre Preferred / Relative Frequency by Age →	Age of Respondent			Total Frequency
	21 and Under	22-40	Over 40	
Romance	$\frac{3}{10} = 30\%$	$\frac{5}{10} = \frac{1}{2} = 50\%$	$\frac{2}{10} = \frac{1}{5} = 20\%$	$\frac{10}{10} = 1 = 100\%$
Horror	$\frac{4}{14} = \frac{2}{7} \approx 28.6\%$	$\frac{5}{14} \approx 35.7\%$	$\frac{5}{14} \approx 35.7\%$	$\frac{14}{14} = 1 = 100\%$
Comedy	$\frac{2}{13} \approx 15.4\%$	$\frac{3}{13} \approx 23.1\%$	$\frac{8}{13} \approx 61.5\%$	$\frac{13}{13} = 1 = 100\%$
Action	$\frac{9}{13} \approx 69.2\%$	$\frac{1}{13} \approx 7.7\%$	$\frac{3}{13} \approx 23.1\%$	$\frac{13}{13} = 1 = 100\%$

Each number from the frequency table age category for the row for Romance is set in a ratio with the denominator of the total number of respondents for that category, which was 10. Then, the fraction is converted to decimal form, rounded to the nearest tenth, if necessary. This process is repeated for each of the other rows. The total for each row of fractions should be 1, and the total for each row of percents should be 100%. This total assures that all the data from the frequency table has been converted to the relative frequency table.

Example 3

Determine the relative frequency for each movie genre preferred from Example 1. Give the results in fraction and percent form.

Answer:

Relative Frequency Table by Movie Genre Preferred

	Age of Respondent		
Relative Frequency by Genre ↓	21 and Under	22–40	Over 40
Romance	$\frac{3}{18} = \frac{1}{6} \approx 16.7\%$	$\frac{5}{14} \approx 35.7\%$	$\frac{2}{18} = \frac{1}{9} \approx 11.1\%$
Horror	$\frac{4}{18} = \frac{2}{9} \approx 22.2\%$	$\frac{5}{14} \approx 35.7\%$	$\frac{5}{18} \approx 27.8\%$
Comedy	$\frac{2}{18} = \frac{1}{9} \approx 11.1\%$	$\frac{3}{14} \approx 21.4\%$	$\frac{8}{18} = \frac{4}{9} \approx 44.4\%$
Action	$\frac{9}{18} = \frac{1}{2} = 50\%$	$\frac{1}{14} \approx 7.1\%$	$\frac{3}{18} = \frac{1}{6} \approx 16.7\%$
Total Frequency	$\frac{18}{18} = 1 = 100\%$	$\frac{14}{14} = 1 = 100\%$*	$\frac{18}{18} = 1 = 100\%$

*Due to rounding, this column adds up to 99.9%.

Guided Practice

1. Fifty middle school students were surveyed and each answered two questions:

   Do you own a smartphone? and Do you receive an allowance?

   The results of the survey are in the two-way table below:

	Yes, I Own a Smartphone	No, I Do Not Own a Smartphone
Yes, I Receive an Allowance	//// //// //// ////	//// //// //// /
No, I Do Not Receive an Allowance	//// //// /	////

   A. Complete a frequency table for the data above.
   B. Complete a relative frequency table for smartphones with results in both fraction and percent forms.
   C. Complete a relative frequency table for allowance with results in both fraction and percent forms.
   D. Answer the following questions from the results of the two-way table, the frequency table, and the relative frequency tables.
      1. Which of the following represents the number of students who do not own a smartphone but do receive an allowance?
         ○ A. 16   ○ B. 19   ○ C. 4   ○ D. 11
      2. How many students who own smartphones do not receive an allowance? ☐
      3. Which of the following statements are true based on the results of the relative frequency tables? Select all that apply.
         ☐ A. Of the students who receive an allowance, less than half do not own a smartphone.
         ☐ B. More students receive an allowance than own a smartphone.
         ☐ C. Twenty percent of all the students surveyed receive an allowance but do not own a smartphone.
         ☐ D. Half of all the surveyed students neither receive an allowance nor own a smartphone.
      4. Give the percent (to the nearest whole percent) of all the students surveyed who receive an allowance and own a smartphone.

Patterns and Relationships in Data • 187

Guided Practice Answers Explained

1.

A. The frequency table is as follows:

	Yes, I Own a Smartphone	No, I Do Not Own a Smartphone	Total
Yes, I Receive an Allowance	19	16	35
No, I Do Not Receive an Allowance	11	4	15
Total	30	20	50

B. The relative frequency table for smartphones is as follows:

	Yes, I Own a Smartphone	No, I Do Not Own a Smartphone	Total
Yes, I Receive an Allowance	$\frac{19}{35} \approx 54.3\%$	$\frac{16}{35} \approx 45.7\%$	$\frac{35}{35} = 100\%$
No, I Do Not Receive an Allowance	$\frac{11}{15} \approx 73.3\%$	$\frac{4}{15} \approx 26.7\%$	$\frac{15}{15} = 100\%$

C. The relative frequency table for allowance is as follows:

	Yes, I Own a Smartphone	No, I Do Not Own a Smartphone
Yes, I Receive an Allowance	$\frac{19}{30} \approx 63.3\%$	$\frac{16}{20} = 80\%$
No, I Do Not Receive an Allowance	$\frac{11}{30} \approx 36.7\%$	$\frac{4}{20} = 20\%$
Total	$\frac{30}{30} = 1 = 100\%$	$\frac{20}{20} = 1 = 100\%$

D.

1. **(A)** 16 students do not own a smartphone but do receive an allowance.

2. **11 students**

3. **(A)** and **(B)**

   Choice (A): Of the students who receive an allowance, less than half do not own a smartphone. (35 students receive an allowance, and 16 of them (45.7%) do not own a smartphone.) *True*

   Choice (B): More students receive an allowance than own a smartphone. (35 students receive an allowance, and 30 students own a smartphone.) *True*

   Choice (C): Twenty percent of all the students surveyed receive an allowance but do not own a smartphone. (16 out of 50 students surveyed receive an allowance but do not own a smartphone, which is 32%.) *False*

   Choice (D): Half of all the surveyed students neither receive an allowance nor own a smartphone. (4 out of 50 students surveyed neither receive an allowance nor own a smartphone, which is 8%.) *False*

4. **38%** (19 out of 50 students surveyed receive an allowance and own a smartphone, which is 38%.)

SBAC Challenge Questions

1. Pollsters surveyed citizens to determine whether they were interested in expanding the city sports complex to include an indoor pool and what their age range is.

   The results of the survey are recorded in the frequency table below:

Pollster Results for Interest in Expanding the City Sports Complex to Include an Indoor Pool				
	Yes	No	No Opinion	Total
Age 18-30	25	10	5	40
Age 31-40	20	6	10	36
Age 41-50	10	12	5	27
Age 51-60	10	6	5	21
Age 61-70	5	10	11	26
Age 71 and Over	2	3	7	12
Total	72	47	43	162

   A. Complete a relative frequency table for each age group range with results in both fraction and percent forms.
   B. Complete a relative frequency table for each type of response (Yes, No, or No Opinion) with results in both fraction and percent forms.

2. Which of the statements below are true based on the relative frequency tables for Question 1? Select all that apply.

   ☐ A. A person who is Age 18-30 is just as likely to not want the indoor pool added as someone over 70 years of age.
   ☐ B. A person who is Age 51-60 years old is twice as likely to have responded Yes about the indoor pool as compared to someone in that age group who responded No Opinion.
   ☐ C. A person who is Age 61-70 years old is more than twice as likely to not want the pool as a person Age 51-60 years old is to have No Opinion.

   (Answers are on page 310.)

Geometry—Two and Three Dimensions

CHAPTER 7

Common Core Standard 8.G.A.5
Use informal arguments to establish facts about the angle sum and exterior angle of triangles, about the angles created when parallel lines are cut by a transversal, and the angle-angle criterion for similarity of triangles.

Common Core Standard 8.G.C.9
Know the formulas for the volumes of cones, cylinders, and spheres and use them to solve real-world and mathematical problems.

Angles Formed by Intersecting Lines

Key Concepts

- A **straight angle** occurs when the two rays that form the angle point in opposite directions, forming a line. A straight angle measures 180°.

- **Adjacent angles** are a pair of angles that share a common vertex and a common side.

- **Vertical angles** are two nonadjacent angles formed when two lines intersect. Vertical angles are congruent.

- When the sum of the measures of a pair of angles is 90°, they are **complementary angles**. Complementary angles can be adjacent or nonadjacent.

- When the sum of the measures of a pair of angles is 180°, they are **supplementary angles**. Supplementary angles can be adjacent or nonadjacent.

- When a pair of adjacent angles whose nonadjacent sides form a straight angle, they are called a **linear pair**. These angles are supplementary.

Example 1

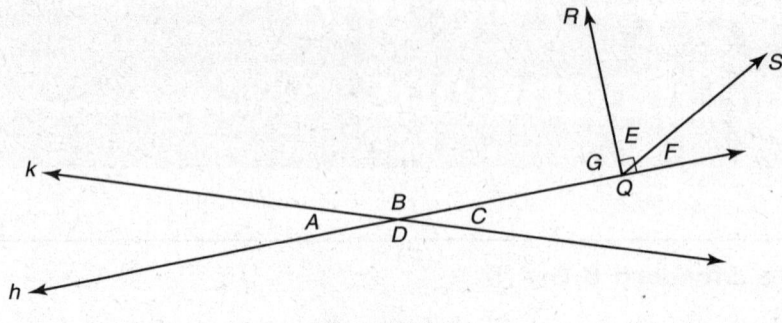

Figure 7-1.

In Figure 7-1, Line *k* and Line *h* intersect, forming ∠A, ∠B, ∠C, and ∠D. Ray QR and Ray QS intersect Line *h* at Point Q, forming ∠E and ∠F.

∠A and ∠B are **adjacent angles** because they share a common vertex and a common side.

∠E and ∠F are **complementary angles** because they form a right angle, which means the sum of the measures of their angles is 90°.

∠A and ∠C are **vertical angles** because they are nonadjacent angles formed by two intersecting lines. ∠A and ∠C are congruent.

∠A and ∠B are a **linear pair** because they are adjacent angles whose nonadjacent sides form Line *h*. Since the angles are a linear pair and their nonadjacent sides form a line, which is a **straight angle**, the sum of their measures is 180°. Since the measures of the linear pair have a sum of 180°, these angles are **supplementary**.

Guided Practice

Use Figure 7-1 to answer the following questions.

1. Determine all pairs of adjacent angles.

2. Determine all sets of supplementary angles that are not linear pairs.

3. Name all sets of linear pairs.

4. If the measure of ∠C is 48° and ∠F is 22°, give the measure of each of the following angles:

   A. ∠A   B. ∠B   C. ∠D   D. ∠E   E. ∠G

Guided Practice Answers Explained

1. ∠A and ∠B, ∠B and ∠C, ∠C and ∠D, ∠D and ∠A, ∠E and ∠F, and ∠E and ∠G

2. **The only supplementary angles are the linear pairs in Figure 7-1.**

3. ∠A and ∠B, ∠B and ∠C, ∠C and ∠D, and ∠D and ∠A

4.
   A. **m∠A = 48°** because it is vertical to ∠C, so they are congruent.

   B. **m∠B = 132°** because it is supplementary to ∠C (they are a linear pair). Also, ∠B is supplementary to ∠A because they are a linear pair.

   C. **m∠D = 132°** because it is vertical to ∠B, so they are congruent. Also, it is supplementary to ∠C because they are a linear pair. It is also supplementary to ∠A because they are a linear pair.

   D. **m∠E = 68°** because it is complementary to ∠F, with a sum of 90° because Figure 7-1 shows that Ray QR is perpendicular to Line h, forming right angles. One right angle is formed by the pair of complementary angles, ∠E and ∠F.

   E. **m∠G = 90°** because it is supplementary to the adjacent right angle.

Independent Practice

Use Figure 7-1 to answer the following questions.

1. Name the types of angles that each pair represents:

   A. ∠G and ∠E   B. ∠B and ∠D

2. Johnny says that ∠E, ∠F, and ∠G are supplementary angles because they form a straight angle and the sum of their measures is 180°. Is he correct? Explain.

3. If the measure of ∠D is 145° and ∠E is 60°, give the measure of each of the following angles:

   A. ∠A   B. ∠B   C. ∠C   D. ∠F

(Answers are on page 312.)

Three or More Intersecting Lines

A **transversal** is a line or segment that intersects two or more other lines or segments. The angles formed by transversals have specific characteristics and are named by their position along the transversal relative to the intersected lines.

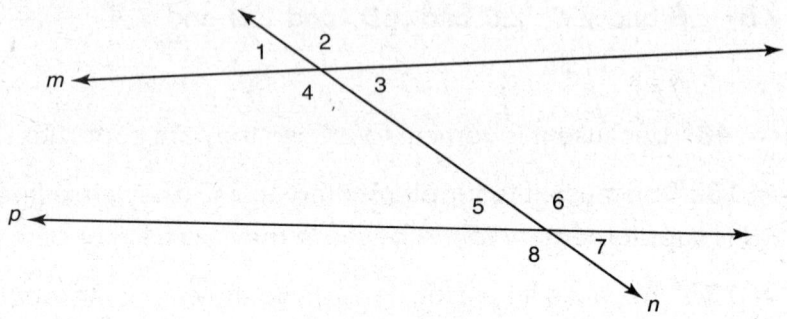

Figure 7-2.

In Figure 7-2, Line n is a transversal for Lines m and p and forms Angles 1 through 8. In this figure, there are different types of angles formed.

Key Concepts

- **Corresponding angles** are pairs of angles in the same position along the transversal as it intersects each of the two respective lines.

- **Alternate exterior angles** are pairs of angles on alternate sides of the transversal, one located above and one located below each of the intersecting lines.

- **Same side exterior angles** are pairs of angles on the same side of the transversal, one located above and one located below each of the intersecting lines.

- **Alternate interior angles** are pairs of angles on alternate sides of the transversal located between the two intersecting lines.

- **Same side interior angles** are pairs of angles on the same side of the transversal located between the two intersecting lines.

Example 1

From Figure 7-2, name: (A) a pair of corresponding angles, (B) a pair of alternate exterior angles, (C) a pair of same side exterior angles, (D) a pair of alternate interior angles, and (E) a pair of same side interior angles.

<u>Answer:</u>

(A) ∠1 and ∠5 are corresponding angles along Transversal n. These angles are along the left-hand hand side of the transversal, above Line m and above Line p. Another pair of corresponding angles is ∠3 and ∠7. These angles are located along the right-hand side of the transversal, below Line m and below Line p.

(B) ∠1 and ∠7 are alternate exterior angles. They are located on alternate sides of the transversal, with ∠1 above Line m and ∠7 below Line p.

(C) ∠1 and ∠8 are same side exterior angles. They are located on the left-hand side of the transversal, with ∠1 above Line m and ∠8 below Line p.

(D) ∠4 and ∠6 are alternate interior angles. They are located on alternate sides of the transversal in the area between Line m and Line p.

(E) ∠3 and ∠6 are same side interior angles. They are located on the right-hand side of the transversal in the area between Line m and Line p.

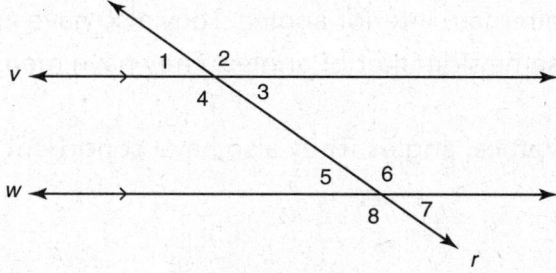

Figure 7-3.

In Figure 7-3, Line v is parallel to Line w, and both are intersected by Transversal Line r.

When a transversal intersects parallel lines:

- Pairs of corresponding angles, pairs of alternate exterior angles, and pairs of alternate interior angles are congruent in measure.
- The measures of pairs of same side exterior and pairs of same side interior angles are supplementary.

Conversely, the two lines intersected by the transversal are parallel when:

- Pairs of corresponding angles, pairs of alternate exterior angles, or pairs of alternate interior angles are congruent in measure.
- Pairs of same side exterior angles or pairs of same side interior angles are supplementary.

Example 2

From Figure 7-3, name: (A) a pair of corresponding angles, (B) a pair of alternate exterior angles, (C) a pair of same side exterior angles, (D) a pair of alternate interior angles, (E) a pair of same side interior angles, and (F) a pair of vertical angles. Determine whether the angle pairs are congruent, supplementary, or neither.

Answer:

(A) ∠1 and ∠5 are corresponding angles. They also have congruent angle measures.
(B) ∠1 and ∠7 are alternate exterior angles. They also have congruent angle measures.
(C) ∠1 and ∠8 are same side exterior angles. They have measures that are supplementary.
(D) ∠3 and ∠5 are alternate interior angles. They also have congruent measures.
(E) ∠3 and ∠6 are same side interior angles. They have measures that are supplementary.
(F) ∠1 and ∠3 are vertical angles. They also have congruent angle measures.

Table 7-1 is a summary of the measures of angles formed by transversals.

Table 7-1. Angles Formed by Transversals

Angle Type	Definition	Angle Measures When Transversal Intersects Parallel Lines	When Transversal Intersects Nonparallel Lines
Corresponding Angles	A pair of angles in the same position along the transversal as it intersects each of the two lines (i.e., top left of each intersected line).	Congruent	The angles are not congruent.
Alternate Exterior Angles	A pair of angles on alternate sides of the transversal, one located above and one located below each of the intersecting lines.	Congruent	The angles are not congruent.
Alternate Interior Angles	A pair of angles located between the two intersecting lines on alternate sides of the transversal	Congruent	The angles are not congruent.
Same Side Exterior Angles	A pair of angles, one located above and one located below each of the intersecting lines, on the same side of the transversal.	Supplementary	The angles are not supplementary.
Same Side Interior Angles	A pair of angles located between the two intersecting lines and on the same side of the transversal.	Supplementary	The angles are not supplementary.

> **HELPFUL HINT**
>
> ∠7 means "angle 7," the object or place where the two rays form the angle.
>
> m∠7 means "the measure of angle 7," in degrees.

Example 3

In Figure 7-4, Line *f* is parallel to Line *g*. Use what you've learned about parallel lines and transversals to show why the sum of the measures of the interior angles of a triangle is 180°.

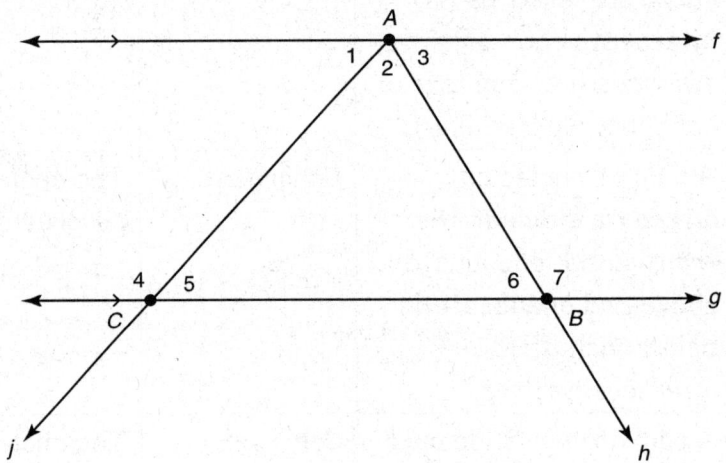

Figure 7-4.

Answer:

∠1 ≅ ∠5   (because Transversal *j* intersects parallel Lines *f* and *g* and the alternate interior angles formed are congruent)

∠3 ≅ ∠6   (because Transversal *h* intersects parallel Lines *f* and *g* and the alternate interior angles formed are congruent)

m∠1 + m∠2 + m∠3 = 180°   (because the three angles form a straight angle)

m∠5 + m∠2 + m∠6 = 180°   (by substitution for congruent angle measures)

m∠5 + m∠2 + m∠6 = 180°   (The sum of the measures of the interior angles of a triangle = 180°.)

Example 4

Use what you've learned about the parallel lines and transversals from Figure 7-4 to show why the exterior angle measure of a triangle is equal to the sum of the two nonadjacent angles of the triangle.

Answer:

$m\angle 5 + m\angle 2 + m\angle 6 = 180°$	(The sum of the measures of the interior angles of a triangle = 180°.)
$m\angle 7 + m\angle 6 = 180°$	(These angles form a linear pair, and a linear pair is supplementary.)
$m\angle 5 + m\angle 2 + m\angle 6 = m\angle 7 + m\angle 6$	(By the transitive property, both equations are equal to 180°, since if $a = b$ and $b = c$, then $a = c$.)
$-m\angle 6 = -m\angle 6$	(Subtract $m\angle 6$ from both sides.)
$m\angle 5 + m\angle 2 = m\angle 7$	(The measure of exterior $\angle 7$ for Triangle ABC is equal to the sum of the measures of the two nonadjacent angles of the triangle.)

In Figure 7-5, Line r is parallel to Line s.

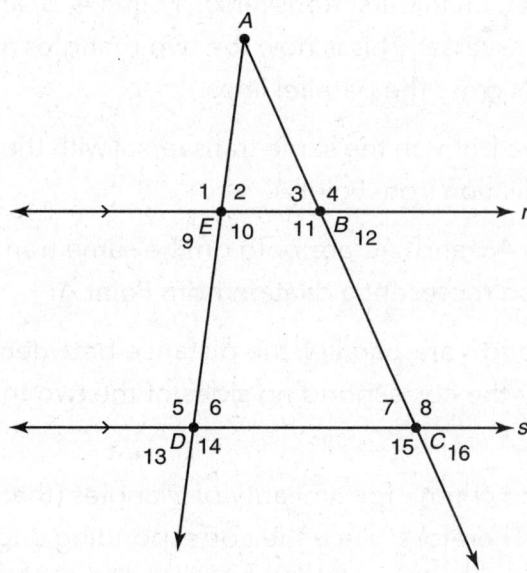

Figure 7-5.

Example 5

For Figure 7-5, use what you've learned about parallel lines and transversals to show that similarity between triangles can be demonstrated by the angle-angle criterion (A-A criterion: If two angles of one triangle are congruent to two angles of another triangle, the two triangles are similar).

<u>Answer:</u> For two triangles to be similar, corresponding angles must be congruent and corresponding sides must be proportional. Also, if two angles of one triangle are congruent to two angles of a second triangle, the third angle of both triangles must also be congruent because the sum of the angles of any triangle is 180°.

$\angle 2 \cong \angle 6$ (When a transversal intersects parallel lines, corresponding angles are congruent.)

$\angle 3 \cong \angle 7$ (When a transversal intersects parallel lines, corresponding angles are congruent.)

Since two of the corresponding angles of Triangle *AEB* and Triangle *ADC* are congruent, and the third angle ($\angle A$) is in both triangles, all three corresponding angles in the triangles are congruent. This meets the first criteria for similarity of triangles (that corresponding angles must be congruent.)

$\frac{AE}{AD} = \frac{AB}{AC}$ (Parallel lines maintain the same distance between them. Points *A*, *E*, and *D* are all on the first transversal. Points *A*, *B*, and *C* are all on the second transversal. This is how the two triangles are formed when the transversals cross the parallel lines.)

Since $\overline{AE}$ and $\overline{AD}$ are both on the same transversal with the same vertex (Point *A*), they must represent a dilation from Point *A*.

In addition, because $\overline{AB}$ and $\overline{AC}$ are both on the same transversal with the same vertex (Point *A*), they also represent a dilation from Point *A*.

Finally, since Lines *r* and *s* are parallel, the distance between them is the same, so the dilation factor for the corresponding sides of the two triangles must be the same.

This meets the second criteria for similarity of triangles (that corresponding sides must be proportional). Therefore, since the corresponding angles of Triangle *AEB* and Triangle *ADC* are congruent and the corresponding sides are proportional, Triangle *AEB* is similar to Triangle *ADC*.

Guided Practice

1. In the figure below, Line *m* and Line *n* are parallel. Fill in the circle for either True or False for each of the following statements:

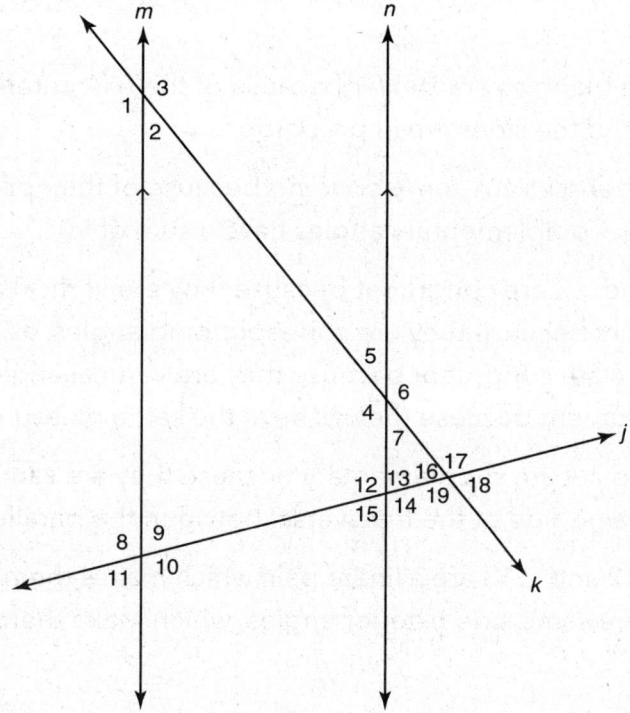

	True	False
A. ∠2 and ∠5 are congruent because they are alternate interior angles.	○	○
B. The two triangles formed by Transversals *j* and *k* intersecting Lines *m* and *n* are congruent triangles because of the A-A criterion.	○	○
C. ∠10 and ∠14 are complementary angles because they are on the upper right of each of the two parallel lines where they are intersected by Transversal *j*.	○	○
D. ∠1, ∠3, ∠4, and ∠6 are all congruent angles.	○	○
E. ∠2 and ∠4 are supplementary.	○	○

2. Which of the following pairs of angles are supplementary? Select all that apply.

☐ A. ∠12 and ∠13 ☐ B. ∠9 and ∠11 ☐ C. ∠3 and ∠6 ☐ D. ∠11 and ∠14

Guided Practice Answers Explained

1.
   A. True These angles are on alternate sides of the transversal and in the area between the two parallel lines. Alternate interior angles on parallel lines are congruent.

   B. False These triangles are *similar* because of the A-A criterion. The angles are congruent and the sides are in proportion.

   C. False These angles are *corresponding* because of their position, not *complementary*. Complementary angles have a sum of 90°.

   D. True ∠1 and ∠3 are congruent because they are vertical angles. ∠1 and ∠4 are congruent because they are corresponding angles, as are ∠3 and ∠6. Also, ∠4 and ∠6 are congruent because they are vertical angles. This means they are all congruent because they all have the same measure.

   E. True ∠2 and ∠4 are supplementary because they are same side interior angles on the same side of the transversal between the parallel lines.

2. **(A)** and **(D)** ∠12 and ∠13 are a linear pair, which makes them supplementary. ∠11 and ∠14 are same side exterior angles, which make them supplementary.

Independent Practice

1. Daniel tells his math class that given a set of parallel lines and a transversal, if he knows the measure of one angle, he can determine the measures of all of the rest of the angles formed. Karen says that he needs to know at least two of the angles to be able to determine the measures. Who is correct and why?

2. Hannah says that if a transversal crosses a pair of lines, she can prove the lines are parallel by knowing only one pair of congruent angles. Joe says that she must know a specific pair of angles is congruent to prove the transversal crosses parallel lines. Who is correct and why?

(Answers are on page 313.)

Volume of Rectangular Prisms, Cylinders, Cones, and Spheres

The volume of a three-dimensional solid is the space that the shape occupies.

> **TIP:** Since a right **rectangular prism** has lateral faces (sides) that meet the parallel bases (top and bottom) at right angles, the formula for the volume of this solid is $V = Bh$, where the uppercase B represents the area of the base, h represents the height, and V represents the volume of the solid. All faces of a right rectangular prism are rectangles. Examples of a right rectangular prism are a fish tank or a box.
>
>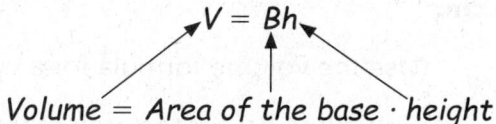
>
> Volume = Area of the base · height
>
> In this case, the area of the rectangular base can be found by using the formula $A = lw$, where l represents the length, w represents the width, and A represents the area of the rectangle.
>
> For example, if you had a carton, and you covered the base of the carton (a two-dimensional rectangle) with 1×1 cubes, the number of cubes would represent the area of the base in square units. The number of columns of cubes along the base would represent the width and the number of rows would represent the length. Stacking more layers of cubes would represent the height.

Example 1

Find the volume of a rectangular prism that has a height of 8 inches, a length of 4 inches, and a width of 2 inches.

<u>Answer:</u> **64 in.³**

$V = Bh$	(Use the volume formula for a rectangular prism.)
$V = lwh$	(Substitute lw for the area of the base because, in a rectangular prism, the base will be a rectangle.)
$V = (4\text{ in.})(2\text{ in.})(8\text{ in.})$	(Substitute the given dimensions.)
$V = 64\text{ in.}^3$	(Simplify.)

A **cylinder** is another type of three-dimensional shape that uses the same formula. In this case, the bases (top and bottom) are circles, so when substituting for B, use πr^2 to represent the area of the circle. Examples of cylinders are a can, a pipe, a battery or a glue stick.

Example 2

A can of pasteurized eggnog has a radius of 5 centimeters and a height of 23 centimeters. Determine the volume of the can of eggnog.

<u>Answer:</u> **about 1,805.5 cm.^{3}**

$V = Bh$ (Use the volume formula for a cylinder.)

$V = \pi r^2 h$ (Substitute πr^2 for the area of the base because, in a cylinder, the base will be a circle.)

$V \approx (3.14)(5 \text{ cm.})^2 (23 \text{ cm.})$ (Substitute the given dimensions.)

$V \approx (3.14)(25 \text{ cm.}^2)(23 \text{ cm.})$ (Simplify the exponent before multiplying.)

$V \approx 1{,}805.5 \text{ cm.}^3$ (Simplify.)

A **cone** is a three-dimensional shape that has a flat base (usually a circle or an ellipse) and whose lateral face gradually and smoothly tapers to a point called a vertex. Examples of cones with a circle base are an ice cream cone, a traffic cone, or a party hat. The formula for the volume of a cone with a base that is a circle is $V = \frac{1}{3}\pi r^2 h$.

Example 3

Winnie will bake cupcakes in specialty party hat cupcake tins, which each have a diameter of 3 inches and a height of 4 inches. What will be the volume of each cupcake?

Answer: **about 9.42 in.³**

$V = \frac{1}{3}\pi r^2 h$	(Use the volume formula for a cone.)
$V \approx \frac{1}{3}(3.14)(1.5 \text{ in.})^2(4 \text{ in.})$	(Substitute 3.14 for π and 4 inches for the height. The diameter is given, but the radius is what is needed for the formula. The length of the radius is half the length of the diameter, so substitute 1.5 for the radius.)
$V \approx \frac{1}{3}(3.14)(2.25 \text{ in.}^2)(4 \text{ in.})$	(Simplify the exponent before multiplying.)
$V \approx \frac{1}{3}(28.26 \text{ in.}^3)$	(Multiply all of the decimals together before multiplying by the fraction. Since $\frac{1}{3}$ transforms to a repeating decimal, it is more accurate to multiply it in fraction form.)
$V \approx 9.42 \text{ in.}^3$	(Simplify.)

A **sphere** is a three-dimensional shape with all points on its surface equidistant from its center. Examples of a sphere are a bowling ball, a marble, a globe, or a holiday ornament. The formula for the volume of a sphere is $V = \frac{4}{3}\pi r^3$.

Example 4

A tennis ball has an approximate diameter of 2.6 inches. Use a calculator to determine the volume of the tennis ball to the nearest whole inch.

Answer: **9 in.³**

$V = \frac{4}{3}\pi r^3$	(Use the volume formula for a sphere.)
$V \approx \frac{4}{3}(3.14)(1.3 \text{ in.})^3$	(Substitute 3.14 for π. The diameter is given, but the radius is what is needed for the formula. The length of the radius is half the length of the diameter, so substitute 1.3 for the radius.)
$V \approx \frac{4}{3}(3.14)(2.197 \text{ in.}^3)$	(Simplify the exponent before multiplying.)
$V \approx \frac{4}{3}(6.89858 \text{ in.}^3)$	(Multiply all of the decimals together before multiplying by the fraction. Since $\frac{4}{3}$ will convert to a repeating decimal, it is more accurate to multiply it in fraction form.)
$V \approx 9.1981066 \text{ in.}^3$	(Simplify.)
$V \approx 9 \text{ in.}^3$	(Round to the nearest whole inch.)

Guided Practice

Use a calculator to answer each of the following questions.

1. Determine if each of the following situations results in a volume greater or less than the volume of a baseball with a diameter of approximately 3 inches. Fill in the correct circle next to each situation.

	Less Volume	**Greater Volume**
A. Half of a can of broken potato crisps with an approximate diameter of 4 inches and a height of 7 inches	○	○
B. A toy plastic megaphone (cone shaped), with an approximate diameter of 3 inches and a height of 6 inches, has a small piece cut off the tip for the mouth piece. This small piece has a volume of approximately 0.5 inches^3.	○	○

2. A display has a spherical snow globe resting on a pedestal cube. The area of the base of the pedestal is 36 square inches. If the snow globe's diameter is the same as the width of the pedestal, find the total volume of the snow globe and the pedestal display to the nearest whole inch.

Guided Practice Answers Explained

1. Situation A has greater volume; Situation B has less volume

In each case, the diameter was given, but the radius is needed, so take half of the diameter for the length of the radius.

Baseball	Potato Crisps Can (Whole)	Plastic Megaphone (Whole)
$V = \frac{4}{3}\pi r^3$	$V = Bh$	$V = \frac{1}{3}\pi r^2 h$
	$V = \pi r^2 h$	
$V \approx \frac{4}{3}(3.14)(1.5 \text{ in.})^3$	$V \approx (3.14)\left(\frac{4}{2} \text{ in.}\right)^2 (7 \text{ in.})$	$V \approx \frac{1}{3}(3.14)\left(\frac{3}{2} \text{ in.}\right)^2 (6 \text{ in.})$
$V \approx \frac{4}{3}(3.14)(3.375 \text{ in.}^3)$	$V \approx (3.14)(4 \text{ in.}^2)(7 \text{ in.})$	$V \approx \frac{1}{3}(3.14)(2.25 \text{ in.}^2)(6 \text{ in.})$
$V \approx \frac{4}{3}(10.5975 \text{ in.}^3)$	$V \approx (3.14)(28 \text{ in.}^3)$	$V \approx \frac{1}{3}(3.14)(13.5 \text{ in.}^3)$
$V \approx 14.13 \text{ in.}^3$	$V \approx 87.92 \text{ in.}^3$	$V \approx \frac{1}{3}(42.39 \text{ in.}^3)$
		$V \approx 14.13 \text{ in.}^3$

Only half of the can of broken potato crisps is full, for a volume of 43.96 in.³ This volume is greater than the volume of the baseball.

Whole cone − cut off piece (14.13 in.³ − 0.5 in.³) = 13.63 in.³ With the small piece cut off, the volume of the toy megaphone is less than the volume of the baseball.

2. 329.04 in.³

Since the area of a square is s^2, the side of the square pedestal base is 6 inches, so the diameter of the sphere is also 6 inches. Half of the length of the diameter length of 6 inches gives the length of the radius of the sphere as 3 inches. Since the pedestal is a cube, each dimension will be 6 inches.

Volume of the Snow Globe	Volume of the Pedestal	
$V = \frac{4}{3}\pi r^3$	$V = Bh$	Snow Globe: 113.04 in.^{3}
$V \approx \frac{4}{3}(3.14)(3 \text{ in.})^3$	$V = (36 \text{ in.}^2)(6 \text{ in.})$	+ Pedestal: 216.00 in.^{3}
$V \approx \frac{4}{3}(3.14)(27 \text{ in.}^3)$	$V = 216 \text{ in.}^3$	Total Volume: 329.04 in.^{3}
$V \approx \frac{4}{3}(84.78 \text{ in.}^3)$		
$V \approx 113.04 \text{ in.}^3$		

Independent Practice

1. Two scoops of ice cream and a waffle cone are the Double Dip special at the local ice cream shop. These oversized spherical scoops of ice cream have an approximate diameter of 4 inches. The waffle cone for the ice cream has an approximate diameter of 4 inches and a height of 6 inches. One ice cream cone is prepared, but not delivered to the customer, and melts onto the counter. If the cone is still filled to the top with melted ice cream, what is the volume of the ice cream that melted onto the counter? Use a calculator and round to the nearest tenth.

2. A sharpened pencil can be perceived as a cylinder topped by a cone. One specific pencil has a length of 6 inches plus the sharpened portion has a length of an additional inch, and the diameter of the eraser is approximately 0.3 inches. What is the volume of the pencil?

(Answers are on page 314.)

SBAC Challenge Questions

1. The circumference of an NFL football at its widest part is approximately 558.92 millimeters. The length of the football from end to end is approximately 300 millimeters. If the football was split in half through the widest part, it would form two approximately cone shaped pieces, each with a circular base. Use a calculator to determine the volume of the whole football to the nearest whole millimeter. Give your answer in scientific notation. (Hint: Circumference = $\pi \cdot$ diameter.)

2. A hollow cement tube is created by setting a cylindrical mold with a diameter of 20 centimeters inside another cylindrical mold with a diameter of 30 centimeters and pouring cement into the space between the molds. If the hollow cement tube is 60 centimeters long, which of the expressions below represents the amount of cement needed to fill the ring of space between the two cylindrical molds to form the hollow tube?

   ○ A. 125π cm.^{3} ○ B. $7,500\pi$ cm.^{3} ○ C. 200π cm.^{3} ○ D. $3,750\pi$ cm.^{3}

   (Answers are on page 315.)

Integer Exponents and Scientific Notation

CHAPTER 8

Common Core Standard 8.EE.A.1

Know and apply the properties of integer exponents to generate equivalent numerical expressions.

Common Core Standard 8.EE.A.3

Use numbers expressed in the form of a single digit times an integer power of 10 to estimate very large or very small quantities, and to express how many times as much one is than the other.

Common Core Standard 8.EE.A.4

Perform operations with numbers expressed in scientific notation, including problems where both decimal and scientific notation are used. Use scientific notation and choose units of appropriate size for measurements of very large or very small quantities (e.g., use millimeters per year for seafloor spreading). Interpret scientific notation that has been generated by technology.

Properties of Integer Exponent Expressions

Positive integer exponents are used to express repeated multiplication of a base.

For example,

$$4 \cdot 4 \cdot 4 \cdot 4 \cdot 4 = 4^5$$

Base — Exponent

Zero and Negative Exponents

> **Key Concepts**
> - Any base with a negative exponent is simplified as the reciprocal of that base to the positive exponent.
> - Any *non zero* base written with a zero exponent is simplified as equal to 1.

HELPFUL HINT

A negative sign in the exponent *does not* affect the sign of the answer.

Example 1

Rewrite the following term with a positive exponent, and then simplify: 4^{-2}

Answer: $\dfrac{1}{16}$

4^{-2}

$= \left(\dfrac{1}{4}\right)^2$ (Write the reciprocal $\left(\dfrac{1}{4}\right)$ of the base (4) to the positive exponent.)

$= \dfrac{1}{4} \cdot \dfrac{1}{4}$ (Expand the multiplication of the base as indicated by the exponent.)

$= \dfrac{1}{16}$ (Simplify.)

Example 2

Rewrite the following term with a positive exponent, and then simplify: $(-5)^{-2}$

Answer: $\dfrac{1}{25}$

$(-5)^{-2}$

$= \left(-\dfrac{1}{5}\right)^2$ (Write the reciprocal $\left(-\dfrac{1}{5}\right)$ of the base (-5) to the positive exponent.)

$= \left(-\dfrac{1}{5}\right) \cdot \left(-\dfrac{1}{5}\right)$ (Expand the multiplication of the base as indicated by the exponent.)

$= \dfrac{1}{25}$ (Simplify.)

Example 3

Rewrite the following term with a positive exponent, and then simplify: $\left(\dfrac{2}{3}\right)^{-4}$

Answer: $\dfrac{81}{16}$

$\left(\dfrac{2}{3}\right)^{-4}$

$= \left(\dfrac{3}{2}\right)^4$ (Write the reciprocal $\left(\dfrac{3}{2}\right)$ of the base $\left(\dfrac{2}{3}\right)$ to the positive exponent.)

$= \dfrac{3}{2} \cdot \dfrac{3}{2} \cdot \dfrac{3}{2} \cdot \dfrac{3}{2}$ (Expand the multiplication of the base as indicated by the exponent.)

$= \dfrac{81}{16}$ (Simplify.)

Example 4

Rewrite the following term with a positive exponent, and then simplify: $\left(-\dfrac{1}{3}\right)^{-3}$

Answer: **−27**

$\left(-\dfrac{1}{3}\right)^{-3}$

$= (-3)^3$ (Write the reciprocal (-3) of the base $\left(-\dfrac{1}{3}\right)$ to the positive exponent.)

$= (-3) \cdot (-3) \cdot (-3)$ (Expand the multiplication of the base as indicated by the exponent.)

$= -27$ (Simplify.)

Example 5

Simplify the following:

A. $\left(\dfrac{3}{8}\right)^0$ B. 5^0 C. 9.75^0

Answers:

A. $\left(\dfrac{3}{8}\right)^0 = \mathbf{1}$

B. $5^0 = \mathbf{1}$

C. $9.75^0 = \mathbf{1}$

(Any non zero base raised to a zero power is equal to 1.)

Guided Practice

Write each of the following with a positive exponent, and then simplify.

1. $\left(-\dfrac{5}{2}\right)^{-3}$ 2. $(2.7)^0$ 3. $\left(9\dfrac{1}{2}\right)^{-2}$ 4. 1^0

Integer Exponents and Scientific Notation • 215

Guided Practice Answers Explained

1. $-\dfrac{8}{125}$

   $\left(-\dfrac{5}{2}\right)^{-3}$

   $= \left(-\dfrac{2}{5}\right)^{3}$ (Write the reciprocal $\left(-\dfrac{2}{5}\right)$ of the base $\left(-\dfrac{5}{2}\right)$ to the positive exponent.)

   $= \left(-\dfrac{2}{5}\right) \cdot \left(-\dfrac{2}{5}\right) \cdot \left(-\dfrac{2}{5}\right)$ (Expand the multiplication of the base as indicated by the exponent.)

   $= -\dfrac{8}{125}$ (Simplify.)

2. **1** Any non zero base raised to a zero power is equal to 1.

3. $\dfrac{4}{361}$

   $\left(9\dfrac{1}{2}\right)^{-2}$

   $= \left(\dfrac{19}{2}\right)^{-2}$ (Write the mixed number as an improper fraction.)

   $= \left(\dfrac{2}{19}\right)^{2}$ (Write the reciprocal $\left(\dfrac{2}{19}\right)$ of the base $\left(\dfrac{19}{2}\right)$ to the positive exponent.)

   $= \left(\dfrac{2}{19}\right) \cdot \left(\dfrac{2}{19}\right)$ (Expand the multiplication of the base as indicated by the exponent.)

   $= \dfrac{4}{361}$ (Simplify.)

4. **1** Any non zero base raised to a zero power is equal to 1.

Independent Practice

Rewrite each term with a positive exponent, and then simplify.

1. $\left(-\dfrac{2}{9}\right)^{-2}$

2. $\left(1\dfrac{1}{3}\right)^{0}$

3. $\left(\dfrac{7}{5}\right)^{-2}$

4. $(-3)^{0}$

(Answers are on page 317.)

When simplifying more complex multiplication and division of exponent expressions, specific properties can provide shortcuts for powers of a common base rather than having to expand the expression into repeated multiplication or division and then simplifying the like bases.

 HELPFUL HINT

- The words **exponent** and **power** do not share the same meaning.
- The word **exponent** is the small raised number that tells how many times the base repeats its multiplication.
- The word **power** means the entire expression (2^5) or the simplified answer (32).
- It is also correct to say "two raised to the fifth power."

Product of Powers Property

Key Concepts

- When multiplying terms that contain exponents, first multiply the coefficients.
- Then, add the exponents of the like bases.

Example 1

Simplify the expression $(4a^2b^3c)(3a^3bc^4)$.

Answer: **$12a^5b^4c^5$**

$(4a^2b^3c)(3a^3bc^4)$

$= 4 \cdot 3 \cdot a^{2+3}b^{3+1}c^{1+4}$ (First, multiply the coefficients. Then, add the exponents of the like bases.)

$= 12a^5b^4c^5$ (Simplify.)

OR

Answer by Expanded Multiplication:

$(4a^2b^3c)(3a^3bc^4)$

$= 4 \cdot a \cdot a \cdot b \cdot b \cdot b \cdot c \cdot 3 \cdot a \cdot a \cdot a \cdot b \cdot c \cdot c \cdot c \cdot c$ (Expand the multiplication as indicated by the exponents.)

$= 4 \cdot 3 \cdot a \cdot a \cdot a \cdot a \cdot a \cdot b \cdot b \cdot b \cdot b \cdot c \cdot c \cdot c \cdot c \cdot c$ (Use the Commutative Property of Multiplication to collect the coefficients and to collect the like bases.)

$= 12a^5b^4c^5$ (Simplify the like bases with exponents.)

Guided Practice

Simplify the following expressions:

1. $(3u^3v^4)(2u^2v^2w)(4uvw^2)$

2. $(6x^2)(3xy)(x^2y^3)$

Guided Practice Answers Explained

1. **$24u^6v^7w^3$**

   $(3u^3v^4)(2u^2v^2w)(4uvw^2)$

   $= 24u^{3+2+1}v^{4+2+1}w^{1+2}$ (First, multiply the coefficients. Then, add the exponents of the like bases.)

   $= 24u^6v^7w^3$ (Simplify.)

OR

Answer by Expanded Multiplication:

$(3u^3v^4)(2u^2v^2w)(4uvw^2)$

$= 3 \cdot u \cdot u \cdot u \cdot v \cdot v \cdot v \cdot v \cdot 2 \cdot u \cdot u \cdot v \cdot v \cdot w \cdot 4 \cdot u \cdot v \cdot w \cdot w$ (Expand the multiplication as indicated by the exponents.)

$= 3 \cdot 2 \cdot 4 \cdot u \cdot u \cdot u \cdot u \cdot u \cdot u \cdot v \cdot v \cdot v \cdot v \cdot v \cdot v \cdot v \cdot w \cdot w \cdot w$ (Use the Commutative Property of Multiplication to collect the coefficients and to collect the like bases.)

$= 24u^6v^7w^3$ (Simplify the like bases with exponents.)

2. $18x^5y^4$

$(6x^2)(3xy)(x^2y^3)$

$= 18x^{2+1+2}y^{1+3}$ (First, multiply the coefficients. Then, add the exponents of the like bases.)

$= 18x^5y^4$ (Simplify.)

OR

Answer by Expanded Multiplication:

$(6x^2)(3xy)(x^2y^3)$

$= 6 \cdot x \cdot x \cdot 3 \cdot x \cdot y \cdot x \cdot x \cdot y \cdot y \cdot y$ (Expand the multiplication as indicated by the exponents.)

$= 6 \cdot 3 \cdot x \cdot x \cdot x \cdot x \cdot x \cdot y \cdot y \cdot y \cdot y$ (Use the Commutative Property of Multiplication to collect the coefficients and to collect the like bases.)

(Simplify the like bases with exponents.)

$= 18x^5y^4$

Independent Practice

Simplify the following expressions.

1. $(2a^2c^3)(5a^3bc^2)(2a^2b)$

2. $(4x^5)(x^3y^4)$

3. $(3m^2n^2p)(2mnp)(2m^3n^3p^4)$

(Answers are on page 318.)

Power of Powers Property

> **Key Concepts**
> - When raising a term to a power, first raise the coefficient to that power.
> - Then, multiply each variable exponent by the exponent of the expression.

Example 1

$(3x^3yz^2)^3$

Answer: **$27x^9y^3z^6$**

$(3x^3yz^2)^3$

$= 3^3 x^{3 \cdot 3} y^{1 \cdot 3} z^{2 \cdot 3}$ (First, raise the coefficient to the power. Then, multiply each variable exponent by the exponent of the expression.)

$= 27x^9y^3z^6$ (Simplify.)

OR

Answer by Expanded Multiplication:

$(3x^3yz^2)^3$

$= (3x^3yz^2)(3x^3yz^2)(3x^3yz^2)$ (Expand the multiplication as indicated by the exponent of the expression.)

$= 3 \cdot x \cdot x \cdot x \cdot y \cdot z \cdot z \cdot 3 \cdot x \cdot x \cdot x \cdot y \cdot z \cdot z \cdot 3 \cdot x \cdot x \cdot x \cdot y \cdot z \cdot z$ (Expand the multiplication as indicated by the variable exponents.)

$= 3 \cdot 3 \cdot 3 \cdot x \cdot x \cdot x \cdot x \cdot x \cdot x \cdot x \cdot x \cdot x \cdot y \cdot y \cdot y \cdot z \cdot z \cdot z \cdot z \cdot z \cdot z$ (Use the Commutative Property of Multiplication to collect the coefficients and to collect the like bases.)

$= 27x^9y^3z^6$ (Simplify the like bases with exponents.)

Guided Practice

Simplify each expression.

1. $(-4ab^3c^4)^3$

2. $(5x^2y^2z)^2$

3. $(-3c^2d^3e^2)^3$

Guided Practice Answers Explained

1. $-64a^3b^9c^{12}$

   $(-4ab^3c^4)^3$

   $= (-4)^3 a^{1\cdot 3} b^{3\cdot 3} c^{4\cdot 3}$ (First, raise the coefficient to the power. Then, multiply each variable exponent by the exponent of the expression.)

   $= -64a^3b^9c^{12}$ (Simplify.)

   OR

   Answer by Expanded Multiplication:

   $(-4ab^3c^4)^3$

   $= (-4ab^3c^4)(-4ab^3c^4)(-4ab^3c^4)$ (Expand the multiplication as indicated by the exponent of the expression.)

   $= (-4)\cdot a\cdot b\cdot b\cdot b\cdot c\cdot c\cdot c\cdot c\cdot (-4)\cdot a\cdot b\cdot b\cdot b\cdot c\cdot c\cdot c\cdot c\cdot (-4)\cdot a\cdot b\cdot b\cdot b\cdot c\cdot c\cdot c\cdot c$ (Expand the multiplication as indicated by the variable exponents.)

   $= (-4)(-4)(-4)\cdot a\cdot a\cdot a\cdot b\cdot b\cdot b\cdot b\cdot b\cdot b\cdot b\cdot b\cdot b\cdot c\cdot c\cdot c\cdot c\cdot c\cdot c\cdot c\cdot c\cdot c\cdot c\cdot c\cdot c$ (Use the Commutative Property of Multiplication to collect the coefficients and to collect the like bases.)

   $= -64a^3b^9c^{12}$ (Simplify the like bases with exponents.)

2. **$25x^4y^4z^2$**

   $(5x^2y^2z)^2$

   $= 5^2 x^{2 \cdot 2} y^{2 \cdot 2} z^{1 \cdot 2}$ (First, raise the coefficient to the power. Then, multiply each variable exponent by the exponent of the expression.)

   $= 25x^4y^4z^2$ (Simplify.)

   OR

   Answer by Expanded Multiplication:

   $(5x^2y^2z)^2$

   $= (5x^2y^2z)(5x^2y^2z)$ (Expand the multiplication as indicated by the exponent of the expression.)

   $= 5 \cdot x \cdot x \cdot y \cdot y \cdot z \cdot 5 \cdot x \cdot x \cdot y \cdot y \cdot z$ (Expand the multiplication as indicated by the variable exponents.)

   $= 5 \cdot 5 \cdot x \cdot x \cdot x \cdot x \cdot y \cdot y \cdot y \cdot y \cdot z \cdot z$ (Use the Commutative Property of Multiplication to collect the coefficients and to collect the like bases.)

   $= 25x^4y^4z^2$ (Simplify the like bases with exponents.)

3. **$-27c^6d^9e^6$**

   $(-3c^2d^3e^2)^3$

   $= (-3)^3 c^{2 \cdot 3} d^{3 \cdot 3} e^{2 \cdot 3}$ (First, raise the coefficient to the power. Then, multiply each variable exponent by the exponent of the expression.)

   $= -27c^6d^9e^6$ (Simplify.)

OR

Answer by Expanded Multiplication:

$(-3c^2d^3e^2)^3$

$= (-3c^2d^3e^2)(-3c^2d^3e^2)(-3c^2d^3e^2)$ (Expand the multiplication as indicated by the exponent of the expression.)

$= (-3)\cdot c\cdot c\cdot d\cdot d\cdot d\cdot e\cdot e\cdot(-3)\cdot c\cdot c\cdot d\cdot d\cdot d\cdot e\cdot e\cdot(-3)\cdot c\cdot c\cdot d\cdot d\cdot d\cdot e\cdot e$ (Expand the multiplication as indicated by the variable exponents.)

$= (-3)\cdot(-3)\cdot(-3)\cdot c\cdot c\cdot c\cdot c\cdot c\cdot c\cdot d\cdot d\cdot d\cdot d\cdot d\cdot d\cdot d\cdot d\cdot d\cdot e\cdot e\cdot e\cdot e\cdot e\cdot e$ (Use the Commutative Property of Multiplication to collect the coefficients and to collect the like bases.)

$= -27c^6d^9e^6$ (Simplify the like bases with exponents.)

Independent Practice

Simplify each expression.

1. $(5a^2b^2c^5)^2$

2. $(-2x^3y^3z^0)^4$

(Answers are on page 319.)

Integer Exponents and Scientific Notation • 223

Quotient of Powers Property

Key Concepts
- When dividing terms with variables that have exponents, first divide the coefficients.
- Then, subtract the exponents of the like bases.

Example 1

Simplify the expression $\dfrac{3.9x^3y^4z^2}{1.3x^2y^2z}$.

Answer: **$3xy^2z$**

$\dfrac{3.9x^3y^4z^2}{1.3x^2y^2z}$

$= 3x^{3-2}y^{4-2}z^{2-1}$ (First, divide the coefficients. Then, subtract the exponents of the like bases.)

$= 3xy^2z$ (Simplify.)

OR

Answer by Expanded Multiplication:

$\dfrac{3.9x^3y^4z^2}{1.3x^2y^2z}$

$= \dfrac{(3.9)\cdot x \cdot x \cdot x \cdot y \cdot y \cdot y \cdot y \cdot z \cdot z}{(1.3)\cdot x \cdot x \cdot y \cdot y \cdot z}$ (Expand the multiplication as indicated by the variable exponents.)

$= \dfrac{(3.9)\cdot \cancel{x} \cdot \cancel{x} \cdot x \cdot \cancel{y} \cdot \cancel{y} \cdot y \cdot y \cdot \cancel{z} \cdot z}{(1.3)\cdot \cancel{x} \cdot \cancel{x} \cdot \cancel{y} \cdot \cancel{y} \cdot \cancel{z}}$ (Divide the coefficients. Cancel all forms of 1.)

$= 3xy^2z$ (Simplify.)

Guided Practice

Simplify each expression.

1. $\dfrac{4a^2b^3c^2}{8abc^4}$

2. $\dfrac{15x^2y^4}{3x^2y^2z^2}$

3. $\dfrac{1.44u^4v^5w^2}{12u^2v^2w^2}$

Guided Practice Answers Explained

1. $\dfrac{1ab^2}{2c^2}$

$$\dfrac{4a^2b^3c^2}{8abc^4}$$

$= \dfrac{1}{2}a^{2-1}b^{3-1}c^{2-4}$ (First, divide the coefficients. Then, subtract the exponents of the like bases.)

$= \dfrac{1ab^2}{2c^2}$ (Simplify.)

OR

Answer by Expanded Multiplication:

$$\dfrac{4a^2b^3c^2}{8abc^4}$$

$= \dfrac{4 \cdot a \cdot a \cdot b \cdot b \cdot b \cdot c \cdot c}{4 \cdot 2 \cdot a \cdot b \cdot c \cdot c \cdot c \cdot c}$ (Expand the multiplication as indicated by the variable exponents.)

$= \dfrac{\cancel{4} \cdot a \cdot \cancel{a} \cdot \cancel{b} \cdot b \cdot b \cdot \cancel{c} \cdot \cancel{c}}{\cancel{4} \cdot 2 \cdot \cancel{a} \cdot \cancel{b} \cdot c \cdot c \cdot \cancel{c} \cdot \cancel{c}}$ (Divide the coefficients. Cancel all forms of 1.)

$= \dfrac{1ab^2}{2c^2}$ (Simplify.)

2. $\dfrac{5y^2}{z^2}$

$\dfrac{15x^2y^4}{3x^2y^2z^2}$

$= \dfrac{5x^{2-2}y^{4-2}}{z^2}$ (First, divide the coefficients. Then, subtract the exponents of the like bases.)

$= \dfrac{5y^2}{z^2}$ (Simplify.)

OR

Answer by Expanded Multiplication:

$\dfrac{15x^2y^4}{3x^2y^2z^2}$

$= \dfrac{3 \cdot 5 \cdot x \cdot x \cdot y \cdot y \cdot y \cdot y}{3 \cdot x \cdot x \cdot y \cdot y \cdot z \cdot z}$ (Expand the multiplication as indicated by the variable exponents.)

$= \dfrac{\cancel{3} \cdot 5 \cdot \cancel{x} \cdot \cancel{x} \cdot \cancel{y} \cdot \cancel{y} \cdot y \cdot y}{\cancel{3} \cdot \cancel{x} \cdot \cancel{x} \cdot \cancel{y} \cdot \cancel{y} \cdot z \cdot z}$ (Divide the coefficients. Cancel all forms of 1.)

$= \dfrac{5y^2}{z^2}$ (Simplify.)

3. **$0.12u^2v^3$**

$\dfrac{1.44u^4v^5w^2}{12u^2v^2w^2}$

$= 0.12u^{4-2}v^{5-2}w^{2-2}$ (First, divide the coefficients. Then, subtract the exponents of the like bases.)

$= 0.12u^2v^3$ (Simplify.)

OR

Answer by Expanded Multiplication:

$$\frac{1.44u^4v^5w^2}{12u^2v^2w^2}$$

$$= \frac{1.44 \cdot u \cdot u \cdot u \cdot u \cdot v \cdot v \cdot v \cdot v \cdot v \cdot w \cdot w}{12 \cdot u \cdot u \cdot v \cdot v \cdot w \cdot w}$$ (Expand the multiplication as indicated by the variable exponents.)

$$= \frac{1.44 \cdot u \cdot u \cdot \cancel{u} \cdot \cancel{u} \cdot v \cdot \cancel{v} \cdot \cancel{v} \cdot v \cdot v \cdot \cancel{w} \cdot \cancel{w}}{12 \cdot \cancel{u} \cdot \cancel{u} \cdot \cancel{v} \cdot \cancel{v} \cdot \cancel{w} \cdot \cancel{w}}$$ (Divide the coefficients. Cancel all forms of 1.)

$$= 0.12u^2v^3$$ (Simplify.)

Independent Practice

Simplify the following expressions.

1. $\dfrac{1.4x^2y^2z^3}{0.2xyz^4}$

2. $\dfrac{18xy^3}{9x^2yz^2}$

3. $\dfrac{25u^2v^2w}{15u^3v^3w^2}$

(Answers are on page 320.)

Table 8-1. Exponent Rules

Property	Coefficients	Variable	Example
Negative Integer Exponents	Reciprocal to the Positive Exponent	Reciprocal to the Positive Exponent	5^{-2} $= \left(\dfrac{1}{5}\right)^2$ $= \dfrac{1}{5} \cdot \dfrac{1}{5}$ $= \dfrac{1}{25}$
Zero Exponents	Any Non Zero Base Is Equal to One	Any Non Zero Base Is Equal to One	$9^0 = 1$
Product of Powers Property	Multiply the Coefficients	Add the Exponents of the Like Bases	$(4x^2y^3)(5xyz)$ $= 20x^{2+1}y^{3+1}z$ $= 20x^3y^4z$
Power of Powers Property	Calculate the Coefficient Raised to the Power	Multiply Each Variable Exponent by the Expression Exponent	$(3a^3b^4)^2$ $= 3^2 a^{3 \cdot 2} b^{4 \cdot 2}$ $= 9a^6b^8$
Quotient of Powers Property	Divide the Coefficients	Subtract the Exponents of the Like Bases	$\dfrac{27a^3b^2c}{9a^2bc}$ $= 3a^{3-2}b^{2-1}c^{1-1}$ $= 3abc^0$ $= 3ab(1)$ $= 3ab$

Scientific Notation

Scientific notation is used by scientists and others to manage very large or very small numbers.

Key Concepts
• Scientific notation is written as the product of a factor (greater than or equal to 1 and less than 10) and a power of 10.
• For standard notation numbers greater than 1, the scientific notation will use a positive power of 10.
• For standard notation numbers less than 1, the scientific notation will use a negative power of 10.

Example 1

The distance from Earth to the Sun is 93,000,000 miles. Write that distance in scientific notation.

Answer: **9.3×10^7 miles**

93,000,000	
The first factor is **9.3**, which is greater than or equal to 1 and less than 10.	• The original number is greater than 1. • The decimal point in the original number is at the far right, but, in the first factor, it is between the digits 9 and 3. • To return the decimal point to the original position, it would need to move 7 places to the right. • This direction indicates that the power of 10 is positive and the number of places is 7. • Therefore, the power of 10 is positive 7.
9.3×10^7	

Example 2

The measure of a wavelength of green light is 0.000000543 meters. Write this measure in scientific notation.

Answer: **5.43 × 10⁻⁷ meters**

0.000000543	
The first factor is **5.43**, which is greater than or equal to 1 and less than 10.	• The original number is less than 1. • The decimal point in the original number is at the far left, but, in the first factor, it is between the digits 5 and 4. • To return the decimal point to the original position, it would need to move 7 places to the left. • This direction indicates that the power of 10 is negative and the number of places is 7. • Therefore, the power of 10 is −7. Note: Since the original number is less than 1, the 0 in the unit place of the original number is not considered when determining the power of 10.
5.43×10^{-7}	

Guided Practice

Convert each of the following numbers from standard notation to scientific notation.

1. 43,562,000,000

2. 0.000000039

3. 2,427,500

4. 0.700325

Guided Practice Answers Explained

1. **4.3562×10^{10}**

43,562,000,000	
The first factor is **4.3562**, which is greater than or equal to 1 and less than 10.	• The original number is greater than 1. • The decimal point in the original number is at the far right, but, in the first factor, it is between the digits 4 and 3. • To return the decimal point to the original position, it would need to move 10 places to the right. • This direction indicates that the power of 10 is positive and the number of places is 10. • Therefore, the power of 10 is positive 10.
4.3562×10^{10}	

2. **3.9×10^{-8}**

0.000000039	
The first factor is **3.9**, which is greater than or equal to 1 and less than 10.	• The original number is less than 1. • The decimal point in the original number is at the far left, but, in the first factor, it is between the digits 3 and 9. • To return the decimal point to the original position, it would need to move 8 places to the left. • This direction indicates that the power of 10 is negative and the number of places is 8. • Therefore, the power of 10 is −8. Note: Since the original number is less than 1, the 0 in the unit place of the original number is not considered when determining the power of 10.
3.9×10^{-8}	

3. **2.4275 × 10⁶**

	2,427,500
The first factor is **2.4275**, which is greater than or equal to 1 and less than 10.	• The original number is greater than 1. • The decimal point in the original number is at the far right, but, in the first factor, it is between the digits 2 and 4. • To return the decimal point to the original position, it would need to move 6 places to the right. • This direction indicates that the power of 10 is positive and the number of places is 6. • Therefore, the power of 10 is positive 6.
	2.4275×10^6

4. **7.00325 × 10⁻¹**

	0.700325
The first factor is **7.00325**, which is greater than or equal to 1 and less than 10.	• The original number is less than 1. • The decimal point in the original number is at the far left, but, in the first factor, it is between the digits 7 and 0. • To return the decimal point to the original position, it would need to move 1 place to the left. • This direction indicates that the power of 10 is negative and the number of places is 1. • Therefore, the power of 10 is −1. Note: Since the original number is less than 1, the 0 in the unit place of the original number is not considered when determining the power of 10.
	7.00325×10^{-1}

Independent Practice

1. Order the following numbers from least to greatest:

   3.4×10^4 7.943×10^3 5.0745×10^4 7.04×10^4 22,500

2. Order the following numbers from least to greatest:

   5.01×10^{-4} 0.00048 5.2×10^{-2} 4.8×10^{-3} 5.001×10^{-3}

(Answers are on page 322.)

Operations with Scientific Notation

Key Concepts

MULTIPLICATION:

- Multiply the first factors as coefficients of the powers of 10.
- Then, add the exponents for the powers of 10.
- Simplify the product coefficient, if necessary, to scientific notation.
- Then, if necessary, simplify the powers of 10.

DIVISION:

- Divide the first factors as coefficients of the powers of 10.
- Then, subtract the exponents for the powers of 10.
- Simplify the quotient coefficient, if necessary, to scientific notation.
- Then, if necessary, simplify the powers of 10.

Note: The final answer after all operations must be in scientific notation!

Example 1

One nanometer = 0.000000001 meters. One average wavelength of red light is 650 nanometers.

   Express the average length (in meters) of one wavelength of red light in scientific notation.

<u>Answer:</u> **6.5×10^{-7} meters**

$(650)(0.000000001)$	(This problem requires multiplication.)
$= (6.5 \times 10^2)(1.0 \times 10^{-9})$	(Express each of the lengths in scientific notation.)
$= (6.5)(1.0) \times (10^2)(10^{-9})$	(Use the Commutative Property of Multiplication to collect the coefficients and to collect the powers of 10 (like bases) together.)
$= 6.5 \times 10^{2 + (-9)}$	(Multiply the coefficients. Use the Product of Powers Property to add the exponents of the powers of 10 (like bases).)
$= 6.5 \times 10^{-7}$	(Simplify.)

Example 2

There were approximately 60.2 billion aluminum cans recycled in 2013. If the population of the United States in 2013 was approximately 315 million, express the approximate average number of cans recycled by one person, on average, in 2013. Give the answer in scientific notation and standard notation.

<u>Answer:</u> **The approximate average number of cans recycled by one person in the United States in 2013 was 1.9×10^2 (scientific notation) or approximately 190 (standard notation) recycled aluminum cans per person.**

$$\text{One million} = 1 \times 10^6$$

$$\text{One billion} = 1 \times 10^9$$

$$\frac{60.2 \text{ billion recycled aluminum cans}}{315 \text{ million people in 2013 U.S. population}} = \frac{(60.2)(1 \times 10^9)}{(315)(1 \times 10^6)}$$

$$= \frac{(60.2)(1 \times 10^9)}{(315)(1 \times 10^6)}$$

$$= \frac{(60.2 \times 10^9)}{(315 \times 10^6)} \quad \text{(Multiply the coefficients in the numerator and in the denominator.)}$$

$$\approx 0.19 \times 10^{9-6} \quad \text{(Divide the coefficients. Round to the nearest hundredth. Use the Quotient of Powers Property to subtract the exponents of the powers of 10 (like bases).)}$$

$$\approx (1.9 \times 10^{-1}) \times 10^3 \quad \text{(Convert the coefficient of the quotient (0.19) to scientific notation } (1.9 \times 10^{-1}).)$$

$$\approx 1.9 \times 10^{-1+3} \quad \text{(Use the Product of Powers Property to add the exponents of the powers of 10 (like bases).)}$$

$$\approx 1.9 \times 10^2 \quad \text{(Simplify.)}$$

Guided Practice

1. A small dog's heart beats approximately 64,500,000 times in a year. If there are 8,760 hours in a year, approximately how many times does a small dog's heart beat per minute? Express your answer in scientific notation and standard notation.

2. A human body contains approximately 32,000 microliters of blood for every pound of body weight. If each microliter of blood contains approximately 5,000,000 red blood cells, approximately how many red blood cells are in the body of a 165 pound wrestler? Express your answer in scientific notation.

Guided Practice Answers Explained

1. **1.2×10^2 (scientific notation) or 120 (standard notation) heartbeats per minute**

$$64{,}500{,}000 \text{ heartbeats per year} = 6.45 \times 10^7$$
$$8{,}760 \text{ hours in a year} = 8.76 \times 10^3$$
$$60 \text{ minutes per hour} = 6.0 \times 10^1$$

$$\frac{\text{\# heartbeats per year}}{(\text{\# hours in a year})(\text{\# minutes per hour})} = \frac{6.45 \times 10^7}{(8.76 \times 10^3)(6.0 \times 10^1)}$$

$\dfrac{6.45 \times 10^7}{(8.76 \times 10^3)(6.0 \times 10^1)}$

$= \dfrac{6.45 \times 10^7}{(8.76 \times 6.0)(10^3 \times 10^1)}$ (Use the Commutative Property of Multiplication to collect the coefficients and to collect the powers of 10 (like bases).)

$= \dfrac{6.45 \times 10^7}{52.56 \times 10^{3+1}}$ (Multiply the coefficients in the denominator. Use the Product of Powers Property to add the exponents of the powers of 10 (like bases).)

$\approx 0.12 \times 10^{7-4}$ (Divide the coefficients. Use the Quotient of Powers Property to subtract the exponents of the powers of 10 (like bases).)

$\approx (1.2 \times 10^{-1}) \times 10^3$ (Convert the coefficient of the quotient (0.12) to scientific notation (1.2×10^{-1}).)

$\approx 1.2 \times 10^{-1+3}$ (Use the Product of Powers Property to add the exponents of the powers of 10 (like bases).)

$\approx 1.2 \times 10^2$ (Simplify.)

A small dog's heart beats approximately 1.2×10^2 or about 120 times per minute.

2. 2.64×10^{13} red blood cells

$$32{,}000 \text{ microliters per pound} = 3.2 \times 10^4$$
$$5{,}000{,}000 \text{ red blood cells} = 5.0 \times 10^6$$
$$165 \text{ pounds} = 1.65 \times 10^2$$

$$\frac{(3.2 \times 10^4) \text{ microliter}}{\text{pound}} \cdot \frac{(5.0 \times 10^6) \text{ red blood cells}}{1 \text{ microliter}} \cdot \frac{(1.65 \times 10^2) \text{ pounds}}{1} =$$

$$\frac{[(3.2)(5.0)(1.65)][(10^4)(10^6)(10^2)] \text{ red blood cells}}{1}$$

(Use the Commutative Property of Multiplication to collect the coefficients and to collect the powers of 10.)

$= 26.4 \times 10^{4+6+2}$ (Multiply the coefficients in the numerator. Use the Product of Powers Property to add the exponents of the powers of 10 (like bases).)

$= (2.64 \times 10^1) \times 10^{12}$ (Convert the coefficient of the product to scientific notation.)

$= 2.64 \times 10^{1+12}$ (Use the Product of Powers Property to add the exponents of the powers of 10 (like bases).)

$= 2.64 \times 10^{13}$ (Simplify.)

There are about 2.64×10^{13} red blood cells in a 165 pound wrestler.

Independent Practice

1. The mass of an elephant is 8.6×10^4 kilograms. The mass of a shrew is about 0.0018 kilograms. Approximately, how many times the mass of a shrew is the mass of an elephant? Give your answer in scientific notation.

2. The distance an object travels in feet in t seconds is given by the formula $d = 64t^2$. How many feet would the object travel in 25 minutes? Give your answer in scientific notation.

(Answers are on page 323.)

SBAC Challenge Questions

Simplify each expression for Questions 1–3.

1. $\dfrac{(3a^2b^2c)^2(4ab^3c)}{12ab^3c^4}$

2. $\dfrac{(1.8m^3n^3p^2)(3m^2np^2)}{(0.3m^2n^3p^3)^2}$

3. $\dfrac{(2a^2b^0c)(4a^3b^2c^2)^2}{8a^3bc^4}$

4. Determine which of the following expressions is equivalent to $2x^2yz^2$. Fill in the circle next to Yes or No for each expression.

		Yes	No
A.	$\dfrac{(2xyz)^2}{2y}$	○	○
B.	$\dfrac{(3xyz^0)(2x^2y)^2}{2y}$	○	○
C.	$\dfrac{(2x^2y^2z^2)(x^2yz^2)(9xz)}{(3x^2yz^2)^2}$	○	○
D.	$\dfrac{(15x^{-1}z^2)(4x^2y^2z^2)}{(10x^{-1}y^{-1}z^2)(3x^2yz^0)}$	○	○
E.	$\dfrac{8x^3y^2z^3}{4xyz}$	○	○

5. The kinetic energy, in joules, of a moving object is found by using the formula $E = \dfrac{1}{2}mv^2$, where m is the mass in kilograms and v is the speed of the object in seconds. The mass of a car is 1,625 kilograms. The car is traveling at 30 meters per second. Determine the kinetic energy of the car. Give your answer in scientific notation.

6. Medical x-rays have a wavelength of approximately 10^{-10} meters. Visible light wavelengths are between 4×10^7 meters and 7.5×10^{-7} meters. If ultraviolet rays are approximately 1,000 times the length of a medical x-ray wavelength, are visible light wavelengths longer or shorter than ultraviolet rays?

7. Infrared rays are approximately 10^{-5} meters in length. Microwaves average 5×10^{-1} meters in length. Using the data you obtained from Question 6, order the wavelengths of medical x-rays, ultraviolet rays, infrared rays, and microwaves from least to greatest length in meters.

(Answers are on page 324.)

Performance Task Overview

CHAPTER 9

As mentioned in the Introduction, the SBAC Grade 8 Math exam is made up of two parts. The second part is the Performance Task. The Performance Task will have between four and six questions related to one main idea. The mathematics necessary to complete the task will require multiple concepts and ideas from the Grade 8 mathematics standards as well as math content learned from previous school years.

The Performance Task will be presented in two columns. You will be able to scroll up and down each column separately. All of the information that you will consult to calculate and make decisions about will be located on the left-hand side of the screen. The four to six questions you will need to answer will be on the right-hand side and will include questions requiring explanations or mathematical justifications for decisions made. Explanations will be typed into text boxes on the screen.

> **The first and second questions** from the Performance Task generally require some data analysis and/or calculation but require little, if any, explanation.

Sample First and Second Questions

1. Kimberly has two boxes with the dimensions given. Complete the chart below.

Table 1

	Length	Width	Height	Volume
Box 1	15 inches	12 inches	10 inches	
Box 2	15 inches	5 inches	12 inches	

2. Use a calculator to determine the diagonal for each of the faces for Box 1 and for each of the faces for Box 2. Organize the data in Table 2.

Table 2

Faces	Box 1	Box 2
Diagonal for Front and Back		
Diagonal for Left and Right		
Diagonal for Top and Bottom		

(Answers are on page 241.)

> **The third and fourth questions** from the Performance Task usually require a decision to be made based on the results from the first two questions or from further analysis.

Sample Third and Fourth Questions

3. Kimberly wants to store a right triangle-shaped pennant in one of the boxes, but she cannot have it lie flat on the bottom of the box.

    - The pennant must be stored upright so that the shorter leg of the right triangle is along the height of the box, and the longer leg of the right triangle is along the diagonal of the base of the box.
    - Any face of the box can be considered the base.

Use the information in Table 2 and a calculator to determine the largest area that Kimberly's pennant can have and still be able to be stored in one of the boxes in the way described.

4. Explain how you determined the largest area that Kimberly's pennant can have for Question 3. Inside which box should she store the pennant? Which dimensions of the box should she consider as the base?

(Answers are on page 242.)

> **The fifth and sixth questions** from the Performance Task usually involve further analysis of the data, using results in a different way, or making a final decision and justifying that decision with evidence from the previous questions.

Sample Fifth and Sixth Questions

5. Determine the perimeter of the pennant with the largest area, as determined in Question 3.

6. Explain how you determined the perimeter of the pennant with the largest area for Question 5.

(Answers are on page 243.)

Sample Performance Task Answers Explained

1.

	Length	Width	Height	Volume
Box 1	15 inches	12 inches	10 inches	1,800 in.³
Box 2	15 inches	5 inches	12 inches	900 in.³

Box 1

Volume = length · width · height
V = 15 inches · 12 inches · 10 inches
V = 1,800 in.³

Box 2

Volume = length · width · height
V = 15 inches · 5 inches · 12 inches
V = 900 in.³

Scoring: One point for both answers correct. Zero points for one or both answers incorrect.

2. Since each face of each box is a rectangle, each of the rectangles has a diagonal that creates two right triangles on that face. Use the Pythagorean theorem to find the lengths of the diagonals.

Faces	Box 1	Box 2
Diagonal for Front and Back	15 × 12 inches ≈ **19.2 inches**	15 × 5 inches ≈ **15.8 inches**
Diagonal for Left and Right	12 × 10 inches ≈ **15.6 inches**	5 × 12 inches = **13 inches**
Diagonal for Top and Bottom	15 × 10 inches ≈ **18.0 inches**	15 × 12 inches ≈ **19.2 inches**

Note: The dimensions must correspond to the faces for each box. That is, if the length and width represent the rectangular dimensions of the front and back faces of Box 1, then the length and width must represent the rectangular dimensions of the front and back faces of Box 2.

Box 1

$$a^2 + b^2 = c^2$$
$$15^2 + 12^2 = x^2$$
$$225 + 144 = x^2$$
$$369 = x^2$$
$$\sqrt{369} = \sqrt{x^2}$$
$$19.2 \approx x$$

$$a^2 + b^2 = c^2$$
$$12^2 + 10^2 = x^2$$
$$144 + 100 = x^2$$
$$244 = x^2$$
$$\sqrt{244} = \sqrt{x^2}$$
$$15.6 \approx x$$

$$a^2 + b^2 = c^2$$
$$15^2 + 10^2 = x^2$$
$$225 + 100 = x^2$$
$$325 = x^2$$
$$\sqrt{325} = \sqrt{x^2}$$
$$18.0 \approx x$$

Box 2

$$a^2 + b^2 = c^2$$
$$15^2 + 5^2 = x^2$$
$$225 + 25 = x^2$$
$$250 = x^2$$
$$\sqrt{250} = \sqrt{x^2}$$
$$15.8 \approx x$$

$$a^2 + b^2 = c^2$$
$$5^2 + 12^2 = x^2$$
$$25 + 144 = x^2$$
$$169 = x^2$$
$$\sqrt{169} = \sqrt{x^2}$$
$$13 = x$$

$$a^2 + b^2 = c^2$$
$$15^2 + 12^2 = x^2$$
$$225 + 144 = x^2$$
$$369 = x^2$$
$$\sqrt{369} = \sqrt{x^2}$$
$$19.2 \approx x$$

Scoring: Two points for all three diagonals correctly calculated for both boxes. One point for three diagonals of one box correctly calculated. Zero points for neither box correctly calculated.

3. **The largest area possible for the right triangle-shaped pennant is approximately 117 in.²**

Diagonal of Face Used for Pennant's Base	Box 1 Base Diagonal	Height Used as Pennant's Shortest Leg	Area of Pennant $A = \frac{1}{2}bh$
Front or Back	15 × 12 in. ≈ 19.2 inches	10 inches	96 in.²
Left or Right	12 × 10 in. ≈ 15.6 inches	15 inches	117 in.²
Top or Bottom	15 × 10 in. ≈ 18.0 inches	12 inches	108 in.²

Diagonal of Face Used for Pennant's Base	Box 2 Base Diagonal	Height Used as Pennant's Shortest Leg	Area of Pennant $A = \frac{1}{2}bh$
Front or Back	$\sqrt{15 \times 5}$ in. $\approx$ 15.8 inches	12 inches	94.8 in.²
Left or Right	$\sqrt{5 \times 12}$ in. $=$ 13 inches	15 inches	97.5 in.²
Top or Bottom	$\sqrt{15 \times 12}$ in. $\approx$ 19.2 inches	5 inches	48 in.²

<u>Scoring:</u> One point for identifying the largest area possible for the pennant. (Note: Full credit is awarded if the calculations are correct based on an incorrect answer for Question 2.) Zero points for an incorrect largest area (perhaps from a calculation error).

4. To find the largest possible area for the two-dimensional pennant, the area formula requires the measures of both the base and the height of the pennant. Kimberly expects the base of the pennant to be stored along the diagonal of one face of the box. Since any face of the box can be its base (this would be the length measure and width measure of the box), it follows that whichever measure is used as the height of the box must also be the height of the pennant. The third side of the pennant is its hypotenuse. The measure of the hypotenuse of the two-dimensional pennant will be the measure of the three-dimensional diagonal of the box because of the way it will be stored.

Using the results from Question 3 and the area formula (with height and the diagonal length as the base of the pennant), it can be determined that the largest area for the pennant is 117 in.²

She must use Box 1 to store a pennant with that area. Using Box 1, the 12 inch × 10 inch dimensions would have to be the dimensions of the rectangular base, and the height would have to be 15 inches.

<u>Scoring:</u> Three points for complete and correct responses for all three parts of the explanation and identification. (Note: Full credit is earned if the explanations are complete and correct based on incorrect calculations for Question 2.)

Two points for complete and correct responses for two parts of the explanation and identification.

One point for a correct response to one part of the explanation or identification.

5. **The perimeter of the pennant with the largest area is approximately 52.2 inches.**

To determine the perimeter of the pennant with the largest area, the lengths of all three sides must be calculated. For this right triangle pennant, the base from Box 1 (12 in. by 10 in. face) is approximately 15.6 inches, the height is 15 inches, and the hypotenuse must be determined for the length of the third side of the pennant. This is the three-dimensional diagonal of the box.

The pennant is a right triangle, so the Pythagorean theorem is used to find the length of the missing side.

$$a^2 + b^2 = c^2$$
$$15.6^2 + 15^2 = x^2$$
$$243.36 + 225 = x^2$$
$$468.36 = x^2$$
$$\sqrt{468.36} = \sqrt{x^2}$$
$$21.6 \approx x$$

$$P \approx 15.6 + 15 + 21.6$$
$$P \approx 52.2 \text{ inches}$$

Scoring: Two points for the correct calculation of the third side and the correct calculation of the perimeter of the triangle. (Note: Full credit is earned if the answer results from the correct calculation of the perimeter based on an incorrect response to Question 3.)

One point for either the correct calculation of the third side or the correct calculation of the perimeter of the triangle based on an incorrect value for the third side.

Zero points for an incorrect calculation of the third side and an incorrect calculation of the perimeter of the triangle.

6. Explain how you determined the perimeter of the pennant with the largest area.

(See the answer explanation for Question 5 to answer Question 6.)

Scoring: Three points if the explanation includes how all three side lengths were determined, how you used the Pythagorean theorem to determine the length of the hypotenuse, referring to the right triangle, and how you added all three side lengths together to determine the perimeter. (Note: Full credit is earned if the answer results from a correct explanation based on an incorrect response to Question 3.)

Two points if the answer includes a precise explanation of how the three side lengths were determined and how you used the Pythagorean theorem to determine the length of the hypotenuse, but the explanation does not refer to the right triangle and does not discuss how you added all three side lengths together to determine the perimeter.

One point if somewhat of an explanation is given for calculating the perimeter, but there is no mention of the right triangle or the use of the Pythagorean theorem.

Zero points if there is no demonstration of an understanding as to how the side lengths were determined, how the Pythagorean theorem was used, what the right triangle is, and how the perimeter was calculated.

Practice Test

CHAPTER 10

Computer Adaptive Test

Directions: Read each question carefully. Be sure to answer each question completely.

1. Rectangle *ABCD* is formed on a Cartesian plane with vertices at *A* (–3, –4), *B* (–3, 1), *C* (3, 1), and *D* (*x*, *y*). Determine the coordinates of the missing vertex.

2. Determine the length of Segment *EG*, with Endpoint *E* at (4, 2) and Endpoint *G* at (–3, –7), to the nearest tenth of a unit, using a calculator.

3. From Rectangle *ABCD*, Side *AB* and Side *CD* are rotated 90° clockwise around the origin. Are image Side *A'B'* and image Side *C'D'* parallel, perpendicular, or neither in each of the following situations?

   Image Side *A'B'* and image Side *C'D'* are:

Parallel	**Perpendicular**	**Neither**	
○	○	○	A. to each other
○	○	○	B. to Side *BC*
○	○	○	C. to Diagonal *BD*
○	○	○	D. to Sides *AB* and *CD*

4. Lindsay has five more trading cards than Lena. Yu-Fen has eight less trading cards than Lindsay. Together they have 62 trading cards. If Stephen has four times as many trading cards as Yu-Fen, how many more trading cards does Stephen have than the other three have together?

5. Determine whether each of the following equations has one solution, no solutions, or infinite solutions.

	One Solution	No Solutions	Infinite Solutions
A. $3(x + 5) - 12 = 2(x + 8) + x$	○	○	○
B. $3(x + 5) - 12 = 2(x + 8) + 2x$	○	○	○
C. $3(x + 5) - 12 = 2(x + 1) + (x + 1)$	○	○	○
D. $7x - 3 + 5x - 4 = 11x$	○	○	○
E. $5(2x - 3) = 9(x - 1) + (x - 6)$	○	○	○

6. A photo is copied onto a sheet of paper 8.5 inches by 10 inches. A 1.5 inch margin is left all around the photo. To the nearest tenth, what is the diagonal length of the photo? (You may need to use a calculator to answer this question.)

7. A container shaped like a cylinder is filled to the top with damp sand and has a lid in the shape of half a sphere. When the lid is removed, the sand compressed by the lid remains in place. The sand will be removed from the container and used to fill cubes with an edge of 2 inches. To the nearest whole cube, how many cubes will be filled by the damp sand in the container if the container is 3 feet high and has a diameter of 3 feet? (You may need to use a calculator to answer this question.)

8. An eight-inch-tall plastic party hat in the shape of a cone has a diameter of 5 inches. One of the games at the party is to fill the hat with water, carry it a short distance, and fill a cylindrical container with the water collected. Assuming that Pat can carry the party hat without spilling any water, how many trips (to the nearest whole trip) will she need to make if the cylindrical container has a radius of 3 inches and is 12 inches tall? (You may need to use a calculator to answer this question.)

9. Sixty students were surveyed to see if they own a smartphone. Of the girls who were surveyed, 32 own a smartphone. Of the boys who were surveyed, 22 own a smartphone. If 36 of those surveyed were girls, complete the chart below.

	Own a Smartphone	Do Not Own a Smartphone	Total
Girls			
Boys			
Total			

10. Of the choices below, choose an expression that contains only irrational terms that have a simplified sum value less than 10.

    ○ A. $\sqrt{9} + \sqrt{16}$
    ○ B. $\sqrt{5} + \sqrt[3]{16} + \sqrt{17}$
    ○ C. $3.\overline{97} + 4.\overline{5} + \pi$
    ○ D. $5\pi - \sqrt{10}$

11. Simplify the following expression and express the answer in scientific notation.

    $$(3.7 \times 10^{-6})(2.1 \times 10^4)(5.0 \times 10^8)$$

    ○ A. 3.885×10^6
    ○ B. 3.885×10^5
    ○ C. 3.885×10^7
    ○ D. 3.885×10^{-192}

12. Select the expression that is equivalent to $\dfrac{450v^3w^2x}{15v^{-3}w^{-2}x^2}$.

    ○ A. $\dfrac{300v^3w^2}{10x}$

    ○ B. $\dfrac{(5x^2)(6v^6)(2w^2)^3}{8x^3}$

    ○ C. $\dfrac{(5v^2w^2x^2)^2}{25x}$

    ○ D. $\dfrac{v^8w^6x^2}{(30)^{-1}v^2w^2x^3}$

13. Loren is 650 miles from home. If he drives 210 miles further from home in 3 hours, write an equation that represents his distance from home, d, after t hours.

14. Which equation below represents the least steep line?

    ○ A. $4x + 6y = 9$
    ○ B. $3y - 12x = -9$
    ○ C. $y - 5x = -\dfrac{3}{5}$
    ○ D. $2x + y = 9$

15. What is the solution to the system of equations graphed below?

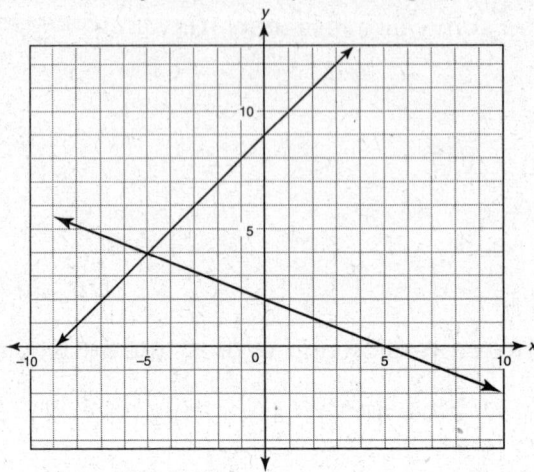

16. Deirdre can buy two sweatshirts and five T-shirts for $32.25 or she can buy five sweatshirts and two T-shirts for $46.50. How much does one sweatshirt cost, and how much does one T-shirt cost?

17. In a race, Diane's distance in miles, d, was represented by the equation $d = 4.5t$, where t represented her time in hours. Erin's time and distance is represented by the table below. Who was running faster?

Time (minutes)	10	25	35
Distance (miles)	0.8	2	2.8

18. Which of the following functions is not linear?

  ○ A. $y = x^2 + 4$

  ○ B.

x	11	10	5	2
y	4	4	4	4

  ○ C. $y = 3x + 4$

  ○ D.

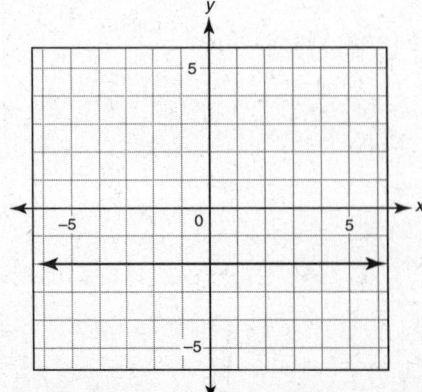

19. Triangle *DEF* is translated 4 units up and 3 units to the left. If the coordinates of Point *E* are (–4, 5), what are the coordinates of Point *E'*?

20. Pentagon *QRSTU* is rotated 90° counterclockwise around the origin, reflected across the *y*-axis, translated 2 units down, and dilated, from the origin, at a scale factor of $\frac{2}{3}$. Which of the following can be determined about the image from the transformations given?

- A. The image is located in Quadrant 1.
- B. All of the *x*-coordinates of the image are the opposite of the *x*-coordinates of the pre-image.
- C. The image is a reduction of the pre-image.
- D. The image is congruent to the pre-image.

21. Find the measure of angle *m*.

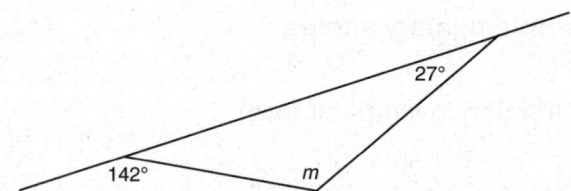

22. The ordered pairs on a scatter plot have a negative linear association. Which of the following statements must be true about the data in the ordered pairs?

- A. As the *x*-coordinates increase, the *y*-coordinates increase.
- B. As the *x*-coordinates increase, the *y*-coordinates decrease.
- C. The data in the ordered pairs form a curve.
- D. The data set has no outliers.

23. For a line of best fit on a scatter plot, the line should

- A. intersect as many points as possible on the scatter plot.
- B. not intersect any points on the scatter plot.
- C. have a positive slope.
- D. be as close to as many points on the scatter plot as possible.

24. Determine whether the following statements are True or False for the figure below. Line 1 is parallel to Line 2.

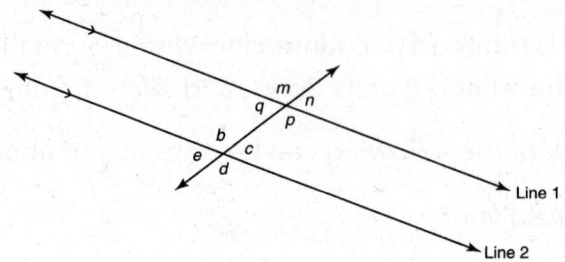

	True	False
A. ∠b and ∠p are alternate interior angles.	O	O
B. ∠b and ∠d are vertical angles.	O	O
C. ∠e and ∠m are corresponding angles.	O	O
D. ∠p ≅ ∠d	O	O
E. ∠q = ∠m	O	O
F. ∠c and ∠p are supplementary angles.	O	O

25. Convert $0.\overline{21}$ to a fraction in simplest form.

26. Donna says that doubling the length of the edge of a cube doubles the volume. Jim disagrees. Who is correct? Explain.

27. Determine the *first* step that contains an error in solving the following system of equations by substitution.

$$y = 2x + 6 \quad 2y - 5x = 12$$

Step One: $\quad 2y - 5(2x + 6) = 12$
Step Two: $\quad 2y - 10y - 30 = 12$
Step Three: $\quad -8y - 30 = 12$
Step Four: $\quad \underline{+ 30 = +30}$
Step Five: $\quad \dfrac{-8y}{-8} = \dfrac{42}{-8}$
Step Six: $\quad y = -5.25$

28. Ed's dad is 15 years older than twice Ed's age. If the sum of their ages is 90, what are their ages?

29. If Line p passes through the points (6, 3) and (−7, −5), determine the slope of the line that would be perpendicular to Line p.

30. Line Segments RS and VW are parallel. They are translated 5 units down and 1 unit to the right. They are then reflected across the x-axis and dilated from Point R using a scale factor of 5. Which of the following statements must be true? Select all that apply.

- ☐ A. Line Segment RS and image R'S' are congruent.
- ☐ B. Line Segments R'S' and V'W' are parallel.
- ☐ C. Line Segments RS and V'W' are parallel.
- ☐ D. Line Segments RS and VW are perpendicular to Line Segments R'S' and V'W'.
- ☐ E. Line Segments RS and VW are one-fifth the size of Line Segments R'S' and V'W'.

Performance Task

Directions: One of the concepts that you learned this year focused on your understanding of equations and the relationships between equations and their graphs. Answer the following series of questions, which will demonstrate your understanding of this concept. Read each question carefully. Be sure to answer each question completely.

1. Determine the slope of the linear function represented by the table below.

x	4	−8	−16	48
y	−3	6	12	−36

2. Write the equation of the line represented by the data in this table.

3. Write an equation for a line that will intersect the line determined in Question 2. How do you know this line will intersect the first line?

4. Which of the following statements is false about the equations for the two lines determined in Question 2 and Question 3?

   ○ A. The point of intersection is a solution to each of the equations.
   ○ B. The equations are parallel.
   ○ C. The equations have one solution in common, called the solution of the system.
   ○ D. Each of the equations has an infinite number of solutions that are not common to the other.

5. A. Graph the equations from Question 2 and from Question 3.

   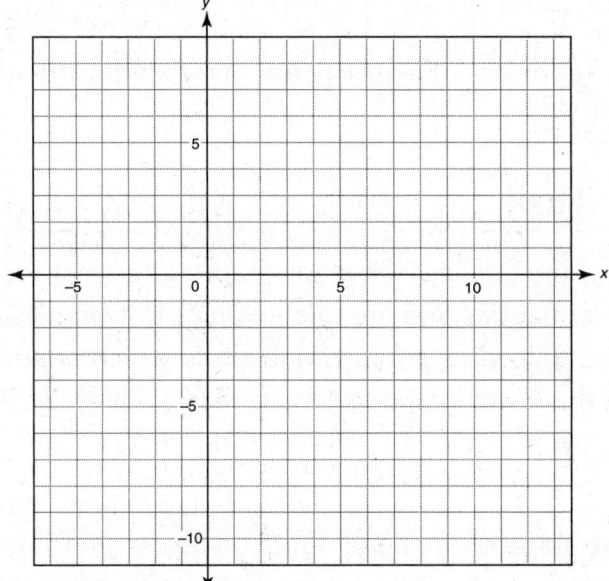

   B. Write an equation for a third line that will form a right triangle when its graph intersects the lines graphed from the equations from Question 2 and Question 3.

   C. Justify mathematically how you know that a right triangle will be formed by the three equations.

6. Deb says that any system of three equations will form a triangle. Is she correct? Explain why or why not.

(Answers are on page 335.)

Answers Explained for Chapters 1-8

Chapter 1: Functions and Proportional Relationships

Identifying Functions—Independent Practice (pages 21-22)

1. **(B)** and **(D)** In choice (B), the vertical line test shows that there is only one input that has infinite outputs. In choice (D), the input 2 has two different outputs (5 and 3). In choices (A), (C), and (E), each of the inputs has exactly one output, meaning that they are functions.

2. **(A)**, **(B)**, and **(C)** Each of these three choices has exactly one output for each input. In choice (D), when $x = 4$, there are two possible values for y (2 and -2) that make the equation true. This would give two outputs for the input 4, so this equation does not represent a function. In choice (E), the input, 5, is in two ordered pairs with two different outputs (-2 and 2), so this set of ordered pairs does not represent a function.

3. **(D)** This ordered pair could not be on the graph of this function because it has the same input, -4, which is the x-coordinate, with a different output, 5, which is the y-coordinate, as the given point. Choices (B), (C), and (E) each have different inputs, and these inputs each have a unique output. Note that choice (A) is the same point used in the question.

Linear Functions and Slope—Independent Practice (pages 30-31)

1. A. **Less Than**

   B. **Greater Than**

   C. **Equal To**

   D. **Less Than**

The slope of the line shown in the graph is $\frac{3}{4}$. Using the points on the graph (5, 0) and (1, −3), the slope can be calculated as follows:

$$\text{slope} = \frac{y_2 - y_1}{x_2 - x_1}$$

$$\text{slope} = \frac{0 - (-3)}{5 - 1}$$

$$\text{slope} = \frac{3}{4}$$

A. The slope of this equation is $\frac{5}{8}$, which is less than $\frac{3}{4}$ $\left(\frac{3}{4} = \frac{6}{8}\right)$. Since this equation is in slope-intercept form, $y = mx + b$, the slope is m, which is the coefficient of x.

B. The slope of the linear function represented by this set of ordered pairs is 2. The slope 2 $\left(2 = \frac{8}{4}\right)$ is greater than $\frac{3}{4}$. Using the points (3, 5) and (4, 7), the slope can be calculated as follows:

$$\text{slope} = \frac{y_2 - y_1}{x_2 - x_1}$$

$$\text{slope} = \frac{7 - 5}{4 - 3}$$

$$\text{slope} = \frac{2}{1}$$

C. In this situation, the slope is $\frac{3}{4}$, which is equal to the slope of the graph. This slope can be calculated by using the information in the situation as ordered pairs: (4, 3) and (12, 9).

$$\text{slope} = \frac{y_2 - y_1}{x_2 - x_1}$$

$$\text{slope} = \frac{9 - 3}{12 - 4}$$

$$\text{slope} = \frac{6}{8} = \frac{3}{4}$$

D. The slope of the linear function represented by this table is $\frac{1}{2}$ $\left(\frac{1}{2} = \frac{2}{4}\right)$, which is less than $\frac{3}{4}$. This slope can be calculated using two ordered pairs from the table: $(-2, 0)$ and $(6, 4)$.

$$\text{slope} = \frac{y_2 - y_1}{x_2 - x_1}$$

$$\text{slope} = \frac{4 - 0}{6 - (-2)}$$

$$\text{slope} = \frac{4}{8} = \frac{1}{2}$$

Function Analysis—Independent Practice (pages 43-44)

1. **Answers will vary.** A sample graph is given below. The requirements for a correct answer are explained below the graph.

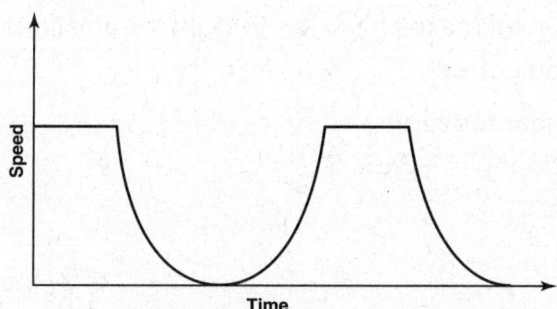

Requirements for a correct answer:
- The graph must start at a speed greater than zero.
- A horizontal line must be used to indicate a consistent speed.
- The graph should then curve down to zero to indicate gradually slowing down and then stopping.
- Some time passes so there should be a horizontal line at zero speed.
- The graph should then curve up to reach the same consistent speed as at the start of his journey.
- A horizontal line must be used to indicate a consistent speed.
- The graph should then curve down to zero to indicate gradually slowing down and then stopping.

2. **Answers will vary.** The requirements for a correct answer for A–F are explained below.

   A. Increasing linear function
      Sample equation: $y = 2x - 1$
      Sample graph:

      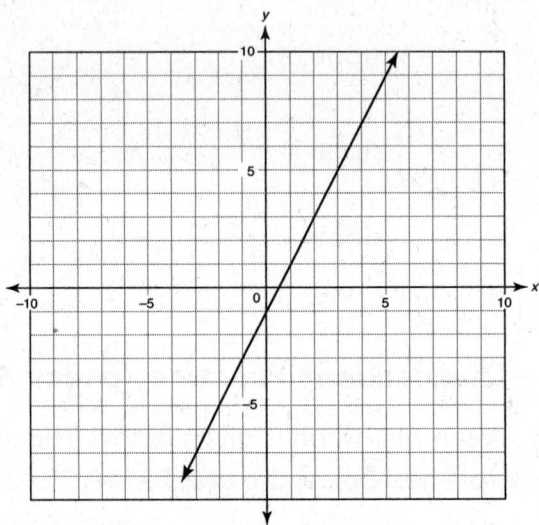

   Any linear graph, that increases from left to right, or any linear equation with a positive slope would be correct.

   B. Decreasing linear function
      Sample equation: $y = -3x + 5$
      Sample graph:

      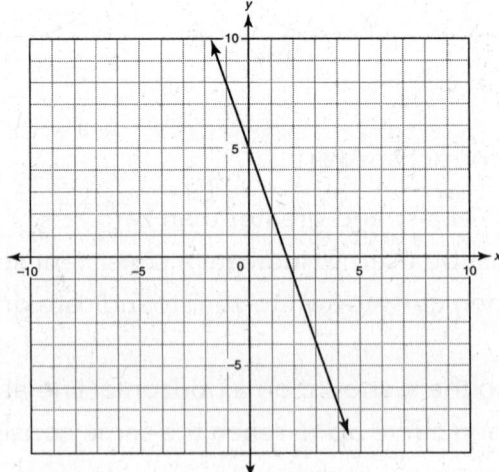

   Any linear graph, that decreases from left to right, or any linear equation with a negative slope would be correct.

C. Increasing nonlinear function

Sample graphs:

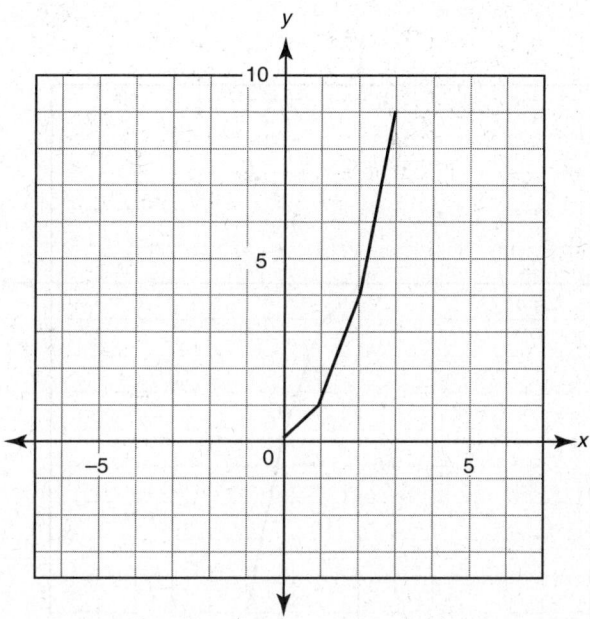

or

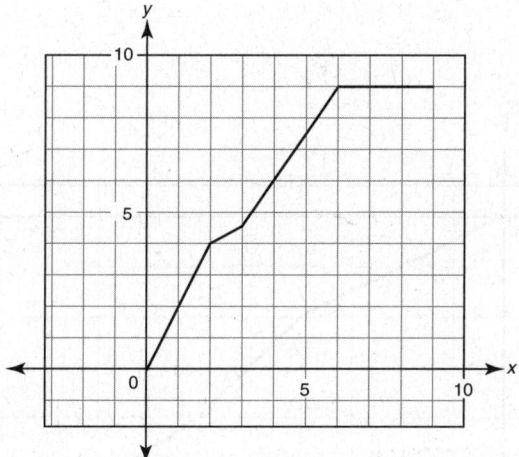

The graph must include multiple parts of linear or curved functions for which the y-values increase or remain constant as the x-values increase.

D. Decreasing nonlinear function

Sample graphs:

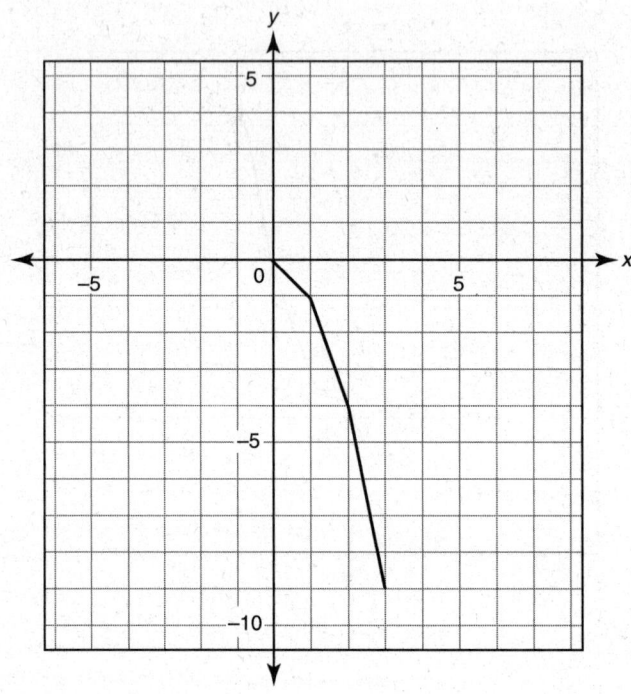

or

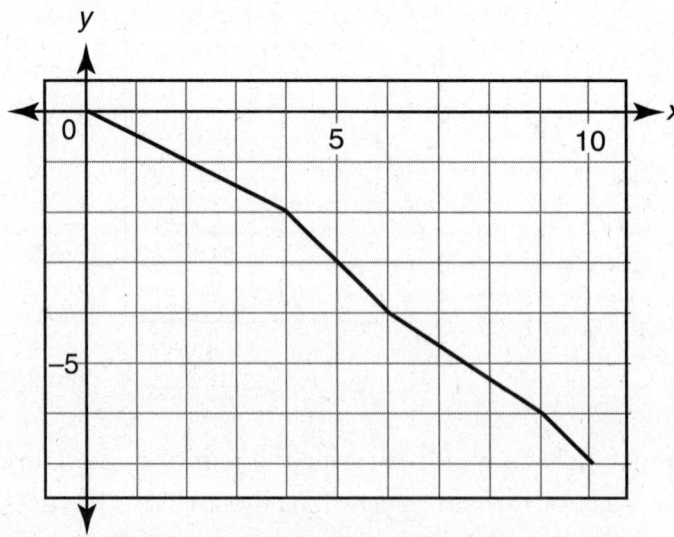

The graph must include multiple parts of linear or curved functions for which the y-values decrease or remain constant as the x-values increase.

Answers Explained for Chapters 1–8 • 259

E. Linear function that neither increases nor decreases

Sample equation: $y = 3$

Sample graph:

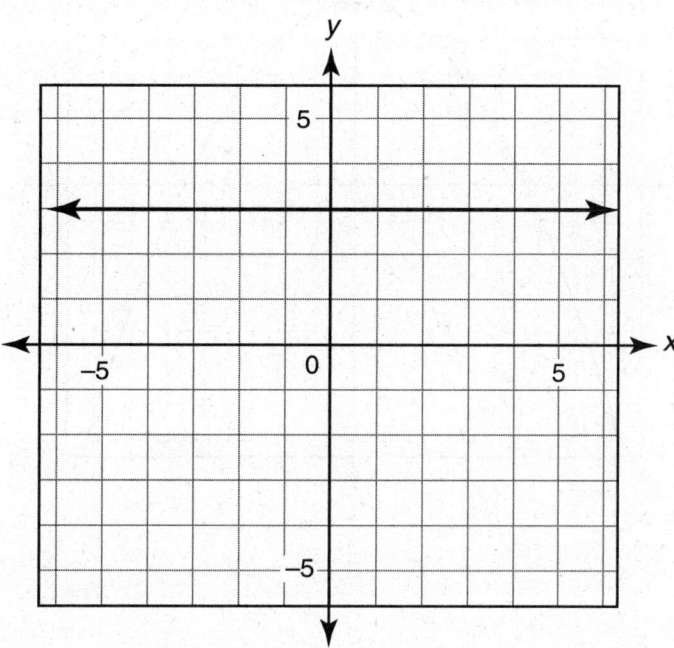

Any graph that is a horizontal line or any linear equation with zero slope would be correct.

F. Increasing and decreasing nonlinear function

Sample equation: $y = |x|$

Sample graphs:

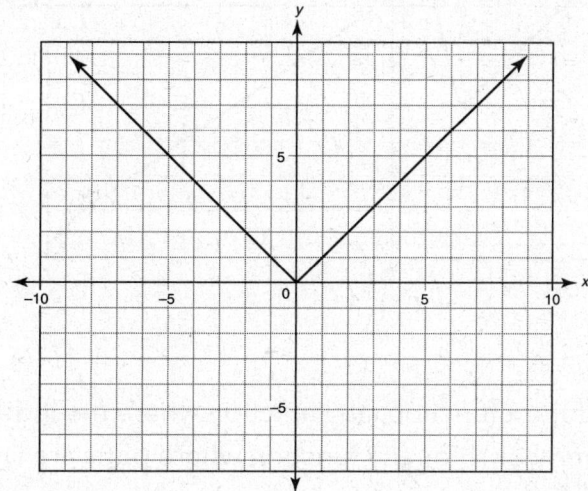

or

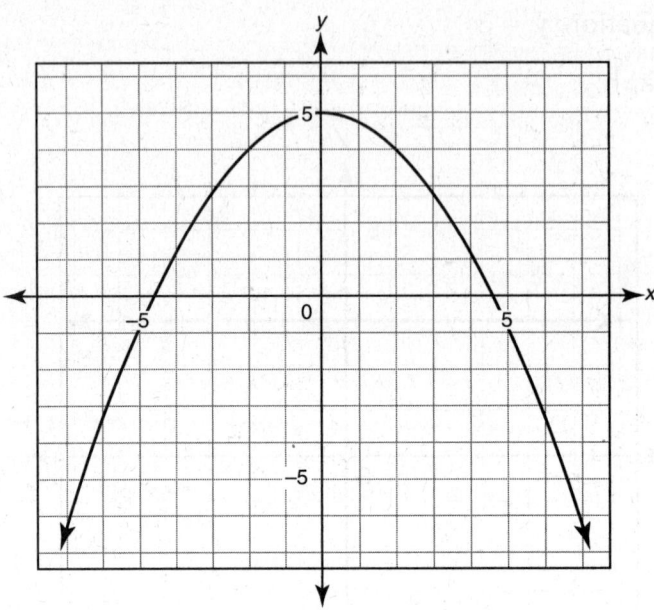

or

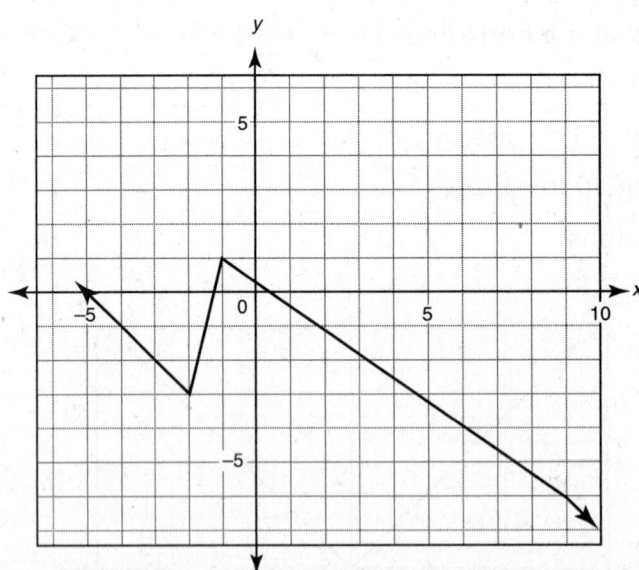

The absolute value of the x function, any function where the independent variable (x) has an exponent other than 1, or any function where parts are linear but not a single line would be correct.

3. **Answers will vary.** The requirements for a correct answer are explained below.

The equation $y = -\frac{4}{5}x + 1$ is in slope-intercept form, $y = mx + b$. The slope is $-\frac{4}{5}$, which is the m value, and the y-intercept is 1.

A. Sample: $y = -\frac{4}{5}x + 2$. Any linear equation with a slope of $-\frac{4}{5}$ and a y-intercept other than 1 would be a correct response. Parallel lines have the same slope but different y-intercepts.

B. Sample: $y = \frac{5}{4}x + 9$. Any linear equation with a slope of $\frac{5}{4}$ and any value for a y-intercept, or no y-intercept listed, would be a correct response. Perpendicular lines have slopes that are opposite reciprocals.

C. Sample: $y = 2x + 3$. Any linear equation with a slope other than $-\frac{4}{5}$, or its opposite reciprocal $\frac{5}{4}$, and any value for a y-intercept (including zero) would be a correct response. Any line with a slope other than $-\frac{4}{5}$, or its opposite reciprocal $\frac{5}{4}$, will intersect, but not be perpendicular.

D. Sample: $y = 3x - 2$. For the slope to be steeper, the slope would need to have a larger absolute value than $\frac{4}{5}$ (which is the absolute value of the slope $-\frac{4}{5}$ from the equation $y = -\frac{4}{5}x + 1$). An equation with a slope greater than $\frac{4}{5}$, and any value for a y-intercept or no y-intercept listed at all, would be a correct response. In this sample equation, the slope is 3.

E. Sample: $y = -\frac{1}{2}x + 3$. For the slope to be less steep, the slope would need to have a smaller absolute value than $\frac{4}{5}$ (which is the absolute value of the slope $-\frac{4}{5}$ from the equation $y = -\frac{4}{5}x + 1$). In this sample equation, the slope is $-\frac{1}{2}$, which has an absolute value of $\frac{1}{2}$.

F. Sample: $y = 2$. Any linear equation with a slope of zero would be a correct response. An equation with a slope of zero would result in a horizontal line. In this sample linear equation, since a slope of zero would mean that 0 is the coefficient of x, by multiplying x by 0, x is eliminated from the equation, leaving only the y-intercept.

SBAC Challenge Questions (pages 46–47)

1. **Dale is correct (the cost of admission is a function of the age of the customer)**

    Using function notation, the cost of admission equals f (the age of the customer). The age of the customer represents the independent variable x (input), and the cost of admission is the dependent variable y (output). The cost of admission *depends* on the customer's age.

    For example, if the input is any value less than the age of 12, the output will be $8. If the input is any value between the ages of 12 and 60, the output will be $12. If the input is any age greater than 60, the output will be $10. There will be no other output for these values, so each input has exactly one output.

    The customer's age cannot be a function of the cost of admission as Patti suggests. Using function notation, the age of the customer does not equal f (cost of admission). The customer's age does not depend on the price of admission. If the input is the cost of admission, there will be multiple outputs for age.

    For example, if the input is $8, the output could be 11 years of age or 8 years of age. If the input is $12, the output might be 27 years of age or 40 years of age. By definition, each input must have exactly one output, so Patti's suggestion is not a function.

2. **(A), (B), and (E)** If Elaine adds any one of these three ordered pairs to the set, one of the original ordered pairs will have two y-coordinates for one of the x-coordinates. For example, (2, 9) added to Elaine's set of ordered pairs will give a second output value of 9 to the input 2 whereas the output of input 2 was already established as 6 in the original set. Choices (C) and (D) would maintain this function because each of these ordered pairs has a new input, so there would not be a duplicate input with a second output.

3. **$y = 0.5x - 1$** Begin with the facts that the slope of the original equation is 0.5 and its y-intercept is 4. For the graphs of linear equations to be parallel, they must have the same slope but different y-intercepts. That means that for any linear equation, $y = 0.5x + b$, the slope will be the same.

Next, to meet the criteria for (4, 1) to be a solution, the x- and y-coordinates of the ordered pair must make the equation true. By using the equation frame, $y = 0.5x + b$, and substituting the ordered pair coordinates for x and y in the equation, the frame can be solved for b to finish the equation frame.

$$y = 0.5x + b$$
$$1 = 0.5(4) + b$$
$$1 = 2 + b$$
$$\underline{-2 = -2}$$
$$-1 = b$$

Finally, use the value of b to finish the equation frame. Then, test the ordered pair in the new equation.

$y = 0.5x - 1$ (The equation has the same slope, 0.5, but a different y-intercept, −1. Determine if the ordered pair (4, 1) is a solution to the equation.)

$1 = 0.5(4) - 1$ (Substitute the ordered pair into the new equation.)

$1 = 2 - 1$

$1 = 1$ (The ordered pair (4, 1) is a solution to the new equation.)

The equation $y = 0.5x - 1$ is a linear equation in slope-intercept form that is parallel (has the same slope but a different y-intercept) and has the ordered pair (4, 1) as a solution.

4. **$y = \dfrac{3}{2}x - 10$** Begin with the facts that the slope of the original equation is $-\dfrac{2}{3}$ and its y-intercept is 5. For the graphs of linear equations to be perpendicular, they must have slopes that are opposite reciprocals. In this case, $\dfrac{3}{2}$ is the opposite reciprocal of $-\dfrac{2}{3}$.

Next, to meet the criteria for (6, −1) to be a solution, the *x*- and *y*-coordinates of the ordered pair must make the equation true. By using the equation frame, $y = \frac{3}{2}x + b$, and substituting the ordered pair coordinates for *x* and *y* in the equation, the frame can be solved for *b* to finish the equation frame.

$$y = \frac{3}{2}x + b$$

$$-1 = \frac{3}{2}(6) + b$$

$$-1 = 9 + b$$

$$\underline{-9 = -9}$$

$$-10 = b$$

Finally, use the value of *b* to finish the equation frame. Then, test the ordered pair in the new equation.

$y = \frac{3}{2}x - 10$ (The equation has the opposite reciprocal slope. Determine if the ordered pair (6, −1) is a solution to the equation.)

$-1 = \frac{3}{2}(6) - 10$ (Substitute the ordered pair into the new equation.)

$-1 = 9 - 10$

$-1 = -1$ (The ordered pair (6, −1) is a solution to the new equation.)

The equation $y = \frac{3}{2}x - 10$ is a linear equation in slope-intercept form that is perpendicular (has the opposite reciprocal slope) and has the ordered pair (6, −1) as a solution.

5. **Answers will vary.** A sample answer is worked out below.

Sample Answer: The equation $-5x + y = -17$ is in standard form. It will intersect the graph of $y = 3x - 9$, but not be perpendicular to it. It also has the ordered pair (3, −2) as a solution.

Begin with the facts that the slope of the original equation is 3 and its *y*-intercept is −9. For the graphs of linear equations to intersect, they must have different slopes. This means that any linear equation that meets all three of the following criteria would be a correct response:

- has a slope other than 3 or its opposite reciprocal $\left(-\dfrac{1}{3}\right)$
- is in standard form, $Ax + By = C$
- has $(3, -2)$ as a solution

Choose a slope other than 3 or its opposite reciprocal, $-\dfrac{1}{3}$, such as 5. By using the equation frame $y = 5x + b$, and substituting the ordered pair coordinates for x and y in the equation, the frame can be solved for b to finish the equation frame.

$$y = 5x + b$$
$$-2 = 5(3) + b$$
$$-2 = 15 + b$$
$$\underline{-15 = -15}$$
$$-17 = b$$

Finally, use the value of b to finish the equation frame. Then, test the ordered pair in the new equation.

$y = 5x - 17$ (The equation has the selected slope but needs to change form.)
$\underline{-5x = -5x}$
$-5x + y = -17$ (The equation is now in standard form, $Ax + By = C$. Determine if the ordered pair $(3, -2)$ is a solution to the equation.)

$-5(3) + (-2) = -17$ (Substitute the ordered pair into the new equation.)
$-15 + (-2) = -17$
$-17 = -17$ (The ordered pair $(3, -2)$ is a solution to the new equation.)

The equation $-5x + y = -17$ is a linear equation in standard form that will intersect the graph of the line $y = 3x - 9$ because it has a different slope, 5. (However, these equations will not be perpendicular because the slopes are not opposite reciprocals.) Finally, $-5x + y = -17$ has the ordered pair $(3, -2)$ as a solution.

Chapter 2: Linear Equations in One Variable

Solving Multi-Step Linear Equations—Independent Practice (pages 55–56)

1. **−3**

    $3x + 9x + 3 = \dfrac{1}{2}(6x - 18) + 5x$

    $12x + 3 = 3x - 9 + 5x$ (Simplify.)

    $12x + 3 = 8x - 9$ (Use the Subtraction Property of Equality to subtract $8x$ from both sides.)

    $\underline{-8x \quad\quad = -8x}$

    $4x + 3 = -9$ (Simplify.)

    $\underline{\quad -3 = -3\quad}$ (Use the Subtraction Property of Equality to subtract 3 from both sides.)

    $\dfrac{4x}{4} = \dfrac{-12}{4}$ (Use the Division Property of Equality to divide both sides by 4.)

    $x = -3$

2. A. **Yes**

    B. **No**

    C. **Yes**

    D. **No**

    To determine which equations have the same solution, solve the original equation first.

    $-4x + 5 = 2x + 17$ (Use the Subtraction Property of Equality to subtract $2x$ from both sides.)

    $\underline{-2x \quad\quad = -2x\quad}$

    $-6x + 5 = 17$ (Use the Subtraction Property of Equality to subtract 5 from both sides.)

    $\underline{\quad -5 = -5\quad}$

    $\dfrac{-6x}{-6} = \dfrac{12}{-6}$ (Simplify. Use the Division Property of Equality to divide both sides by −6.)

    $x = -2$ (The solution of the original equation is −2.)

A. **Yes**

$6(x - 3) + 4 = \dfrac{1}{2}(6x - 8) + 8x$ (Simplify both sides of the equation before solving.)

$6x - 18 + 4 = 3x - 4 + 8x$

$6x - 14 = 11x - 4$

$\underline{-11x = -11x}$ (Simplify. Use the Subtraction Property of Equality to subtract $11x$ from both sides.)

$-5x - 14 = -4$

$\underline{+ 14 = +14}$ (Use the Addition Property of Equality to add 14 to both sides.)

$\dfrac{-5x}{-5} = \dfrac{10}{-5}$ (Use the Division Property of Equality to divide both sides by -5.)

$x = -2$ (The solution is -2, which is the same solution as that of the original equation.)

B. **No**

$3x - 5 = 12x + 11$ (Use the Subtraction Property of Equality to subtract $12x$ from both sides.)

$\underline{-12x = -12x}$

$-9x - 5 = 11$ (Use the Addition Property of Equality to add 5 to both sides.)

$\underline{+ 5 = +5}$

$\dfrac{-9x}{-9} = \dfrac{16}{-9}$ (Use the Division Property of Equality to divide both sides by -9.)

$x = \dfrac{-16}{9}$ $\left(\text{The solution is } \dfrac{-16}{9}, \text{ which is not the same solution as that of the original equation.}\right)$

C. **Yes**

$5x + 5 + 9x + 2 = 13x + 5$ (Simplify both sides of the equation before solving.)

$14x + 7 = 13x + 5$ (Use the Subtraction Property of Equality to subtract $13x$ from both sides.)

$\underline{-13x = -13x}$

$x + 7 = 5$ (Use the Subtraction Property of Equality to subtract 7 from both sides.)

$\underline{-7 = -7}$

$x = -2$ (The solution is -2, which is the same solution as that of the original equation.)

D. **No**

$12\left(\dfrac{2}{3}x + \dfrac{3}{4}x = 17\right)$ (Use the Multiplication Property of Equality to multiply the equation by the common denominator to eliminate the fractional coefficients.)

$8x + 9x = 204$ (Simplify.)

$\dfrac{17x}{17} = \dfrac{204}{17}$ (Use the Division Property of Equality to divide both sides by 17.)

$x = 12$ (The solution is 12, which is not the same solution as that of the original equation.)

3. **The charge will be the same for 22 game rentals.**

   Define the variables:

   x = the number of games rented

   $\$2.50x + \$33$ = the total cost for the membership fee plus $2.50 per game rental

   $\$4x$ = the total cost for games at $4 per game rental

   The equation $\$2.50x + \$33 = \$4x$ represents when the two costs will be the same. Solve to determine the number of game rentals that will cost the same amount using either payment method.

   $\$2.50x + \$33 = \$4x$ (Use the Subtraction Property of Equality to subtract $2.50x from both sides.)
   $-\$2.50x \quad\quad = -\$2.50x$

   $\dfrac{\$33}{\$1.50} = \dfrac{\$1.50x}{\$1.50}$ (Use the Division Property of Equality to divide both sides by $1.50.)

   $22 = x$

   The charge will be the same for 22 game rentals.

4. **−8**

   $3x - 2(x + 7) = 3(x - 5) - (x - 9)$ (Simplify both sides of the equation before solving.)
   $3x - 2x - 14 = 3x - 15 - x + 9$

   $x - 14 = 2x - 6$ (Use the Subtraction Property of Equality to subtract $2x$ from both sides.)
   $-2x \quad\quad = -2x$

   $-x - 14 = -6$ (Use the Addition Property of Equality to add 14 to both sides.)
   $+14 = +14$

   $\dfrac{-x}{-1} = \dfrac{8}{-1}$ (Use the Multiplication Property of Equality to divide both sides by -1.)

   $x = -8$

Determining the Number of Solutions to Linear Equations—Independent Practice (page 61)

1. **You should disagree with Ellie.** A solution of $x = 0$ means that x has one solution, and that numerical solution is 0. For an equation to have no solutions, the variables would need to cancel from both sides of the equation, and the remaining constants on either side of the equal sign would not make a true statement. Think of $3 = 5$ as an example. In this case, since $3 \neq 5$, the variables canceled, but the constants on either side of the equal sign do not make a true statement. Thus, this example equation would have no solutions.

2. A. **No solutions**
   B. **Infinite solutions**
   C. **One solution**
   D. **One solution**

   A. **No solutions**

   $12 - 2x + 5 = -2x + 7$ (Simplify both sides of the equation before solving.)
   $17 - 2x = -2x + 7$ (Use the Addition Property of Equality to add $2x$ to both sides.)
   $\underline{+2x = +2x}$
   $17 \neq 7$ (The variables canceled. The constants on either side of the equal sign do not make a true statement. Therefore, this equation has no solutions.)

   B. **Infinite solutions**

   $-x + 7 = -(-7 + x)$ (Simplify both sides of the equation before solving.)
   $-x + 7 = 7 - x$ (Use the Addition Property of Equality to add x to both sides.)
   $\underline{+x \quad = \quad +x}$
   $7 = 7$ (The variables canceled. The constants on either side of the equal sign make a true statement. Therefore, this equation has infinite solutions.)

   C. **One solution**

   $x - 2x = -5x + 4 + 2x$ (Simplify both sides of the equation before solving.)
   $-x = -3x + 4$ (Use the Addition Property of Equality to add $3x$ to both sides.)
   $\underline{+3x = +3x}$
   $\dfrac{2x}{2} = \dfrac{4}{2}$ (Use the Division Property of Equality to divide both sides by 2.)
   $x = 2$ (The variable is equal to 2. This equation has one solution.)

D. **One solution**

$6x + 3x - 5 = 6(3x - 2) + 1$ (Simplify both sides of the equation before solving.)

$9x - 5 = 18x - 12 + 1$

$9x - 5 = 18x - 11$ (Use the Subtraction Property of Equality to subtract 18x from both sides.)

$\underline{-18x = -18x}$

$-9x - 5 = -11$ (Use the Addition Property of Equality to add 5 to both sides.)

$\underline{+5 = +5}$

$\dfrac{-9x}{-9} = \dfrac{-6}{-9}$ (Use the Division Property of Equality to divide both sides by −9.)

$x = \dfrac{2}{3}$ $\left(\text{The variable is equal to } \dfrac{2}{3}. \text{ This equation has one solution.}\right)$

SBAC Challenge Questions (page 62)

1. **25 feet**

    Define the variables:

    x = the length of the base of the triangle

    $3x - 5$ = the length of each of the congruent sides

    $x + 2(3x - 5) = 60$ represents the perimeter of the isosceles triangle

    Solve to find the length of the base.

    $x + 2(3x - 5) = 60$ (Simplify both sides of the equation before solving.)

    $x + 6x - 10 = 60$

    $7x - 10 = 60$ (Use the Addition Property of Equality to add 10 to both sides.)

    $\underline{+10 = +10}$

    $\dfrac{7x}{7} = \dfrac{70}{7}$ (Use the Division Property of Equality to divide both sides by 7.)

    $x = 10$ (The solution is 10. The base is 10 feet.)

    $3x - 5 = 3(10) - 5 = 25$ (The congruent sides are 25 feet each.)

    The length of each congruent side is 25 feet.

2. **The width of the first painting is 36 inches. The length of the first painting is 138 inches. The width of the second painting is 66 inches. The length of the second painting is 108 inches.**

   Define the variables:

   $$x = \text{the width of the first painting}$$
   $$4x - 6 = \text{the length of the first painting}$$
   $$x + 30 = \text{the width of the second painting}$$
   $$3x = \text{the length of the second painting}$$

   The perimeter of the first painting is $2(x) + 2(4x - 6)$

   The perimeter of the second painting is $2(x + 30) + 2(3x)$

   $2(x) + 2(4x - 6) = 2(x + 30) + 2(3x)$ represents the perimeters of the two paintings as equal

$2(x) + 2(4x - 6) = 2(x + 30) + 2(3x)$	(Simplify both sides of the equation before solving.)
$2x + 8x - 12 = 2x + 60 + 6x$	
$10x - 12 = 8x + 60$	(Use the Subtraction Property of Equality to subtract $8x$ from both sides.)
$\underline{-8x \qquad = -8x}$	
$2x - 12 = 60$	(Use the Addition Property of Equality to add 12 to both sides.)
$\underline{+12 = +12}$	
$\dfrac{2x}{2} = \dfrac{72}{2}$	(Use the Division Property of Equality to divide both sides by 2.)
$x = 36$	(The solution is 36.)

   $x = $ the width of the first painting $= 36$ inches
   $4x - 6 = $ the length of the first painting $= 138$ inches
   $x + 30 = $ the width of the second painting $= 66$ inches
   $3x = $ the length of the second painting $= 108$ inches

3. **(C)** The first error is in Step Three. On the left side of the equation, $2x$ was subtracted, and, on the right side, $2x$ was added. It should have been added on both sides.

Chapter 3: Systems of Equations

Solving Systems of Equations by Substitution—Independent Practice (page 69)

1. $(8, -7)$

Step One: **Isolate**

$2x + y = 9$ (Isolate y since it already has a coefficient of 1.)

$\underline{-2x \quad\quad = -2x}$ (Use the Subtraction Property of Equality to subtract 2x from both sides.)

$y = -2x + 9$

Step Two: **Substitute**

$3.5x - 4y = 56$ (Substitute the expression $-2x + 9$ for y into the original second equation. When distributing multiplication of a negative, be certain to multiply each term by the negative.)

$3.5x - 4(-2x + 9) = 56$

$3.5x + 8x - 36 = 56$

$11.5x - 36 = 56$ (Use the Addition Property of Equality to add 36 to both sides.)

$\underline{\quad\quad +36 = +36}$

$\dfrac{11.5x}{11.5} = \dfrac{92}{11.5}$ (Use the Division Property of Equality to divide both sides by 11.5.)

$x = 8$ (The result is a numerical value of 8 for x.)

Step Three: **Substitute**

$2x + y = 9$ (Substitute the numerical value 8 for x into the original first equation.)

$2(8) + y = 9$

$16 + y = 9$ (Use the Subtraction Property of Equality to subtract 16 from both sides.)

$\underline{-16 \quad\quad = -16}$

$y = -7$ (The result is a numerical value of -7 for y.)

Step Four: **Solution**

$(8, -7)$ (Use 8 for the x-coordinate and -7 for the y-coordinate of the ordered pair.)

Step Five: **Check**

$3.5x - 4y = 56$ (Substitute the ordered pair (8, −7) into the original second equation to determine if the ordered pair makes the equation true.)

$3.5(8) - 4(-7) = 56$

$28 + 28 = 56$

$56 = 56$ (The statement is true. The ordered pair (8, −7) checks.)

2. **(0, −2)**

Step One: **Isolate**

$y - x = -2$ (Isolate y since it already has a coefficient of 1.)

$\underline{+x = +x}$ (Use the Addition Property of Equality to add x to both sides.)

$y = x - 2$

Step Two: **Substitute**

$4x + 3y = -6$ (Substitute the expression $x - 2$ for y into the original second equation.)

$4x + 3(x - 2) = -6$

$4x + 3x - 6 = -6$

$7x - 6 = -6$ (Use the Addition Property of Equality to add 6 to both sides.)

$\underline{+6 = +6}$

$\dfrac{7x}{7} = \dfrac{0}{7}$ (Use the Division Property of Equality to divide both sides by 7.)

$x = 0$ (The result is a numerical value of 0 for x.)

Step Three: **Substitute**

$y - x = -2$ (Substitute the numerical value 0 for x into the original first equation.)

$y - 0 = -2$

$y = -2$ (The result is a numerical value of −2 for y.)

Step Four: **Solution**

(0, −2)   (Use 0 for the x-coordinate and −2 for the y-coordinate of the ordered pair.)

Step Five: **Check**

$$4x + 3y = -6$$
$$4(0) + 3(-2) = -6$$
$$0 + (-6) = -6$$
$$-6 = -6$$

(Substitute the ordered pair (0, −2) into the original second equation to determine if the ordered pair makes the equation true.)

(The statement is true. The ordered pair (0, −2) checks.)

3. **(A)** and **(C)**

   A. The *y*-coordinate is −2.

Step One: **Isolate**

$$6x + y = 34$$
$$\underline{-6x = -6x}$$
$$y = -6x + 34$$

(Use the Subtraction Property of Equality to subtract $6x$ from both sides to isolate y.)

Step Two: **Substitute**

$$3x - 6y = 30$$
$$3x - 6(-6x + 34) = 30$$
$$3x + 36x - 204 = 30$$
$$39x - 204 = 30$$
$$\underline{+204 = +204}$$
$$\frac{39x}{39} = \frac{234}{39}$$
$$x = 6$$

(Substitute the expression $-6x + 34$ for y into the original second equation. When distributing multiplication of a negative, be certain to multiply each term by the negative.)

(Use the Addition Property of Equality to add 204 to both sides.)

(Use the Division Property of Equality to divide both sides by 39.)

(The result is a numerical value of 6 for x.)

Step Three: **Substitute**

$$6x + y = 34$$
$$6(6) + y = 34$$
$$36 + y = 34$$
$$\underline{-36 = -36}$$
$$y = -2$$

(Substitute the numerical value 6 for x into the original first equation.)

(Use the Subtraction Property of Equality to subtract 36 from both sides.)

(The result is a numerical value of −2 for y.)

Step Four: **Solution**

(6, −2)

(Use 6 for the *x*-coordinate and −2 for the *y*-coordinate of the ordered pair.)

Step Five: **Check**

$3x - 6y = 30$ (Substitute the ordered pair (6, −2) into the original second equation to determine if the ordered pair makes the equation true.)

$3(6) - 6(-2) = 30$

$18 + 12 = 30$

$30 = 30$ (The statement is true. The ordered pair (6, −2) checks.)

The y-coordinate is −2.

B. Neither coordinate is −2.

Step One: **Isolate**

$6x = y + 8$ (Use the Subtraction Property of Equality to subtract 8 from both sides to isolate y.)

$\underline{-8 = -8}$

$6x - 8 = y$

Step Two: **Substitute**

$2y - 4x = 0$ (Substitute the expression $6x - 8$ for y into the original second equation.)

$2(6x - 8) - 4x = 0$

$12x - 16 - 4x = 0$

$8x - 16 = 0$ (Use the Addition Property of Equality to add 16 to both sides.)

$\underline{+16 = +16}$

$\dfrac{8x}{8} = \dfrac{16}{8}$ (Use the Division Property of Equality to divide both sides by 8.)

$x = 2$ (The result is a numerical value of 2 for x.)

Step Three: **Substitute**

$6x = y + 8$ (Substitute the numerical value 2 for x into the original first equation.)

$6(2) = y + 8$

$12 = y + 8$ (Use the Subtraction Property of Equality to subtract 8 from both sides.)

$\underline{-8 = -8}$

$4 = y$ (The result is a numerical value of 4 for y.)

Step Four: **Solution**

(2, 4) (Use 2 for the x-coordinate and 4 for the y-coordinate of the ordered pair.)

Step Five: Check

$2y - 4x = 0$ (Substitute the ordered pair (2, 4) into the original second equation to determine if the ordered pair makes the equation true.)
$2(4) - 4(2) = 0$
$8 - 8 = 0$
$0 = 0$ (The statement is true. The ordered pair (2, 4) checks.)

Neither coordinate is −2.

C. The x-coordinate is −2.

Step One: Isolate

$-4x + y = 12.5$ (Use the Addition Property of Equality to add $4x$ to both sides to isolate y.)
$\underline{+4x \quad = +4x}$
$y = 4x + 12.5$

Step Two: Substitute

$2y = 0.5x + 10$ (Substitute the expression $4x + 12.5$ for y into the original second equation.)
$2(4x + 12.5) = 0.5x + 10$
$8x + 25 = 0.5x + 10$ (Use the Subtraction Property of Equality to subtract $0.5x$ from both sides.)
$\underline{-0.5x \quad\quad = -0.5x}$
$7.5x + 25 = 10$ (Use the Subtraction Property of Equality to subtract 25 from both sides.)
$\underline{\quad\quad -25 = -25}$
$\dfrac{7.5x}{7.5} = \dfrac{-15}{7.5}$ (Use the Division Property of Equality to divide both sides by 7.5.)
$x = -2$ (The result is a numerical value of −2 for x.)

Step Three: Substitute

$-4x + y = 12.5$ (Substitute the numerical value −2 for x into the original first equation.)
$-4(-2) + y = 12.5$
$8 + y = 12.5$ (Use the Subtraction Property of Equality to subtract 8 from both sides.)
$\underline{-8 \quad\quad = -8}$
$y = 4.5$ (The result is a numerical value of 4.5 for y.)

Step Four: Solution

$(-2, 4.5)$ (Use −2 for the x-coordinate and 4.5 for the y-coordinate of the ordered pair.)

Step Five: **Check**

$2y = 0.5x + 10$ (Substitute the ordered pair $(-2, 4.5)$ into the original second equation to determine if the ordered pair makes the equation true.)

$2(4.5) = 0.5(-2) + 10$

$9 = -1 + 10$

$9 = 9$ (The statement is true. The ordered pair $(-2, 4.5)$ checks.)

The x-coordinate is -2.

Solving Systems of Equations by Elimination—Independent Practice (page 74)

1. **(−1, 7)**

Step One: **Multiply**

$7(3x + 5y = 32) = 21x + 35y = 224$ (Multiply the first equation by 7 and the second equation by 3 to create opposite coefficients for x.)

$3(-7x - 8y = -49) = -21x - 24y = -147$

Step Two: **Solve**

$21x + 35y = 224$

$+ \; -21x - 24y = -147$ (Combine the equations to eliminate the x-terms.)

$\dfrac{11y}{11} = \dfrac{77}{11}$ (Use the Division Property of Equality to divide both sides by 11.)

$y = 7$ (The result is a numerical value of 7 for y.)

Step Three: **Substitute**

$3x + 5y = 32$ (Substitute 7 for y into the original first equation.)

$3x + 5(7) = 32$

$3x + 35 = 32$ (Use the Subtraction Property of Equality to subtract 35 from both sides.)

$\underline{-35 = -35}$

$\dfrac{3x}{3} = \dfrac{-3}{3}$ (Use the Division Property of Equality to divide both sides by 3.)

$x = -1$ (The result is a numerical value of -1 for x.)

Step Four: **Solution**

$(-1, 7)$ (Use -1 for the x-coordinate and 7 for the y-coordinate of the ordered pair.)

Step Five: **Check**

$$-7x - 8y = -49$$
$$-7(-1) - 8(7) = -49$$
$$7 - 56 = -49$$
$$-49 = -49$$

(Substitute the ordered pair $(-1, 7)$ into the original second equation to determine if the ordered pair makes the equation true.)

(The statement is true. The ordered pair $(-1, 7)$ checks.)

2. **(4, −6)**

Step One: **Multiply**

$$3(2x + 5y = -22) = 6x + 15y = -66$$
$$-5(10x + 3y = 22) = -50x - 15y = -110$$

(Multiply the first equation by 3 and the second equation by -5 to create opposite coefficients for y.)

Step Two: **Solve**

$$6x + 15y = -66$$
$$+\ -50x - 15y = -110$$

$$\frac{-44x}{-44} = \frac{-176}{-44}$$

$$x = 4$$

(Combine the equations to eliminate the y-terms.)

(Use the Division Property of Equality to divide both sides by -44.)

(The result is a numerical value of 4 for x.)

Step Three: **Substitute**

$$2x + 5y = -22$$
$$2(4) + 5y = -22$$
$$8 + 5y = -22$$
$$\underline{-8 = -8}$$
$$\frac{5y}{5} = \frac{-30}{5}$$
$$y = -6$$

(Substitute 4 for x into the original first equation.)

(Use the Subtraction Property of Equality to subtract 8 from both sides.)

(Use the Division Property of Equality to divide both sides by 5.)

(The result is a numerical value of -6 for y.)

Step Four: **Solution**

$(4, -6)$

(Use 4 for the x-coordinate and -6 for the y-coordinate of the ordered pair.)

Step Five: **Check**

$$10x + 3y = 22$$
$$10(4) + 3(-6) = 22$$
$$40 + (-18) = 22$$
$$22 = 22$$

(Substitute the ordered pair (4, −6) into the original second equation to determine if the ordered pair makes the equation true.)

(The statement is true. The ordered pair (4, −6) checks.)

3. **(A)**, **(B)**, and **(C)**

   A. The x-coordinate is 1.

Step One: **Multiply**

$$-2x = -15y - 32 \quad \rightarrow \quad -2x + 15y = -32 \quad \rightarrow \quad -2x + 15y = -32$$
$$-7x + 5y = -17 \quad \rightarrow \quad -3(-7x + 5y = -17) \quad \rightarrow \quad 21x - 15y = 51$$

(Transform the first equation to line up the like variable terms for each equation. Multiply the second equation only by −3 to create opposite coefficients for y.)

Step Two: **Solve**

$$-2x + 15y = -32$$
$$+\ 21x - 15y = 51$$

$$\frac{19x}{19} = \frac{19}{19}$$

$$x = 1$$

(Combine the equations to eliminate the y-terms.)

(Use the Division Property of Equality to divide both sides by 19.)

(The result is a numerical value of 1 for x.)

Step Three: **Substitute**

$$-2x = -15y - 32$$
$$-2(1) = -15y - 32$$
$$-2 = -15y - 32$$
$$+\ 32 = \ + 32$$

$$\frac{30}{-15} = \frac{-15y}{-15}$$

$$-2 = y$$

(Substitute 1 for x into the original first equation.)

(Use the Addition Property of Equality to add 32 to both sides.)

(Use the Division Property of Equality to divide both sides by −15.)

(The result is a numerical value of −2 for y.)

Step Four: **Solution**

(1, −2) (Use 1 for the x-coordinate and −2 for the y-coordinate of the ordered pair.)

Step Five: **Check**

$-7x + 5y = -17$ (Substitute the ordered pair (1, −2) into the original second equation to determine if the ordered pair makes the equation true.)
$-7(1) + 5(-2) = -17$
$-7 + (-10) = -17$
$-17 = -17$ (The statement is true. The ordered pair (1, −2) checks.)

The x-coordinate is 1. It is best to completely solve the system to check your work.

B. The y-coordinate is 1.

Step One: **Multiply**

$2x + 5y = 17$ → $2(2x + 5y = 17)$ → $4x + 10y = 34$
$2y − 3x = −16$ → $-5(-3x + 2y = -16)$ → $15x − 10y = 80$

(Multiply the first equation by 2 and the second equation by −5 to create opposite coefficients for y.)

Step Two: **Solve**

$4x + 10y = 34$ (Combine the equations to eliminate the y-terms.)
$+ 15x − 10y = 80$

$\dfrac{19x}{19} = \dfrac{114}{19}$ (Use the Division Property of Equality to divide both sides by 19.)

$x = 6$ (The result is a numerical value of 6 for x.)

Step Three: **Substitute**

$2x + 5y = 17$ (Substitute 6 for x into the original first equation.)
$2(6) + 5y = 17$
$12 + 5y = 17$
$\underline{-12 \quad\quad = -12}$ (Use the Subtraction Property of Equality to subtract 12 from both sides.)

$\dfrac{5y}{5} = \dfrac{5}{5}$ (Use the Division Property of Equality to divide both sides by 5.)

$y = 1$ (The result is a numerical value of 1 for y.)

Step Four: **Solution**

    (6, 1)   (Use 6 for the x-coordinate and 1 for the y-coordinate of the ordered pair.)

Step Five: **Check**

$2y - 3x = -16$ (Substitute the ordered pair (6, 1) into the original second equation to determine if the ordered pair makes the equation true.)

$2(1) - 3(6) = -16$

$2 - 18 = -16$

$-16 = -16$ (The statement is true. The ordered pair (6, 1) checks.)

The y-coordinate is 1. It is best to completely solve the system to check your work.

  C. The x-coordinate is 1.

Step One: **Multiply**

$8(9x + 4y = 29) = 72x + 32y = 232$ (Multiply the first equation by 8 and the second equation by 9 to create opposite coefficients for x.)

$9(-8x + 2y = 2) = -72x + 18y = 18$

Step Two: **Solve**

$72x + 32y = 232$ (Combine the equations to eliminate the x-terms.)

$+\ -72x + 18y = 18$

$\dfrac{50y}{50} = \dfrac{250}{50}$ (Use the Division Property of Equality to divide both sides by 50.)

$y = 5$ (The result is a numerical value of 5 for y.)

Step Three: **Substitute**

$9x + 4y = 29$ (Substitute 5 for y into the original first equation.)

$9x + 4(5) = 29$

$9x + 20 = 29$ (Use the Subtraction Property of Equality to subtract 20 from both sides.)

$\underline{\ -20 = -20\ }$

$\dfrac{9x}{9} = \dfrac{9}{9}$ (Use the Division Property of Equality to divide both sides by 9.)

$x = 1$ (The result is a numerical value of 1 for x.)

Step Four: **Solution**

    (1, 5)   (Use 1 for the x-coordinate and 5 for the y-coordinate of the ordered pair.)

Step Five: **Check**

$$-8x + 2y = 2$$
$$-8(1) + 2(5) = 2$$
$$-8 + 10 = 2$$
$$2 = 2$$

(Substitute the ordered pair (1, 5) into the original second equation to determine if the ordered pair makes the equation true.)

(The statement is true. The ordered pair (1, 5) checks.)

The x-coordinate is 1. It is best to completely solve the system to check your work.

Solving Systems of Equations by Graphing—Independent Practice (page 79)

1. (3, −4)

Step One: **Graph**

Determine the slope and y-intercept for each equation. This is done by transforming each equation into slope-intercept form ($y = mx + b$).

$$-x + 3y = -15 \qquad\qquad 4x + y = 8$$
$$\underline{+x \qquad\quad = +x} \qquad\qquad \underline{-4x \qquad = -4x}$$
$$\frac{3y}{3} = \frac{x-15}{3} \qquad\qquad y = -4x + 8$$
$$y = \frac{1}{3}x - 5$$

The slope = $\frac{1}{3}$; the y-intercept = (0, −5)   The slope = $-\frac{4}{1}$; the y-intercept = (0, 8)

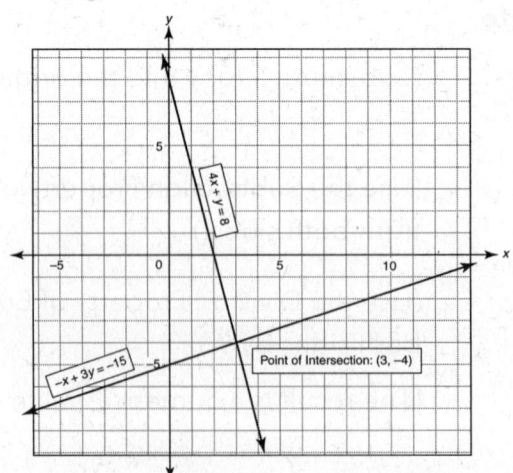

Step Two: **Solution**

Determine the point of intersection. The solution to this system of equations is (3, −4).

Step Three: **Check**

Check the ordered pair (3, −4) algebraically in each equation.

$$-x + 3y = -15 \qquad 4x + y = 8$$
$$-(3) + 3(-4) = -15 \qquad 4(3) + (-4) = 8$$
$$-3 + (-12) = -15 \qquad 12 - 4 = 8$$
$$-15 = -15 \qquad 8 = 8$$

2. **(6, −1)**

Step One: **Graph**

Determine the slope and y-intercept for each equation. This is done by transforming each equation into slope-intercept form ($y = mx + b$).

$$y = -\frac{1}{3}x + 1 \qquad\qquad -x + 3y = -9$$
$$\phantom{y = -\frac{1}{3}x + 1 \qquad\qquad} +x = +x$$
$$\phantom{y = -\frac{1}{3}x + 1 \qquad\qquad} \frac{3y}{3} = \frac{x - 9}{3}$$
$$\phantom{y = -\frac{1}{3}x + 1 \qquad\qquad} y = \frac{1}{3}x - 3$$

The slope $= -\frac{1}{3}$; the y-intercept = (0, 1)   The slope $= \frac{1}{3}$; the y-intercept = (0, −3)

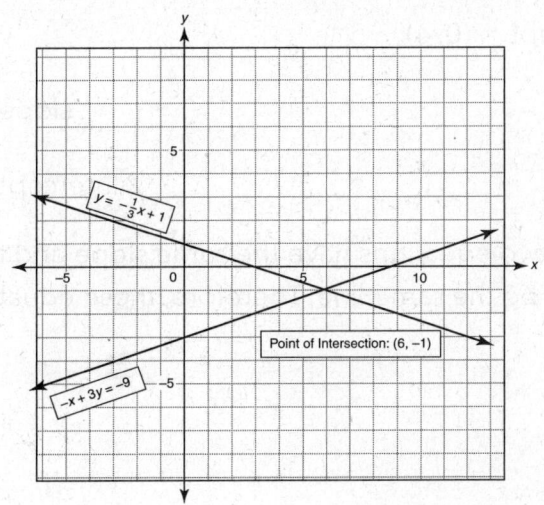

Step Two: **Solution**

Determine the point of intersection. The solution to this system of equations is (6, −1).

Step Three: **Check**

Check the ordered pair (6, −1) algebraically in each equation.

$$y = -\frac{1}{3}x + 1 \qquad\qquad -x + 3y = -9$$

$$-1 = -\frac{1}{3}(6) + 1 \qquad\qquad -(6) + 3(-1) = -9$$

$$-1 = -2 + 1 \qquad\qquad -6 + (-3) = -9$$

$$-1 = -1 \qquad\qquad -9 = -9$$

3. A. **Infinite solutions**
   B. **No solutions**
   C. **One solution**

Determine the slope and y-intercept for each equation. This is done by transforming each equation into slope-intercept form ($y = mx + b$).

A. **Infinite solutions**

$$y = 3x + 4 \qquad\qquad -12x + 4y = 16$$

$$\underline{+12x \qquad\qquad = +12x}$$

$$\text{slope} = \frac{3}{1} \qquad\qquad \frac{4y}{4} = \frac{12x + 16}{4}$$

y-intercept = (0, 4) $\qquad\qquad y = 3x + 4$

$$\text{slope} = \frac{3}{1}$$

y-intercept = (0, 4)

Since these two equations have the same slope and the same y-intercepts, the graphs will be the same line. Therefore, these equations will have infinite solutions.

B. **No solutions**

$$2x + y = 7 \qquad\qquad y = -2x + 3$$
$$\underline{-2x = -2x}$$
$$y = -2x + 7$$
$$\text{slope} = -\frac{2}{1} \qquad\qquad \text{slope} = -\frac{2}{1}$$
$$y\text{-intercept} = (0, 7) \qquad\qquad y\text{-intercept} = (0, 3)$$

Since these two equations have the same slope but different y-intercepts, the graphs will be parallel. Therefore, these equations will have no solutions.

C. **One solution**

$$3x + 4y = 12 \qquad\qquad 2x + 4y = 8$$
$$\underline{-3x = -3x} \qquad\qquad \underline{-2x = -2x}$$
$$\frac{4y}{4} = \frac{-3x + 12}{4} \qquad\qquad \frac{4y}{4} = \frac{-2x + 8}{4}$$
$$y = -\frac{3}{4}x + 3 \qquad\qquad y = -\frac{1}{2}x + 2$$
$$\text{slope} = -\frac{3}{4} \qquad\qquad \text{slope} = -\frac{1}{2}$$
$$y\text{-intercept} = (0, 3) \qquad\qquad y\text{-intercept} = (0, 2)$$

Since these two equations have different slopes (that are not opposite reciprocals), the graphs will intersect at one point. Therefore, these equations will have one solution.

Real-World and Mathematical Problems—Independent Practice (page 88)

1. **They will have the same amount of money in their savings accounts after 3 months.**

    Define the variables:

    x = number of months

    y = the total amount in each savings account

    Sarah's account is represented by $y = \$25x + \$90$ because the total amount in her savings account has an initial value of $90 plus the number of months multiplied by $25 saved per month.

    Camber's account is represented by $y = \$15x + \$120$ because her initial value is $120 plus the number of months multiplied by $15 saved per month.

Step One: **Graph**

Determine the slope and *y*-intercept for each equation. This is done by recognizing that each equation is in slope-intercept form ($y = mx + b$).

$$y = \$25x + \$90 \qquad\qquad y = \$15x + \$120$$

$$\text{slope} = \frac{25}{1} \qquad\qquad \text{slope} = \frac{15}{1}$$

$$y\text{-intercept} = (0, 90) \qquad\qquad y\text{-intercept} = (0, 120)$$

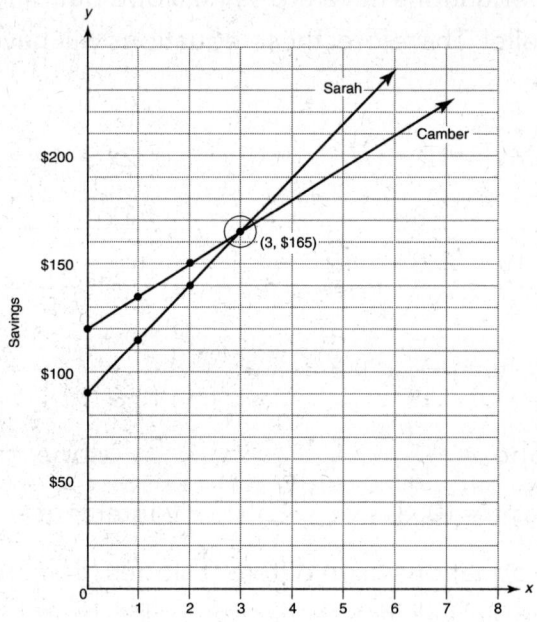

Step Two: **Solution**

Determine the point of intersection. The solution to this system of equations is (3, $165).

Step Three: **Check**

Check the ordered pair (3, $165) algebraically in each equation.

$$y = \$25x + \$90 \qquad\qquad y = \$15x + \$120$$

$$\$165 = \$25(3) + \$90 \qquad\qquad \$165 = \$15(3) + \$120$$

$$\$165 = \$75 + \$90 \qquad\qquad \$165 = \$45 + \$120$$

$$\$165 = \$165 \qquad\qquad \$165 = \$165$$

The ordered pair (3, $165) is the solution to this system of equations. This represents (3 months, total of $165) in each account. It will be three months until they have the same amount of money in their savings accounts.

2. **An admission ticket is $25, and a meal deal is $11.95.**

   Define the variables:

   a = the cost of an admission ticket

   m = the cost of a meal deal

   The Lee family is represented by the equation $5a + 2(5m) = \$244.50$. (Each member of the Lee family received two meal deals.)

   The Nogal family is represented by the equation $3a + 3m = \$110.85$.

   The elimination method is a good choice for this system of equations because neither of the equations has a variable that can easily be isolated.

Step One: **Multiply**

$3(5a + 2(5m) = \$244.50) \quad \rightarrow \quad 15a + 30m = \$733.50$

$-5(3a + 3m = \$110.85) \quad \rightarrow \quad -15a - 15m = -\$554.25$

(Multiply the first equation by 3 and the second equation by -5 to create opposite coefficients for a.)

Step Two: **Solve**

$15a + 30m = \$733.50$ (Combine the equations to eliminate the a-terms.)

$+\ -15a - 15m = -\$554.25$

$\dfrac{15m}{15} = \dfrac{\$179.25}{15}$ (Use the Division Property of Equality to divide both sides by 15.)

$m = \$11.95$ (The result is a numerical value of $11.95 for m.)

Step Three: **Substitute**

$5a + 2(5m) = \$244.50$ (Substitute $11.95 for m in the original first equation.)

$5a + 10(\$11.95) = \$244.50$

$5a + \$119.50 = \$244.50$ (Use the Subtraction Property of Equality to subtract $119.50 from both sides.)

$\underline{-\$119.50 = -\$119.50}$

$\dfrac{5a}{5} = \dfrac{\$125}{5}$ (Use the Division Property of Equality to divide both sides by 5.)

$a = \$25$ (The result is a numerical value of $25 for a.)

Step Four: **Solution**

($25, $11.95) (Use $25 for the *a*-coordinate and $11.95 for the *m*-coordinate of the ordered pair.)

Step Five: **Check**

$$3a + 3m = \$110.85$$
$$3(\$25) + 3(\$11.95) = \$110.85$$
$$\$75 + \$35.85 = \$110.85$$
$$\$110.85 = \$110.85$$

(Substitute the ordered pair ($25, $11.95) into the original second equation to determine if the ordered pair makes the equation true.)

(The statement is true. The ordered pair ($25, $11.95) checks.)

Admission tickets are $25 each, and meal deals are $11.95 each.

3. **Taylor's Toys produced 465 blue pennants.**

   Define the variables:

   Let x = the number of orange pennants; y = the number of blue pennants

   The equation $x + y = 600$ represents the total number of orange and blue pennants.

   The equation $y = 3x + 60$ represents the number of blue pennants in terms of the number of orange pennants.

   Solving this system of equations by substitution is logical in this situation because the second equation already has the variable y isolated.

Step One: **Isolate**

$y = 3x + 60$ (The variable y is already isolated in terms of x.)

Step Two: **Substitute**

$$x + y = 600$$
$$x + 3x + 60 = 600$$
$$4x + 60 = 600$$
$$\underline{-60 = -60}$$
$$\frac{4x}{4} = \frac{540}{4}$$
$$x = 135$$

(Substitute the expression $3x + 60$ for y into the original second equation.)

(Use the Subtraction Property of Equality to subtract 60 from both sides.)

(Use the Division Property of Equality to divide both sides by 4.)

(The result is a numerical value of 135 for x.)

Step Three: **Substitute**

$y = 3x + 60$ (Substitute the numerical value 135 for x into the original first equation.)

$y = 3(135) + 60$

$y = 405 + 60$

$y = 465$ (The result is a numerical value of 465 for y.)

Step Four: **Solution**

(135, 465) (Use 135 for the x-coordinate and 465 for the y-coordinate of the ordered pair.)

Step Five: **Check**

$x + y = 600$ (Substitute the ordered pair (135, 465) into the original second equation to determine if the ordered pair makes the equation true.)

$135 + 465 = 600$

$600 = 600$ (The statement is true. The ordered pair (135, 465) checks.)

The solution to this system of equations is (135, 465). This represents (number of orange pennants, number of blue pennants). Taylor's Toys produced 135 orange pennants and 465 blue pennants.

SBAC Challenge Questions (page 89)

1. **After 5 monthly projects, their total earnings will be the same ($6,500).**

   Define the variables:

   p = the number of monthly projects they will design

   e = total earnings

   The equation $e = \$500p + \$4,000$ will represent Colin's earnings.

   The equation $e = \$1,000p + \$1,500$ will represent Daniel's earnings.

   Graphing would be the most logical method to solve this problem. The equations are already in slope-intercept form.

Step One: Graph

Determine the slope and y-intercept for each equation. This is done by examining each equation in slope-intercept form ($y = mx + b$).

$$e = \$500p + \$4{,}000 \qquad\qquad e = \$1{,}000p + \$1{,}500$$

$$\text{slope} = \frac{\$500}{1} \qquad\qquad \text{slope} = \frac{\$1{,}000}{1}$$

$$y\text{-intercept} = (0, \$4{,}000) \qquad\qquad y\text{-intercept} = (0, \$1{,}500)$$

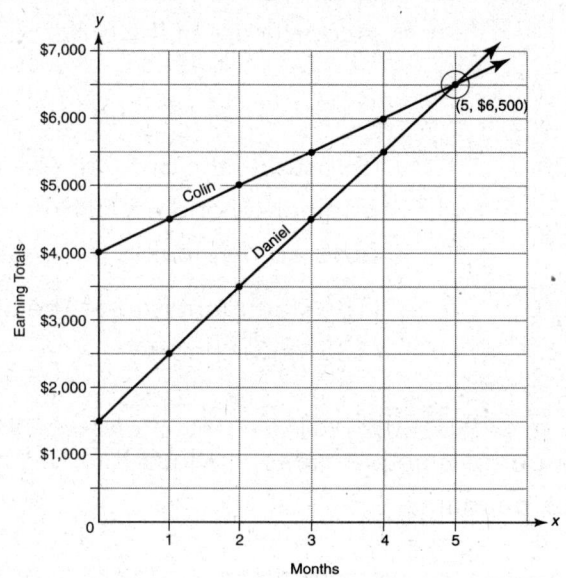

Step Two: Solution

Determine the point of intersection. The solution to this system of equations is (5, $6,500).

Step Three: Check

Check the ordered pair (5, $6,500) algebraically in each equation.

$$e = \$500p + \$4{,}000 \qquad\qquad e = \$1{,}000p + \$1{,}500$$
$$\$6{,}500 = \$500(5) + \$4{,}000 \qquad\qquad \$6{,}500 = \$1{,}000(5) + \$1{,}500$$
$$\$6{,}500 = \$2{,}500 + \$4{,}000 \qquad\qquad \$6{,}500 = \$5{,}000 + \$1{,}500$$
$$\$6{,}500 = \$6{,}500 \qquad\qquad \$6{,}500 = \$6{,}500$$

The ordered pair (5, $6,500) is the solution to this system of equations. After 5 monthly projects, they will have the same total earnings ($6,500).

2. **He threw 539 passes for touchdowns.**

   Define the variables:

   x = the number of passes thrown for interceptions

   y = the number of passes thrown for touchdowns

   The equation $x + y = 790$ represents the total number of passes.

   The equation $y = 2x + 37$ represents the number of passes that were touchdowns.

This system of equations can be solved by substitution. The second equation has one variable already isolated.

<u>Step One:</u> **Isolate**

$y = 2x + 37$ (The variable y is already isolated in terms of x.)

<u>Step Two:</u> **Substitute**

$x + y = 790$ (Substitute the expression $2x + 37$ for y into the original second equation.)

$x + 2x + 37 = 790$

$3x + 37 = 790$ (Use the Subtraction Property of Equality to subtract 37 from both sides.)

$ -37 = -37$

$\dfrac{3x}{3} = \dfrac{753}{3}$ (Use the Division Property of Equality to divide both sides by 3.)

$x = 251$ (The result is a numerical value of 251 for x.)

<u>Step Three:</u> **Substitute**

$y = 2x + 37$ (Substitute the numerical value 251 for x into the original first equation.)

$y = 2(251) + 37$

$y = 502 + 37$

$y = 539$ (The result is a numerical value of 539 for y.)

<u>Step Four:</u> **Solution**

(251, 539)   (Use 251 for the x-coordinate and 539 for the y-coordinate of the ordered pair.)

Step Five: **Check**

$x + y = 790$ (Substitute the ordered pair (251, 539) into the original second equation to determine if the ordered pair makes the equation true.)

$251 + 539 = 790$

$790 = 790$ (The statement is true. The ordered pair (251, 539) checks.)

The solution to this system of equations is (251, 539). This represents (number of passes thrown for interceptions, number of passes thrown for touchdowns). The football player threw 539 passes for touchdowns.

3. **Jamie has 13 dolls on the display shelves.**

   Define the variables:

   j = the number of dolls Jamie has on the display shelves

   d = the number of dolls that Deirdre has on the display shelves

   The equation $j + d = 3(6)$ represents the dolls they display together on the shelves.

   The equation $j = d + 8$ represents the number of dolls that Jamie has on the display shelves in terms of the number of dolls Deirdre has.

The logical method for solving these equations is elimination. The second equation can be transformed to eliminate the variable d when the equations are combined.

Step One: **Multiply**

$j + d = 3(6) \rightarrow j + d = 18$

$j = d + 8 \rightarrow j - d = 8$

(Use the Subtraction Property of Equality to subtract d from both sides of the second equation. This will cancel the variable d when simplified.)

Step Two: **Solve**

$j + d = 18$ (Combine the equations to eliminate the d-terms.)

$+ j - d = 8$

$\dfrac{2j}{2} = \dfrac{26}{2}$ (Use the Division Property of Equality to divide both sides by 2.)

$j = 13$ (The result is a numerical value of 13 for j.)

Step Three: **Substitute**

$j + d = 3(6)$ (Substitute 13 for j in the original first equation.)

$13 + d = 18$
$\underline{-13 = -13}$ (Use the Subtraction Property of Equality to subtract 13 from both sides.)
$d = 5$ (The result is a numerical value of 5 for d.)

Step Four: **Solution**

(5, 13) (Use 5 for the d-coordinate and 13 for the j-coordinate of the ordered pair.)

Step Five: **Check**

$j = d + 8$
$13 = 5 + 8$ (Substitute the ordered pair (5, 13) into the original second equation to determine if the ordered pair makes the equation true.)

$13 = 13$ (The statement is true. The ordered pair (5, 13) checks.)

The solution to this system of equations is (5, 13). The ordered pair represents (number of Deirdre's dolls, number of Jamie's dolls). Therefore, Jamie has 13 dolls displayed on the shelves.

Chapter 4: Real Numbers and the Pythagorean Theorem

Estimating Values of Expressions That Contain Irrational Numbers—Independent Practice (page 100)

1. A. $\dfrac{4}{27}$

$x = 0.148148\ldots$ (Set the repeating decimal equal to x. Write any repeated digits, followed by an ellipsis.)

$1{,}000(x = 0.148148\ldots)$ (Multiply by 10^3 because three digits repeat.)

$1{,}000x = 148.148148\ldots$
$\underline{-(x = 0.148148\ldots)}$ (Subtract the original equation from the transformed equation, eliminating the repeating part of the decimal.)

$\dfrac{999x}{999} = \dfrac{148}{999}$ (Solve the new equation for x.)

$x = \dfrac{148 \div 37}{999 \div 37}$ (Simplify. Listing the factors of 148 (2×74, 4×37) will help you find a common factor.)

$x = \dfrac{4}{27}$

B. $2\frac{2}{3}$

$x = 2.666\ldots$ (Set the repeating decimal equal to x. Write any repeated digits, followed by an ellipsis.)

$10(x = 2.666\ldots)$ (Multiply by 10^1 because only one digit repeats.)

$10x = 26.666\ldots$ (Subtract the original equation from the transformed
$-(x = 2.666\ldots)$ equation, eliminating the repeating part of the decimal.)

$9x = 24$

$\frac{9x}{9} = \frac{24}{9}$ (Solve the new equation for x.)

$x = 2\frac{6 \div 3}{9 \div 3}$ (Simplify.)

$x = 2\frac{2}{3}$

2. The solution is the expressions in order from least to greatest:

$$\left(\sqrt{17}\right)^2 + 1,\ 5\left(\sqrt{13}\right),\ \sqrt[3]{216} + \sqrt{20} + 2\left(\sqrt{18}\right),\ 2(\pi)^2$$

The decimal approximations are as follows:

$\left(\sqrt{17}\right)^2 + 1$	$5\left(\sqrt{13}\right)$	$\sqrt[3]{216} + \sqrt{20} + 2\left(\sqrt{18}\right)$	$2(\pi)^2$
$= 17 + 1$	$\approx 5(3.6055512)$	$\approx 6 + 4.4721359 + 2(4.2426406)$	$\approx 2(3.14)^2$
$= 18$	≈ 18.02776	$\approx 6 + 4.4721359 + 8.4852812$	$\approx 2(9.8596)$
		≈ 18.95742	≈ 19.7192

The Pythagorean Theorem—Independent Practice (pages 114–115)

1. **about 16.5 feet high**

The ladder forms the hypotenuse of a right triangle when the height of the building intersects the ground at a right angle, and the distance to the base of the ladder forms the other leg. Use the Pythagorean theorem to find the missing measure.

$$a^2 + b^2 = c^2$$
$$4^2 + b^2 = 17^2 \quad \text{(Substitute the lengths of the one leg and the hypotenuse.)}$$
$$16 + b^2 = 289 \quad \text{(Use the Subtraction Property of Equality to subtract 16 from}$$
$$\underline{-16 \quad\quad = -16} \quad \text{both sides.)}$$
$$b^2 = 273$$
$$\sqrt{b^2} = \sqrt{273} \quad \text{(Take the square root of each side.)}$$
$$b \approx 16.5 \quad (\sqrt{273} \text{ is irrational. } (16.5)^2 = 272.25, \text{ and } (16.6)^2 = 275.56. \text{ To the nearest whole tenth, } \sqrt{273} \text{ is closer to 16.5.)}$$

2. **about 12 feet of rope**

A right angle is formed by the length of the pole and the ground. The length of rope needed for one edge of the net is the hypotenuse of the right triangle formed. Enough rope is needed for *two* stake ropes. Use the Pythagorean theorem to find the length of one rope first.

$$a^2 + b^2 = c^2$$
$$5^2 + 3^2 = c^2 \quad \text{(Substitute the lengths of the two legs that form the right angle.)}$$
$$25 + 9 = c^2 \quad \text{(Simplify.)}$$
$$34 = c^2$$
$$\sqrt{34} = \sqrt{c^2} \quad \text{(Take the square root of each side.)}$$
$$6 \approx c \quad (\sqrt{34} \text{ is irrational. } 5^2 = 25, \text{ and } 6^2 = 36. \text{ To the nearest whole foot, } \sqrt{34} \text{ is closer to 6.)}$$

Be careful! The problem asks for enough rope for *both* stake ropes, so for two stake ropes, about 12 feet of rope is needed.

3. **The snail crawls about 17.0 inches diagonally across the patio stone.**

Two edges of the square patio stone form a right angle. The diagonal of the square patio stone is the hypotenuse of the right triangle formed. If the area of the square patio stone is 144 square inches, then using the area formula $A = s^2$, it can be determined that one edge of the patio stone is 12 inches long. The Pythagorean theorem can then be used to find the length of the hypotenuse.

$a^2 + b^2 = c^2$

$12^2 + 12^2 = c^2$ (Substitute the lengths of the two legs that form the right angle.)

$144 + 144 = c^2$ (Simplify.)

$288 = c^2$

$\sqrt{288} = \sqrt{c^2}$ (Take the square root of each side.)

$17.0 \approx c$ ($\sqrt{288}$ is irrational. $(16.9)^2 = 285.61$, and $(17.0)^2 = 289$. To the nearest tenth of an inch, $\sqrt{288}$ is closer to 17.0.)

Note: 17.0 is the correct answer, not just 17, because the tenths place must be included as mentioned in the question.

4. **The stem does not need to be trimmed at all. It is shorter than the three-dimensional diagonal, which is about 17.2 inches.**

The box is a rectangular prism. The three-dimensional diagonal is the hypotenuse of the right triangle formed by the diagonal of the rectangular base as one leg and the height of the box as the other leg. Use the Pythagorean theorem to calculate the diagonal of the base of the box, using the length and width as the legs that form the right angle of the rectangular base.

$a^2 + b^2 = c^2$

$15^2 + 6^2 = c^2$ (Substitute the lengths of the two legs that form the right angle.)

$225 + 36 = c^2$ (Simplify.)

$261 = c^2$

$\sqrt{261} = \sqrt{c^2}$ (Take the square root of each side.)

$\sqrt{261} = c$ ($\sqrt{261}$ is irrational. Since it will be squared in the next step, it is not necessary to approximate it.)

Use the Pythagorean theorem to calculate the three-dimensional diagonal of the box with the hypotenuse of the right triangle formed with the diagonal of the rectangular base as one leg and the height of the box as the other leg.

$a^2 + b^2 = c^2$

$(\sqrt{261})^2 + 6^2 = c^2$ (Substitute the lengths of the two legs that form the right angle.)

$261 + 36 = c^2$ (Simplify.)

$297 = c^2$

$\sqrt{297} = \sqrt{c^2}$ (Take the square root of each side.)

$17.2 \approx c$ ($\sqrt{297}$ is irrational. $(17.2)^2 = 295.84$, and $(17.3)^2 = 299.29$. $\sqrt{297}$ is closer to 17.2.)

SBAC Challenge Questions (page 115)

1. A. **The perimeter of the triangle is about 27.2 units.**

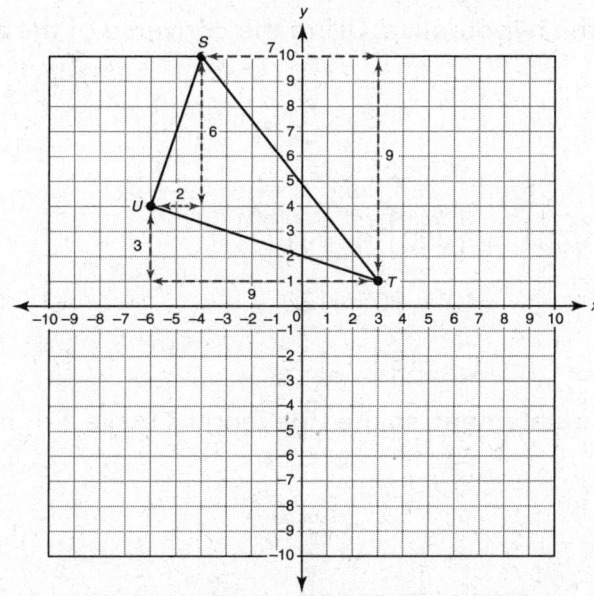

Graph the three ordered pairs. On the graph, create a right triangle using side *ST* as its hypotenuse. Use the vertical and horizontal distances between the endpoints as the lengths of the legs. Use the Pythagorean theorem to determine the length of side *ST*. Repeat this process with sides *TU* and *US* to determine the lengths of the three sides of Triangle *STU*. The perimeter is the sum of the lengths of the three calculated sides of Triangle *STU*.

Side *ST*	Side *TU*	Side *US*
$a^2 + b^2 = c^2$	$a^2 + b^2 = c^2$	$a^2 + b^2 = c^2$
$7^2 + 9^2 = c^2$	$3^2 + 9^2 = c^2$	$2^2 + 6^2 = c^2$
$49 + 81 = c^2$	$9 + 81 = c^2$	$4 + 36 = c^2$
$130 = c^2$	$90 = c^2$	$40 = c^2$
$\sqrt{130} = \sqrt{c^2}$	$\sqrt{90} = \sqrt{c^2}$	$\sqrt{40} = \sqrt{c^2}$
$11.4 \approx c$	$9.5 \approx c$	$6.3 \approx c$

The perimeter is the sum of the lengths of the three sides of the triangle: 11.4 + 9.5 + 6.3 = 27.2.

   B. **The lengths of the sides in order from least to greatest are Side US, Side TU, and Side ST.**

   C. **This triangle is a right triangle based on the converse of the Pythagorean theorem.**

Use the irrational square roots, which are the exact measures of the side lengths, rather than the approximations used to order the side lengths. Side ST is the longest side, so it is the hypotenuse. Using the converse of the Pythagorean theorem:

$$a^2 + b^2 = c^2$$
$$\left(\sqrt{40}\right)^2 + \left(\sqrt{90}\right)^2 = \left(\sqrt{130}\right)^2$$
$$40 + 90 = 130$$
$$130 = 130$$

This results in a true statement, so the side lengths make a right triangle.

2. **(A), (C),** and **(D)**

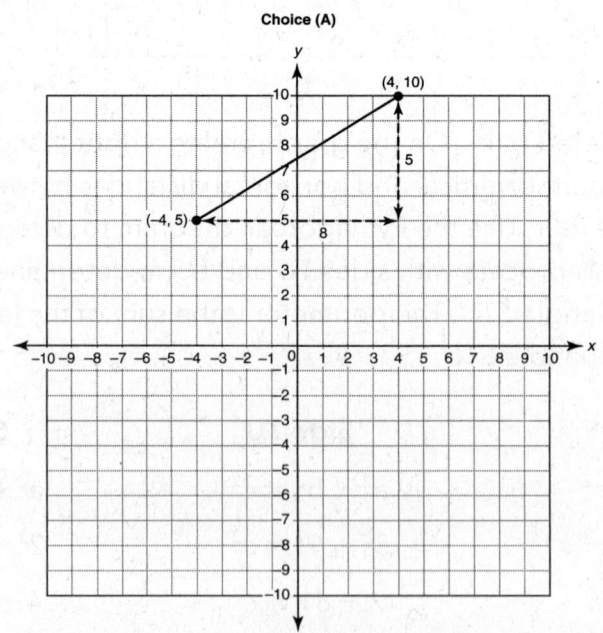

Choice (A)

Choice (B)

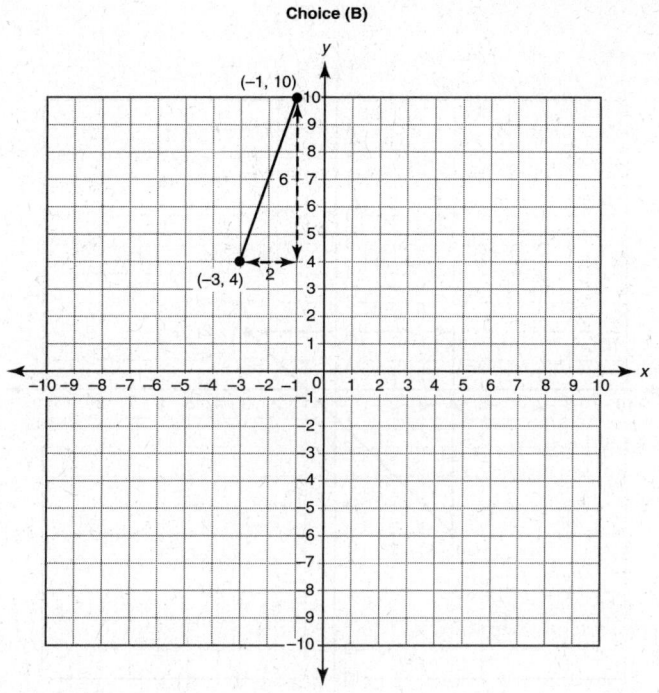

Choice (C)

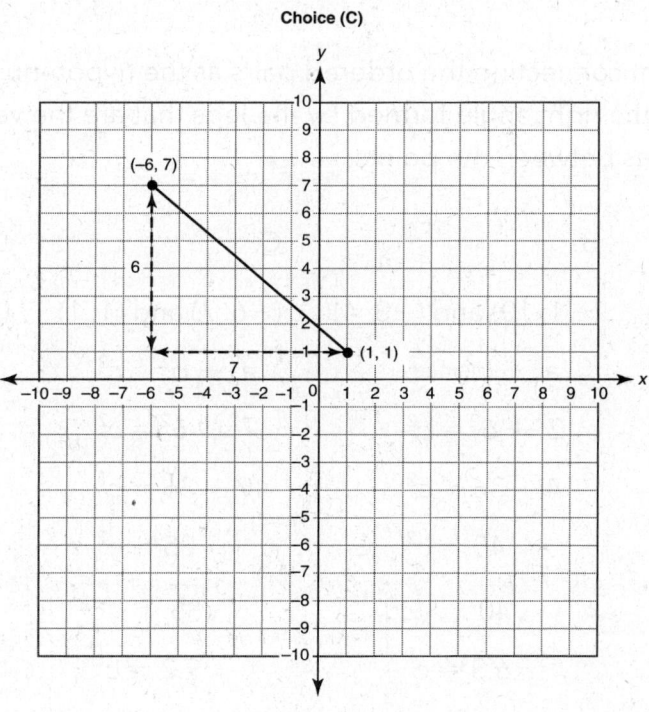

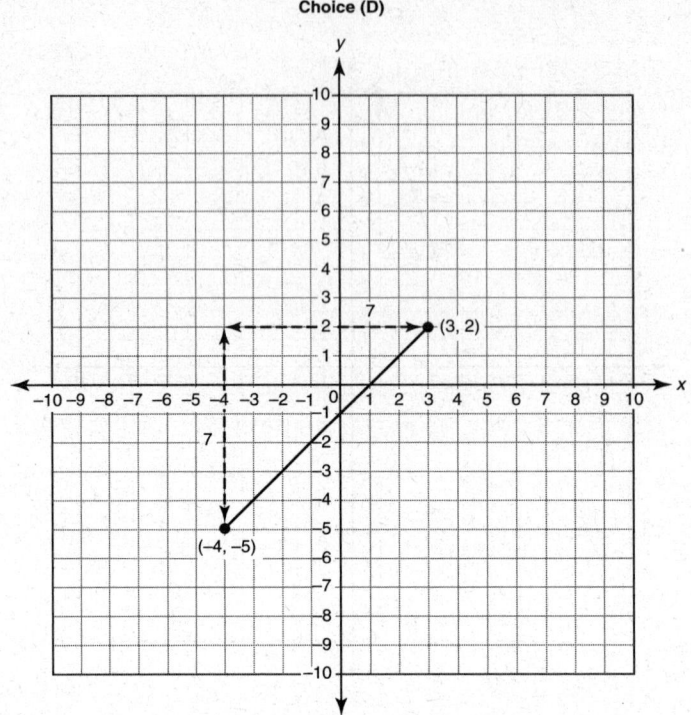

Use the segment connecting the ordered pairs as the hypotenuse of a right triangle opposite the right angle formed by the legs that are the vertical and horizontal distances between the points.

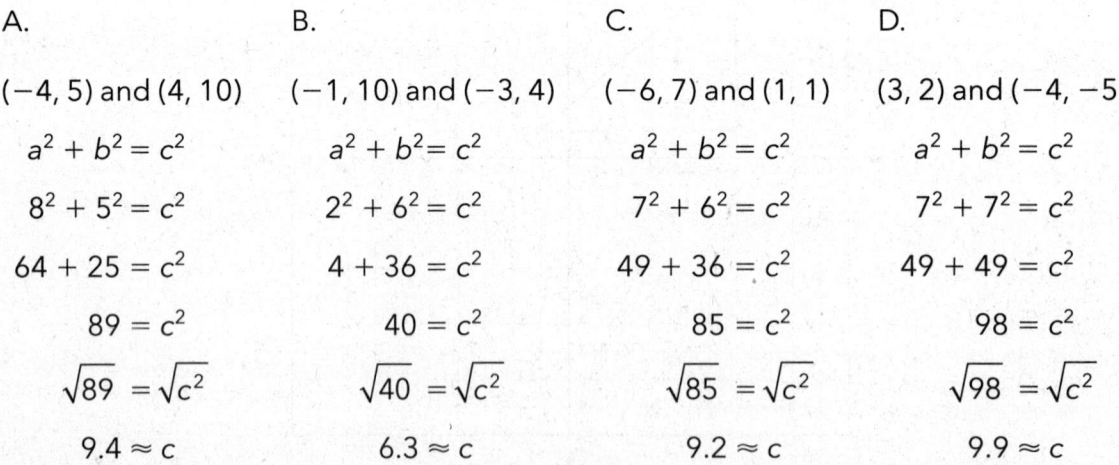

The lengths between 9 and 10 units are choices (A), (C), and (D).

Chapter 5: Geometry—Transformations

Translations—Independent Practice (page 124)

1. **The coordinates of Triangle R'S'T' are R' (−1, 5), S' (3, 2), and T' (−3, 2).**

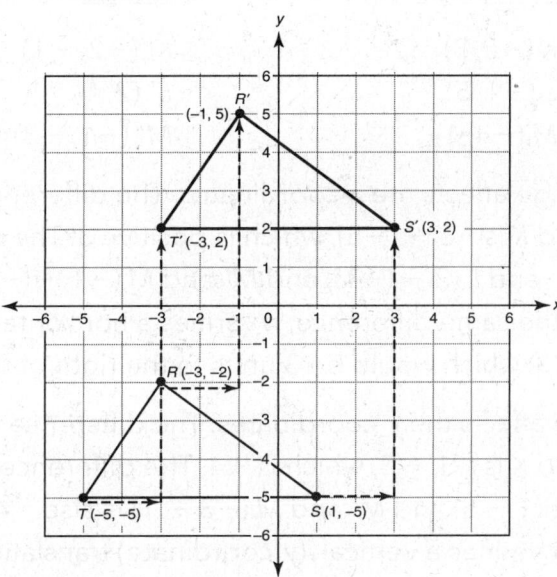

Each vertex was translated to the right 2 units and up 7 units. The alternate notation for this is $(x + 2, y + 7)$.

2. **The endpoints are Y' (−5, 4) and X' (−2, −1).**

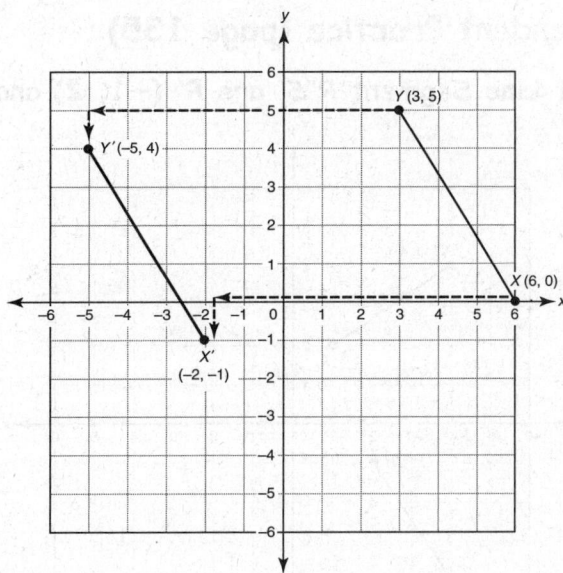

Each endpoint of the pre-image was translated to the left 8 units and down 1 unit. The alternate notation for this is $(x − 8, y − 1)$.

3. **The ordered pair notation is (x + 3, y − 4).**

To determine the translation, calculate the differences in the coordinates for each vertex by subtracting the pre-image coordinates from the image coordinates.

Pre-Image	Image
K (−5, 3)	K' (−2, −1)
L (−1, 5)	L' (2, 1)
M (−4, 1)	M' (−1, −3)

The horizontal change affects the x-coordinates. The difference between the x-coordinates of K' and K is −2 − (−5), which is positive 3. The difference between the x-coordinates of L' and L (2 − (−1)) and M' and M (−1 − (−4)) is also positive 3. Since they all have the same difference, it verifies a horizontal (x-coordinate) translation of positive 3, which would be 3 units to the right of the pre-image.

The vertical change affects the y-coordinates. The difference between the y-coordinates of K' and K is −1 − 3, which is −4. The difference between the y-coordinates L' and L (1 − 5) and M' and M (−3 − 1) is also −4. Since they all have the same difference, it verifies a vertical (y-coordinate) translation of −4, which would be 4 units down from the pre-image.

This means that all image vertices result from the pre-image translated 3 units to the right and 4 units down. This is represented by the ordered pair (x, y) for the pre-image and the ordered pair (x + 3, y − 4) for the image.

Rotations—Independent Practice (page 135)

1. **The endpoints of Line Segment R'S' are R' (−1, 2) and S' (−4, 4).**

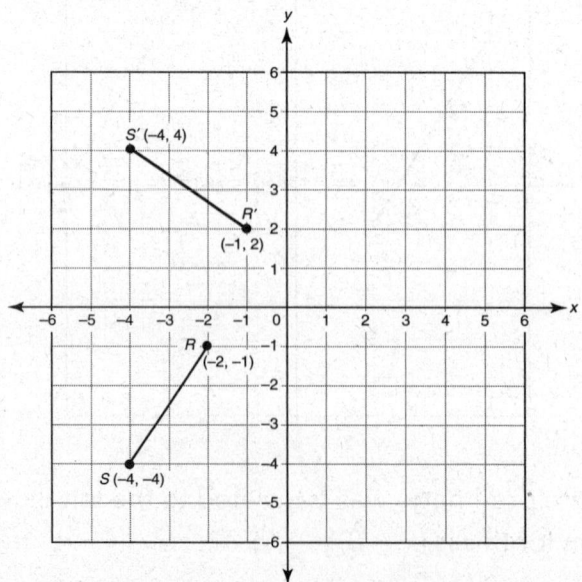

The change of the coordinates R(−2, −1) and S(−4, −4) for a clockwise rotation of 90° around the origin is from (x, y) to (y, −x). The y-coordinate value of the pre-image becomes the x-coordinate value of the image. Then, the opposite of the x-coordinate value from the pre-image becomes the y-coordinate value of the image.

2. **The rotation is 90° counterclockwise around the origin.**

The change for the coordinates J(5, 1), K(1, −3), and L(3, −5) to J'(−1, 5), K'(3, 1), and L'(5, 3) indicates a change from (x, y) to (−y, x). The opposite of the y-coordinate value from the pre-image becomes the x-coordinate value of the image. The x-coordinate value for the pre-image becomes the y-coordinate value for the image. This notation indicates a counterclockwise rotation of 90° around the origin.

Reflections—Independent Practice (page 145)

1. **The vertices are U'(−1, −3), V'(3, 1), and W'(−4, 0).**

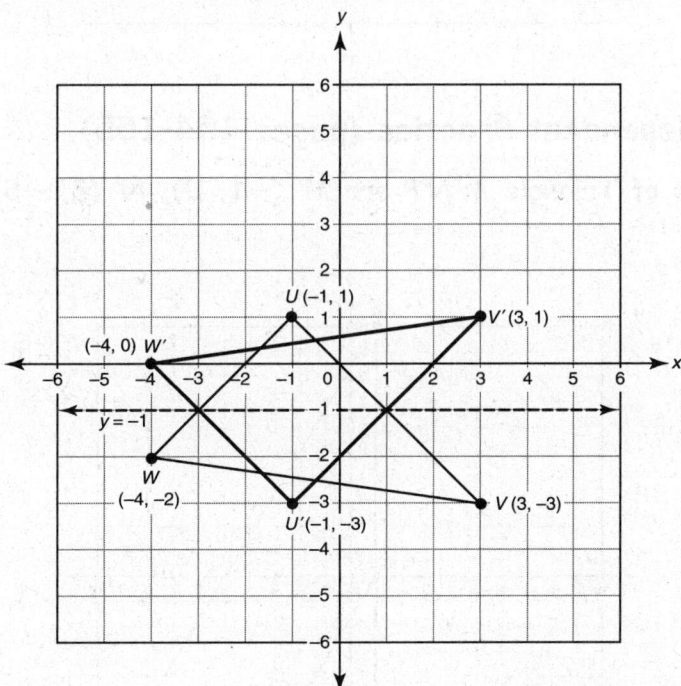

Vertex U is 2 units above y = −1, and its reflection should be 2 units below that line.

Vertex V is 2 units below y = −1, and its reflection should be 2 units above that line.

Vertex W is 1 unit below y = −1, and its reflection should be 1 unit above that line.

2. Image Angle A″B″C″ is a reflection of pre-image Angle ABC across the y-axis to form Angle A′B′C′, which was then reflected across the line y = 3.

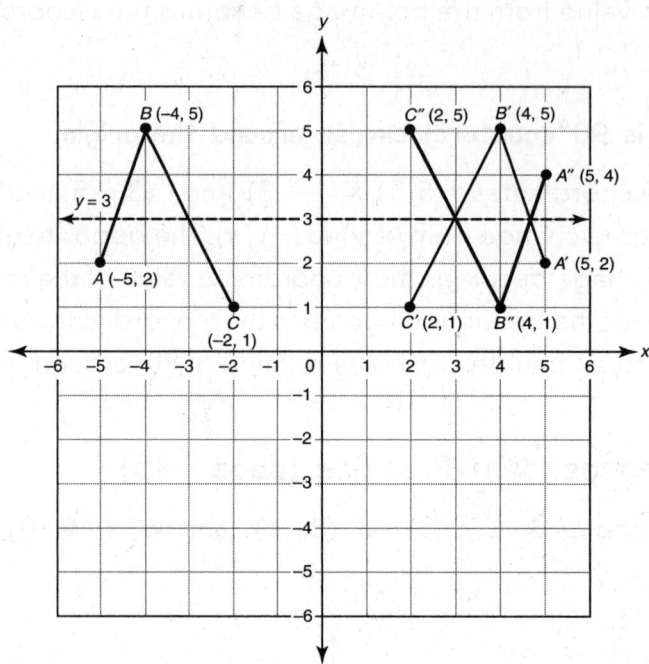

Dilations—Independent Practice (pages 154–155)

1. The vertices of Triangle M′N′P are M′ (−1, 0), N′ (2, −5), and P (−1, −5).

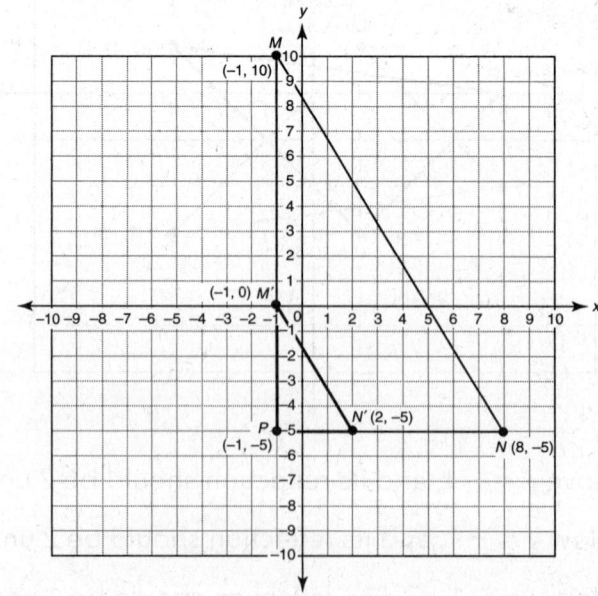

Vertex M had a vertical distance of 15 from Vertex P. Multiplied by $\frac{1}{3}$, M′'s vertical distance would be 5 units up from Vertex P at (−1, 0).

Vertex N had a horizontal distance of 9 from Vertex P. Multiplied by $\frac{1}{3}$, N''s horizontal distance would be 3 units to the right of Vertex P at (2, −5).

Vertex P is in the same location, (−1, −5), for the pre-image and for the image because it is given as the point of dilation.

2. **The vertices of Parallelogram A'B'C'D' are A' (2, 0), B' (8, 0), C' (6, −4), and D' (0, −4).**

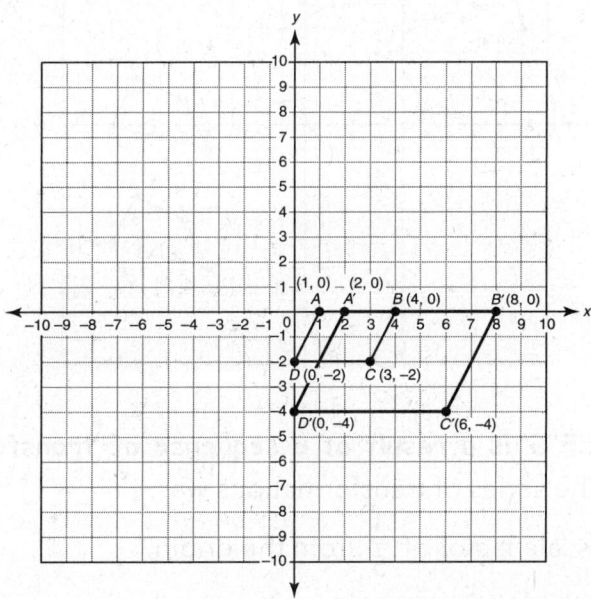

Using the origin as the point of dilation, the scale factor of 2 multiplies each of the pre-image vertex coordinates by 2 to determine the vertices of the image.

Congruence and Similarity—Independent Practice (pages 169-170)

1. **The sequence of transformations was:**

    A. Reflection across the line $x = -4$. Image vertices after reflection:

    $$F' (0, 8), G' (-2, 7), H' (-1, 5), J' (1, 4)$$

    B. Rotation of 90° clockwise around the origin. Image vertices after rotation:

    $$F'' (8, 0), G'' (7, 2), H'' (5, 1), J'' (4, -1)$$

C. Translation down 5 units. Image vertices after translation:

$$F'''(8, -5), G'''(7, -3), H'''(5, -4), J'''(4, -6)$$

Quadrilateral $F'''G'''H'''J'''$ is **congruent** to Quadrilateral $FGHJ$. The transformations preserve the size and the shape and just change the location.

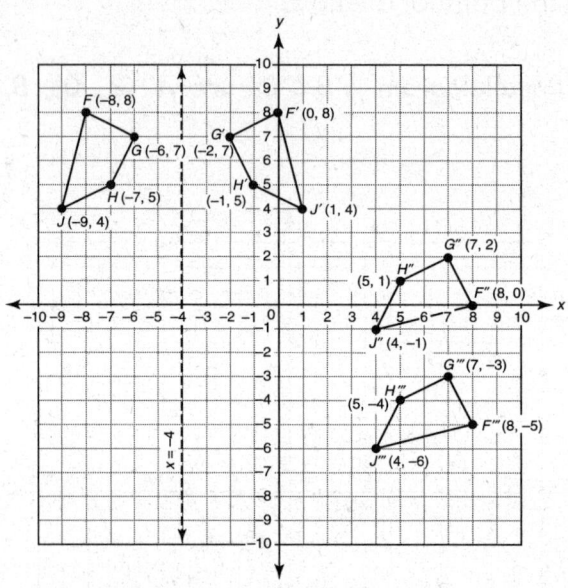

2. **Yes, Triangle $E'F''G''$ is a result of a sequence of transformations to Triangle EFG.** The series of transformations was:

   A. Dilation by a scale factor of $\frac{1}{5}$ from the origin.

   B. Translation to the left 8 units and up 6 units.

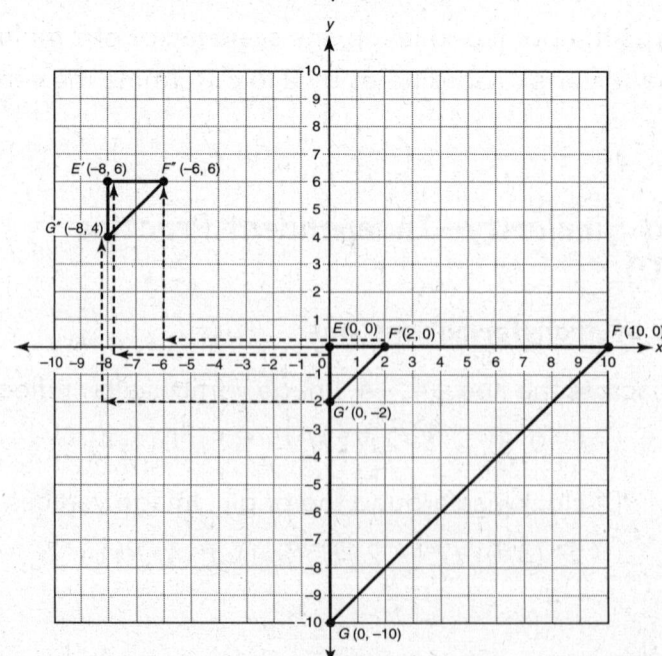

The triangles are **similar** because the dilation creates an image that has congruent angles and sides that are in proportion.

SBAC Challenge Questions (page 171)

1. **The translation that will determine the image is 2 units to the right and 4 units down.**

Pre-Image	**Image**
W (5, 6)	W' (7, 2)
V (−1, −1)	V' (1, −5)

   To determine the translation, calculate the differences in the coordinates for each endpoint by subtracting the pre-image coordinates from the image coordinates.

   The horizontal change affects the x-coordinates. The difference between the x-coordinates of W' and W is 7 − 5, which is 2, and the difference between the x-coordinates of V' and V is 1 − (−1), which is also 2. Since both have the same difference, it verifies a horizontal (x-coordinate) translation of positive 2, which would be 2 units to the right of the pre-image.

   The vertical change affects the y-coordinates. The difference between the y-coordinates of W' and W is 2 − 6, which is −4, and the difference between the y-coordinates of V' and V is −5 − (−1), which is also −4. Since both have the same difference, it verifies a vertical (y-coordinate) translation of −4, which would be 4 units down from the pre-image.

   This means that both image endpoints result from the pre-image translated 2 units to the right and 4 units down. This can be represented by the ordered pair (x, y) for the pre-image and the ordered pair $(x + 2, y - 4)$ for the image.

2. **(B)**, **(D)**, and **(E)**

   Choice (A): The translation and the reflection will only change the location, but the dilation by a scale factor of $\frac{1}{5}$ will result in a smaller figure. The pre-image and the image will be similar, but the scale factor is less than 1, so the image will be a reduction and will have a *smaller* area.

Choice (B): The rotation and the translation will only change the location. The figures will be similar because of the dilation. The dilation by a scale factor of $\frac{3}{2}$ is greater than 1, resulting in an enlargement with a *larger* area.

Choice (C): The rotation and the reflection will only change the location, but the dilation by a scale factor of $\frac{2}{3}$ will result in a smaller figure. The figures will be similar, but the scale factor is less than 1, so the image will be a reduction and will have a *smaller* area.

Choice (D): The translation and the reflection will only change the location. The figures will be similar because of the dilation. The dilation by a scale factor of $\frac{7}{5}$ is greater than 1, resulting in an enlargement with a *larger* area.

Choice (E): The rotation and the translation will only change the location. The figures will be similar because of the dilation. The dilation by a scale factor of 3 is greater than 1, resulting in an enlargement with a *larger* area.

3. **Wendy is correct.**

A clockwise (or counterclockwise) rotation of 180° around the origin will take the vertex of a shape from (x, y) to (−x, −y). This means that the rotation will result in the opposite of the *x*-coordinate and the opposite of the *y*-coordinate.

A reflection across the *x*-axis will result in the opposite *y*-coordinate, while the *x*-coordinate will remain the same. This will result in the vertex of a shape from (x, y) to (x, −y).

Following that with a reflection across the *y*-axis will result in a point with the opposite of the *x*-coordinate, while the *y*-coordinate will remain the same. This will result in the vertex (x, −y) becoming (−x, −y).

Wendy is correct that both transformations will result in the same image.

HELPFUL HINT

Wendy's statement would also be correct if the reflection was across the *y*-axis first, followed by a reflection across the *x*-axis. The result would still be (−x, −y).

Chapter 6: Patterns and Relationships in Data

Scatter Plots and Lines of Best Fit—Independent Practice (pages 181–182)

1. **(A)** Choice (A) is correct because approximately half of the data points are above the line and half are below the line, and the data points are clustered near the line. An outlier appears at (21, 1). Choice (B) is incorrect because, although half of the data points are above the line and half are below the line, the data points are not clustered near the line. Choice (C) is incorrect because the data points are not divided in half, and the data points are not clustered near the line. Choice (D) is incorrect because, although the data points are clustered near the line, all the data points are on the line or are on one side of the line, not split in half by the line.

2. **The equation of the line of best fit is $y = -\dfrac{7}{6}x + 20$.**

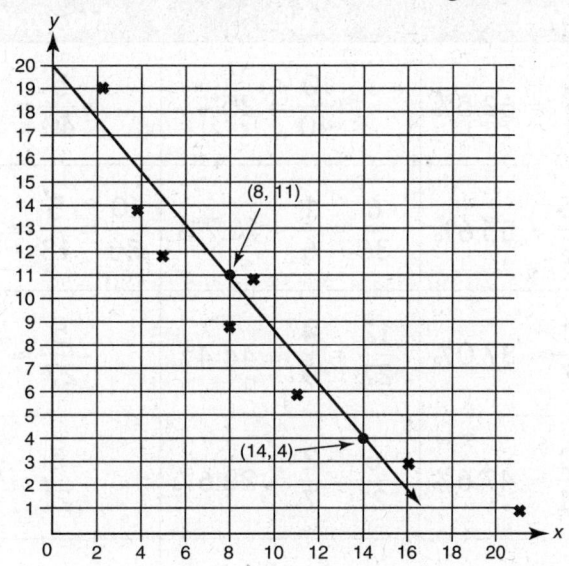

Step 1: The line is sketched so that approximately half of the data points are above the line and half are below the line, and the data points are clustered near the line.

Step 2: Choose two points *on* the line to find the slope: (8, 11) and (14, 4).

$$\dfrac{y_2 - y_1}{x_2 - x_1} = \dfrac{4 - 11}{14 - 8} = \dfrac{-7}{6}$$

Step 3: Extend the line to determine the *y*-intercept of 20.

Step 4: Write the equation of the line in slope-intercept form.

$$y = -\dfrac{7}{6}x + 20$$

3. **(B) and (D)** The slope indicates that it will be 5 minutes per each mile, with x representing the number of miles. The y-intercept 20 represents that it will take 20 minutes on average to locate the dry-cleaned product. This can be checked by substituting 0 miles driven into the equation, and the fixed 20 minutes is left as the time necessary to locate the product.

SBAC Challenge Questions (page 189)

1. **A. The correct relative frequency table is displayed below.**

Pollster Results for Interest in Expanding the City Sports Complex to Include an Indoor Pool

	Relative Frequency by Age Group Range			
	Yes	No	No Opinion	Total
Age 18–30	$\frac{25}{40} = 62.5\%$	$\frac{10}{40} = 25\%$	$\frac{5}{40} = 12.5\%$	$\frac{40}{40} = 1 = 100\%$
Age 31–40	$\frac{20}{36} = \frac{5}{9} \approx 55.6\%$	$\frac{6}{36} = \frac{1}{6} \approx 16.7\%$	$\frac{10}{36} = \frac{5}{18} \approx 27.8\%$	$\frac{36}{36} = 1 \approx 100\%$*
Age 41–50	$\frac{10}{27} \approx 37.0\%$	$\frac{12}{27} = \frac{4}{9} \approx 44.4\%$	$\frac{5}{27} \approx 18.5\%$	$\frac{27}{27} = 1 \approx 100\%$*
Age 51–60	$\frac{10}{21} \approx 47.6\%$	$\frac{6}{21} = \frac{2}{7} \approx 28.6\%$	$\frac{5}{21} \approx 23.8\%$	$\frac{21}{21} = 1 = 100\%$
Age 61–70	$\frac{5}{26} \approx 19.2\%$	$\frac{10}{26} = \frac{5}{13} \approx 38.5\%$	$\frac{11}{26} \approx 42.3\%$	$\frac{26}{26} = 1 = 100\%$
Age 71 and Over	$\frac{2}{12} = \frac{1}{6} \approx 16.7\%$	$\frac{3}{12} = \frac{1}{4} = 25\%$	$\frac{7}{12} \approx 58.3\%$	$\frac{12}{12} = 1 = 100\%$

*Due to rounding, this row is off by 0.1%.

B. **The correct relative frequency table is displayed below.**

Pollster Results for Interest in Expanding the City Sports Complex to Include an Indoor Pool

	Relative Frequency By Response		
	Yes	No	No Opinion
Age 18–30	$\frac{25}{72} = 34.7\%$	$\frac{10}{47} \approx 21.3\%$	$\frac{5}{43} \approx 11.6\%$
Age 31–40	$\frac{20}{72} = \frac{5}{18} \approx 27.8\%$	$\frac{6}{47} \approx 12.8\%$	$\frac{10}{43} \approx 23.3\%$
Age 41–50	$\frac{10}{72} = \frac{5}{36} \approx 13.9\%$	$\frac{12}{47} \approx 25.5\%$	$\frac{5}{43} \approx 11.6\%$
Age 51–60	$\frac{10}{72} = \frac{5}{36} \approx 13.9\%$	$\frac{6}{47} \approx 12.8\%$	$\frac{5}{43} \approx 11.6\%$
Age 61–70	$\frac{5}{72} \approx 6.9\%$	$\frac{10}{47} \approx 21.3\%$	$\frac{11}{43} \approx 25.6\%$
Age 71 and Over	$\frac{2}{72} = \frac{1}{36} \approx 2.8\%$	$\frac{3}{47} \approx 6.4\%$	$\frac{7}{43} \approx 16.3\%$
Total	$\frac{72}{72} = 1 = 100\%$	$\frac{47}{47} = 1 = 100\%*$	$\frac{43}{43} = 1 = 100\%$

*Due to rounding, this column is off by 0.1%.

2. **(A)** and **(B)**

Choice (A): A person who is Age 18–30 is just as likely to not want the indoor pool added as someone over 70 years of age. (25% of both of those age groups responded No.) *True*

Choice (B): A person who is Age 51–60 years old is twice as likely to have responded Yes about the indoor pool as compared to someone in that age group who responded No Opinion. (In this age group, 47.6% responded Yes and 23.8% responded No Opinion.) *True*

Choice (C): A person who is Age 61–70 years old is more than twice as likely to not want the pool as a person Age 51–60 years old is to have No Opinion. (In the Age 61–70 age group, 38.5% responded No, and in the Age 51–60 age group, 23.8% responded No Opinion.) *False*

Chapter 7: Geometry—Two and Three Dimensions

Angles Formed By Intersecting Lines—Independent Practice (page 193)

1. A. **∠G and ∠E are adjacent angles.** These angles share a common vertex and a common side.

    B. **∠B and ∠D are vertical angles.** Formed by intersecting lines, they share a common vertex, but they do *not* share a common side.

2. **Johnny is not correct.** Johnny is correct in part of his answer, that the sum of the angles forming the straight angle is 180°. However, part of his answer is incorrect because supplementary angles are a *pair* of angles that have a sum of 180°, and Johnny has named *three* angles, not *two*. Therefore, he is not correct.

3. A. **m∠A = 35°** because it is a linear pair with ∠D, and they are supplementary, with a sum of 180°.

    B. **m∠B = 145°** because it is vertical to ∠D, and they are congruent. Also, ∠B is supplementary to ∠A because they form a linear pair.

    C. **m∠C = 35°** because it is vertical to ∠A.

    D. **m∠F = 30°** because it is complementary to ∠E.

Three or More Intersecting Lines—Independent Practice (page 202)

1. **Daniel is correct.** For an example, see the figure below which contains Lines *a* and *b*, which are parallel, crossed by Transversal *c*.

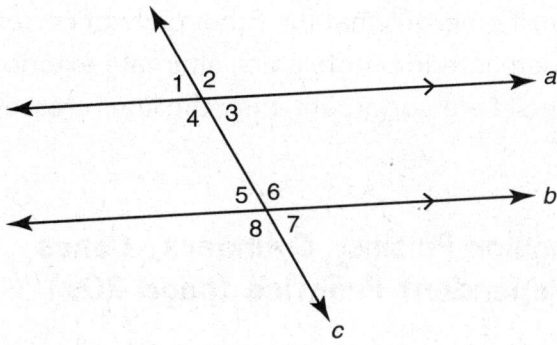

For the figure above, if Daniel knows the measure of ∠1, he can determine that ∠3 is vertical and congruent to ∠1. He knows that ∠1 and ∠2 are a linear pair, which makes them supplementary, so he can determine the measure of ∠2. ∠2 is congruent to ∠4 because they are vertical angles. Also, if the lines are parallel, ∠1 and ∠5 are corresponding, which makes them congruent. Then, he could follow the same series of steps with ∠5 and its respective vertical angles and linear pairs. Since he knows the measures for ∠1 through ∠4, with parallel lines, ∠2 and ∠6, ∠3 and ∠7, and ∠4 and ∠8 are also all pairs of corresponding congruent angles.

2. **Joe is correct.** See the figure below.

Hannah might know that a pair of vertical angles are congruent, but that would only generate one other pair of congruent vertical angles. The definition of vertical angles states that they are formed by any two intersecting lines. Vertical angles are not formed on parallel lines because they do not intersect.

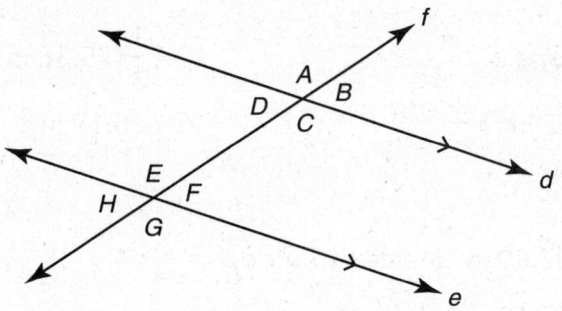

If Joe knows, for example, that ∠A ≅ ∠E, because they are corresponding, then he can prove that all of the other pairs of corresponding angles are congruent by being linear pairs or vertical angles. If Joe knows that ∠A ≅ ∠G because they are alternate exterior angles, he can prove that the angles that make linear pairs with these angles are congruent, which leads to alternate interior angles ∠D and ∠F being congruent. Then, it emerges that the other pairs of corresponding angles are congruent. If alternate interior angle pairs, alternate exterior angle pairs, and corresponding angle pairs are congruent, then the lines crossed by the transversal must be parallel.

Volume of Rectangular Prisms, Cylinders, Cones, and Spheres—Independent Practice (page 209)

1. **41.9 in.³** Each scoop of ice cream is approximately 33.5 in.³ Two scoops would be 67 in.³ Since the waffle cone would hold 25.12 in.³, the rest would melt onto the counter. In each case, the diameter is given as 4 inches, but the radius is needed. Dividing the diameter in half gives a radius of 2 inches.

Scoop of Ice Cream

$V = \frac{4}{3}\pi r^3$

$V \approx \frac{4}{3}(3.14)(2 \text{ in.})^3$

$V \approx \frac{4}{3}(3.14)(8 \text{ in.}^3)$

$V \approx \frac{4}{3}(25.12 \text{ in.}^3)$

$V \approx 33.5 \text{ in.}^3$

Two Scoops

$V \approx 2(33.5 \text{ in.}^3)$

$V \approx 67 \text{ in.}^3$

Waffle Cone

$V = \frac{1}{3}\pi r^2 h$

$V \approx \frac{1}{3}(3.14)(2 \text{ in.})^2(6 \text{ in.})$

$V \approx \frac{1}{3}(3.14)(4 \text{ in.}^2)(6 \text{ in.})$

$V \approx \frac{1}{3}(3.14)(24 \text{ in.}^3)$

$V \approx \frac{1}{3}(3.14)(24 \text{ in.}^3)$

$V \approx \frac{1}{3}(75.36 \text{ in.}^3)$

$V \approx 25.12 \text{ in.}^3$

$$\begin{array}{r} 67.00 \text{ in.}^3 \text{ ice cream scoops} \\ - 25.12 \text{ in.}^3 \text{ waffle cone} \\ \hline \approx 41.88 \text{ in.}^3 \end{array}$$

≈ 41.9 in.³ of ice cream melted onto the counter

2. **0.44745 in.³**

Volume of Pencil	Volume of Sharpened Point
$V = Bh$	$V = \frac{1}{3}\pi r^2 h$
$V = \pi r^2 h$	$V \approx \frac{1}{3}(3.14)(0.15 \text{ in.})^2(1 \text{ in.})$
$V \approx (3.14)(0.15 \text{ in.})^2(6 \text{ in.})$	$V \approx \frac{1}{3}(3.14)(0.0225 \text{ in.}^2)(1 \text{ in.})$
$V \approx (3.14)(0.0225 \text{ in.}^2)(6 \text{ in.})$	$V \approx \frac{1}{3}(3.14)(0.0225 \text{ in.}^3)$
$V \approx (3.14)(0.135 \text{ in.}^3)$	$V \approx \frac{1}{3}(0.07065 \text{ in.}^3)$
$V \approx 0.4239 \text{ in.}^3$	$V \approx 0.02355 \text{ in.}^3$

Pencil + Sharpened tip = 0.4239 in.³ + 0.02355 in.³ = a total pencil volume of 0.44745 in.³

SBAC Challenge Questions (page 210)

1. **The volume of the whole football is approximately 2.487194×10^6 mm.³**

To find the volume of the cones formed by cutting the football in half, it is first necessary to find the radius of each of the circular bases. Since the circumference is 558.92 millimeters, you can use the circumference formula to find the diameter.

$C = \pi d$

$558.92 = (3.14)d$ (Substitute the information given and solve to find d.)

$\frac{558.92}{3.14} = \frac{(3.14)d}{3.14}$ (Isolate the variable by dividing both sides by 3.14.)

$178 = d$ (Simplify.)

The diameter of the football is 178 millimeters.

To find the radius of the football from the diameter, divide by two to determine that the radius of the football is 89 millimeters. Also, remember that the football was cut in half, so the height of one cone-shaped half is half the length of the football, or 150 millimeters.

Volume of One Cone

$V = \dfrac{1}{3}\pi r^2 h$

$V \approx \dfrac{1}{3}(3.14)(89 \text{ mm.})^2(150 \text{ mm.})$

$V \approx \dfrac{1}{3}(3.14)(7{,}921 \text{ mm.}^2)(150 \text{ mm.})$

$V \approx \dfrac{1}{3}(3.14)(1{,}188{,}150 \text{ mm.}^3)$

$V \approx \dfrac{1}{3}(3{,}730{,}791 \text{ mm.}^3)$

$V \approx 1{,}243{,}597 \text{ mm.}^3$

Volume of Both Cones

$V \approx 2(1{,}243{,}597 \text{ mm.}^3)$

$V \approx 2{,}487{,}194 \text{ mm.}^3$

$V \approx (2.487194 \times 10^6) \text{ mm.}^3$

Since the volume of both cones (the whole football) is a number greater than 1, it requires a positive power of 10 for scientific notation.

$$2{,}487{,}194 \text{ mm.}^3 = (2.487194 \times 10^6) \text{ mm.}^3$$

2. **(B)** Since each of the molds is a cylinder, the volume of the small cylinder subtracted from the volume of the large cylinder will leave the volume of the space between them, forming the hollow cement tube. Since all of the choices are in terms of π, it is not necessary to substitute 3.14 in either calculation before subtracting. Refer to the figure below.

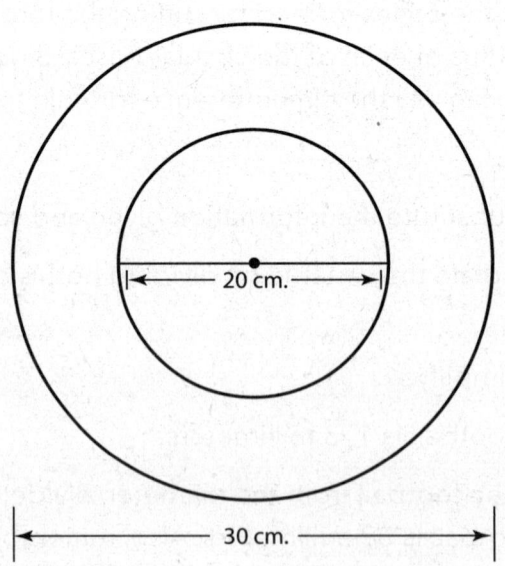

Volume of Large Cylinder

$V = Bh$

$V = \pi r^2 h$

$V = \pi(15 \text{ cm.})^2(60 \text{ cm.})$

Volume of Small Cylinder

$V = Bh$

$V = \pi r^2 h$

$V = \pi(10 \text{ cm.})^2(60 \text{ cm.})$

Answers Explained for Chapters 1–8 • 317

$$V = \pi(225 \text{ cm.}^2)(60 \text{ cm.}) \qquad V = \pi(100 \text{ cm.}^2)(60 \text{ cm.})$$
$$V = \pi(13{,}500 \text{ cm.}^3) \qquad V = \pi(6{,}000 \text{ cm.}^3)$$

Volume of Large Cylinder − Volume of Small Cylinder = Volume of Hollow Tube

$$13{,}500\pi \text{ cm.}^3 - 6{,}000\pi \text{ cm.}^3 = 7{,}500\pi \text{ cm.}^3$$

Chapter 8: Integer Exponents and Scientific Notation

Zero and Negative Exponents—Independent Practice (page 216)

1. $\dfrac{81}{4}$

$$\left(-\dfrac{2}{9}\right)^{-2}$$

$$= \left(-\dfrac{9}{2}\right)^{2} \qquad \left(\text{Write the reciprocal } \left(-\dfrac{9}{2}\right) \text{ of the base } \left(-\dfrac{2}{9}\right) \text{ to the positive exponent.}\right)$$

$$= \left(-\dfrac{9}{2}\right)\left(-\dfrac{9}{2}\right) \qquad \text{(Expand the multiplication of the base as indicated by the exponent.)}$$

$$= \dfrac{81}{4} \qquad \text{(Simplify. Remember the negative sign in the exponent does not affect the sign of the answer.)}$$

2. **1** Any non zero base raised to a zero power is equal to 1.

3. $\dfrac{25}{49}$

$$\left(\dfrac{7}{5}\right)^{-2}$$

$$= \left(\dfrac{5}{7}\right)^{2} \qquad \left(\text{Write the reciprocal } \left(\dfrac{5}{7}\right) \text{ of the base } \left(\dfrac{7}{5}\right) \text{ to the positive exponent.}\right)$$

$$= \left(\dfrac{5}{7}\right)\left(\dfrac{5}{7}\right) \qquad \text{(Expand the multiplication of the base as indicated by the exponent.)}$$

$$= \dfrac{25}{49} \qquad \text{(Simplify. Remember the negative sign in the exponent does not affect the sign of the answer.)}$$

4. **1** Any non zero base raised to a zero power is equal to 1.

Product of Powers Property—Independent Practice (page 218)

1. $20a^7b^2c^5$

   $(2a^2c^3)(5a^3bc^2)(2a^2b)$

   $= 20a^{2+3+2}b^{1+1}c^{3+2}$ (First, multiply the coefficients. Then, add the exponents of the like bases.)

   $= 20a^7b^2c^5$ (Simplify.)

   You could also answer this question by using expanded multiplication.

   $(2a^2c^3)(5a^3bc^2)(2a^2b)$

   $= 2 \cdot a \cdot a \cdot c \cdot c \cdot c \cdot 5 \cdot a \cdot a \cdot a \cdot b \cdot c \cdot c \cdot 2 \cdot a \cdot a \cdot b$ (Expand the multiplication as indicated by the exponents.)

   $= 2 \cdot 5 \cdot 2 \cdot a \cdot a \cdot a \cdot a \cdot a \cdot a \cdot a \cdot b \cdot b \cdot c \cdot c \cdot c \cdot c \cdot c$ (Use the Commutative Property of Multiplication to collect the coefficients and to collect the like bases.)

   $= 20a^7b^2c^5$ (Simplify the like bases with exponents.)

2. $4x^8y^4$

   $(4x^5)(1x^3y^4)$

   $= 4x^{5+3}y^4$ (First, multiply the coefficients. Then, add the exponents of the like bases.)

   $= 4x^8y^4$ (Simplify.)

   You could also answer this question by using expanded multiplication.

   $(4x^5)(1x^3y^4)$

   $= 4 \cdot x \cdot x \cdot x \cdot x \cdot x \cdot 1 \cdot x \cdot x \cdot x \cdot y \cdot y \cdot y \cdot y$ (Expand the multiplication as indicated by the exponents.)

   $= 4 \cdot 1 \cdot x \cdot x \cdot x \cdot x \cdot x \cdot x \cdot x \cdot x \cdot y \cdot y \cdot y \cdot y$ (Use the Commutative Property of Multiplication to collect the coefficients and to collect the like bases.)

   $= 4x^8y^4$ (Simplify the like bases with exponents.)

Answers Explained for Chapters 1–8 • 319

3. **$12m^6n^6p^6$**

$(3m^2n^2p)(2mnp)(2m^3n^3p^4)$

$= 12m^{2+1+3}n^{2+1+3}p^{1+1+4}$ (First, multiply the coefficients. Then, add the exponents of the like bases.)

$= 12m^6n^6p^6$ (Simplify.)

You could also answer this question by using expanded multiplication.

$(3m^2n^2p)(2mnp)(2m^3n^3p^4)$

$= 3 \cdot m \cdot m \cdot n \cdot n \cdot p \cdot 2 \cdot m \cdot n \cdot p \cdot 2 \cdot m \cdot m \cdot m \cdot n \cdot n \cdot n \cdot p \cdot p \cdot p \cdot p$ (Expand the multiplication as indicated by the exponents.)

$= 3 \cdot 2 \cdot 2 \cdot m \cdot m \cdot m \cdot m \cdot m \cdot m \cdot n \cdot n \cdot n \cdot n \cdot n \cdot n \cdot p \cdot p \cdot p \cdot p \cdot p \cdot p$ (Use the Commutative Property of Multiplication to collect the coefficients and to collect the like bases.)

$= 12m^6n^6p^6$ (Simplify the like bases with exponents.)

Power of Powers Property—Independent Practice (page 222)

1. **$25a^4b^4c^{10}$**

$(5a^2b^2c^5)^2$

$= 5^2a^{2\cdot2}b^{2\cdot2}c^{5\cdot2}$ (First, raise the coefficient to the power. Then, multiply each variable exponent by the exponent of the expression.)

$= 25a^4b^4c^{10}$ (Simplify.)

You could also answer this question by using expanded multiplication.

$(5a^2b^2c^5)^2$

$= (5a^2b^2c^5)(5a^2b^2c^5)$ (Expand the multiplication as indicated by the exponent of the expression.)

$= 5 \cdot a \cdot a \cdot b \cdot b \cdot c \cdot c \cdot c \cdot c \cdot c \cdot 5 \cdot a \cdot a \cdot b \cdot b \cdot c \cdot c \cdot c \cdot c \cdot c$ (Expand the multiplication as indicated by the variable exponents.)

$= 5 \cdot 5 \cdot a \cdot a \cdot a \cdot a \cdot b \cdot b \cdot b \cdot b \cdot c \cdot c \cdot c \cdot c \cdot c \cdot c \cdot c \cdot c \cdot c \cdot c$ (Use the Commutative Property of Multiplication to collect the coefficients and to collect the like bases.)

$= 25a^4b^4c^{10}$ (Simplify the like bases with exponents.)

2. $16x^{12}y^{12}$

$(-2x^3y^3z^0)^4$

$= (-2)^4 x^{3 \cdot 4} y^{3 \cdot 4} z^{0 \cdot 4}$ (First, raise the coefficient to the power. Then, multiply each variable exponent by the exponent of the expression.)

$= 16x^{12}y^{12}$ (Simplify.)

You could also answer this question by using expanded multiplication.

$(-2x^3y^3z^0)^4$

$= (-2x^3y^3z^0)(-2x^3y^3z^0)(-2x^3y^3z^0)(-2x^3y^3z^0)$ (Expand the multiplication as indicated by the exponent of the expression.)

$= (-2) \cdot x \cdot x \cdot x \cdot y \cdot y \cdot y \cdot 1 \cdot (-2) \cdot x \cdot x \cdot x \cdot y \cdot y \cdot y \cdot 1 \cdot (-2) \cdot x \cdot x \cdot x \cdot y \cdot y \cdot y \cdot 1 \cdot (-2) \cdot x \cdot x \cdot x \cdot y \cdot y \cdot y \cdot 1$

(Expand the multiplication as indicated by the variable exponents. Note: $z^0 = 1$.)

$= (-2) \cdot (-2) \cdot (-2) \cdot (-2) \cdot 1 \cdot 1 \cdot 1 \cdot 1 \cdot x \cdot x \cdot x \cdot x \cdot x \cdot x \cdot x \cdot x \cdot x \cdot x \cdot x \cdot x \cdot y \cdot y \cdot y \cdot y \cdot y \cdot y \cdot y \cdot y \cdot y \cdot y \cdot y \cdot y$

(Use the Commutative Property of Multiplication to collect the coefficients and to collect the like bases.)

$= 16x^{12}y^{12}$ (Simplify the like bases with exponents.)

Quotient of Powers Property—Independent Practice (page 226)

1. $\dfrac{7xy}{z}$

$\dfrac{1.4x^2y^2z^3}{0.2xyz^4}$

$= 7x^{2-1}y^{2-1}z^{3-4}$ (First, divide the coefficients. Then, subtract the exponents of the like bases.)

$= 7xyz^{-1}$ (Simplify. To simplify z^{-1}, it will need to be written as a reciprocal with a positive exponent, $\left(\dfrac{1}{z}\right)$.)

$= \dfrac{7xy}{z}$ (Simplify.)

You could also answer this question by using expanded multiplication.

$$\frac{1.4x^2y^2z^3}{0.2xyz^4}$$

$$= \frac{(1.4)x \cdot x \cdot y \cdot y \cdot z \cdot z \cdot z}{(0.2)x \cdot y \cdot z \cdot z \cdot z \cdot z} \quad \text{(Expand the multiplication as indicated by the variable exponents.)}$$

$$= \frac{(1.4)x \cdot \cancel{x} \cdot \cancel{y} \cdot y \cdot \cancel{z} \cdot \cancel{z} \cdot \cancel{z}}{(0.2)\cancel{x} \cdot \cancel{y} \cdot z \cdot \cancel{z} \cdot \cancel{z} \cdot \cancel{z}} \quad \text{(Divide the coefficients. Cancel all forms of 1.)}$$

$$= \frac{7xy}{z} \quad \text{(Simplify.)}$$

2. $\dfrac{2y^2}{xz^2}$

$$\frac{18xy^3}{9x^2yz^2}$$

$$= 2x^{1-2}y^{3-1}z^{0-2} \quad \text{(First, divide the coefficients. Then, subtract the exponents of the like bases.)}$$

$$= 2x^{-1}y^2z^{-2} \quad \text{(Simplify.)}$$

$$= 2 \cdot \frac{1}{x} \cdot y^2 \cdot \frac{1}{z^2} \quad \left(\text{To simplify } x^{-1} \text{ and } z^{-2}, \text{ they will need to be written as reciprocals with positive exponents: } \left(\frac{1}{x}\right) \text{ and } \left(\frac{1}{z^2}\right).\right)$$

$$= \frac{2y^2}{xz^2} \quad \text{(Simplify.)}$$

You could also answer this question by using expanded multiplication.

$$\frac{18xy^3}{9x^2yz^2}$$

$$= \frac{18 \cdot x \cdot y \cdot y \cdot y}{9 \cdot x \cdot x \cdot y \cdot z \cdot z} \quad \text{(Expand the multiplication as indicated by the variable exponents.)}$$

$$= \frac{18 \cdot \cancel{x} \cdot y \cdot \cancel{y} \cdot y}{9 \cdot \cancel{x} \cdot x \cdot \cancel{y} \cdot z \cdot z} \quad \text{(Divide the coefficients. Cancel all forms of 1.)}$$

$$= \frac{2y^2}{xz^2} \quad \text{(Simplify.)}$$

3. $\dfrac{5}{3uvw}$

$\dfrac{25u^2v^2w}{15u^3v^3w^2}$

$= \dfrac{5}{3}u^{2-3}v^{2-3}w^{1-2}$ (First, divide the coefficients. Then, subtract the exponents of the like bases.)

$= \dfrac{5}{3}u^{-1}v^{-1}w^{-1}$ (Simplify.)

$= \dfrac{5}{3} \cdot \dfrac{1}{u} \cdot \dfrac{1}{v} \cdot \dfrac{1}{w}$ $\left(\text{To simplify } u^{-1}, v^{-1}, \text{ and } w^{-1}, \text{ they will need to be written as reciprocals with positive exponents: } \left(\dfrac{1}{u}\right), \left(\dfrac{1}{v}\right), \text{ and } \left(\dfrac{1}{w}\right).\right)$

$= \dfrac{5}{3uvw}$ (Simplify.)

You could also answer this question by using expanded multiplication.

$\dfrac{25u^2v^2w}{15u^3v^3w^2}$

$= \dfrac{5 \cdot 5 \cdot u \cdot u \cdot v \cdot v \cdot w}{5 \cdot 3 \cdot u \cdot u \cdot u \cdot v \cdot v \cdot v \cdot w \cdot w}$ (Expand the multiplication as indicated by the variable exponents.)

$= \dfrac{\cancel{5} \cdot 5 \cdot \cancel{u} \cdot \cancel{u} \cdot \cancel{v} \cdot \cancel{v} \cdot \cancel{w}}{\cancel{5} \cdot 3 \cdot u \cdot \cancel{u} \cdot \cancel{u} \cdot \cancel{v} \cdot \cancel{v} \cdot v \cdot \cancel{w} \cdot w}$ (Divide the coefficients. Cancel all forms of 1.)

$= \dfrac{5}{3uvw}$ (Simplify.)

Scientific Notation—Independent Practice (page 232)

1. From least to greatest:

   7.943×10^3 $22{,}500$ 3.4×10^4 5.0745×10^4 7.04×10^4

   Convert all of the numbers to standard notation to compare.

   $3.4 \times 10^4 = 34{,}000$

   $7.943 \times 10^3 = 7{,}943$

   $5.0745 \times 10^4 = 50{,}745$

   $7.04 \times 10^4 = 70{,}400$

   $22{,}500 = 22{,}500$

Standard notation from least to greatest:

| 7,943 | 22,500 | 34,000 | 50,745 | 70,400 |

Then, match the order with the scientific notations and standard notations in the form they were given in the question:

| 7.943×10^3 | 22,500 | 3.4×10^4 | 5.0745×10^4 | 7.04×10^4 |

2. From least to greatest:

0.00048 5.01×10^{-4} 4.8×10^{-3} 5.001×10^{-3} 5.2×10^{-2}

Convert all of the numbers to standard notation to compare, and add zeros where necessary to compare at the same place value:

$$5.01 \times 10^{-4} = 0.000501$$
$$0.00048 = 0.000480$$
$$5.2 \times 10^{-2} = 0.052000$$
$$4.8 \times 10^{-3} = 0.004800$$
$$5.001 \times 10^{-3} = 0.005001$$

Standard notation from least to greatest:

| 0.000480 | 0.000501 | 0.004800 | 0.005001 | 0.052000 |

Then, match the order with the scientific notations and standard notations in the form they were given in the question:

| 0.00048 | 5.01×10^{-4} | 4.8×10^{-3} | 5.001×10^{-3} | 5.2×10^{-2} |

Operations with Scientific Notation—Independent Practice (page 236)

1. **The mass of an elephant is about 4.8×10^7 times the mass of a shrew.**

    $\dfrac{\text{Mass of an elephant}}{\text{Mass of a shrew}}$ Elephant $= 8.6 \times 10^4$ Shrew $= 1.8 \times 10^{-3}$

    $\dfrac{8.6 \times 10^4 \text{ kg}}{1.8 \times 10^{-3} \text{ kg}}$ (Divide the coefficients. Use the Quotient of Power Property to subtract the exponents for the powers of 10 (like bases). Units cancel.)

    $4.\overline{7} \times 10^{4-(-3)}$ (Round to the nearest tenth.)

    4.8×10^7 (Simplify the exponents.)

2. **The distance the object would travel is 1.44×10^8 feet in 25 minutes.**

$$60 \text{ seconds} = 1 \text{ minute}$$
$$1{,}500 \text{ seconds} = 25 \text{ minutes}$$
$$1.5 \times 10^3 \text{ seconds} = 25 \text{ minutes}$$

$d = 64t^2$

$d = 64(1.5 \times 10^3)^2$ (Substitute the number of seconds in 25 minutes.)

$d = 64(1.5)^2 \times 10^{3 \cdot 2}$ (Raise the coefficient to the power. Multiply the exponent of the base with the exponent of the expression.)

$d = 64(2.25 \times 10^6)$ (Multiply.)

$d = 144 \times 10^6$ (Simplify.)

$d = (1.44 \times 10^2) \times 10^6$ (Convert the first factor (coefficient) to scientific notation.)

$d = 1.44 \times 10^{2+6}$ (Add the exponents of the like bases.)

$d = 1.44 \times 10^8$ (Simplify.)

SBAC Challenge Questions (pages 237–238)

1. $\dfrac{3a^4b^4}{c}$

$\dfrac{(3a^2b^2c)^2(4ab^3c)}{12ab^3c^4}$

$= \dfrac{(3^2 a^{2 \cdot 2} b^{2 \cdot 2} c^{1 \cdot 2})(4ab^3c)}{12ab^3c^4}$ (Raise the coefficient to the power. Multiply the exponent of each variable by the expression exponent.)

$= \dfrac{(9a^4b^4c^2)(4ab^3c)}{12ab^3c^4}$ (Simplify.)

$= \dfrac{36a^{4+1}b^{4+3}c^{2+1}}{12ab^3c^4}$ (Multiply the coefficients in the numerator. Add the exponents of the like bases.)

$= 3a^{5-1}b^{7-3}c^{3-4}$ (Divide the coefficients. Then, subtract the exponents of the like bases.)

$= \dfrac{3a^4b^4}{c}$ (Simplify.)

You could also answer this question by using expanded multiplication.

$$\frac{(3a^2b^2c)^2(4ab^3c)}{12ab^3c^4}$$

$$= \frac{(3a^2b^2c)(3a^2b^2c)(4ab^3c)}{12ab^3c^4}$$ (Expand the multiplication for the expression exponent.)

$$= \frac{3 \cdot a \cdot a \cdot b \cdot b \cdot c \cdot 3 \cdot a \cdot a \cdot b \cdot b \cdot c \cdot 4 \cdot a \cdot b \cdot b \cdot b \cdot c}{3 \cdot 4 \cdot a \cdot b \cdot b \cdot b \cdot c \cdot c \cdot c \cdot c}$$ (Expand the multiplication as indicated by the variable exponents.)

$$= \frac{3 \cdot 3 \cdot 4 \cdot a \cdot a \cdot a \cdot a \cdot a \cdot b \cdot b \cdot b \cdot b \cdot b \cdot b \cdot b \cdot c \cdot c \cdot c}{3 \cdot 4 \cdot a \cdot b \cdot b \cdot b \cdot c \cdot c \cdot c \cdot c}$$ (Use the Commutative Property of Multiplication to collect the coefficients and to collect the like bases.)

$$= \frac{3 \cdot 3 \cdot \cancel{4} \cdot a \cdot a \cdot a \cdot a \cdot \cancel{a} \cdot \cancel{b} \cdot \cancel{b} \cdot \cancel{b} \cdot b \cdot b \cdot b \cdot b \cdot \cancel{b} \cdot \cancel{c} \cdot \cancel{c} \cdot \cancel{c}}{\cancel{3} \cdot \cancel{4} \cdot \cancel{a} \cdot \cancel{b} \cdot \cancel{b} \cdot \cancel{b} \cdot c \cdot \cancel{c} \cdot \cancel{c} \cdot \cancel{c}}$$ (Cancel all forms of 1.)

$$= \frac{3a^4b^4}{c}$$ (Simplify.)

2. $\dfrac{60m}{n^2p^2}$

$$\frac{(1.8m^3n^3p^2)(3m^2np^2)}{(0.3m^2n^3p^3)^2}$$

$$= \frac{(1.8m^3n^3p^2)(3m^2np^2)}{(0.3)^2 m^{2 \cdot 2} n^{3 \cdot 2} p^{3 \cdot 2}}$$ (Raise the coefficient in the denominator to the expression exponent. Multiply the variable exponents with the expression exponent.)

$$= \frac{5.4m^{3+2}n^{3+1}p^{2+2}}{0.09m^4n^6p^6}$$ (Multiply the coefficients, and add the exponents of the like terms in the numerator. Simplify the denominator.)

$$= 60m^{5-4}n^{4-6}p^{4-6}$$ (Divide the coefficients. Subtract the exponents of the like bases.)

$$= (60m)\left(\frac{1}{n^2}\right)\left(\frac{1}{p^2}\right)$$ $\Bigg($ Simplify. The negative exponents must be simplified $\left(n^{-2} = \dfrac{1}{n^2} \text{ and } p^{-2} = \dfrac{1}{p^2}\right)$ as the reciprocal to the positive power. $\Bigg)$

$$= \frac{60m}{n^2p^2}$$

You could also answer this question by using expanded multiplication.

$$\frac{(1.8m^3n^3p^2)(3m^2np^2)}{(0.3m^2n^3p^3)^2}$$

$$= \frac{(1.8m^3n^3p^2)(3m^2np^2)}{(0.3m^2n^3p^3)(0.3m^2n^3p^3)}$$ (Expand the multiplication as indicated by the expression exponent.)

$$= \frac{1.8 \cdot m \cdot m \cdot m \cdot n \cdot n \cdot n \cdot p \cdot p \cdot 3 \cdot m \cdot m \cdot n \cdot p \cdot p}{0.3 \cdot m \cdot m \cdot n \cdot n \cdot n \cdot p \cdot p \cdot p \cdot 0.3 \cdot m \cdot m \cdot n \cdot n \cdot n \cdot p \cdot p \cdot p}$$ (Expand the multiplication as indicated by the variable exponents.)

$$= \frac{1.8 \cdot 3 \cdot \cancel{m} \cdot \cancel{m} \cdot \cancel{m} \cdot \cancel{m} \cdot m \cdot \cancel{n} \cdot \cancel{n} \cdot \cancel{n} \cdot \cancel{n} \cdot p \cdot p \cdot p \cdot p}{0.3 \cdot 0.3 \cdot \cancel{m} \cdot \cancel{m} \cdot \cancel{m} \cdot \cancel{m} \cdot n \cdot \cancel{n} \cdot \cancel{n} \cdot \cancel{n} \cdot \cancel{n} \cdot p \cdot p \cdot p \cdot p \cdot p \cdot p}$$ (Use the Commutative Property of Multiplication to collect the coefficients and to collect the like variables. Cancel all forms of 1.)

$$= \frac{60m}{n^2p^2}$$ (Simplify.)

3. **$4a^5b^3c$**

$$\frac{(2a^2b^0c)(4a^3b^2c^2)^2}{8a^3bc^4}$$

$$= \frac{(2a^2b^0c)(4^2a^{3 \cdot 2}b^{2 \cdot 2}c^{2 \cdot 2})}{8a^3bc^4}$$ (In the numerator, raise the coefficient to the expression exponent. Multiply the variable exponents with the expression exponent.)

$$= \frac{(2a^2b^0c)(16a^6b^4c^4)}{8a^3bc^4}$$ (Simplify.)

$$= \frac{(32a^{2+6}b^{0+4}c^{1+4})}{8a^3bc^4}$$ (Multiply the coefficients in the numerator. Add the exponents of the like terms.)

$= 4a^{8-3}b^{4-1}c^{5-4}$ (Simplify. Divide the coefficients. Subtract the exponents of the like terms.)

$= 4a^5b^3c$ (Simplify.)

You could also answer this question by using expanded multiplication.

$$\frac{(2a^2b^0c)(4a^3b^2c^2)^2}{8a^3bc^4}$$

$= \dfrac{(2a^2b^0c)(4a^3b^2c^2)(4a^3b^2c^2)}{8a^3bc^4}$ (Expand the multiplication as indicated by the expression exponent.)

$= \dfrac{2 \cdot a \cdot a \cdot 1 \cdot c \cdot 4 \cdot a \cdot a \cdot a \cdot b \cdot b \cdot c \cdot c \cdot 4 \cdot a \cdot a \cdot a \cdot b \cdot b \cdot c \cdot c}{8 \cdot a \cdot a \cdot a \cdot b \cdot c \cdot c \cdot c \cdot c}$ (Expand the multiplication as indicated by the variable exponents.)

$= \dfrac{2 \cdot 1 \cdot 4 \cdot 4 \cdot a \cdot a \cdot a \cdot a \cdot a \cdot a \cdot a \cdot a \cdot b \cdot b \cdot b \cdot b \cdot c \cdot c \cdot c \cdot c \cdot c}{8 \cdot a \cdot a \cdot a \cdot b \cdot c \cdot c \cdot c \cdot c}$ (Use the Commutative Property of Multiplication to collect the coefficients and to collect the like variables. Cancel all forms of 1.)

$= 4a^5b^3c$ (Divide the coefficients. Simplify.)

4. A. **Yes**
   B. **No**
   C. **No**
   D. **No**
   E. **Yes**

A. **Yes**

$$\frac{(2xyz)^2}{2y}$$

$$= \frac{2^2 x^{1\cdot 2} y^{1\cdot 2} z^{1\cdot 2}}{2y}$$ (Raise the coefficient to the expression exponent. Multiply the variable exponents with the expression exponent.)

$$= \frac{4x^2 y^{2-1} z^2}{2}$$ (Simplify. Subtract the exponents of the like variables.)

$$= 2x^2 yz^2$$ (Simplify.)

You could also answer this question by using expanded multiplication.

$$\frac{(2xyz)^2}{2y}$$

$$= \frac{(2xyz)(2xyz)}{2y}$$ (Expand the multiplication as indicated by the expression exponent.)

$$= \frac{2\cdot x\cdot y\cdot z\cdot 2\cdot x\cdot y\cdot z}{2\cdot y}$$ (Expand the multiplication as indicated by the variable exponents.)

$$= \frac{2\cdot \cancel{2}\cdot x\cdot x\cdot y\cdot \cancel{y}\cdot z\cdot z}{\cancel{2}\cdot \cancel{y}}$$ (Use the Commutative Property of Multiplication to collect the coefficients and to collect the like variables. Cancel all forms of 1.)

$$= 2x^2 yz^2$$ (Simplify.)

B. **No**

$$\frac{(3xyz^0)(2x^2y)^2}{2y}$$

$$= \frac{(3xyz^0)(2^{2}x^{2\cdot 2}y^{1\cdot 2})}{2y}$$ (Raise the coefficient to the expression exponent. Multiply the variable exponents by the expression exponent.)

$$= \frac{(3xyz^0)(4x^4y^2)}{2y}$$ (Simplify.)

$$= \frac{(12x^{1+4}y^{1+2}z^0)}{2y}$$ (Multiply the coefficients in the numerator. Add the exponents of the like bases.)

$$= \frac{(12x^5y^{3-1}z^0)}{2}$$ (Simplify. Subtract the exponents of the like bases.)

$$= 6x^5y^2(1)$$ (Divide the coefficients. Any non zero base to the zero power is simplified as 1.)

$$= 6x^5y^2$$ (Simplify.)

You could also answer this question by using expanded multiplication.

$$\frac{(3xyz^0)(2x^2y)^2}{2y}$$

$$= \frac{(3xyz^0)(2x^2y)(2x^2y)}{2y}$$ (Expand the multiplication as indicated by the expression exponent.)

$$= \frac{3 \cdot x \cdot y \cdot 1 \cdot 2 \cdot x \cdot x \cdot y \cdot 2 \cdot x \cdot x \cdot y}{2 \cdot y}$$ (Expand the multiplication as indicated by the variable exponents.)

$$= \frac{3 \cdot 1 \cdot 2 \cdot \cancel{2} \cdot x \cdot x \cdot x \cdot x \cdot x \cdot \cancel{y} \cdot y \cdot y}{\cancel{2} \cdot \cancel{y}}$$ (Use the Commutative Property of Multiplication to collect the coefficients and to collect the like variables. Cancel all forms of 1.)

$$= 6x^5y^2$$ (Simplify.)

C. **No**

$$\frac{(2x^2y^2z^2)(x^2yz^2)(9xz)}{(3x^2yz^2)^2}$$

$$= \frac{(2x^2y^2z^2)(x^2yz^2)(9xz)}{(3^2 x^{2 \cdot 2} y^{1 \cdot 2} z^{2 \cdot 2})} \quad \text{(Raise the coefficient to the expression exponent in the denominator. Multiply the variable exponents with the expression exponent.)}$$

$$= \frac{18x^{2+2+1} y^{2+1} z^{2+2+1}}{9x^4 y^2 z^4} \quad \text{(Multiply the coefficients. Add the exponents of the like variables.)}$$

$$= \frac{2x^5 y^3 z^5}{x^4 y^2 z^4} \quad \text{(Divide the coefficients. Simplify.)}$$

$$= 2x^{5-4} y^{3-2} z^{5-4} \quad \text{(Subtract the coefficients of the like bases.)}$$

$$= 2xyz \quad \text{(Simplify.)}$$

You could also answer this question by using expanded multiplication.

$$\frac{(2x^2y^2z^2)(x^2yz^2)(9xz)}{(3x^2yz^2)^2}$$

$$= \frac{(2x^2y^2z^2)(x^2yz^2)(9xz)}{(3x^2yz^2)(3x^2yz^2)} \quad \text{(Expand the multiplication as indicated by the expression exponent.)}$$

$$= \frac{2 \cdot x \cdot x \cdot y \cdot y \cdot z \cdot z \cdot x \cdot x \cdot y \cdot z \cdot z \cdot 9 \cdot x \cdot z}{3 \cdot x \cdot x \cdot y \cdot z \cdot z \cdot 3 \cdot x \cdot x \cdot y \cdot z \cdot z} \quad \text{(Expand the multiplication as indicated by the variable exponents.)}$$

$$= \frac{2 \cdot 9 \cdot \cancel{x} \cdot \cancel{x} \cdot \cancel{x} \cdot \cancel{x} \cdot x \cdot \cancel{y} \cdot \cancel{y} \cdot y \cdot \cancel{z} \cdot \cancel{z} \cdot \cancel{z} \cdot \cancel{z} \cdot z}{3 \cdot 3 \cdot \cancel{x} \cdot \cancel{x} \cdot \cancel{x} \cdot \cancel{x} \cdot \cancel{y} \cdot \cancel{y} \cdot \cancel{z} \cdot \cancel{z} \cdot \cancel{z} \cdot \cancel{z}} \quad \text{(Use the Commutative Property of Multiplication to collect the coefficients and to collect the like variables.)}$$

$$= 2xyz \quad \text{(Simplify.)}$$

D. **No**

$$\frac{(15x^{-1}z^2)(4x^2y^2z^2)}{(10x^{-1}y^{-1}z^2)(3x^2yz^0)}$$

$$= \frac{(60x^{-1+2}y^2z^{2+2})}{(30x^{-1+2}y^{-1+1}z^{2+0})}$$ (Multiply the coefficients. Add the exponents of the like bases.)

$$= 2x^{1-1}y^{2-0}z^{4-2}$$ (Simplify. Divide the coefficients. Subtract the exponents of the like bases.)

$$= 2x^0y^2z^2$$ (Simplify.)

$$= 2(1)y^2z^2$$ (Any non zero base raised to the zero power simplifies to 1.)

$$= 2y^2z^2$$ (Simplify.)

You could also answer this question by using expanded multiplication.

$$\frac{(15x^{-1}z^2)(4x^2y^2z^2)}{(10x^{-1}y^{-1}z^2)(3x^2yz^0)}$$

$$= \frac{15 \cdot \frac{1}{x} \cdot z \cdot z \cdot 4 \cdot x \cdot x \cdot y \cdot y \cdot z \cdot z}{10 \cdot \frac{1}{x} \cdot \frac{1}{y} \cdot z \cdot z \cdot 3 \cdot x \cdot x \cdot y \cdot (1)}$$ (Expand the multiplication as indicated by the variable exponents. All negative exponents simplify to the reciprocal to the positive power.)

$$= \frac{15 \cdot 4 \cdot \frac{1}{x} \cdot x \cdot x \cdot y \cdot y \cdot z \cdot z \cdot z \cdot z}{10 \cdot 3 \cdot (1) \cdot \frac{1}{x} \cdot x \cdot x \cdot \frac{1}{y} \cdot y \cdot z \cdot z}$$ (Use the Commutative Property of Multiplication to collect the coefficients and to collect the like variables.)

$$= \frac{15 \cdot 4 \cdot \left(\frac{1}{\cancel{x}} \cdot \cancel{x}\right) \cdot x \cdot y \cdot y \cdot z \cdot z \cdot \cancel{z} \cdot \cancel{z}}{10 \cdot 3 \cdot (1) \cdot \left(\frac{1}{\cancel{x}} \cdot \cancel{x}\right) \cdot x \cdot \left(\frac{1}{\cancel{y}} \cdot \cancel{y}\right) \cdot \cancel{z} \cdot \cancel{z}}$$ (Cancel all forms of 1.)

$$= \frac{60(1)y^2z^2}{30(1)(1)(1)}$$ (Simplify.)

$$= 2y^2z^2$$ (Divide the coefficients. Simplify.)

E. **Yes**

$$\frac{8x^3y^2z^3}{4xyz}$$

$= 2x^{3-1}y^{2-1}z^{3-1}$ (Divide the coefficients. Subtract the exponents of the like bases.)

$= 2x^2y^1z^2$ (Simplify.)

You could also answer this question by using expanded multiplication.

$$\frac{8x^3y^2z^3}{4xyz}$$

$= \dfrac{8 \cdot x \cdot x \cdot x \cdot y \cdot y \cdot z \cdot z \cdot z}{4 \cdot x \cdot y \cdot z}$ (Expand the multiplication as indicated by the variable exponents.)

$= \dfrac{8 \cdot x \cdot x \cdot \cancel{x} \cdot \cancel{y} \cdot y \cdot \cancel{z} \cdot z \cdot z}{4 \cdot \cancel{x} \cdot \cancel{y} \cdot \cancel{z}}$ (Use the Commutative Property of Multiplication to collect the coefficients and to collect the like variables. Cancel all forms of 1.)

$= 2x^2yz^2$ (Divide the coefficients. Simplify the like bases with exponents.)

5. **7.3125×10^5 joules**

Mass of the car = 1,625 kilograms

Speed of the car = 30 meters per second

E = joules (measure of kinetic energy)

$E = \dfrac{1}{2}mv^2$ (Formula given.)

$E = \dfrac{1}{2}(1{,}625)(30)^2$ (Substitute the given measures into the formula.)

$E = \dfrac{1}{2}(1{,}625)(900)$ (Calculate using the exponent.)

$E = \dfrac{1}{2}(1{,}462{,}500)$ (Multiply.)

$E = 731{,}250$ (Multiply.)

$E = 7.3125 \times 10^5$ (The number 7.3125 is the first factor. It is greater than 1 and less than 10. The decimal in the original number is on the far right To move it back to the original position, it will need to be moved five places to the right. The direction is positive so the power of 10 is positive 5.)

6. **The wavelengths of ultraviolet rays are shorter than even the shortest wavelengths of visible light.**

$$\text{Medical x-rays} = 1.0 \times 10^{-10}$$
$$\text{Ultraviolet rays} = 1,000 \times 1.0 \times 10^{-10}$$
$$7.5 \times 10^{-7} < \text{Visible light} < 4 \times 10^{7}$$

Ultraviolet rays

$= 1,000 \times 1.0 \times 10^{-10}$

$= (1.0 \times 10^{3})(1.0 \times 10^{-10})$ (Convert 1,000 to scientific notation.)

$= (1.0 \times 1.0)(10^{3} \times 10^{-10})$ (Use the Commutative Property of Multiplication to collect the coefficients and to collect the like bases.)

$= 1.0 \times 10^{3 + -10}$ (Multiply the coefficients. Use the Product of Powers Property to add the exponents of powers of 10 (like bases).)

$= 1.0 \times 10^{-7}$ (Simplify.)

Comparing the length of ultraviolet rays and visible light wavelengths, with the same power of 10, the coefficient of visible light (7.5) and the coefficient of the ultraviolet rays (1.0) shows that the shortest wavelengths of visible light are longer than the wavelengths of ultraviolet rays.

7. From least to greatest wavelengths in meters:

   medical x-rays, ultraviolet rays, infrared rays, microwaves

   Medical x-rays $= 1.0 \times 10^{-10} \rightarrow 0.0000000001$ meters
   Ultraviolet rays $= 1.0 \times 10^{-7} \rightarrow 0.0000001$ meters
   Infrared rays $= 1.0 \times 10^{-5} \rightarrow 0.00001$ meters
   Microwaves $= 5.0 \times 10^{-1} \rightarrow 0.5$ meters

   The larger the negative exponent of the power of 10, the smaller the number will be in standard notation.

Answers Explained for the Practice Test

APPENDIX B

Computer Adaptive Test (pages 245–251)

1. **(3, −4)** Once the three ordered pairs are graphed, completing the rectangle requires opposite sides to be equal. The vertical distance between A and B is 5 units, which means that the vertical distance between C and D must also be 5 units. Moving 5 units down changes the y-coordinate of C by −5 and puts D at (3, −4). The horizontal distance can be checked as well. Between B and C is 6 units. Therefore, between A and D must also be 6 units. Moving 6 units right changes the x-coordinate of A by +6, which puts D at (3, −4).

2. **about 11.4 units** The vertical distance between the points is 9 units, the horizontal distance is 7 units, and the vertical distance and the horizontal distance form a right triangle. You can use the Pythagorean theorem to find the length of the hypotenuse, which is represented by Segment EG:

$$a^2 + b^2 = c^2$$
$$9^2 + 7^2 = c^2$$
$$81 + 49 = c^2$$
$$130 = c^2$$
$$\sqrt{130} = \sqrt{c^2}$$
$$11.4 \approx c$$

335

3. A. **Parallel**
   B. **Parallel**
   C. **Neither**
   D. **Perpendicular**

   A. Parallel sides remain parallel when rotated.
   B. Side AB and Side BC are perpendicular in the pre-image rectangle. If Side AB is rotated 90° clockwise around the origin, it would then be parallel to Side BC.
   C. Since Side AB and Side CD were originally neither parallel nor perpendicular to Diagonal BD, they would still be neither parallel nor perpendicular to Diagonal BC after the rotation of 90° clockwise around the origin.
   D. The 90° rotation from their initial position puts them perpendicular to their initial position.

4. **Stephen has 6 more trading cards than the other three have together.**

Define the variables:

$x =$ the number of trading cards that Lena has

$x + 5 =$ the number of trading cards that Lindsay has

$(x + 5) - 8 =$ the number of trading cards that Yu-Fen has

$x + (x + 5) + (x + 5) - 8 = 62 =$ the equation that represents the number of cards that Lena, Lindsay, and Yu-Fen have together

$$x + (x + 5) + (x + 5) - 8 = 62$$

$$3x + 2 = 62$$

$$\underline{-2 = -2}$$

$$\frac{3x}{3} = \frac{60}{3}$$

$$x = 20$$

Lena has 20 trading cards, Lindsay has $(x + 5)$ or 25 trading cards, and Yu-Fen has $(x + 5) - 8$ or 17 trading cards. Since Stephen has 4 times as many trading cards as Yu-Fen, Stephen has 4(17) or 68 trading cards. Stephen's 68 trading cards − (Lena's 20 + Lindsay's 25 + Yu-Fen's 17 total of 62) = 6 cards. That means that Stephen has 6 more trading cards than the other three have combined.

5. A. **No solutions**
   B. **One solution**
   C. **Infinite solutions**
   D. **One solution**
   E. **Infinite solutions**

   A.
   $$3(x + 5) - 12 = 2(x + 8) + x$$
   $$3x + 15 - 12 = 2x + 16 + x$$
   $$3x + 3 = 3x + 16$$
   $$\underline{-3x = -3x}$$
   $$3 \neq 16$$

   There are no solutions. The variables canceled, and the remaining statement is not true.

   B.
   $$3(x + 5) - 12 = 2(x + 8) + 2x$$
   $$3x + 15 - 12 = 2x + 16 + 2x$$
   $$3x + 3 = 4x + 16$$
   $$\underline{-4x = -4x}$$
   $$-x + 3 = 16$$
   $$\underline{-3 = -3}$$
   $$\frac{-x}{-1} = \frac{13}{-1}$$
   $$x = -13$$

   This has one solution. The variable did not cancel.

   C.
   $$3(x + 5) - 12 = 2(x + 1) + (x + 1)$$
   $$3x + 15 - 12 = 2x + 2 + x + 1$$
   $$3x + 3 = 3x + 3$$
   $$\underline{-3x = -3x}$$
   $$3 = 3$$

   This is an identity. It has infinite solutions. The variables canceled, and the remaining statement is true.

D.
$$7x - 3 + 5x - 4 = 11x$$
$$12x - 7 = 11x$$
$$\underline{-12x = -12x}$$
$$\frac{-7}{-1} = \frac{-x}{-1}$$
$$7 = x$$

This has one solution. The variable did not cancel.

E.
$$5(2x - 3) = 9(x - 1) + (x - 6)$$
$$10x - 15 = 9x - 9 + x - 6$$
$$10x - 15 = 10x - 15$$
$$\underline{-10x = -10x}$$
$$-15 = -15$$

This is an identity. It has infinite solutions. The variables canceled, and the remaining statement is true.

6. **about 8.9 inches** Given that the copy paper is 8.5 inches by 10 inches and that the photo has a border of 1.5 inches all around, a total of 3 inches should be subtracted from both paper dimensions. Accounting for 1.5 inches on the left and on the right, the border leaves a photo width of 5.5 inches. The 1.5 inches on the top and on the bottom leaves a photo length of 7 inches. The Pythagorean theorem can then be used to find the length of the diagonal. Since the corners of the rectangle (the paper and the photo) are 90°, the diagonal will form right triangles.

$$a^2 + b^2 = c^2$$
$$(5.5)^2 + (7)^2 = c^2$$
$$30.25 + 49 = c^2$$
$$79.25 = c^2$$
$$\sqrt{79.25} = \sqrt{c^2}$$
$$8.9 \approx c$$

The diagonal length is about 8.9 inches.

7. The sand will fill 6,104 cubes.

First, find the volumes of the cylinder and the half sphere. Remember that there are 12 inches in 1 foot, and you must convert all feet measures to inches.

<u>Cylinder</u>

$V = Bh$

$V = \pi r^2 h$

$V = \pi(18 \text{ inches})^2(36 \text{ inches})$

$V = \pi(324 \text{ inches}^2)(36 \text{ inches})$

$V = 11{,}664\pi \text{ inches}^3$

<u>Half Sphere</u>

$V = \frac{4}{3}\pi r^3$

$V = \frac{4}{3}\pi (18 \text{ inches})^3$

$V = \frac{4}{3}\pi (5{,}832 \text{ inches}^3)$

$V = 7{,}776\pi \text{ inches}^3$

Remember to take half of this volume since this is a half sphere. Half of $7{,}776\pi$ inches^3 is $3{,}888\pi$ inches.^{3}

Next, find the volume of the container.

Volume of the cylinder + volume of the half sphere = volume of the container

$11{,}664\pi$ inches^3 + $3{,}888\pi$ inches^3 = volume of the container

$15{,}552\pi$ inches^3 = volume of the container

$15{,}552(3.14)$ inches^3 = volume of the container

$48{,}833.28$ inches^3 = volume of the container

Then, find the volume of one cube.

$V = s^3$

$V = (2 \text{ inches})^3$

$V = 8 \text{ inches}^3$

Finally, divide the sand in the container by the sand in one cube to find the number of cubes filled.

$$\frac{\text{Sand in the container}}{\text{Sand in one cube}} = \text{number of cubes filled}$$

$$\frac{48{,}833.28 \text{ inches}^3}{8 \text{ inches}^3} = 6{,}104.16 \text{ cubes}$$

$$\approx 6{,}104 \text{ cubes}$$

8. **7 trips**

The volume of the cylindrical container divided by the volume of the party hat will determine how many times the party hat will need to be filled with water to fill the cylindrical container.

Volume of Cylindrical Container

$V = Bh$

$V = \pi r^2 h$

$V = \pi(3 \text{ inches})^2(12 \text{ inches})$

$V = \pi(9 \text{ inches}^2)(12 \text{ inches})$

$V \approx 108(3.14) \text{ inches}^3$

$V \approx 339.12 \text{ inches}^3$

Volume of Party Hat

$V = \frac{1}{3}\pi r^2 h$

$V = \frac{1}{3}\pi(2.5 \text{ inches})^2(8 \text{ inches})$

$V = \frac{1}{3}\pi(6.25 \text{ inches}^2)(8 \text{ inches})$

$V = \frac{1}{3}\pi(50 \text{ inches}^3)$

$V \approx 16.7(3.14) \text{ inches}^3$

$V \approx 52.438 \text{ inches}^3$

$$\frac{\text{Volume of cylindrical container}}{\text{Volume of party hat}} = \text{number of trips}$$

$$\frac{339.12 \text{ inches}^3}{52.438 \text{ inches}^3} \approx 6:5 \text{ trips}$$

Pat will need to make 7 trips to fill the container.

9.

	Own a Smartphone	Do Not Own a Smartphone	Total
Girls	32	4	36
Boys	22	2	24
Total	54	6	60

10. **(B)** Choice (A) is incorrect. Both of the terms are rational. They are square roots that can be simplified. Choice (B) is correct. All three terms are irrational. $\sqrt{5}$ is slightly greater than 2. $\sqrt[3]{16}$ is slightly greater than 2 but less than 3 ($2^3 = 8$, $3^3 = 27$). $\sqrt{17}$ is slightly greater than 4. The sum of these is less than 10. Choice (C) is incorrect. Although π is irrational, both of the other terms are repeating decimals, which are rational numbers. Choice (D) is incorrect. Although π and $\sqrt{10}$ are both irrational, 5π is slightly greater than 15, $\sqrt{10}$ is slightly greater than 3, and $15 - 3$ is greater than 10. The question stated that the simplified expression had to have a sum value less than 10.

Answers Explained for the Practice Test • 341

11. **(C)**

$(3.7 \times 10^{-6})(2.1 \times 10^4)(5.0 \times 10^8)$

$(3.7 \times 2.1 \times 5.0)(10^{-6} \times 10^4 \times 10^8)$ (Use the Commutative Property of Multiplication to collect the coefficients and to collect the powers of 10.)

38.85×10^6 (Multiply the coefficients. Add the exponents of the like bases.)

$(3.885 \times 10^1) \times 10^6$ (Convert the coefficient of the product to scientific notation.)

3.885×10^7 (Add the exponents of the like bases.)

12. **(D)** First, simplify the original expression in the question. Then, simplify each answer choice to find which is equivalent to the simplified original expression.

$$\frac{450v^3w^2x}{15v^{-3}w^{-2}x^2}$$

$= 30v^{3-(-3)}w^{2-(-2)}x^{1-2}$ (Divide the coefficients. Subtract the exponents of the like bases.)

$= 30v^6w^4x^{-1}$ (Simplify.)

$= (30v^6w^4)\left(\dfrac{1}{x}\right)$ (Negative exponents are simplified as the reciprocal of the base to the positive exponent.)

$= \dfrac{30v^6w^4}{x}$ (Simplify.)

You could also use expanded multiplication.

$$\frac{450v^3w^2x}{15v^{-3}w^{-2}x^2}$$

$= \dfrac{450 \cdot v \cdot v \cdot v \cdot w \cdot w \cdot x}{15 \cdot \frac{1}{v} \cdot \frac{1}{v} \cdot \frac{1}{v} \cdot \frac{1}{w} \cdot \frac{1}{w} \cdot x \cdot x}$ (Expand the multiplication as indicated by the variable exponents.)

$= \dfrac{30 \cdot v \cdot v \cdot v \cdot v \cdot v \cdot v \cdot w \cdot w \cdot w \cdot w \cdot \cancel{x}}{x \cdot \cancel{x}}$ (Divide the coefficients. Simplify. Cancel all forms of 1.)

$= \dfrac{30v^6w^4}{x}$ (Simplify the like bases with exponents.)

Choice (A) is incorrect.

$$\frac{300v^3w^2}{10x}$$ (Divide the coefficients. The numerator and the denominator do not have like bases.)

$$= \frac{30v^3w^2}{x}$$

You could also use expanded multiplication. However, because there are no like bases in the numerator or in the denominator, no forms of 1 will cancel after simplifying the coefficients.

Choice (B) is incorrect.

$$\frac{(5x^2)(6v^6)(2w^2)^3}{8x^3}$$

$$= \frac{(5x^2)(6v^6)(2^3w^{2 \cdot 3})}{8x^3}$$ (Raise the coefficient and the variable exponent to the expression exponent.)

$$= \frac{(5x^2)(6v^6)(8w^6)}{8x^3}$$ (Simplify.)

$$= \frac{240x^{2-3}v^6w^6}{8}$$ (Multiply the coefficients. Subtract the exponents of the like bases.)

$$= 30x^{-1}v^6w^6$$ (Divide the coefficients.)

$$= 30 \cdot \frac{1}{x} \cdot v^6w^6$$ (The negative exponent simplifies to the reciprocal of the base to the positive exponent.)

$$= \frac{30v^6w^6}{x}$$

You could also use expanded multiplication.

$$\frac{(5x^2)(6v^6)(2w^2)^3}{8x^3}$$

$$= \frac{5 \cdot x \cdot x \cdot 6 \cdot v \cdot v \cdot v \cdot v \cdot v \cdot v \cdot 2 \cdot w \cdot w \cdot 2 \cdot w \cdot w \cdot 2 \cdot w \cdot w}{2 \cdot 2 \cdot 2 \cdot x \cdot x \cdot x}$$

(Expand the multiplication as indicated by the exponents, including the expression exponent and the variable exponents.)

$$= \frac{5 \cdot 6 \cdot 2 \cdot 2 \cdot 2 \cdot x \cdot x \cdot v \cdot v \cdot v \cdot v \cdot v \cdot v \cdot w \cdot w \cdot w \cdot w \cdot w \cdot w}{2 \cdot 2 \cdot 2 \cdot x \cdot x \cdot x}$$

(Use the Commutative Property of Multiplication to collect the coefficients and to collect the like bases.)

$$= \frac{5 \cdot 6 \cdot \cancel{2} \cdot \cancel{2} \cdot \cancel{2} \cdot \cancel{x} \cdot \cancel{x} \cdot v \cdot v \cdot v \cdot v \cdot v \cdot v \cdot w \cdot w \cdot w \cdot w \cdot w \cdot w}{\cancel{2} \cdot \cancel{2} \cdot \cancel{2} \cdot \cancel{x} \cdot \cancel{x} \cdot x}$$

(Cancel all forms of 1.)

$$= \frac{30v^6 w^6}{x}$$

(Simplify the like bases with exponents.)

Choice (C) is incorrect.

$$\frac{(5v^2 w^2 x^2)^2}{25x}$$

$$= \frac{5^2 v^{2 \cdot 2} w^{2 \cdot 2} x^{2 \cdot 2}}{25x}$$

(Raise the coefficient to the expression exponent. Multiply the variable exponents with the expression exponent.)

$$= \frac{25 v^4 w^4 x^{4-1}}{25}$$

(Simplify. Subtract the exponents of the like bases.)

$$= v^4 w^4 x^3$$

(Divide the coefficients. Simplify.)

You could also use expanded multiplication.

$$\frac{(5v^2w^2x^2)^2}{25x}$$

$$= \frac{5 \cdot v \cdot v \cdot w \cdot w \cdot x \cdot x \cdot 5 \cdot v \cdot v \cdot w \cdot w \cdot x \cdot x}{5 \cdot 5 \cdot x}$$ (Expand the multiplication as indicated by the expression exponent and the variable exponents.)

$$= \frac{5 \cdot 5 \cdot v \cdot v \cdot v \cdot v \cdot w \cdot w \cdot w \cdot w \cdot x \cdot x \cdot x \cdot x}{5 \cdot 5 \cdot x}$$ (Use the Commutative Property of Multiplication to collect the coefficients and to collect the like bases.)

$$= \frac{\cancel{5 \cdot 5} \cdot v \cdot v \cdot v \cdot v \cdot w \cdot w \cdot w \cdot w \cdot \cancel{x} \cdot x \cdot x \cdot x}{\cancel{5 \cdot 5} \cdot \cancel{x}}$$ (Cancel all forms of 1.)

$$= v^4w^4x^3$$ (Simplify the like bases with exponents.)

Choice (D) is correct.

$$\frac{v^8w^6x^2}{(30)^{-1}v^2w^2x^3}$$

$$= \frac{v^{8-2}w^{6-2}x^{2-3}}{\frac{1}{30}}$$ (Subtract the exponents of the like bases. The negative exponent simplifies to the reciprocal raised to the positive exponent.)

$$= 30v^6w^4x^{-1}$$ (Simplify.)

$$= 30v^6w^4 \cdot \frac{1}{x}$$ (The negative exponent simplifies to the reciprocal raised to the positive exponent.)

$$= \frac{30v^6w^4}{x}$$ (Simplify.)

You can also use expanded multiplication.

$$\frac{v^8w^6x^2}{(30)^{-1}v^2w^2x^3}$$

$$= \frac{v \cdot v \cdot v \cdot v \cdot v \cdot v \cdot v \cdot v \cdot w \cdot w \cdot w \cdot w \cdot w \cdot w \cdot x \cdot x}{\frac{1}{30} \cdot v \cdot v \cdot w \cdot w \cdot x \cdot x \cdot x}$$ (Expand the multiplication as indicated by the variable exponents.)

$$= \frac{30 \cdot \cancel{v \cdot v} \cdot v \cdot v \cdot v \cdot v \cdot v \cdot v \cdot \cancel{w \cdot w} \cdot w \cdot w \cdot w \cdot w \cdot \cancel{x \cdot x}}{\cancel{v \cdot v} \cdot \cancel{w \cdot w} \cdot \cancel{x \cdot x} \cdot x}$$ (Cancel all forms of 1.)

$$= \frac{30v^6w^4}{x}$$ (Simplify.)

13. **$d = 70t + 650$** Since Loren is already 650 miles from home after 0 additional hours, 650 is the y-intercept. The unit rate (slope) of speed is 70 miles for 1 hour $\left(\frac{210}{3} = 70\right)$. Since distance is the dependent variable, because it depends on how long (time) Loren travels, distance takes the place of y and the slope is 70. In slope-intercept form, the equation is $d = 70t + 650$.

14. **(A)** To compare steepness, the equations must be in slope-intercept form. The equation that has the slope with the smallest absolute value will be the least steep line.

    Choice (A):
    $$4x + 6y = 9$$
    $$-4x = -4x$$
    $$\frac{6y}{6} = \frac{-4x + 9}{6}$$
    $$y = -\frac{4}{6}x + \frac{9}{6}$$
    $$y = -\frac{2}{3}x + \frac{3}{2}$$
    $$\text{slope} = -\frac{2}{3}$$
    $$\left|-\frac{2}{3}\right| = \frac{2}{3}$$

    Choice (B):
    $$3y - 12x = -9$$
    $$+12x = +12x$$
    $$\frac{3y}{3} = \frac{12x - 9}{3}$$
    $$y = 4x - 3$$
    $$\text{slope} = 4$$
    $$|4| = 4$$

Choice (C):
$$y - 5x = -\frac{3}{5}$$
$$+5x = +5x$$
$$y = 5x - \frac{3}{5}$$
$$\text{slope} = 5$$
$$|5| = 5$$

Choice (D):
$$2x + y = 9$$
$$-2x \quad = -2x$$
$$y = -2x + 9$$
$$\text{slope} = -2$$
$$|-2| = 2$$

The slope of $-\frac{2}{3}$ is the smallest absolute value of all the slopes. Therefore, choice (A) will be the least steep line.

15. **The solution to this system of equations is (−5, 4).** Each line graphed shows an infinite number of solutions. The point of intersection is the point that makes both equations true. It is called the solution of the system.

16. **One sweatshirt costs $8, and one T-shirt costs $3.25.**

    Define the variables:

    s = the cost of one sweatshirt

    t = the cost of one T-shirt

    The first situation can be represented with the equation $2s + 5t = \$32.25$, and the second situation can be represented with the equation $5s + 2t = \$46.50$. Solve the system by elimination.

    $$5(2s + 5t = 32.25)$$
    $$-2(5s + 2t = 46.50)$$

    $$10s + 25t = 161.25$$
    $$+ -10s - 4t = -93.00$$

    $$\frac{21t}{21} = \frac{68.25}{21}$$
    $$t = 3.25$$

Answers Explained for the Practice Test • 347

$$2s + 5t = 32.25$$
$$2s + 5(3.25) = 32.25$$
$$2s + 16.25 = 32.25$$
$$-16.25 = -16.25$$
$$\frac{2s}{2} = \frac{16}{2}$$
$$s = 8$$

Therefore, $(s, t) = (8, 3.25)$. Check to be sure.

$$5s + 2t = 46.50$$
$$5(8) + 2(3.25) = 46.50$$
$$40 + 6.50 = 46.50$$
$$46.50 = 46.50$$

Remember to always substitute into the original equations. Also, remember to alternate equations. Do not use the same equation twice in a row.

17. **Erin was running faster.** In Diane's equation, $d = 4.5t$, her rate of speed is 4.5 miles per hour. To compare to the data in the table, it is necessary to determine Diane's rate of speed per minute. That would be 4.5 miles in 60 minutes:

$$\frac{4.5}{60} \cdot \frac{10}{10} = \frac{45}{600}$$

To eliminate the decimal in the numerator, multiply by a form of 1. Simplifying the fraction gives $\frac{45 \div 15}{600 \div 15} = \frac{3}{40}$, which converts to 0.075 miles per minute.

In Erin's table, choosing the ordered pairs (10, 0.8) or (25, 2) converts to $\frac{0.8}{10} \cdot \frac{10}{10} = \frac{8}{100}$ and $\frac{2}{25}$, which each convert to 0.08 miles per minute. Since Erin's 0.08 miles per minute is greater than Diane's 0.075 miles per minute, Erin's speed is greater.

18. **(A)** The function in choice (A) is not linear. This equation has an independent variable with an exponent other than 1. Since x has an exponent of 2, the graph will be curved. It will not be a linear function. The function in choice (B) is linear. This will actually graph as a horizontal line since all of the y-coordinates are the same and only the x-coordinates change. The function in choice (C) is linear. Given an equation where x has a coefficient of 1, this will result in a function that is linear. The function in choice (D) is linear. This graph has a horizontal line that indicates a linear function.

19. **(−7, 9)** A translation of 4 units up is an increase in the y-coordinate of 4, and 3 units to the left is a decrease in the x-coordinate of 3. It moves from (x, y) to $(x − 3, y + 4)$.

20. **(C)** Choice (A) is incorrect. Since no information is given as to where the pentagon pre-image began, a change in quadrant cannot be determined. Choice (B) is incorrect. If the x-coordinates are the opposite of the pre-image, the y-coordinates would also have to be the opposite of the pre-image, and that would only result with a rotation of 180°, not the 90° counterclockwise rotation stated. Choice (C) is correct. The scale factor for the dilation is less than 1, so the image would be smaller than the pre-image, which is a reduction. Choice (D) is incorrect. Since the pre-image was dilated, it would be similar, not congruent. The angles would be the same, but the sides would be proportional based on the scale factor.

21. **115°** The exterior angle is equal to the sum of the remote interior angles. Also, the exterior angle is a linear pair with the adjacent angle, which is inside the triangle. Linear pairs are supplementary. The sum of the measures of the interior angles of a triangle is 180.°

    $\angle m + 27° = 142°$ OR $\angle m + 27° +$ supplement of $142° = 180°$
    $ -27° = -27°$ $\angle m + 27° + 38° = 180°$
    $ \angle m = 115°$ $\angle m + 65° = 180°$
    $ -65° = -65°$
    $ \angle m = 115°$

22. **(B)** Choice (A) is false. If the y-coordinates increase as the x-coordinates increase, it is a positive linear association. Choice (B) is a true statement. Choice (C) is false. If the data form a curve, it would not be linear. It would be nonlinear. Choice (D) is false. Without knowing the data or seeing the scatter plot, this cannot be determined.

23. **(D)** When working with lines of best fit on a scatter plot, the line needs to be as close to as many points on the scatter plot as possible.

24. A. **True** Alternate interior angles are on opposite sides of a transversal, between the parallel lines, and they are congruent.
    B. **True** Vertical angles are nonadjacent angles formed by two lines that intersect.
    C. **False** One is above the line and one is below the line. They are same side exterior angles, not corresponding angles.
    D. **True** These angles are corresponding (same position along the transversal, but on the other parallel line), and they are congruent.
    E. **False** These angles are only adjacent angles, which form a linear pair. They are supplementary.
    F. **True** These are same side interior angles, which are supplementary.

25. $\frac{7}{33}$

    $x = 0.\overline{21}$ (Set the repeating decimal equal to x.)
    $100(x = 0.212121\ldots)$ (Multiply the equation by a power of 10 equal to the number of repeating digits.)
    $100x = 21.212121\ldots$ (Subtract the original equation from the transformed
    $\underline{-(x = 0.212121\ldots)}$ equation, eliminating the repeating part of the decimal.)
    $\frac{99x}{99} = \frac{21}{99}$ (Isolate the variable by dividing both sides by 99.)
    $x = \frac{7}{33}$ (Simplify.)

26. **Jim is correct.** Doubling each dimension of a cube will multiply the volume by 2 for each dimension. That will make the volume of the new cube 8 times as large as the original. For example, if a 3 inch cube has each dimension doubled, the new cube has each dimension as 6 inches. The volume of the first cube is 27 inches cubed, while the volume of the second cube is 216 inches cubed. $216 \div 27 = 8$. Alternatively, if each dimension is doubled, the volume is 2^3 as large, or 8 times as large.

27. **The first error was made in Step One.** The substitution should have been made for y, but it was mistakenly made for x instead.

28. **Ed is 25 years old, and his dad is 65 years old.**

Define the variables:

$$x = \text{Ed's age}$$
$$y = \text{Dad's age}$$
$$x + y = 90 = \text{the equation to represent the sum of their ages}$$
$$y = 2x + 15 = \text{the equation to represent the relationship of their ages}$$

Solve the system by substitution:

$$x + y = 90$$
$$x + 2x + 15 = 90$$
$$3x + 15 = 90$$
$$\underline{-15 = -15}$$
$$\frac{3x}{3} = \frac{75}{3}$$
$$x = 25$$

$$y = 2x + 15$$
$$y = 2(25) + 15$$
$$y = 50 + 15$$
$$y = 65$$

$$(x, y) = (25, 65)$$

Check:

$$x + y = 90$$
$$25 + 65 = 90$$
$$90 = 90$$

29. **The slope of the line that would be perpendicular to Line p is $-\frac{13}{8}$.** The slope of the line that passes through the two points is as follows:

$$\text{slope} = \frac{y_2 - y_1}{x_2 - x_1}$$

$$\text{slope} = \frac{3 - (-5)}{6 - (-7)}$$

$$\text{slope} = \frac{8}{13}$$

The slopes of perpendicular lines are opposite reciprocals. That would make the perpendicular slope $-\frac{13}{8}$.

30. **(B), (C), and (E)** Choice (A) is false. Once the dilation occurs, the image is 5 times as large as the pre-image. Choice (B) is true. Since the pre-image has parallel segments, then the image will also have parallel segments. The transformations preserve the shape and the distance between the lines. Choice (C) is true. The two segments in the pre-image maintain their distance throughout the transformations. The given transformations do not change the direction of the pre-image, so the pre-image segments and the image segments are parallel as well. That means that one of the segments from the pre-image would be parallel to one of the segments from the image. Choice (D) is false. Since the segments are not rotated 90° either clockwise or counterclockwise, the image segments will not be perpendicular to the pre-image segments. Choice (E) is true. The image is 5 times as large as the pre-image, so, the pre-image is one-fifth the size of the image.

Performance Task (pages 251–252)

1. $-\frac{3}{4}$ Choose two ordered pairs from the table: $(4, -3)$ and $(-8, 6)$. Calculate using the slope formula:

$$\text{slope} = \frac{y_2 - y_1}{x_2 - x_1}$$

$$\text{slope} = \frac{6 - (-3)}{-8 - 4}$$

$$\text{slope} = \frac{9 \div 3}{-12 \div 3}$$

$$\text{slope} = -\frac{3}{4}$$

2. $y = -\dfrac{3}{4}x$ Substitute the slope of the ordered pairs into slope-intercept form of an equation, and solve for a value for b.

$$(4, -3) \text{ and slope} = -\dfrac{3}{4}$$

$$y = mx + b$$
$$-3 = -\dfrac{3}{4}(4) + b$$
$$-3 = -3 + b$$
$$\underline{+3 = +3}$$
$$0 = b$$

$$y = mx + b$$

$$y = -\dfrac{3}{4}x + 0$$

$$y = -\dfrac{3}{4}x$$

3. **Answers will vary** A sample answer is provided below.

   <u>Sample Answer:</u> One possible equation is $y = 3x - 5$. An equation with any slope different from $-\dfrac{3}{4}$ will intersect the line indicated by the data in the table. If the second equation has the same slope and a different y-intercept (other than zero), it will be parallel to the first line, and they will not intersect. If the second equation has the same slope and the same y-intercept, the equations would be the same line (not intersecting in one point).

   Other sample equations would be:

   $$y = \dfrac{2}{3}x + 2$$
   $$y = 5x - 1$$
   $$y = 0.4x - 7$$

4. **(B)** Choice (A) is true. The point of intersection is a solution to each of the equations because it lies on each equation. Every point on a line is a solution to the equation represented by that line. Choice (B) is false. The equations do not have the same slope. Therefore, they are not parallel. (Note: In order to be parallel, the equations would need to have different y-intercepts AND the same slope.) Choice (C) is true. The equations intersect. Therefore, they have one solution in common. It is the solution to the system. Choice (D) is true. Each of the equations has an infinite number of solutions. Although they have one solution in common, they still have an infinite number of solutions that they do not have in common.

5. A. **Answers will vary** A sample graph is provided below. Note that if the equations have different slopes, the equations will intersect.

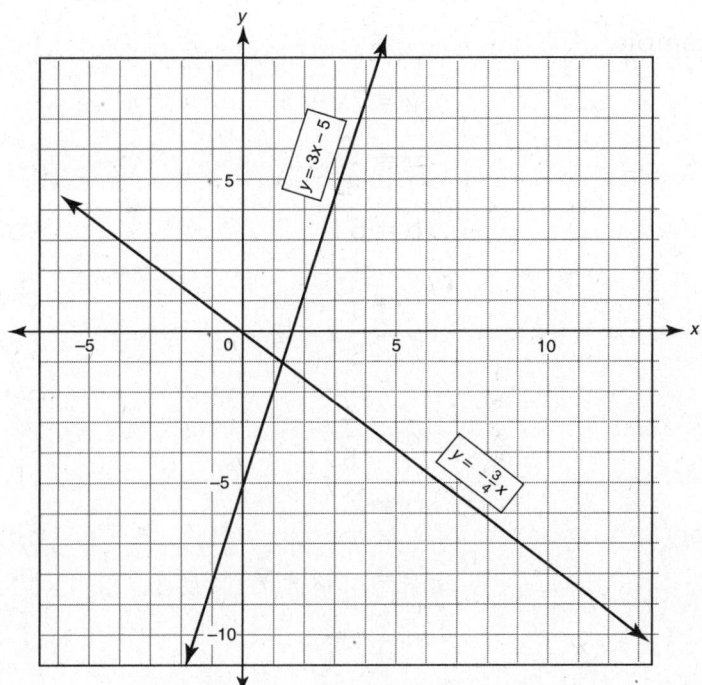

B. **Answers will vary** A sample answer is provided below.

Sample Answer: $y = \frac{4}{3}x + 1$ (would be perpendicular to $y = -\frac{3}{4}x$)

The slope of $y = \frac{4}{3}x + 1$ is $\frac{4}{3}$ which is the opposite reciprocal for $-\frac{3}{4}$, the slope of $y = -\frac{3}{4}x$. It also has a slope different from 3, which is the slope of $y = 3x - 5$. Since this equation is perpendicular to one equation and intersects the other equation, together they will form a right triangle.

C. **Answers will vary** A sample answer is provided below.

An equation that will form a right triangle must be perpendicular to one of the two graphed equations and intersect the other.

6. **Deb is incorrect.** It is not true that the graphs of *any* three equations will form a triangle. If two of the equations graphed were to have the same slope (and different *y*-intercepts), those two lines would be parallel, and there would be no way for a third line, that intersects them both, to form a triangle. However, it *is sometimes* possible for the graphs of three equations to form a triangle. They must all have different slopes so that they will intersect each other. (Two might have the same *y*-intercept or all three *y*-intercepts might be different.) The easiest way to see this is to visualize the equations graphed, knowing that the points of intersection would be the vertices of the triangle formed.

For example:

$$y = 7x + 5$$
$$m = \frac{7}{1}$$
$$b = 5$$

$$y = \frac{4}{5}x + 2$$
$$m = \frac{4}{5}$$
$$b = 2$$

$$y = -4x + 7$$
$$m = -\frac{4}{1}$$
$$b = 7$$

These three equations have different slopes and different *y*-intercepts, so each will intersect the others. The three points of intersection will form a triangle.

Possible Scoring for this Performance Task

1. 1 point = the correct answer (decimal equivalent is acceptable)
   0 points = an incorrect answer

2. 1 point = the correct answer
   0 points = an incorrect answer

3. 1 point = any equation with a slope other than $-\frac{3}{4}$

   0 points = any equation with the same slope $\left(-\frac{3}{4}\right)$ (making the two lines parallel) or with the same slope and the same y-intercept (making the two lines the same line)

4. 1 point = the correct answer choice
   0 points = an incorrect choice

5. 3 points = ALL of the following:

   A. Both equations are graphed correctly. (Note: Scoring for this graph is based on actual answers to Questions 2 and 3, even if they are incorrect.)

   AND

   B. A correct perpendicular equation (representing the opposite reciprocal slope)

   AND

   C. A clear explanation that discusses that the equation in B. is perpendicular to one of the two graphed equations and intersects the other

   2 points = one part of the above criteria is not complete or correct (parts B. and C. are either correct or incorrect)
   1 point = two parts of the above criteria are not complete or correct
   0 points = all three parts of the above criteria are not complete or correct

6. 3 points = ALL of the following:
   - The response correctly states that Deb is incorrect.
   - The response contains a strong, clear, convincing explanation that states that different slopes must occur for lines to intersect. The response might include a discussion of parallel lines (which do not intersect) and perpendicular lines (which do intersect) and/or an example.
   - A top scoring answer may include a specific example.

2 points =

- The response correctly states that Deb is incorrect.
- The response contains a good explanation and all correct information, and it demonstrates a clear understanding.

1 point =

- The response incorrectly states that Deb is correct, or it does not state whether she is correct or incorrect.
- The response contains an explanation that includes many correct points, but it does not demonstrate a clear understanding.

0 points =

- The response incorrectly states that Deb is correct, or it does not state whether she is correct or incorrect.
- The response contains an explanation that is unclear, or it does not contain an explanation at all.

Common Core Standards

APPENDIX C

The Number System

Know that there are numbers that are not rational, and approximate them by rational numbers.

CCSS.MATH.CONTENT.8.NS.A.1 Know that numbers that are not rational are called irrational. Understand informally that every number has a decimal expansion; for rational numbers show that the decimal expansion repeats eventually, and convert a decimal expansion which repeats eventually into a rational number.

CCSS.MATH.CONTENT.8.NS.A.2 Use rational approximations of irrational numbers to compare the size of irrational numbers, locate them approximately on a number line diagram, and estimate the value of expressions (e.g., π^2). *For example, by truncating the decimal expansion of $\sqrt{2}$, show that $\sqrt{2}$ is between 1 and 2, then between 1.4 and 1.5, and explain how to continue on to get better approximations.*

Expressions and Equations

Expressions and equations work with radicals and integer exponents.

CCSS.MATH.CONTENT.8.EE.A.1 Know and apply the properties of integer exponents to generate equivalent numerical expressions. *For example,*
$$3^2 \times 3^{-5} = 3^{-3} = \left(\frac{1}{3}\right)^3 = \left(\frac{1}{27}\right).$$

CCSS.MATH.CONTENT.8.EE.A.2 Use square root and cube root symbols to represent solutions to equations of the form $x^2 = p$ and $x^3 = p$, where p is a positive rational number. Evaluate square roots of small perfect squares and cube roots of small perfect cubes. Know that $\sqrt{2}$ is irrational.

CCSS.MATH.CONTENT.8.EE.A.3 Use numbers expressed in the form of a single digit times an integer power of 10 to estimate very large or very small quantities, and to express how many times as much one is than the other. *For example, estimate the population of the United States as 3 times 10^8 and the population of the world as 7 times 10^9, and determine that the world population is more than 20 times larger.*

CCSS.MATH.CONTENT.8.EE.A.4 Perform operations with numbers expressed in scientific notation, including problems where both decimal and scientific notation are used. Use scientific notation and choose units of appropriate size for measurements of very large or very small quantities (e.g., use millimeters per year for seafloor spreading). Interpret scientific notation that has been generated by technology.

Understand the connections between proportional relationships, lines, and linear equations.

CCSS.MATH.CONTENT.8.EE.B.5 Graph proportional relationships, interpreting the unit rate as the slope of the graph. Compare two different proportional relationships represented in different ways. *For example, compare a distance-time graph to a distance-time equation to determine which of two moving objects has greater speed.*

CCSS.MATH.CONTENT.8.EE.B.6 Use similar triangles to explain why the slope m is the same between any two distinct points on a non-vertical line in the coordinate plane; derive the equation $y = mx$ for a line through the origin and the equation $y = mx + b$ for a line intercepting the vertical axis at b.

Analyze and solve linear equations and pairs of simultaneous linear equations.

CCSS.MATH.CONTENT.8.EE.C.7 Solve linear equations in one variable.

CCSS.MATH.CONTENT.8.EE.C.7.A Give examples of linear equations in one variable with one solution, infinitely many solutions, or no solutions. Show which of these possibilities is the case by successively transforming the given equation into simpler forms, until an equivalent equation of the form $x = a$, $a = a$, or $a = b$ results (where a and b are different numbers).

CCSS.MATH.CONTENT.8.EE.C.7.B Solve linear equations with rational number coefficients, including equations whose solutions require expanding expressions using the distributive property and collecting like terms.

CCSS.MATH.CONTENT.8.EE.C.8 Analyze and solve pairs of simultaneous linear equations.

CCSS.MATH.CONTENT.8.EE.C.8.A Understand that solutions to a system of two linear equations in two variables correspond to points of intersection of their graphs, because points of intersection satisfy both equations simultaneously.

CCSS.MATH.CONTENT.8.EE.C.8.B Solve systems of two linear equations in two variables algebraically, and estimate solutions by graphing the equations. Solve simple cases by inspection. *For example, $3x + 2y = 5$ and $3x + 2y = 6$ have no solution because $3x + 2y$ cannot simultaneously be 5 and 6.*

CCSS.MATH.CONTENT.8.EE.C.8.C Solve real-world and mathematical problems leading to two linear equations in two variables. *For example, given coordinates for two pairs of points, determine whether the line through the first pair of points intersects the line through the second pair.*

Functions

Define, evaluate, and compare functions.

CCSS.MATH.CONTENT.8.F.A.1 Understand that a function is a rule that assigns to each input exactly one output. The graph of a function is the set of ordered pairs consisting of an input and the corresponding output.[1]

CCSS.MATH.CONTENT.8.F.A.2 Compare properties of two functions each represented in a different way (algebraically, graphically, numerically in tables, or by verbal descriptions). *For example, given a linear function represented by a table of values and a linear function represented by an algebraic expression, determine which function has the greater rate of change.*

CCSS.MATH.CONTENT.8.F.A.3 Interpret the equation $y = mx + b$ as defining a linear function, whose graph is a straight line; give examples of functions that are not linear. *For example, the function $A = s^2$ giving the area of a square as a function of its side length is not linear because its graph contains the points (1, 1), (2, 4), and (3, 9), which are not on a straight line.*

Use functions to model relationships between quantities.

CCSS.MATH.CONTENT.8.F.B.4 Construct a function to model a linear relationship between two quantities. Determine the rate of change and initial value of the function from a description of a relationship or from two (x, y) values, including reading these from a table or from a graph. Interpret the rate of change and initial value of a linear function in terms of the situation it models, and in terms of its graph or a table of values.

---

[1] Function notation is not required for Grade 8.

CCSS.MATH.CONTENT.8.F.B.5 Describe qualitatively the functional relationship between two quantities by analyzing a graph (e.g., where the function is increasing or decreasing, linear or nonlinear). Sketch a graph that exhibits the qualitative features of a function that has been described verbally.

Geometry

Understand congruence and similarity using physical models, transparencies, or geometry software.

CCSS.MATH.CONTENT.8.G.A.1 Verify experimentally the properties of rotations, reflections, and translations:

CCSS.MATH.CONTENT.8.G.A.1.A Lines are taken to lines, and line segments to line segments of the same length.

CCSS.MATH.CONTENT.8.G.A.1.B Angles are taken to angles of the same measure.

CCSS.MATH.CONTENT.8.G.A.1.C Parallel lines are taken to parallel lines.

CCSS.MATH.CONTENT.8.G.A.2 Understand that a two-dimensional figure is congruent to another if the second can be obtained from the first by a sequence of rotations, reflections, and translations; given two congruent figures, describe a sequence that exhibits the congruence between them.

CCSS.MATH.CONTENT.8.G.A.3 Describe the effect of dilations, translations, rotations, and reflections on two-dimensional figures using coordinates.

CCSS.MATH.CONTENT.8.G.A.4 Understand that a two-dimensional figure is similar to another if the second can be obtained from the first by a sequence of rotations, reflections, translations, and dilations; given two similar two-dimensional figures, describe a sequence that exhibits the similarity between them.

CCSS.MATH.CONTENT.8.G.A.5 Use informal arguments to establish facts about the angle sum and exterior angle of triangles, about the angles created when parallel lines are cut by a transversal, and the angle-angle criterion for similarity of triangles. *For example, arrange three copies of the same triangle so that the sum of the three angles appears to form a line, and give an argument in terms of transversals why this is so.*

Understand and apply the Pythagorean theorem.

CCSS.MATH.CONTENT.8.G.B.6 Explain a proof of the Pythagorean theorem and its converse.

CCSS.MATH.CONTENT.8.G.B.7 Apply the Pythagorean theorem to determine unknown side lengths in right triangles in real-world and mathematical problems in two and three dimensions.

CCSS.MATH.CONTENT.8.G.B.8 Apply the Pythagorean theorem to find the distance between two points in a coordinate system.

Solve real-world and mathematical problems involving volume of cylinders, cones, and spheres.

CCSS.MATH.CONTENT.8.G.C.9 Know the formulas for the volumes of cones, cylinders, and spheres and use them to solve real-world and mathematical problems.

Statistics and Probability

Investigate patterns of association in bivariate data.

CCSS.MATH.CONTENT.8.SP.A.1 Construct and interpret scatter plots for bivariate measurement data to investigate patterns of association between two quantities. Describe patterns such as clustering, outliers, positive or negative association, linear association, and nonlinear association.

CCSS.MATH.CONTENT.8.SP.A.2 Know that straight lines are widely used to model relationships between two quantitative variables. For scatter plots that suggest a linear association, informally fit a straight line, and informally assess the model fit by judging the closeness of the data points to the line.

CCSS.MATH.CONTENT.8.SP.A.3 Use the equation of a linear model to solve problems in the context of bivariate measurement data, interpreting the slope and intercept. *For example, in a linear model for a biology experiment, interpret a slope of 1.5 cm/hr as meaning that an additional hour of sunlight each day is associated with an additional 1.5 cm in mature plant height.*

CCSS.MATH.CONTENT.8.SP.A.4 Understand that patterns of association can also be seen in bivariate categorical data by displaying frequencies and relative frequencies in a two-way table. Construct and interpret a two-way table summarizing data on two categorical variables collected from the same subjects. Use relative frequencies calculated for rows or columns to describe possible association between the two variables. *For example, collect data from students in your class on whether or not they have a curfew on school nights and whether or not they have assigned chores at home. Is there evidence that those who have a curfew also tend to have chores?*

Index

A
Adjacent angles, 191–192
Alternate exterior angles, 194, 197
Alternate interior angles, 194, 197
Angles
   adjacent, 191–192
   complementary, 191–192
   congruent, 197
   corresponding, 194, 197
   formed by intersecting lines, 191
   formed by transversal, 194, 197
   straight, 191–192
   supplementary, 191–192, 197
   types of, 191–192
Association, of data, 174, 176

B
Bivariate data, 174

C
Categorical data, 174, 182
Circumference formula, 315
Common Core Standards, 357–361
Complementary angles, 191–192
Computer Adaptive Test (CAT)
   expectations, 1–2
   practice test, 245–251
Cone, volume of, 204–205
Congruence and similarity, 157–164
Congruent angles, 197
Congruent shapes, 157
Constructed-response tasks, 5
Coordinate system, distance between two points, 106–108
Correlation, of data, 174
Corresponding angles, 194, 197
Curve, as a nonlinear function, 15
Cylinder, volume of, 204

D
Data
   association of, 174, 176
   bivariate, 174
   categorical, 174, 182
   correlation of, 174
   numerical, 174
   qualitative, 174, 182
   quantitative, 174
Decimal, to a rational number, 93–96
Dependent variable, in functions, 13
Dilation, 146–150, 156
Distance between two points in a coordinate system, 106–108
Division, scientific notation, 232

E
Enlargement, 147
Equations
   converting from decimal to fraction, 94
   slope-intercept form of, 28
   solving by elimination, 70
   solving by graphing, 74
   solving by substitution, 64
   two-variable, 22
   See Linear equations
Exponent, 216
   integer expressions, 211
   rules, 227
   zero and negative, 212–214
Extended constructed-response tasks, 5

F
Formulas
   circumference, 210
   cone, 204–205
   cylinder, 204
   slope, 23, 33–34, 44–46, 76
   sphere, 206
   volume, 203–206
Fraction form, 93–94
Frequency table, 183
Functions
   analysis, 32–38
   coordinates in, 14
   dependent variable, 13
   equation, 16
   graphs and, 15–16
   identifying, 12–18
   independent variable, 13
   mapping diagram and, 12–13
   nonlinear, 15–16, 32
   ordered pairs and, 14–15
   tables and, 13–14
   word problems and, 17–18
   See Linear functions

G

Geometry
- angles formed by intersecting lines, 191–192
- three or more intersecting lines, 194–200
- volume, 203–206

Graphs
- distance between two points in a coordinate system, 106–108
- for nonlinear functions, 32
- rate of change (slope), 23
- systems of equations, 63, 74–76, 80
- to identify functions, 15–16

H

Helpful hints
- angle 7, 198
- calculator, 173
- exponents, 212, 216
- multiple-response questions, 4
- Pythagorean triple, 101
- rate of change (slope), 23
- reflections, 308
- response type, 8
- solving by graphing, 75
- subtracting an expression, 57, 66
- systems of equations, 64, 82, 84, 85, 87
- translations, 120
- triangles and slope, 46
- use of inverse, 57, 66

I

Independent variable in functions, 13
Integer exponent expressions, 211–214
Irrational numbers, 91–92, 98–99

L

Line of best fit, 176–178
Linear association, 176

Linear equations
- number of solutions, 56–58
- solving multi-step, 49–52
- *See* Equations

Linear functions
- graph of, 22
- line, 15
- rate of change (slope) as, 23
- slope characteristics, 33–34
- tables, 37
- word problems and, 36
- *See* Functions

Linear pair, 191–192

M

Mapping diagram, 12–13
Math shifts, 2
Mathematical problems, systems of equations, 81
Multiple-response questions, 4
Multiplication, scientific notation, 232
Multi-step linear equations, 49–52

N

Negative and zero exponents, 212–214
Negative association, 174–175
Nonlinear association, 176
Nonlinear functions, 14–15, 32
Numbers, irrational, 91–92, 98–99
Numerical data, 174

O

Operations with scientific notation, 232–234
Ordered pairs
- rate of change (slope), 27
- to identify functions, 14

Outlier, 174

P

Parallel lines and transversals, 195–196

Performance task
- expectations, 2
- overview of, 6, 239–244
- practice test, 251–252

Positive association, 174–175
Power of Powers Property, 219, 227
Prism, volume of, 203–204
Product of Powers Property, 216–217, 227
Pythagorean theorem
- converse, 101
- distance between two points, 106–108
- in three dimensions, 111–112
- use of, 101–104

Q

Qualitative data, 174, 182
Quantitative data, 174
Quotient of Powers Property, 223, 227

R

Rate of change (slope), 23
Rational and irrational numbers, 91–92
Rational numbers, 91–92, 93–96
Real-world problems. *See* Word problems
Rectangular prism, 203
Reduction, 147
Reflections, 136–140, 156
Relation, set of ordered pairs, 12
Relative frequency tables, 182–185
Rotations, 125–131, 156

S

Same side exterior angles, 194, 197
Same side interior angles, 194, 197
SBAC test
- formatting of, 8
- overview of, 1–2

scoring, 7
task types, 3–6
Scatter plots, 174–176
Scientific notation, 228–229, 232–234
Scoring, 7
Selected-response
 tasks, 3–4
Similar shapes, 157
Similarity and congruence, 157–164
Slope
 determining the, 23
 intercept form, 28, 74–76, 80–81, 176
 linear function and, 33–34
 ordered pairs and, 27
 rate of change, 23
 systems of equations, 76
 triangles, 44–46
 undefined, 33
Solids, volume of, 203–205
Sphere, volume of, 206
Straight angles, 191–192
Supplementary angles, 191–192, 197
Systems of equations
 number of solutions, 81
 overview of, 80
 solving by elimination, 70–71, 80
 solving by graphing, 63, 74–76, 80
 solving by substitution, 64–65, 80

T
Tables
 frequency, 183
 linear function, 37
 rate of change (slope), 26
 to identify functions, 13–14
 two-way, 182–183
Task types
 constructed-response, 5
 performance, 6
 selected response, 3–4
 technology-enhanced, 5–6
Technology-enhanced
 tasks, 5–6
Transformations, 118, 156
Translation, 118–121, 156
Transversal
 and parallel lines, 195–196
 angles formed by, 197
Triangles, and slope, 44–46
Two-variable equation, 22
Two-way table, 182–183

U
Unit rate, 23

V
Verbal description, 12, 17, 23
Vertical angles, 191–192
Vertical line test, 14–15
Visual display
 as line segment, 106
 mapping diagram and, 12–13
 of qualitative (categorical) data, 182
 of quantitative (numerical) data, 174
Volume
 cone, 204–205
 cylinder, 204
 of three-dimensional solids, 203–206
 prism, 203
 sphere, 206

W
Word problems
 functions, 17–18
 linear function, 36
 multi-step linear equations, 51–52
 rate of change (slope), 27–28
 systems of equations, 81–83

X
x-coordinate, in functions, 14

Y
y-coordinate, in functions, 14
y-intercept, 28

Z
Zero and negative exponents, 212–214

Notes

Notes

PREPARE STUDENTS FOR SUCCESS

Let's Prepare for the PARCC . . . Tests

This series of books introduces students to the PARCC assessment administered across the country. It offers comprehensive subject reviews and practice tests designed to familiarize students with the PARCC grade level test and prepares them to do their best on test day.

Students will find everything they need in order to prepare—and succeed— on the PARCC tests.

Let's Prepare for the PARCC Grade 8 ELA/Literacy Test
ISBN 978-1-4380-0821-9

Let's Prepare for the PARCC Grade 8 Math Test
ISBN 978-1-4380-0822-6

Each book: Paperback, 7 13/16" x 10", $12.99, Can$15.50

SBAC Books

This series of books introduces students to the Smarter Balanced Assessment Consortium (SBAC), a series of next-generation assessment tests based on the Common Core Standards. These fair and reliable standards prepare students for 21st century learning, including the use of computers on test day. Each Grade 8 book features one practice test; an overview of the tests, including the computerized format of the exams; all questions thoroughly answered and explained; practice exercises that cover the different types of SBAC questions; test-taking tips and strategies; and more. It's the perfect way to help students reach their highest potential on the grade-specific SBAC tests.

SBAC Grade 8 ELA
ISBN 978-1-4380-1062-5

SBAC Grade 8 Math
ISBN 978-1-4380-1090-8

Each book: Paperback, 7 13/16" x 10", $14.99, Can$18.50

Available at your local bookstore
or visit **www.barronseduc.com**

Barron's Educational Series, Inc.
250 Wireless Blvd.
Hauppauge, NY 11788
Order toll-free: 1-800-645-3476

In Canada: Georgetown Book Warehouse
34 Armstrong Ave.
Georgetown, Ontario L7G 4R9
Canadian orders: 1-800-247-7160

Prices subject to change without notice.

Really. This isn't going to hurt at all...

Learning won't hurt when middle school and high school students open any *Painless* title. These books transform subjects into fun—emphasizing a touch of humor and entertaining brain-tickler puzzles that are fun to solve.

Bonus Online Component—each title followed by (*) includes additional online games to challenge students, including Beat the Clock, a line match game, and a word scramble.

Each book: Paperback

Painless Algebra, 4th Ed.*
Lynette Long, Ph.D.
ISBN 978-1-4380-0775-5, $9.99, Can$11.99

Painless American Government
Jeffrey Strausser
ISBN 978-0-7641-2601-7, $9.99, Can$11.99

Painless American History, 2nd Ed.
Curt Lader
ISBN 978-0-7641-4231-4, $9.99, Can$11.99

Painless Chemistry, 2nd Ed.*
Loris Chen
ISBN 978-1-4380-0771-7, $9.99, Can$11.99

Painless Earth Science
Edward J. Denecke, Jr.
ISBN 978-0-7641-4601-5, $11.99, Can$14.99

Painless English for Speakers of Other Languages, 2nd Ed.
Jeffrey Strausser and José Paniza
ISBN 978-1-4380-0002-2, $9.99, Can$11.50

Painless Fractions, 3rd Ed.
Alyece Cummings, M.A.
ISBN 978-1-4380-0000-8, $10.99, Can$13.99

Painless French, 3rd Ed.*
Carol Chaitkin, M.S., and Lynn Gore, M.A.
ISBN 978-1-4380-0770-0, $9.99, Can$11.99

Painless Geometry, 2nd Ed.
Lynette Long, Ph.D.
ISBN 978-0-7641-4230-7, $9.99, Can$11.99

Painless Grammar, 4th Ed.*
Rebecca Elliott, Ph.D.
ISBN 978-1-4380-0774-8, $9.99, Can$11.99

Painless Italian, 2nd Ed.
Marcel Danesi, Ph.D.
ISBN 978-0-7641-4761-6, $9.99, Can$11.50

Painless Math Word Problems, 2nd Ed.
Marcie Abramson, B.S., Ed.M.
ISBN 978-0-7641-4335-9, $11.99, Can$14.99

Painless Poetry, 2nd Ed.
Mary Elizabeth
ISBN 978-0-7641-4591-9, $9.99, Can$11.99

Painless Pre-Algebra, 2nd Ed.*
Amy Stahl
ISBN 978-1-4380-0773-1, $9.99, Can$11.99

Painless Reading Comprehension, 3rd Ed.*
Darolyn "Lyn" Jones, Ed.D.
ISBN 978-1-4380-0769-4, $9.99, Can$11.99

Painless Spanish, 3rd Ed.*
Carlos B. Vega and Dasha Davis
ISBN 978-1-4380-0772-4, $9.99, Can$11.99

Painless Spelling, 3rd Ed.
Mary Elizabeth
ISBN 978-0-7641-4713-5, $9.99, Can$11.99

Painless Study Techniques
Michael Greenberg
ISBN 978-0-7641-4059-4, $9.99, Can$11.99

Painless Vocabulary, 3rd Ed.*
Michael Greenberg
ISBN 978-1-4380-0778-6, $9.99, Can$11.99

Painless Writing, 3rd Ed.*
Jeffrey Strausser
ISBN 978-1-4380-0784-7, $9.99, Can$11.99

Prices subject to change without notice.

Available at your local bookstore or visit **www.barronseduc.com**

Barron's Educational Series, Inc.
250 Wireless Blvd.
Hauppauge, N.Y. 11788
Order toll-free:
1-800-645-3476

MAXIMIZE YOUR MATH SKILLS!

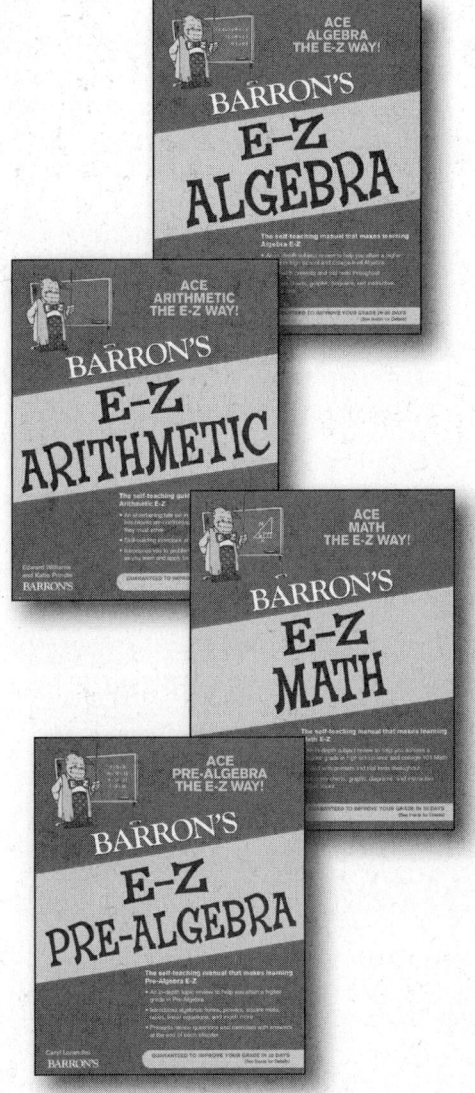

E-Z ALGEBRA
5th Edition
Douglas Downing, Ph.D.
Topics covered in this detailed review of algebra include general rules for dealing with numbers, equations, negative numbers and integers, fractions and rational numbers, exponents, roots and real numbers, algebraic expressions, functions, graphs, systems of two equations, quadratic equations, circles, ellipses, parabolas, polynomials, numerical series, permutations, combinations, the binomial formula, proofs by mathematical induction, exponential functions and logarithms, simultaneous equations and matrices, and imaginary numbers. Exercises follow each chapter with answers at the end of the book.
(978-0-7641-4257-4) $16.99, *Can$19.99*

E-Z ARITHMETIC
5th Edition
Edward Williams and Katie Prindle
A brush-up for students and general readers, this book reviews all arithmetic operations—addition, subtraction, multiplication, and division, and calculations with fractions, decimals, and percentages. Includes practice exercises with answers.
(978-0-7641-4466-0) $16.99, *Can$19.99*

E-Z MATH
5th Edition
Anthony Prindle and Katie Prindle
Barron's *E-Z Math* reviews whole numbers, fractions, percentages, algebra, geometry, trigonometry, word problems, probability, and statistics. The book also presents a diagnostic and a practice test with answers.
(978-0-7641-4132-4) $14.99, *Can$17.99*

E-Z PRE-ALGEBRA
Caryl Lorandini
Barron's *E-Z Pre-Algebra* presents everything students need to prepare themselves for an algebra class. Separate chapters focus on fractions, integers, ratios, proportions, expressions, equations, inequalities, graphing, statistics and probability basics, word problems, and more. Review questions and chapter reviews all have answers.
(978-1-4380-0011-4) $14.99, *Can$16.99*

Available at your local book store
or visit **www.barronseduc.com**

Barron's Educational Series, Inc.
250 Wireless Blvd.
Hauppauge, N.Y. 11788
Order toll-free: 1-800-645-3476

In Canada:
Georgetown Book Warehouse
34 Armstrong Ave.
Georgetown, Ontario L7G 4R9
Canadian orders: 1-800-247-7160

Prices subject to change without notice.

(#142) R 8/16

Test Practice for Common Core

GRADE 8 TEST PRACTICE FOR COMMON CORE

Covers Both ELA & Math

Help students practice and prepare for the all-important Common Core assessment tests at the end of the school year. Every turn of the page provides a new standard with a series of practice questions for students to work on. Features include:

- Hundreds of practice questions complete with detailed answers
- Covers many different question types, including multiple-choice, short-answer, extended-response, and more
- Tip boxes throughout the book provide students with friendly reminders
- Easy-to-follow tabs allow parents and teachers to recognize the types of questions within each standard
- An easy-to-follow, side-by-side layout lets students conquer one standard at a time
- Student-friendly worksheets reinforce what they are learning in the classroom
- Practice tests at the end of each section pinpoint strengths and weaknesses
- A cumulative assessment tests their understanding of everything they have learned

Paperback, 8 3/8" x 10 7/8", ISBN 978-1-4380-0712-0
$14.99, Can$17.99

It's an excellent resource for parents and teachers as they help students meet and exceed grade level expectations on the Common Core assessment tests.

Available at your local book store or visit www.barronseduc.com

Barron's Educational Series, Inc.
250 Wireless Blvd.
Hauppauge, N.Y. 11788
Order toll-free: 1-800-645-3476

In Canada:
Georgetown Book Warehouse
34 Armstrong Ave.
Georgetown, Ontario L7G 4R9
Canadian orders: 1-800-247-7160

Prices subject to change without notice.